CASEBOOK SERIES ON EUROPEAN POLITICS AND SOCIETY NO. 2
Director, Stanley Hoffmann

Culture and Society in Contemporary Europe

CASEBOOK SERIES ON EUROPEAN POLITICS AND SOCIETY

1 THE COMMUNIST PARTIES OF ITALY, FRANCE AND SPAIN:
POSTWAR CHANGE AND CONTINUITY
Edited by Peter Lange and Maurizio Vannicelli
With a Foreword by Stanley Hoffmann

Culture and Society in Contemporary Europe

A Casebook

Edited by
STANLEY HOFFMANN
PASCHALIS KITROMILIDES
Center for European Studies, Harvard University

GEORGE ALLEN & UNWIN
Center for European Studies, Harvard University

First published in 1981

GEORGE ALLEN & UNWIN LTD
40 Museum Street, London WC1A 1LU

British Library Cataloguing in Publication Data

Culture and society in contemporary Europe –
(Casebook series on European politics and society; no. 2)
1. Civilization, Modern – 20th century
I. Hoffmann, Stanley   II. Kitromilides,
Paschalis   III. Series
940.5   CB425

ISBN 0-04-809014-X
ISBN 0-04-809015-8 Pbk

Set in 10 on 12 point Plantin by
Typesetters (Birmingham) Limited
and Printed and bound in Great Britain by
William Clowes (Beccles) Limited, Beccles and London.

Contents

Foreword

The materials selected and presented by Paschalis Kitromilides should be of interest to readers, teachers, and students in the humanities and in the social sciences. The arts and letters of Europe have evolved in ways and for reasons that can be described autonomously – without reference to their political and social context. But this was never the only way of understanding intellectual currents or artistic styles. The context always mattered, and explained a great deal, especially in the case of literature. In the last half-century a consideration of the relation between society and culture has become indispensable to our evaluation of either.

In the first place, at least since the Enlightenment, the makers of European culture have always seen themselves, without excessive modesty, as a special kind of leaders of society – an intellectual ruling class, a spiritual elite that inherited some of the functions of moral guidance from the church and added to them a temporal mission of political and social criticism and prophecy (today Solzhenitzyn is the most forceful heir to this tradition). As a result, except at its most esoteric fringes, European culture has always been engaged in a double quest: about the ideal social and political order, and about the ideal relation between the intelligentsia and that order; there has always been, in other words, both a critical and a self-critical pursuit: how well, or how badly, did existing society conform to the (highly conflicting) imperatives and ideals set up by the artists and writers, how well, or how badly, did the latter perform their own mission in and toward society?

In the second place, the tempests and torments of the twentieth century have shaken European culture to its depths. The material conditions of intellectual production and of the distribution of intellectual and artistic goods have been drastically changed by science, technology, and industry. Artists and writers have been able to reach a much wider audience, but the effects of the mass media on culture, the appearance of a homogenized mass culture that replaces the diversified and fragmented popular cultures of the past, the development of so potent and ambiguous an art form as the cinema, the enormous quantitative expansion of the intelligentsia – which now includes not only the creators of culture but armies of interpreters, transmitters, and executors – all of these factors have provided European intellectuals both with tempting opportunities, and with reasons for revulsion and fear. Whatever the (frequently democratic or even radical) message, the roots of the European intelligentsia were in the aristocratic tradition and class system – denunciations of the bourgeois would have been less virulent, and differently phrased, otherwise. The coming of the age of social mobilization and mass media made intellectuals both potentially more able to act as shapers of opinion and movers of militants, and inevitably more subjected to the laws of the market, the lures and tyranny of money, or the manipulation of temporal rulers in control of the media.

Indeed, the great political upheavals of twentieth-century Europe have injected into the European intelligentsia enormous doses of pride (or *hubris*) and guilt (or self-hatred). The grand totalitarian systems which the First World War unleashed or incited have been at least partly systems of ideas, and the most lasting of these, the communist one, claims as its founding fathers one intellectual giant, Marx, and one great 'action intellectual,' Lenin. Communism, fascism, Nazism, in different ways and degrees, have provided intellectuals with the inebriating illusion of being able to shape history − and yet they have also reduced culture and its makers to a debased and often grotesque condition of stunted service to the state. Intellectuals, as willing or forced slaves, have thus contributed both to mass murder − by their calls as well as by their rationalizations − and to the destruction of culture. It is no surprise if the theme of protest against tyranny is at least as strong as the older and persistent criticism of bourgeois, class society, and if − as in the celebrated controversy between Sartre and Camus − those intellectuals who still claimed that their duty was a commitment to social revolution and to the classless society, and those intellectuals who defined their duty as the denunciation of philosophies of history that sacrifice decency today to the pursuit of hapiness the day after tommorrow, or as the call for limits to messianism and murder, were doomed to a dialogue of the deaf. For each group gave a different answer to the question of the responsibility of the artist, and to the question of the function of culture.

The upheavals of the twentieth century have affected the artists and writers of Europe in diverse ways for another reason as well: European culture may have been single, and unique, because of its roots, and of its position in and attitude toward society, but it has always been fragmented along national lines. It has been, and remains, universal, insofar as the experiences of European political and social history and the experiments of European writers and artists are of worldwide relevance and have, for better or worse, spread all over the globe. But it has also been intensely parochial, insofar as each national intelligentsia has not only been shaped by the special fate of its nation, but also tended to generalize from the national case. In this century the cases could not have been more different, and in this volume several essays examine the imprint different histories have left on the Spanish, or the Greek, or the Czech, or the British world of culture.

The reader will find many traces of intellectual bad conscience. I have tried to suggest some of the reasons for it − the ambivalent relation to technological progress, the debate between the artist's 'subjective' search for self-expression and his 'objective' responsibilities to society, the legacy of totalitarian debauchery, the split between reform and revolution, the difficulties of protest in tyrannical societies, and so on. There is one more: the fear of decadence, which affects a continent half of which is a *glacis* for one superpower, the other half of which is under the protection as well as the strong cultural influence of the other superpower, and all of which seems to have become a stake after having provided for so many centuries the center stage and the cast of actors. Between a past that weighs like the lid of a coffin, and the temptation of escape either into the frayed utopias of total change or into the constraining disciplines of specialized scholarship, European culture today often presents the spectacle of a disarray and an empty rage that sometimes contrasts with the social scene, as in France, England, or Germany, or reflects the turbulence of society, as in Italy. Only in Eastern Europe is there still a focus for anger and protest − even if these risk being as futile as the clamors and gestures in which West European intellectuals often indulge under the glaring lights of the media.

STANLEY HOFFMANN

Acknowledgements

In compiling this anthology, the editors incurred many debts to many friends who generously shared their knowledge of European culture with them. The interest and advice of our colleagues at the Center for European Studies and in the wider Harvard community enabled us to map out the complex universe of contemporary European cultural criticism and to be informed in making our selections. To all those who helped us in this task – too numerous to mention individually here – we express our appreciation. The project, which was conceived after many theoretical discussions, could never have been put into practice without the enthusiasm and dedication of a remarkable group of undergraduate research assistants who surveyed an enormous amount of material and carried innumerable volumes back and forth from Widener Library. If the zeal of Eric Gilioli, Richard Kreindler, Ferenc Molnar, and most notably Neal Johnson, who bore the major burden of the final preparation of the manuscript, is any indication, this book will do well with students. Working with them has been one of the greatest pleasures of teaching at Harvard. The staff of the Center for European Studies have been supportive throughout the project, while Henrik Madsen in Cambridge and Cyril Sarris in Athens were helpful during the last stages of the preparation of the anthology.

P.M.K.
S.H.
Cambridge, Mass.

Acknowledgements

Introductory Essay: A Perspective on the Temper of Twentieth-Century European Culture

I

The purpose of this anthology is to provide a perspective on the relationship between culture and society in contemporary Europe. It attempts to do so through essays surveying important aspects of the cultural life of major European countries and by presenting a selection from the varieties of cultural criticism that have appeared in postwar European thought. The basic assumption underlying this project postulates an organic relationship between forms of cultural expression and their social milieu. The universe of cultural life with its symbolic and emotive content constitutes an essential part of the life of a human community. Grasping its multiple meanings therefore is an integral part of the process of understanding a society. A broad range of difficult theoretical arguments could be made in order to illustrate all the complexities of this relationship between culture and society and to respond to an equally broad range of conceivable objections. These theoretical disputes, however, may be symptomatic of a certain phase in the development of contemporary cultural criticism but are not necessarily fruitful for the illustrative purposes of this project. These purposes are encompassed by the simple statement, a good deal about the character of a society and its politics can be understood by looking at its cultural life. We naturally do not wish to imply any sort of one-to-one mechanistic relationship between the structural and cultural components of a social whole and define a kind of direct causality between them. On the contrary, it is precisely in order to escape the pitfalls of such a simple-minded structural determinism that we voice the plea for the development of an empathetic understanding through the prism of cultural forms in attempting to comprehend social and political phenomena.

The argument concerning the importance of culture as a mode of understanding derives its force from the intuitive ability of writers, artists, and critics to capture and articulate in their works deeper human concerns and yearnings that no academic, social, or political analysis, with its methodological constraints and concentration on arguments based on ascertainable evidence, can ever convey. This is one of the reasons why students often find their assignments in academic social science dry and uninspiring: they find themselves absorbing a great deal of empirical facts about a country or community without gaining a deeper and more intimate awareness of its problems. The same is largely true of the study of political and social ideas. The works of major thinkers are usually read in isolation, without an adequate sense of the circumstances which generated them and the problems to which they responded. The genuine purposes of their authors, the nuances in their meanings, the real import of their arguments and imagery cannot be fully appreciated until even the greatest classics are understood in their pertinent historical and cultural context. The broader cultural climate, the atmosphere of symbols, shared meanings, and social sentiments to which a great work constitutes a creative response, provide the crucial clues for its comprehension. The products of reflection or of the creative imagination in turn provide the most sensitive and eloquent statements that mediate between the situation that gave them birth and the understanding of the student of these situations by capturing what is essential and enduring and lasting in terms that can be readily appreciated and felt by outsiders to the milieu reflected in a particular classic work. The relationship can be characterized as truly 'dialectical.'

Thus the exigencies of understanding the classic works of creative expression and reflection, no less than the development of a full sense of the character of social and political life, point to a study of the cultural environment that connects the two. Context-building is therefore an essential precondition of the process of understanding. This task can be partly accomplished by looking at the insights of criticism which explores precisely the connections between the works of creative expression and reflection and their milieu.

Cultural criticism involves the evaluation and interpretation of all those forms of creative or reflective expression that constitute the cultural production of a society. The task of evaluation and interpretation is discharged naturally by reference to certain prevailing intellectual and moral standards which the critics want either to uphold or to subvert, according to their perception of the quality and function of culture. Cultural criticism therefore opens a double perspective: it provides information on the nature and content of creative and reflective expression in a society at a particular point in time and exposes us to the sense of values and needs guiding the appreciation of these varieties of expression. The movement of cultural criticism, therefore, registers the life-history of a civilization and provides precisely that deeper sense of empathetic understanding that empirical knowledge often loses by describing mere externalities. The pertinence of the study of such intellectual phenomena for political understanding does not need to be argued in any detail. It is enough to recollect that the greatest sources of political philosophy invariably found in cultural criticism their point of departure. Montesquieu and Hegel, no less than Plato, began from a consideration of spiritual principles and the phenomenology of cultural forms in order to proceed to their political criticism.

The pretensions of this project, of course, do not range so far as to raise claims of direct inspiration from these sources. A more concrete model of appreciation of the possibilities of the study of cultural criticism has been found in what is perhaps the most successful essay studying a process of social change through the varieties of cultural criticism it elicited as presented by Raymond Williams in *Culture and Society*. Acknowledging the fruitfulness of that approach, the present project attempts to collect some of the relevant primary materials that might be suggestive of the range of cultural concerns in postwar Europe. This is thus an initial exploratory step in treading a path such as that first followed by Williams, picking up chronologically where he left off, and expanding geographically into the natural and cultural vicinity of his own focus. The proper way to introduce this attempt at context-building is to illustrate the interpretive uses to which the materials in this volume might be put by briefly hinting at some cultural themes and moods that have underwritten the political and social history of twentieth-century Europe. It must be made clear at the outset that this collection is not an exhaustive anthology pretending to survey all aspects of contemporary European culture, but just an indicative casebook which attempts to introduce the case for the relation of culture and society through a selection of some relevant materials. Its only ambition and hope is to stimulate and invite students to think about the problems raised in the following pages and to explore further.

II

At the threshold of the twentieth century, one of the most authentic voices of lyricism in the new age, the German poet Rainer Maria Rilke, captured the deeper meaning of cultural creation in the century ahead in his insistence on loneliness and the loss of certainty as the consitutents of the human condition. He consequently could identify solitude and sorrow as the sources of creativity. In acknowledging the emanation of personal destiny from within and in recognizing the sense of solitude as the precondition of artistic creation, Rilke achieved a reconciliation with the human predicament which he transformed into the sensitive harmony of his poetry.

By taking this aesthetic position, Rilke was in a sense enunciating the cultural temper of the new century. The hermeticism of his poetry and his aesthetic of solitude in cultural creation were an integral part of the 'cultural revolution' that in the years before the First World War inaugurated twentieth-century European culture. The discovery of 'cultural revolutions' has become a favored pastime in contemporary criticism, but the characterization could hardly be more appropriate in defining the large-scale reorientation away from conventional standards in all aspects of European cultural life in the closing years of the 'belle époque'.

The cultural revolution encompassed the advent of atomic physics and the theory of relativity in science, the anti-positivist crusades led by Nietzsche and Bergson in philosophy, and the radical reorientation in social theory toward the forces of the unconscious effectuated by Freud. The impact of these developments was decisive in reshaping twentieth-century European thought in the long run, but the most spectacular manifestations of the cultural revolution were made most immediately apparent in literature and the fine arts. The artistic revolt involved essentially a break with what were felt to be the fetters of representational art, the abandonment of the classic techniques of realism, and the orientation toward abstraction and experimentation with the immanent possibilities of the constituent elements of art whether these might be color and light or words and sounds. The movement was already in the making in the quest of impressionism, but it reached a full awareness of its goals and hypostasis with the achievements of expressionism, cubism, and fauvism during the decade preceding the First World War. If these revolutionary artistic trends found their most concrete expression in painting, the publication in 1913 of the first volume of Marcel Proust's *A la recherche du temps perdu* inaugurated a revolution in literature from the tradition of nineteenth-century realism and naturalism. His lead in the renovation of the twentieth-century European novel was followed by a remarkable succession of authors including Franz Kafka, James Joyce, D. H. Lawrence, André Gide, and Thomas Mann, all of whom focused on the exploration of the inner dimension of existence.

The essence of the revolution that marked the transition from nineteenth- to twentieth-century culture lay in the increasing concern with the exploration of *sub*structure, of the dynamic components of experience, and of forms of expression. If this was obviously the major thrust of the advent of atomic physics, Freudian psychology, and Bergsonian philosophy, in the arts it was consciously described as the objective of the new movements in Wassily Kandinsky's 1912 essay, *Concerning the Spiritual in Art*. In its explanation of the new artistic styles as modes of exploration of the inner structure of the elements of art, this text could be considered as the genuine manifesto of modernism.

The criticism and rejection of prevailing social and cultural values voiced by the modernist revolt during the opening years of the century appeared vindicated by the devastating experience of the First World War. The reversal suffered by the optimism and the belief in progress enshrined in nineteenth-century culture was reflected not only in the disenchantment and gloom of anti-war literature that sprang from the experience of four years in the trenches, but also in the emergence of self-conscious and militant forms of cultural protest such as dadaism and surrealism which were explicitly directed against the dominant values of prewar Europe. Thus the major cultural impact of the First World War was to make the criticisms voiced by the prewar cultural revolution credible. This in turn can largely explain the triumph of cultural modernism in the 1920s, which witnessed the transformation of the prewar *avant-garde* into the mainstream of European culture.

The reception of the prewar *avant-garde* outsiders as insiders into the culture of the 1920s gave a distinctly modernist tone to the postwar cultural outlook. This was most characteristically the case with the culture of Weimar Germany – the country whose politics and society absorbed the most profound impact of the war. The persistence and further development during the next half-century of the modernist temper and values introduced by the outsiders-turned-insiders gave twentieth-century culture a basic aesthetic unity. The social significance of cultural modernism could be best understood as a generalization of the aesthetic attitude immanent in Rilke's premonition about the essence and conditions of artistic creation: a retreat into the self, an exploration of the inner world of human sensibility and personal aesthetic experience were indeed making the sense of solitude the major theme of the new culture. The acclaim with which Proust's second volume was received in 1921, after the relative indifference that met the appearance of the first eight years earlier, was indicative of the strides made by the new outlook. Thirty years after Rilke wrote his *Letters to a Young Poet*, Marc Chagall found in the theme of solitude the appropriate title for a painting depicting an allegory on artistic creation. In the experience of solitude and in the form of retreat from society, European artists continued their revolt against their own bourgeois backgrounds and against the recasting of bourgeois Europe which emerged as the major preoccupation of public policy and recovery programs in the interwar period. In some remarkable instances the flight from bourgeois society took the form of an appeal to a conception of primitive authenticity as exemplified in painting by Chagall and Rousseau, in music by Stravinsky, and by the initiation of Lévi-Strauss's anthropological researches which culminated in one of the most significant intellectual phenomena of the postwar period, structuralism.

In a way it seemed that the flight from society and the retreat to solitude formed the only path open to the representatives of the new culture. To the extent that they might have been interested in extending their cultural dissent to the political sphere, the one outlet available to them was to join the period's politics of protest as it happened with those exponents of Italian futurism, like Marinetti, who embraced fascism or the French surrealists, like André Breton and Louis Aragon, who enlisted under the banner of the new French Communist Party. Witnessing this pattern of political engagement of men of letters, however, the French critic Julien Benda warned that it essentially amounted to an act of treason against the intellectual's vocation. In denouncing the treason of the intellectuals, Benda aimed his attack mostly against those minor *littérateurs* and adventurers like Marinetti who rallied to the causes of nationalism and fascism. By so doing they kindled what Benda saw as the most explosive danger of the era, simmering political passions which might – as they eventually did – escalate into violence and conflict of apocalyptic dimensions. The treason of the intellectuals as defined by Benda amounted to the abandonment of the role of disinterested critics and guardians of ideal values traditionally conceived to be the essence of the intellectuals' vocation, for the sake of enlistment in the service of destructive political passions.

Treason was thus essentially identified with political partisanship, which was considered unbecoming to the proper role of the intellectual in society. If that role, however, was conceived as the disinterested defense of certain ideal values and those values had already been undermined and worn out by the doubts and questioning of the cultural revolution, their defense would amount to still another form of treason. Even worse than treason, it would be nothing less than naked hypocrisy. The only plausible option that remained available, therefore, to all those who cared for intellectual integrity was the solitude of retreat and the exploration of the inner meaning of personal experience. Thus the options of solitude, hypocrisy, or treason that confronted the twentieth-century heirs to the European cultural tradition necessarily led to a set of choices that made the premonitions of Rilke's sensitivity emerge as a prophetic reading of the predicament of twentieth-century culture. The debates over the nature of 'pure poetry' and its relation to society that were triggered by the poetic production of Paul Valéry and dominated interwar literary criticism were characteristic of the new aesthetic attitude.

Solitude, however, might have appeared as the only choice dictated by intellectual integrity, but it had its own serious cost. The outsiders of the *avant-garde* who had become the insiders of modernist culture remained isolated in their societies, lacking the moral sustenance of an appreciative audience. This was acknowledged by one of the major exponents of aesthetic modernism, the painter Paul Klee who in 1923 wrote: 'We seek a people.' The modernist culture of solitude thus appeared to remain in a vacuum even at the moment of its triumph. This paradox was further compounded by the fact that the interwar period witnessed the emergence of mass audiences in European society interested in the consumption of some kind of cultural products once their basic socioeconomic needs were met. This was the age of the 'revolt of the masses' in European history, but these potential mass audiences remained unattracted to the hermeticism of modernist culture and thought. They were captivated instead by the effects of still another cultural revolution that was made possible by the combined impact of the possibilities of modern technology and the new sociological realities. The latter were the effects of the social mobilization of the masses of European populations which until then had remained beyond the purview of national cultures. This other cultural revolution was that of the mass media, which became the transmitters of a popular culture of leisure and entertainment appealing to the needs and tastes of the masses to whom the hermeticism of high culture remained inaccessible.

The split between the two cultural revolutions, the revolution of modernism and the revolution of the mass media, inaugurated the divorce between popular culture and high culture that has developed into a major focus of contemporary cultural thought. At the time of its appearance this divergence was perceived as a symptom of a new sociological configuration that generated a major wave of cultural criticism. The major challenge consisted of a perception of a coming decadence of European civilization in the age of the masses. The appeal of the popular culture of the mass media was interpreted as a symptom of the impending collapse of the great tradition of European culture. Already, at the end of the First World War, Oswald Spengler had predicted the coming decline of the West, but in the 1930s, following on the heels of the triumph of modernism in the previous decade, the new cultural criticism, in voicing its concern about the quality of cultural creation in the society of the masses, enunciated an attack on modernity.

This form of cultural criticism was a transnational phenomenon appearing almost simultaneously in one European society after another. The Spanish philosopher José Ortega y Gasset with his book *The Revolt of the Masses* provided an epigrammatic articulation of the major concern of a whole school of cultural thought. Similar anxieties were voiced by Karl Jaspers in Germany, F. R. Leavis and T. S. Eliot in Britain, while in France Georges Duhamel identified the challenge of mass society and popular culture with a danger of 'Americanization of European civilization.' Although all these constituted conservative responses to a changing society, the new cultural criticism found a left-wing version in the aesthetic views of the Frankfurt school of critical social theory which shared the preoccupation with the dilution of cultural quality and sought to explain the nature of cultural change by looking at the broader systemic forces transforming European society.

It is important to note in considering the arguments of these critics of modernity that generally they did not subject to questioning the modernist values themselves. On the contrary, some of them were major exponents of the culture of modernism: T. S. Eliot was one of the foremost representatives of the hermetic poetry of solitude and Karl Jaspers was intimately involved with the elaboration of existentialism, one of the major waves of twentieth-century philosophic thought. The thinkers of the Frankfurt school in turn attempted to reinterpret and revitalize Marxist social thought by drawing on the esoteric philosophical currents of existentialism and phenomenology as well as on Freud's social theory – all of which had developed in conscious opposition to the nineteenth-century positivist legacy of which Marxism was a major component.

Such were the paradoxes of European cultural criticism in the age that saw the consolidation of the modernist revolution. The basic irony lay in the fact that in the name of modernist values and modes of thought it constituted an attack on the advent of modern society. The modernist values and achievements themselves, however, were far from being universally acceptable. The tension between modernism and modernity was occasionally resolved in the eyes of their common enemies. Caught in the claws of the Nazi Behemoth, the flowering modernist culture of Weimar Germany came to an abrupt end and many of its most creative exponents sought refuge across the Atlantic where twentieth-century culture was destined to bloom in its natural home. Both modernism in art and the claims of modern society were ruthlessly suppressed by the Nazi counter-revolution which denounced the former as decadence and regimented the latter allegedly to prevent anarchy. A parallel fate awaited cultural modernism in Stalinist Russia, where after the spectacular achievements of the modernist 1920s artistic creativity was sacrificed to the requirements of a 'socialist realism' that was expected to motivate the sacrifices required for the construction of an alternative modern society.

All these paradoxes were symptomatic of a profound crisis in European civilization. The falsity of certain haunting dilemmas and contradictions and the emptiness of accepted ideologies were soon made apparent by the choices forced upon the European conscience by the political confrontations of the 1930s. The advent of Nazism in Germany, the construction of 'socialism in one country' in Stalin's Russia, and the collision of the ideological currents of the period in the Spanish Civil War had profound repercussions in the cultural realm and led to an intense politicization of the arts. The wave of fascism during the interwar period attracted the sympathies of some prominent men of letters including Ezra Pound who actually chose to settle in Mussolini's Italy, T. S. Eliot, and also, to some degree, D. H. Lawrence and W. B. Yeats. In France the militants of the Action Française led by Charles Maurras perceived in fascist ideology a means of injecting modern dynamism into their reactionary traditionalism. In Italy itself Gabriele d'Annunzio led a frenzy of nationalist literature. In Nazi Germany the regimentation and ideological cleansing of the arts forced the foremost exponents of German culture either to take the road of exile – like Thomas Mann – or to voice their protest through the silence of their 'inner migration'. One of the most distinguished German philosophers, however, the leading existentialist Martin Heidegger, chose to applaud the coming of Nazism.

On the opposite side stood all those who had found an alternative source of inspiration in the socialist tradition and threw their effort into the cultural mobilization against fascism. André Gide, a leading communist sympathizer in France, had returned disillusioned from a visit to the Soviet Union, but the socialist allegiances of W. H. Auden and Stephen Spender in Britain and of Louis Aragon and Paul Eluard in France contributed creatively to their aesthetic pursuits. In France, furthermore, the papal condemnation of the Action Française in 1926 enabled socially conscious Catholic writers like François Mauriac to join the anti-fascist mobilization. From the direction of the broad alignment of the Popular Front which had been formed in 1936 to defend democratic government from the fascist threat came the social realism of Roger Martin du Gard and Jules Romain. In the case of Italy, anti-fascist resistance inspired the social commentaries of Ignazio Silone.

The fascist attack on the Spanish Republic in 1936 and the subsequent civil war in Spain transformed the confrontation between fascists and anti-fascists into a pan-European crusade which posed such pressing moral choices before the conscience of all thinking persons that it became impossible to maintain the posture of neutrality and retreat. Solitude as an option of cultural life appeared increasingly irrelevant, while political commitment, *engagement*, was felt by many as an ethical necessity. The Spanish Civil War, in short, stirred the European conscience out of the complacency of solitude and retreat. Through his involvement in the Spanish struggle on the republican side, André Malraux showed how political activism could become a source of creative inspiration. W. H. Auden, one of the most authentic exponents of poetic modernism, indicated with his attitude during the Spanish Civil War that solitary hermeticism could not remain immune to the challenges of moral and political choice. That choice was exercised unequivocally not only by the young idealists and democrats who joined the International Brigade to fight for Spanish democracy. It also stimulated the literary responses to the conflict in the works of Franz Borkenau, George Orwell, and Ernest Hemingway. At the same time, it motivated other writers to abandon their earlier pro-fascist positions. This was the case with Georges Bernanos who joined two other prominent Catholic intellectuals, Jacques Maritain and François Mauriac, in condemning the nationalist insurgents in Spain.

Thus the intense politicization of European culture in the 1930s in the context of the confrontation between fascists and anti-fascists culminated in the enlistment of an important segment of Europe's intelligentsia to the struggle in defense of the cherished values of a tradition threatened by barbarism. Support for the cause of republican Spain became a test of conscience for all European democrats. No other posture was indeed possible in view of the coming broader confrontation of which the Spanish conflict was simply a prelude. The fate of Federico Garcia Lorca, Spain's greatest twentieth-century poet, who joined the practice of lyricism to the tragedy of political sacrifice, was the opening episode anticipating the tribulations of cultural life in the global drama just beginning. Lorca's tragic destiny remained a challenge before the conscience of a culture seeking through the holocaust to purify itself.

III

The apocalyptic experience of the first 'total war' during which the very survival of civilization seemed to be at stake had a cathartic impact on European culture. In the presence of such a contest the option of solitude versus hypocrisy and treason as alternative paths of cultural life lost any compelling force it might have possessed. The new experiences, hypostasized in a sense of living through a confrontation between good and evil, made new options and visions appear relevant to cultural creation. The experience of war acted as a catalyst that liberated culture from the impasse of the interwar paradoxes by confronting it with the burning needs and dilemmas of real life. Amidst the traumas of the calamity, not only was the falsity of earlier dilemmas made plain, but also the need for a new cultural configuration was intensely felt.

If a section of the European intelligentsia, mesmerized at the beginning by fascism, was prepared to compromise with it, and if many others, including T. S. Eliot, remained neutral before the tragedy of Spain, the eventual outbreak of the Second World War put the options confronting Europe's future in a much harsher light. This made choices more readily apparent and resulted in the emergence of a search for new values. The experience of resistance provided a point of departure and set the tone of the new cultural quests. Paradoxically, at the darkest moments of the war the cultural outlook that sprang from that supreme struggle was expressed in a literature of hope and expectancy, in an embattled vision of a better future. The catharsis that European culture was going through was expressed in the yearning for recapturing Europe's humanist tradition in a new synthesis encompassing all ideological positions fighting against fascism – the common enemy embodying the total negation of the values of that tradition.

The cultural temper of postwar Europe was thus shaped by the recovery of basic humanist concerns. The end of the war witnessed an outpouring of creativity. Europe's intellectuals appeared to be motivated by great urgency to express the feelings and ideas that remained submerged in the years of holocaust. They wanted to have their say about the experience of war and tyranny and to voice their appraisal of the present and future. The social themes that Silone had introduced in anti-fascist literature were readily taken over and amplified in the social commentaries of Italian neo-realism in the novels of Carlo Levi, Elio Vittorini, and Cesare Pavese and in the films of Vittorio da Sica and Roberto Rosellini. In depicting poverty and human misery, neo-realism combined social criticism with a constructive faith in social change and a more humane future. This was the essence of the new humanism.

In Germany the quest for catharsis found an outlet in the 'literature of ruins' and the shuddering description of life under Nazism in the works of Ernst Wiechert and Eugen Kogon. The haunting sense of guilt in German collective conscience that these authors attempted to impart was soon transformed into the political and moral criticism of 'Group 47' and reached its most distinguished expression in Günter Grass's *The Tin Drum* (1959). While catharsis through criticism proceeded in Germany and Italy, in France the possibilities of a new humanism relevant to the requirements of the time were daringly projected in the wartime novel of 'Vercors', The *Silence of the Sea* (1942). Meanwhile Albert Camus, after his exploration of the psychological structure of nihilism in *The Outsider* (1942), managed, by means of his brilliant allegory of the struggle against barbarism and death, to reach a moral affirmation of life in *The Plague* (1947). England finally produced a counterpart of neo-realism in the protests voiced in the early 1950s by the 'Angry Young Men' in their revolt against the invisible social barriers which planning for social change in the welfare state had allowed to persist. These protests were characteristically registered in the works of John Osborne and John Braine.

Social criticism and social protest provided a refreshingly lively content to the efforts at a cultural reconstruction in postwar Europe. This was achieved without disrupting the basic aesthetic unity of modernism which was carried over from the interwar period in the essential continuity of stylistic forms in literature and the arts. Both Camus and Grass used the possibilities of surrealist fiction to express their vision of the human condition, while in the fine arts the creative longevity of older masters assured the pre-eminence of modernism whose aesthetic resources were employed to express the new concerns. Picasso had shown forcefully with *Guernica* already before the war that it was quite possible to use the expressive styles of modernism in order to depict the intensity of political tragedies. Likewise, Henry Moore and Marino Marini sculpted into visual reality the traumas and suffering of the war experience in their respective monumental creations.

The accentuation of the political aspect of experience provides an important part of the content of various forms of cultural life in the immediate postwar period. It appeared as if the earlier divorce between modernist culture and society was replaced by a concern to be relevant to human needs, even through the medium of modernist expression. The reintegration of political humanism was extended to the esoteric realm of twentieth-century philosophy as well. This was the objective of the ambitious philosophical project that the French existentialists set for themselves in the attempt to combine the insights of psychoanalysis, phenomenology, and Marxism within a framework that still raised the basic existentialist questions. The wartime experiences of collaboration, resistance, and death set the context of extreme situations in which the existentialist imperative of exercising a choice even under ambiguous circumstances would appear eminently pertinent. The making of a choice in the face of moral dilemmas was understood as the essential way in realizing the individual's existence by means of an act of responsibility and freedom. Through the linkage of existentialism to Marxism, Jean-Paul Sartre and Maurice Melreau-Ponty, the most prominent of French existentialists, suggested a choice committing the individual to the struggle of the masses for social change. Their position appeared quite powerful and found wide appeal in the years immediately following the war when Europe's appropriate future paths were still debated by her intellectual leaders. This was the context of one of the most celebrated ideological debates in postwar Europe in the course of which Melreau-Ponty affirmed in *Humanism and Terror* the claims of 'Marxist' existentialism in the face of Arthur Koestler's gruesome revelations in *Darkness at Noon* concerning the Moscow trials of the 1930s. This exchange provided an opportunity to Raymond Aron to denounce the ideological vogue of Marxism as the 'opium' of European intellectuals and to appeal to the values of an older liberal humanism as an alternative.

This debate was an intellectual harbinger of the coming Cold War which for more than a decade absorbed Europe's energies. The intensity of the ideological confrontation of the Cold War submerged a great deal of the creativity of the immediate postwar years which had brought about Europe's cultural reconstruction. The impact of the Cold War on domestic politics in Western Europe contributed to a split between the political leaders and the leading exponents of postwar cultural reconstruction. The latter remained isolated and estranged amidst the shrill hostility toward social change and political criticism elicited by the fear of a perceived communist menace. Despite the pressures and temptations of the ideological Manichaeism of the Cold War, however, European culture proved that the lessons of the war, the dangers of human degradation and annihilation which the interwar generation seemed to have had forgotten too soon, were deeply absorbed and acted as brakes on the reawakened political passions. The content of postwar cultural orientations was transformed but not completely shed. Following the advent of ideological rigidification, a new intolerance did not destroy the recovery of humanism.

The pressures of the Cold War on the societies of Eastern Europe had as a consequence in the realm of culture the continuing regimentation and tight state control over all forms of expression. The restrictions of Zhanovism remained in force after its founder's death in 1948, and even the 'cultural thaw' that followed Stalin's departure in 1953 was at best conditional. Cultural renewal therefore could only come in the form of protest, allusive criticism, and veiled defiance of the regime. This attitude was channeled into the poetry of Yevgeny Yevtushenko, Boris Pasternak's Nobel prize-winning novel, *Doctor Zhivago* (1957), and over the years into the fiction of Alexander Solzhenitsyn. Such questioning often brought sentences to labour-camp terms as it happened in 1965 with two authors, Daniel and Sinyavsky. Elsewhere in Eastern Europe conditions were no less repressive. In East Germany, where Brecht chose to return from his wartime exile, his political irony alone was tolerated – an exception that underlined the grim silence of a fettered culture.

In the West as well the Cold War undermined the cogency of politicized cultural expression and the social criticism that had been voiced by the different forms of neo-realism was muted. The return of modernist abstraction in the guise of explorations of the absurd in one field of cultural creation after another, the retreat into inner mono-logue and artistic experimentation, and the abandonment of speculation for the sake of technical rigor and 'scientific' methodology in philosophy and the social sciences were so many signs of the cultural effects of ideological polarization during the Cold War. The replacement of neo-realism by the 'new wave' which restored fantasy and psycho-logical probing in the novel and in the cinema was a telling sign of this development. The cultural outlook of the 1950s and 1960s could be interpreted as a commentary on the quality of life and the shape of human relations in the advanced industrial society that emerged in Europe as a consequence of postwar economic reconstruction and growth. Thus instead of representing a retreat from society and a reduction of culture to some kind of meaningless solitude, the novels and films of the 'new wave' and the theatre of the absurd could be understood on a certain level as exploratory forms of art in the nature of emotional reality in modern society.

The oblique social commentary of 'new wave' culture did not of course remove the basic problem of communicability that was becoming increasingly apparent. The messages were there but they were almost impossible to capture and interpret. So *avant-garde* culture remained distant from the wide public and appeared locked in a willful 'narcissistic hermeticism', in Michael Biddiss's phrase. Despite its broad success, the theatre of the absurd, represented in France by two adopted authors, Samuel Beckett and Eugene Ionesco, excelled primarily in unintelligibility. The same problem faced the 'new novel' of Robbe-Grillet, Claude Simon, and Natalie Sarautte who attempted to carry forward the tradition of Proust and Joyce, but often lapsed into ambiguity and disorientation. Part of the cinematographic explorations of Truffaut, Goddard, and Alain Resnais exemplified similar difficulties. Esotericism and occasional unintelligibility characterized as well the brilliant attempts to explore the psychological complexities and penetrate in depth into the emotional and perceptual problems in modern society undertaken by the two most prominent branches of con-temporary European cinema, the Swedish school of Ingmar Bergman and the Italian post-neo-realist tradition represented by Federico Fellini and Michelangelo Antonio. In the visual arts the extreme experimentation involved in the adoption of American models of Op and Pop Art created doubts about both the authenticity of European imitation and its relevance, voiced by, among others, Marcel Duchamp, himself a survivor of earlier movements of artistic innovation.

Conceptual esotericism and hermeticism of language remained a major problem for philosophy and social thought as well. While Anglo-Saxon philosophy persisted in the increasingly remote technicalities – and often trivialities – of linguistic and logical analysis, continental philosophy, despite the fertility of its major twentieth-century movements, phenomenology and existentialism, remained clouded in conceptual obscurity. The major tradition of continental social thought furthermore, Marxism, despite the sustained quest of its twentieth-century luminaries from Lukács to Althusser for a philosophical renovation, experienced a form of social retreat and isolation. From a militant theory of political activism, Marxism became increasingly a commentary on consciousness and culture. In a lucid essay, Perry Anderson has explained this development as the consequence of the defeat of the revolutionary movement of the working class in Western Europe. It might be added that it has also been the product of the social success and the vogue of the intellectual leadership of contemporary European Marxism. The cohabitation of diverse schools of thought in a kind of trendy philosophical *avant-garde* has also made possible their intermarriage, as it happened in the case of the Marxist version of existentialism. Whether these inter-changes have had a genuinely fertilizing impact remains open to question. Social theory, by remaining conceptually obscure and stylistically impenetrable, has been an unmistakable form of social and cultural retreat.

This has generally been the case as well with the two other major currents of postwar European thought, structuralism and psychoanalysis. Both provided holistic accounts of social reality and in their versions elaborated respectively by Claude Lévi-Strauss and Jacques Lacan they have proposed synthetic views of human experience. Their brand of intellectual appeal has been explained by Michel Foucault by reference to the fact that 'they dissolve man' by pointing to universal structures of experience and to the force of the unconscious. In essence, therefore, they represent flights from the concrete world of history and politics. According to Foucault, their pursuits suggest that the centrality of man, as an object of knowledge, may be nearing its end – and with it a whole tradition of European humanism.

The debates that have expressed the various currents of cultural criticism in con-temporary Europe, however, appear to have evolved around a retention of humanism as a common denominator of conflicting points of view. Such was the case with the most important of these interchanges, the 'two cultures debate' that unfolded in Britain in the early 1960s between C. P. Snow and F. R. Leavis. Snow argued that the culture and possibilities of modern science and technology held the key to the satisfaction of human needs in modern society. Therefore, a basic understanding of the concepts of modern science was deemed essential to all educated persons. Against this position, Leavis, a survivor of the interwar conservative criticism of mass culture, pointed at the continuing relevance of Europe's classical literary tradition as a source of genuine values and a necessary corrective of the pitfalls, illusions, and dehumanizing risks of the modern culture of scientism. Paradoxically, Leavis's warnings against the dangers of dehumanization in a culture mesmerized by science and technology reverberated in the radical critiques of modern industrial society voiced by the New Left. Marcuse's nightmare about the emerging one-dimensional persons as the human species in post-industrial society constituted essentially a critique of the culture of scientism through an appeal to the humanist ideal of the well-rounded, critically minded individual.

That indeed was expected to be realized through a generalization of the benefits of cultural life, among as wide a segment of national populations as possible. This democratization of culture through the adoption of systematic government policies of cultural diffusion, decentralization, and increased accessibility of cultural products became a central concern in the arguments of cultural critics, who attempted to influence government planning accordingly. Such was the case, for instance, with the French academician Pierre Emmanuel who advocated a conception of culture as a dynamic force in the re-creation of national community.

The role of culture in society has accordingly provided the focus not only for essays in traditional cultural criticism and for inescapably vague appeals to the values of Europe's humanist heritage, but also for the impressive, empirically based explorations of Pierre Bourdieu who has broken new ground in the field of the sociology of culture. On the basis of empirical surveys of an enormous range, Bourdieu and his associates have examined the relations between cultural tastes and standards and the social conditions of existence. They managed to proceed from a statistical mapping of the terrain of cultural phenomena to the articulation of compelling criticism of the social function of aesthetic tastes and of the role of aesthetic creation in post-industrial civilization. Their criticism appears all the more convincing in view of the constant scrutiny and questioning to which they subject their very method of empirical inquiry.

In contrast to interwar cultural criticism, the appeal to cultural quality is no longer employed as an attack on the masses and as a protest against modernity. Culture, by becoming widely accessible, was expected to integrate the masses into the new humanism and to make the great heritage of European civilization a living experience for modern Europeans. In this effort, the resources of modern technology could be reappraised as helpful means rather than as threatening adversaries. A sign of the new approach to culture has been the fact that in one European country after another cultural development became an integral part of government planning and an objective of intergovernmental cooperation either in bilateral agreements or through trans-national organizations.

The increased awareness of the relevance of culture, in turn, could and did provide a medium of criticism of the failures of organized political power, existing academic institutions, and established structures of cultural life, in promoting the democratization of the cultural experience. Furthermore, when the pressures of the Cold War subsided after the mid-1960s, the concerns of cultural criticism in the advanced regions of liberal Europe were reinforced and fertilized by an expanding awareness of the relevance of culture to struggles for political change in the southern and eastern parts of the continent. The struggles against the dictatorships in Europe's southern periphery and the silent ardors required by the effort to endow East European socialism with a human face have been fought to a remarkable extent in the realms of cultural life. These experiences proved decisive catalysts of cultural change in the societies in which they occurred, and in turn provided inspiration and met with the solidarity of major exponents of cultural life elsewhere in Europe. The responsiveness elicited in Western Europe by the cultural articulation of change and protest in the South and East, was reflected in the attention devoted to these phenomena in the context of the major event of organized cultural presence on the continent, the Venice Biennale. Spanish 'artistic *avant-garde* and social reality, 1936–1976' provided one of the themes in 1976 and East European dissidence offered a main focus during the following cycle of the Biennale.

IV

A cosmopolitan humanism constitutes therefore one of the salient dimensions of contemporary European culture. In a sense, of course, European culture has always been cosmopolitan. But earlier forms of cosmopolitanism were rather narrowly based in the areas of cultural influence and mutual awareness of artistic achievements that connected the intellectual elites of different European countries. The new cosmopolitanism is different in two respects. First it points to a unity of values. This is the product of the shared concerns of a modern culture that has appeared to have learnt from the tragedies of the past. In this regard, European culture is returning to a spiritual unity for the first time since the Enlightenment, after the disruptions of the century of nationalisms and the age of the world wars. Furthermore, if the Enlightenment represented a humanist cosmopolitanism achieved by and limited among intellectual elites absorbing the cultural influences of British and French philosophy, the new cosmopolitanism derives from the sense of Europe's diminished dimensions and essential unity in comparison to the larger world and possesses a broad basis through the opening of culture to the masses. This suggests the second distinctive characteristic of the new cosmopolitanism. It is more democratic in aspiration and in practice. This is due naturally to the vastly changed character of European society and to the possibilities of modern technology. Cosmopolitanism is the inevitable effect of the age of the revolution in communication, of the explosion in mobility and travel. Cultural exchange thus becomes daily practice before becoming official policy. Consequently cosmopolitanism is reflected most integrally in the mutual awareness of and responsiveness to each other of formerly isolated cultural regions and traditions. This in turn allows the coming into their own, as creative entities, of former cultural provinces of more dynamic civilizations.

Two substantive aspects of this phenomenon, already alluded to, need to be particularly underlined. First, it is significant that the most genuine yearnings of humanism are voiced in the East which thus provides – maybe for the first time in European history – through its culture of dissent a major inspiration to the shared tradition of European civilization. Dissident humanism comes from the East to revitalize a tradition of values that in the West finds itself constantly confronted with the fears of exhaustion and impasse. Secondly, perhaps for the reason just stated, cultural thought in contemporary Europe has progressively come to appreciate the vitality and authenticity of the contribution of the Mediterranean regions of the continent, where a tradition of lyricism unfolding for many generations has attained a compelling level of artistic achievement. The successive Nobel prizes for literature awarded in the last twenty years to the poetry of Mediterranean Europe in the persons of Salvadore Quasimodo, George Seferis, Eugenio Montale, Vicente Aleixandre, and most recently Odysseus Elytis constitute a circumstantial, but telling, acknowledgement of the cultural equality of the Mediterranean societies in European civilization. The essential contribution of Mediterranean poetry is a vision hammered by the concrete experiences of life and history, which captures in its symbolic language concerns relevant to the anxieties of all humanity. The recognition of Elytis's affirmation of life and luminous beauty through his perception of the aesthetic personality of the Aegean and the poetic re-creation of the transparency of the Greek landscape and outlook is an eloquent indication that the framework of cosmopolitan humanism has broken down the barriers of national isolation. It appears quite capable of goading contemporary criticism to appreciate the relevance of creative achievement even in a poetic universe cast in a language uniquely charged by the poet's own sense of his historical and cultural aesthetic.

The groupings for inspiration beyond the traditional regions of cultural predominance point to an expanding horizon, but at the same time hint at an obverse side to the rather congratulatory picture of contemporary European humanism painted above. Like earlier periods in cultural history, the cultural configuration of present-day Europe is not immune to contradictions and paradoxes. Many of these represent the immediate impact of the constraints of the social environment on cultural life. Culture is often a prisoner of these structural constraints rather than their critic − despite the intellectuals' pretensions to the contrary. It is true that European culture today remains lively and unruly, ready to espouse novelties, to explore new possibilities, and, naturally, to raise the standard of revolt as it happened in 1968. During that elusive revolution the resources of culture were mobilized in a protest against the discontinuities of social change and the failures of organized society to realize the aspirations for which culture stood ready to fight. That may have been a transient outburst of romantic heroism, but it did belie at least one influential diagnosis about Europe's temper: the 'end of ideology' thesis which suggested that affluence and prosperity had nurtured an American-style pragmatism which had drained the appeal of ideas as moving forces in European politics.

The shared frame of humanist thinking identified above, nevertheless, raises the question whether it signifies anything else than the total secularization of European life. The prevalence of a framework of secular humanism as the axis of cultural consensus in a way might betray a cultural temper of resignation, as some perceptive observers of the European scene have suspected. Resignation is most graphically expressed in a ritualization of protest, which in fact amounts to an eloquent acknowledgement of lack of alternatives. Despite a perennial dissatisfaction with the existing order voiced in intellectual circles, things are accepted and enjoyed as they are and criticism itself appears to be a necessary part of the whole configuration. What else could be meant by the existentialists' insistence on making even meaningless choices? The problem basically involves a failure of will and as a consequence intellectual community remains always an aspiration equally elusive to the change it might seek to realize.

The vogue of the social sciences in postwar Europe constitutes a clear sign of cultural secularization and the metamorphosis of the intellectual from critic into technocrat. This has been one of the most far-ranging revolutions in European culture which, by fundamentally altering the pattern of expectations from the intellectual, has contributed toward the ritualization of the protests of the stubborn and has co-opted the more pliable into the technocratic apparatus of post-industrial civilization. The 'cultural revolution' which Michel Crozier was the first to identify as the effect of the quest for social change in postwar Europe can be precisely described in terms of the transition in the position of the intellectual from role to function, from the role of critics voicing a society's conscience to the function of 'think-tank' members and guardians of specialized expertise. The cultural revolution could be thus understood as the process through which the zealots of the social sciences emerged as the most prestigious and best-rewarded segment of the European intelligentsia, charged with the promotion of the secular ends of society: growth, modernization, material prosperity.

This is the context of the resignation of the intellectual to the role of media monger as it has been recently suggested by Régis Debray. Considering this role to which the successors of the critics of mass culture have resigned themselves, one cannot escape some ruminations on the cunning of history. If thus the intellectuals close to the 'establishment' have abandoned every pretension to autonomous intellectual leadership and joined into the exercise of power by assuming the role of ideology fabricators through the media, criticism must have found refuge in the bosom of the left. The intellectual left, however, has been so much isolated and consumed by its ego-centrism that criticism has been submerged in the theoretical esotericism and oracular pronouncements of its internal debates, especially in France and Germany.

In view of these problems that besiege contemporary secular humanism, this overview of present-day European culture will have to break off with a suspended judgement. In this connection, a sobering concluding reflection might be drawn from an analogy recently suggested by Jean Starobinski, between contemporary criticism and the trajectory followed by Montaigne at the dawn of Europe's modern civilization. Montaigne's intellectual itinerary took him from the articulation of protest against, to the acceptance of appearance and of things as they are − for lack of better alternatives. The same message emerges, Starobinski has argued, from the diagnosis offered by some of the most important schools of cultural criticism in contemporary Europe. There is naturally no reason to rejoice in this conclusion. One might add, however, that Montaigne on his way from protest to skepticism probed all the essential questions and thus he has managed to sustain an open dialogue with all thinking individuals concerned with the human condition in subsequent generations. Whether the analogy with Montaigne can be read to suggest as much about contemporary European cultural thought with all its constraints and contradictions is, of course, an entirely different issue. If a future critic nevertheless comes to acknowledge it, it will be no mean achievement. For the time being, however, it must remain an open question.

PASCHALIS KITROMILIDES

References: Introductory Essay

Anderson, Perry, *Considerations on Western Marxism* (London: New Left Books, 1977).

Aron, Raymond, *The Opium of the Intellectuals* (Garden City, NY: Doubleday, 1957).

Benda, Julien, *The Treason of the Intellectuals* (New York: Norton, 1969).

Biddiss, Michael D., *The Age of the Masses* (New York: Harper, 1977).

Bourdieu, Pierre, *La Distinction. Critique sociale de jugement* (Paris: Minuit, 1979).

Debray, Régis, *Le Pouvoir intellectuel en France* (Paris: Editions Ramsay, 1979).

Duhamel, Georges, *America the Menace* (Boston, Mass.: Houghton Mifflin, 1931).

Eliot, T. S., *The Idea of a Christian Society* (London, Faber, 1939).

Eliot, T. S., *Notes towards the Definition of Culture* (London: Faber, 1948).

Emmanuel, Pierre, *Pour une politique de la culture* (Paris: Seuil, 1971).

Foucault, Michel, *The Order of Things* (a translation of *Les Mots et les choses*) (New York: Vintage, 1970).

Gay, Peter, *Weimar Culture: The Outsider as Insider* (New York: Harper & Row, 1968).

Jaspers, Karl, *Man in the Modern Age* (Garden City, NY: Doubleday, 1957).

Jay, Martin, *The Dialectical Imagination: A History of the Frankfurt School and the Institute of Social Research, 1923–1950* (Boston, Mass.: Little, Brown, 1973), ch. 6, 'Aesthetic theory and the critique of mass culture.'

Koestler, Arthur, *Darkness at Noon* (New York: Macmillan, 1941).

Leavis, F. R., *Mass Civilization and Minority Culture* (Cambridge: The Minority Press, 1930).

Leavis, F. R., *Two Cultures? The Significance of C. P. Snow,* (London: Chatto & Windus, 1963).

Marcuse, Herbert, *One-Dimensional Man* (Boston, Mass.: Beacon, 1964).

Merleau-Ponty, Maurice, *Humanism and Terror* (Boston, Mass.: Beacon, 1969).

Ortega y Gasset, José, *The Revolt of the Masses* (New York: Norton, 1932).

Rilke, Rainer Maria, *Letters to a Young Poet* (New York: Norton, 1934).

Snow, C. P., *The Two Cultures and a Second Look* (Cambridge: Cambridge University Press, 1965).

Spengler, Oswald, *The Decline of the West*, 2 vols (New York: Knopf, 1926 and 1928).

Starobinski, Jean, 'Montaigne on illusion: the denunciation of untruth', *Daedalus*, Summer 1979, pp. 85–101.

UNESCO, *Studies and Documents on Cultural Policies* (Paris: UNESCO, 1969–70).

Williams, Raymond, *Culture and Society, 1780–1950* (New York: Columbia University Press, 1958).

PART ONE

The Social Significance of Cultural
Forms: Theoretical Statements

Introduction to Part One

The conception of a certain integral relation between different forms of cultural expression and their social environment provides the basis of the cultural criticism of the four thinkers represented in this section. Their theoretical arguments have exerted a major influence on the understanding of culture in contemporary European thought. Indeed it could be argued that cultural thought in contemporary Europe cannot be comprehended outside the frame of reference that has been set by Lukács, Sartre, Brecht, and Benjamin. Although the relation of culture and society constitutes their major premiss, their interpretation of cultural forms does not in any way represent a kind of mechanistic reductionism. On the contrary, the relation of culture and society is explored in all its complexity in an attempt to capture the meaning of cultural creation by defining what Jean-Paul Sartre characterized as the 'situation' of the exponents of cultural life.

From the vantage point provided by a sense of the social situation of culture, cultural criticism then proceeds to the diagnosis of the social significance, possibilities, and limits of cultural creation. Georg Lukács, after reflecting on the meaning of modernism in twentieth-century literature, is able to point to its failures in regard to what he conceived as essential human concerns. Thus modernism as the ideology of social isolation and retreat becomes the target of a mode of cultural criticism which is inspired by an abiding concern with social change and with the human predicament in modern society.

The same inspiration informs Bertolt Brecht's yearning for a humanist theatre relevant to the concerns of men and women in the modern 'scientific' age. This theatre, according to postwar Europe's most influential dramatist, should be true to its age-old function of responding to the human need for entertainment and pleasure while at the same time it should become a medium of social change by deepening awareness of human relations as they might be a in better world.

One of the most sensitive and original of European cultural critics in the twentieth century, Walter Benjamin, focused the attention of his philosophical reflections on the social significance of artistic creation by identifying a dynamic at work in the history of art akin to that shaping broader configurations of social forces. Thus the social dynamic of revolutions in the means of production is transposed as an interpretive scheme into the understanding of change in artistic creation. The importance of Benjamin's elaboration of this theory lies in the fact that it never lapses into simplistic analogical interpretation that might easily lose the complexity and mystique of the artistic experience. The social significance of change in artistic creation for the public of art is encapsulated in the elusive concept of aura which provides a principle of cultural criticism that is pertinent both to an understanding of the aesthetics of modern art and for an evaluation of its relevance to an ever-widening public. Although Benjamin died tragically in 1940, the full impact of his thought was felt in postwar cultural criticism on which it exerted an enduring influence. His approach, by detecting in the world of art a microcosmic counterpart of the dynamic processes trans-forming society, without however overlooking the independent emotive aspect and the mystique of artistic experience, has remained unmatched in contemporary aesthetics and provides a persisting point of departure for all theories of art since its formulation.

1

GEORG LUKÁCS

The Ideology of Modernism

It is in no way surprising that the most influential contemporary school of writing should still be committed to the dogmas of 'modernist' anti-realism. It is here that we must begin our investigation if we are to chart the possibilities of a bourgeois realism. We must compare the two main trends in contemporary bourgeois literature, and look at the answers they give to the major ideological and artistic questions of our time.

We shall concentrate on the underlying ideological basis of these trends (ideological in the above-defined, not in the strictly philosophical, sense). What must be avoided at all costs is the approach generally adopted by bourgeois-modernist critics themselves: that exaggerated concern with formal criteria, with questions of style and literary technique. This approach may appear to distinguish sharply between 'modern' and 'traditional' writing (i.e. contemporary writers who adhere to the styles of the last century). In fact it fails to locate the decisive formal problems and turns a blind eye to their inherent dialectic. We are presented with a false polarization which, by exaggerating the importance of stylistic differences, conceals the opposing principles actually underlying and determining contrasting styles.

To take an example: the *monologue intérieur*. Compare, for instance, Bloom's monologue in the lavatory or Molly's monologue in bed, at the beginning and at the end of *Ulysses*, with Goethe's early-morning monologue as conceived by Thomas Mann in his *Lotte in Weimar*. Plainly, the same stylistic technique is being employed. And certain of Thomas

Mann's remarks about Joyce and his methods would appear to confirm this.

Yet it is not easy to think of any two novels more basically dissimilar than *Ulysses* and *Lotte in Weimar*. This is true even of the superficially rather similar scenes I have indicated. I am not referring to the – to my mind – striking difference in intellectual quality. I refer to the fact that with Joyce the stream-of-consciousness technique is no mere stylistic device; it is itself the formative principle governing the narrative pattern and the presentation of character. Technique here is something absolute; it is part and parcel of the aesthetic ambition informing *Ulysses*. With Thomas Mann, on the other hand, the *monologue intérieur* is simply a technical device, allowing the author to explore aspects of Goethe's world which would not have been otherwise available. Goethe's experience is not presented as confined to momentary sense-impressions. The artist reaches down to the core of Goethe's personality, to the complexity of his relations with his own past, present and even future experience. The stream of association is only apparently free. The monologue is composed with the utmost artistic rigour: it is a carefully plotted sequence gradually piercing to the core of Goethe's personality. Every person or event, emerging momentarily from the stream and vanishing again, is given a specific weight, a definite position, in the pattern of the whole. However unconventional the presentation, the compositional principle is that of the traditional epic; in the way the pace is controlled, and the transitions and climaxes are organized, the ancient rules of epic narration are faithfully observed.

It would be absurd, in view of Joyce's artistic ambitions and his manifest abilities, to qualify the exaggerated attention he gives to the detailed recording of sense-data, and his comparative neglect of ideas and emotions, as artistic failure. All this was in conformity with Joyce's artistic intentions; and, by use of such techniques, he may be said to have achieved them satisfactorily. But between Joyce's intentions and those of Thomas Mann there is a total opposition. The perpetually oscillating patterns of sense-and memory-data, their powerfully charged – but aimless and directionless – fields of force, give rise to an epic structure which is *static*, reflecting a belief in the basically static character of events.

These opposed views of the world – dynamic and developmental on the one hand, static and sensational on the other – are of crucial importance in examining the two schools of literature I have mentioned. I shall return to the opposition later. Here, I want only to point out that an exclusive emphasis on formal matters can lead to serious misunderstanding of the character of an artist's work.

What determines the style of a given work of art? How does the intention determine the form? (We are concerned here, of course, with the intention realized in the work; it need not coincide with the writer's conscious intention.) The distinctions that concern us are not those between stylistic 'techniques' in the formalistic sense. It is the view of the world, the ideology or *Weltanschauung* underlying a writer's work, that counts. And it is the writer's attempt to reproduce this view of the world which constitutes his 'intention' and is the formative principle underlying the style of a given piece of writing. Looked at in this way, style ceases to be a formalistic category. Rather, it is rooted in content; it is the specific form of a specific content.

Content determines form. But there is no content of which Man himself is not the focal point. However various the *données* of literature (a particular experience, a didactic purpose), the basic question is, and will remain: what is Man?

Here is a point of division: if we put the question in abstract, philosophical terms, leaving aside all formal considerations, we arrive – for the realist school – at the traditional Aristotelian dictum (which was also reached by other than purely aesthetic considerations): Man is *zoon politikon*, a social animal. The Aristotelian dictum is applicable to all great realistic literature. Achilles and Werther, Oedipus and Tom Jones, Antigone and Anna Karenina: their individual existence – their *Sein an sich*, in the Hegelian terminology; their 'ontological being', as a more fashionable terminology has it – cannot be distinguished from their social and historical environment. Their human significance, their specific individuality cannot be separated from the context in which they were created.

The ontological view governing the image of man in the work of leading modernist writers is the exact opposite of this. Man, for these writers, is by nature solitary, asocial, unable to enter into relationships with other human beings. Thomas Wolfe once wrote: 'My view of the world is based on the firm conviction that solitariness is by no means a rare condition, something peculiar to myself or to a few specially solitary human beings, but the inescapable, central fact of human existence.' Man, thus imagined, may establish contact with other individuals, but only in a superficial accidental manner; only, ontologically speaking, by retrospective reflection. For 'the others', too, are basically solitary, beyond significant human relationship.

This basic solitariness of man must not be confused with that individual solitariness to be found in the literature of traditional realism. In the latter case, we are dealing with a particular situation in which a human being may be placed, due either to his character or to the circumstances of his life. Solitariness may be objectively conditioned, as with Sophocles' Philoctetes, put ashore on the bleak island of Lemnos. Or it may be subjective, the product of inner necessity, as with Tolstoy's Ivan Ilyitsch or Flaubert's Frédéric Moreau in the *Education sentimentale*. But it is always merely a fragment, a phase, a climax or anti-climax, in the life of the community as a whole. The fate of such individuals is characteristic of certain human types in specific social or historical circumstances. Beside and beyond their solitariness, the common life, the strife and togetherness of other human beings, goes on as before. In a word, their solitariness is a specific social fate, not a universal *condition humaine*.

The latter, of course, is characteristic of the theory and practice of modernism. I would like, in the present study, to spare the reader tedious excursions into philosophy. But I cannot refrain from drawing the reader's attention to Heidegger's description of human existence as a 'thrownness-into-being' *(Geworfenheit ins Dasein)*. A more graphic evocation of the ontological solitariness of the individual would be hard to imagine. Man is 'thrown-into-being'. This implies, not merely that man is constitutionally unable to establish relationships with things or persons outside himself; but also it is impossible to determine theoretically the origin and goal of human existence.

Man, thus conceived, is an ahistorical being. (The fact that Heidegger does admit a form of 'authentic' historicity in his system is not really relevant. I have shown elsewhere that Heidegger tends to belittle historicity as 'vulgar'; and his 'authentic' historicity is not distinguishable from ahistoricity.) This negation of history takes two different forms in modernist literature. First, the hero is strictly confined within the limits of his own experience. There is not for him – and apparently not for his creator – any pre-existent reality beyond his own self, acting upon him or being acted upon by him. Secondly, the hero himself is without personal history. He is 'thrown-into-the-world': meaninglessly, unfathomably. He does not develop through contact with the world; he neither forms nor is formed by it. The only 'development' in this literature is the gradual revelation of the human condition. Man is now what he has always been and always will be. The narrator, the examining subject, is in motion; the examined reality is static.

Of course, dogmas of this kind are only really viable in philosophical abstraction, and then only with a measure of sophistry. A gifted writer, however extreme his theoretical modernism, will in practice have to compromise with the demands of historicity and of social environment. Joyce uses Dublin, Kafka and Musil the Habsburg monarchy, as the locus of their masterpieces. But the locus they lovingly depict is little more than a backcloth; it is not basic to their artistic intention.

This view of human existence has specific literary consequences, particularly in one category, of primary theoretical and practical importance, to which we must now give our attention: that of *potentiality*. Philosophy distinguishes between *abstract* and *concrete* (in Hegel, 'real') *potentiality*. These two categories, their interrelation and opposition, are rooted in life itself. *Potentiality* – seen abstractly or subjectively – is richer than actual life. Innumerable possibilities for man's development are imaginable, only a small percentage of which will be realized. Modern subjectivism, taking these imagined possibilities for actual complexity of life, oscillates between melancholy and fascination. When the world declines to realize these possibilities, this melancholy becomes tinged with contempt. Hofmannsthal's Sobeide expressed the reaction of the generation first exposed to this experience:

> The burden of those endlessly pored-over
> And now forever perished possibilities . . .

How far were those possibilities even concrete or 'real'? Plainly, they existed only in the imagination of the subject, as dreams or daydreams. Faulkner, in whose work this subjective potentiality plays an important part, was evidently aware that reality must thereby be subjectivized and made to appear arbitrary. Consider this comment of his: 'They were all talking simultaneously, getting flushed and excited, quarrelling, making the unreal into a possibility, then into a probability, then into an irrefutable fact, as human beings do when they put their wishes into words.' The possibilities in a man's mind, the particular pattern, intensity and suggestiveness they assume, will of course be characteristic of that individual. In practice, their number will border on the infinite, even with the most unimaginative individual. It is thus a hopeless undertaking to define the contours of individuality, let alone to come to grips with a man's actual fate, by means of potentiality. The *abstract* character of potentiality is clear from the fact that it cannot determine development – subjective mental states, however permanent or profound, cannot here be decisive. Rather, the development of personality is determined by inherited gifts and qualities; by the factors, external or internal, which further or inhibit their growth.

But in life potentiality can, of course, become reality. Situations arise in which a man is confronted with a choice; and in the act of choice a man's character may reveal itself in a light that surprises even himself. In literature – and particularly in dramatic literature – the denouement often consists in the realization of just such a potentiality, which circumstances have kept from coming to the fore. These potentialities are, then, 'real' or concrete potentialities. The fate of the character depends on the potentiality in question, even if it should condemn him to a tragic end. In advance, while still a subjective potentiality in the character's mind, there is no way of distinguishing it from the innumerable abstract potentialities in his mind. It may even be buried away so completely that, before the moment of decision, it has never entered his mind even as an abstract potentiality. The subject, after taking his decision, may be unconscious of his own motives. Thus Richard Dudgeon, Shaw's Devil's Disciple, having sacrificed himself as Pastor Andersen, confesses: 'I have often asked myself for the motive, but I find no good reason to explain why I acted as I did.'

Yet it is a decision which has altered the direction of his life. Of course, this is an extreme case. But the qualitative leap of the denouement, cancelling and at the same time renewing the continuity of individual consciousness, can never be predicted. The concrete potentiality cannot be isolated from the myriad abstract potentialities. Only actual decision reveals the distinction.

The literature of realism, aiming at a truthful reflection of reality, must demonstrate both the concrete and abstract potentialities of human beings in extreme situations of this kind. A character's concrete potentiality once revealed, his abstract potentialities will appear essentially inauthentic. Moravia, for instance, in his novel *The Indifferent Ones*, describes the young son of a decadent bourgeois family, Michel, who makes up his mind to kill his sister's seducer. While Michel, having made his decision, is planning the murder, a large number of abstract – but highly suggestive – possibilities are laid before us. Unfortunately for Michel the murder is actually carried out; and, from the sordid details of the action, Michel's character emerges as what it is – representative of that background from which, in subjective fantasy, he had imagined he could escape.

Abstract potentiality belongs wholly to the realm of subjectivity; whereas concrete potentiality is concerned with the dialectic between the individual's subjectivity and objective reality. The literary presentation of the latter thus implies a description of actual persons inhabiting a palpable, identifiable world. Only in the interaction of character and environment can the concrete potentiality of a particular individual be singled out from the 'bad infinity' of purely abstract potentialities, and emerge as the determining potentiality of just this individual at just this phase of his development. This principle alone enables the artist to distinguish concrete potentiality from a myriad abstractions.

But the ontology on which the image of man in modernist literature is based invalidates this principle. If the 'human condition' – man as a solitary being, incapable of meaningful relationships – is identified with reality itself, the distinction between abstract and concrete potentiality becomes null and void. The categories tend to merge. Thus Cesare Pavese notes with John Dos Passos, and his German contemporary Alfred Döblin, a sharp oscillation between 'superficial *verisme*' and 'abstract expressionist schematism'. Criticizing Dos Passos, Pavese writes that fictional characters 'ought to be created by deliberate selection and description of individual features' – implying that Dos Passos's characterizations are transferable from one individual to another. He describes the artistic consequences: by exalting man's subjectivity, at the expense of the objective reality of his environment, man's subjectivity itself is impoverished.

The problem, once again, is ideological. This is not to say that the ideology underlying modernist writings is identical in all cases. On the contrary: the ideology exists in extremely various, even contradictory forms. The rejection of narrative objectivity, the surrender to subjectivity, may take the form of Joyce's stream of consciousness, or of Musil's 'active passivity', his 'existence without quality', or of Gide's *'action gratuite'*, where abstract potentiality achieves pseudo-realization. As individual character manifests itself in life's moments of decision, so too in literature. If the distinction between abstract and concrete potentiality vanishes, if man's inwardness is identified with an abstract subjectivity, human personality must necessarily disintegrate.

T. S. Eliot described this phenomenon, this mode of portraying human personality, as

> Shape without form, shade without colour,
> Paralysed force, gesture without motion.

The disintegration of personality is matched by a disintegration of the outer world. In one sense, this is simply a further consequence of our argument. For the identification of abstract and concrete human potentiality rests on the assumption that the objective world is inherently inexplicable. Certain leading modernist writers, attempting a theoretical apology, have admitted this quite frankly. Often this theoretical impossibility of understanding reality is the point of departure, rather than the exaltation of subjectivity. But in any case the connection between the two is plain. The German poet Gottfried Benn, for instance, informs us that 'there is no outer reality, there is only human consciousness, constantly building, modifying, rebuilding new worlds out of its own creativity'. Musil, as always, gives a moral twist to this line of thought. Ulrich, the hero of his *The Man without Qualities*, when asked what he would do if he were in God's place, replies: 'I should be compelled to abolish reality.' Subjective existence 'without qualities' is the complement of the negation of outward reality.

The negation of outward reality is not always demanded with such theoretical rigour. But it is present in almost all modernist literature. In conversation, Musil once gave as the period of his great novel 'between 1912 and 1914'. But he was quick to modify this statement by adding: 'I have not, I must insist, written a historical novel. I am not concerned with actual events ... Events, anyhow, are interchangeable. I am interested in what is typical, in what one might call the ghostly aspect of reality.' The word 'ghostly' is interesting. It points to a major tendency in modernist literature: the attenuation of actuality. In Kafka, the descriptive detail is of an extraordinary immediacy and authenticity. But Kafka's artistic ingenuity is really directed towards substituting his *Angst*-ridden vision of the world for objective reality. The realistic detail is the expression of a ghostly unreality, of a nightmare world, whose function is to evoke *Angst*. The same phenomenon can be seen in writers who attempt to combine Kafka's techniques with a critique of society – like the German writer Wolfgang Koeppen, in his satirical novel about Bonn, *Das Treibhaus*. A similar attenuation of reality underlies Joyce's stream of consciousness. It is, of course, intensified where the stream of consciousness is itself the medium through which reality is presented. And it is carried *ad absurdum* where the stream of consciousness is that of an abnormal subject or of an idiot – consider the first part of Faulkner's *The Sound and the Fury* or, a still more extreme case, Beckett's *Molloy*.

Attenuation of reality and dissolution of personality are thus interdependent: the stronger the one, the stronger the other. Underlying both is the lack of a consistent view of human nature. Man is reduced to a sequence of unrelated experiential fragments; he is as inexplicable to others as to himself. In Eliot's *The Cocktail Party* the psychiatrist, who voices the opinions of the author, describes the phenomemon:

> Ah, but we die to each other daily
> What we know of other people
> Is only our memory of the moments
> During which we knew them. And they have
>   changed since then.
> To pretend that they and we are the same
> Is a useful and convenient social convention
> Which must sometimes be broken. We must
>   also remember
> That at every meeting we are meeting a stranger.

The dissolution of personality, originally the unconscious product of the identification of concrete and abstract potentiality, is elevated to a deliberate principle in the light of consciousness. It is no accident that Gottfried Benn called one of his theoretical tracts *'Doppelleben'*. For Benn, this dissolution of personality took the form of a schizophrenic dichotomy. According to him, there was in man's personality no coherent pattern of motivation or behaviour. Man's animal nature is opposed to his denaturized, sublimated thought-processes. The unity of thought and action is 'backwoods philosophy'; thought and being are 'quite separate entities'. Man must be either a moral or a thinking being – he cannot be both at once.

These are not, I think, purely private, eccentric speculations. Of course, they are derived from Benn's specific experience. But there is an inner connection between these ideas and a certain tradition of bourgeois thought. It is more than a hundred years since Kierkegaard first attacked the Hegelian view that the inner and outer world form an objective dialectical unity, that they are indissolubly married in spite of their apparent opposition. Kierkegaard denied any such unity. According to Kierkegaard, the individual exists within an opaque, impenetrable 'incognito'.

This philosophy attained remarkable popularity after the Second World War – proof that even the most abstruse theories may reflect social reality. Men like Martin Heidegger, Ernst Jünger, the lawyer Carl Schmitt, Gottfried Benn and others passionately embraced this doctrine of the eternal incognito which implies that a man's external deeds are no guide to his motives. In this case, the deeds obscured behind the mysterious incognito were, needless to say, these intellectuals' participation in Nazism: Heidegger, as rector of Freiburg University, had glorified Hitler's seizure of power at his inauguration; Carl Schmitt had put his great legal gifts at Hitler's disposal. The facts were too well known to be simply denied. But, if this impenetrable incognito were the true *'condition humaine'*, might not – concealed within their incognito – Heidegger or Schmitt have been secret opponents of Hitler all the time, only supporting him

in the world of appearances? Ernst von Salomon's cynical frankness about his opportunism in *The Questionnaire* (keeping his reservations to himself or declaring them only in the presence of intimate friends) may be read as an ironic commentary on this ideology of the incognito as we find it, say, in the writings of Ernst Jünger.

This digression may serve to show, taking an extreme example, what the social implications of such an ontology may be. In the literary field, this particular ideology was of cardinal importance; by destroying the complex tissue of man's relations with his environment, it furthered the dissolution of personality. For it is just the opposition between a man and his environment that determines the development of his personality. There is no great hero of fiction – from Homer's Achilles to Mann's Adrian Leverkühn or Sholochov's Grigory Melyekov – whose personality is not the product of such an opposition. I have shown how disastrous the denial of the distinction between abstract and concrete potentiality must be for the presentation of character. The destruction of the complex tissue of man's interaction with his environment likewise saps the vitality of this opposition. Certainly, some writers who adhere to this ideology have attempted, not unsuccessfully, to portray this opposition in concrete terms. But the underlying ideology deprives these contradictions of their dynamic, developmental significance. The contradictions coexist, unresolved, contributing to the further dissolution of the personality in question.

It is to the credit of Robert Musil that he was quite conscious of the implications of his method. Of his hero Ulrich he remarked: 'One is faced with a simple choice: either one must run with the pack (when in Rome, do as the Romans do); or one becomes a neurotic.' Musil here introduces the problem, central to all modernist literature, of the significance of psychopathology.

This problem was first widely discussed in the naturalist period. More than fifty years ago, that doyen of Berlin dramatic critics, Alfred Kerr, was writing: 'Morbidity is the legitimate poetry of naturalism. For what is poetic in everyday life? Neurotic aberration, escape from life's dreary routine.

Only in this way can a character be translated to a rarer clime and yet retain an air of reality.' Interesting, here, is the notion that the poetic necessity of the pathological derives from the prosaic quality of life under capitalism. I would maintain − we shall return to this point − that in modern writing there is a continuity from naturalism to the modernism of our day − a continuity restricted, admittedly, to underlying ideological principles. What at first was no more than dim anticipation of approaching catastrophe developed, after 1914, into an all-pervading obsession. And I would suggest that the ever-increasing part played by psychopathology was one of the main features of the continuity. At each period − depending on the prevailing social and historical conditions − psychopathology was given a new emphasis, a different significance and artistic function. Kerr's description suggests that in naturalism the interest in psychopathology sprang from an aesthetic need; it was an attempt to escape from the dreariness of life under capitalism. The quotation from Musil shows that some years later the opposition acquired a moral slant. The obsession with morbidity had ceased to have a merely decorative function, bringing colour into the greyness of reality, and become a moral protest against capitalism.

With Musil − and with many other modernist writers − psychopathology became the goal, the *terminus ad quem*, of their artistic intention. But there is a double difficulty inherent in their intention, which follows from its underlying ideology. There is, first, a lack of definition. The protest expressed by this flight into psychopathology is an abstract gesture; its rejection of reality is wholesale and summary, containing no concrete criticism. It is a gesture, moreover, that is destined to lead nowhere; it is an escape into nothingness. Thus the propagators of this ideology are mistaken in thinking that such a protest could ever be fruitful in literature. In any protest against particular social conditions, these conditions themselves must have the central place. The bourgeois protest against feudal society, the proletarian against bourgeois society, made their point of departure a criticism of the old order. In both cases the protest − reaching out beyond the point of

departure − was based on a concrete *terminus ad quem*: the establishment of a new order. However indefinite the structure and content of this new order, the will towards its more exact definition was not lacking.

How different the protest of writers like Musil! The *terminus a quo* (the corrupt society of our time) is inevitably the main source of energy, since the *terminus ad quem* (the escape into psychopathology) is a mere abstraction. The rejection of modern reality is purely subjective. Considered in terms of man's relation with his environment, it lacks both content and direction. And this lack is exaggerated still further by the character of the *terminus ad quem*. For the protest is an empty gesture, expressing nausea, or discomfort, or longing. Its content − or rather lack of content − derives from the fact that such a view of life cannot impart a sense of direction. These writers are not wholly wrong in believing that psychopathology is their surest refuge; it is the ideological complement of their historical position.

This obsession with the pathological is not only to be found in literature. Freudian psychoanalysis is its most obvious expression. The treatment of the subject is only superficially different from that in modern literature. As everybody knows, Freud's starting point was 'everyday life'. In order to explain 'slips' and daydreams, however, he had to have recourse to psychopathology. In his lectures, speaking of resistance and repression, he says: 'Our interest in the general psychology of symptom-formation increases as we understand to what extent the study of pathological conditions can shed light on the workings of the normal mind.' Freud believed he had found the key to the understanding of the normal personality in the psychology of the abnormal. This belief is still more evident in the typology of Kretschmer, which also assumes that psychological abnormalities can explain normal psychology. It is only when we compare Freud's psychology with that of Pavlov, who takes the Hippocratic view that mental abnormality is a deviation from a norm, that we see it in its true light.

Clearly, this is not strictly a scientific or literary-critical problem. It is an ideological problem, deriving from the ontological dogma of the solitariness of man. The literature of realism, based on the Aristotelean concept of man as *zoon politikon*, is entitled to develop a new typology for each new phase in the evolution of a society. It displays the contradictions within society and within the individual in the context of a dialectical unity. Here, individuals embodying violent and extraordinary passions are still within the range of a socially normal typology (Shakespeare, Balzac, Stendhal). For, in this literature, the average man is simply a dimmer reflection of the contradictions always existing in man and society; eccentricity is a socially conditioned distortion. Obviously, the passions of the great heroes must not be confused with 'eccentricity' in the colloquial sense: Christian Buddenbrook is an 'eccentric'; Adiran Leverkühn is not.

The ontology of *Geworfenheit* makes a true typology impossible; it is replaced by an abstract polarity of the eccentric and the socially average. We have seen why this polarity – which in traditional realism serves to increase our understanding of social normality – leads in modernism to a fascination with morbid eccentricity. Eccentricity becomes the necessary complement of the average; and this polarity is held to exhaust human potentiality. The implications of this ideology are shown in another remark of Musil's: 'If humanity dreamt collectively, it would dream Moosbrugger.' Moosbrugger, you will remember, was a mentally retarded sexual pervert with homicidal tendencies.

What served, with Musil, as the ideological basis of a new typology – escape into neurosis as a protest against the evils of society – becomes with other modernist writers an immutable *condition humaine*. Musil's statement loses its conditional 'if' and becomes a simple description of reality. Lack of objectivity in the description of the outer world finds its complement in the reduction of reality to a nightmare. Beckett's *Molloy* is perhaps the *ne plus ultra* of this development, although Joyce's vision of reality as an incoherent stream of consciousness had already assumed in Faulkner a nightmare quality. In Beckett's novel we have the same vision twice over. He presents us with an image of the utmost human

degradation – an idiot's vegetative existence. Then, as help is imminent from a mysterious unspecified source, the rescuer himself sinks into idiocy. The story is told through the parallel streams of consciousness of the idiot and of his rescuer.

Along with the adoption of perversity and idiocy as types of the *condition humaine*, we find what amounts to frank glorification. Take Montherlant's *Pasiphae*, where sexual perversity – the heroine's infatuation with a bull – is presented as a triumphant return to nature, as the liberation of impulse from the slavery of convention. The chorus – i.e. the author – puts the following question (which, though rhetorical, clearly expects an affirmative reply): 'Si l'absence de pensée et l'absence de morale ne contribuent pas beaucoup à la dignité des bêtes, des plantes et des eaux . . .?' Montherlant expresses as plainly as Musil, though with different moral and emotional emphasis, the hidden – one might say repressed – social character of the protest underlying this obsession with psychopathology, its perverted Rousseauism, its anarchism. There are many illustrations of this in modernist writing. A poem of Benn's will serve to make the point:

> O that we were our primal ancestors,
> Small lumps of plasma in hot, sultry swamps;
> Life, death, conception, parturition
> Emerging from those juices soundlessly.
>
> A frond of seaweed or a dune of sand,
> Formed by the wind and heavy at the base;
> A dragonfly or gull's wing – already, these
> Would signify excessive suffering.

This is not overtly perverse in the manner of Beckett or Montherlant. Yet, in his primitivism, Benn is at one with them. The opposition of man as animal to man as social being (for instance, Heidegger's devaluation of the social as *'das Man'*, Klages's assertion of the incompatibility of *Geist* and *Seele*, or Rosenberg's racial mythology) leads straight to a glorification of the abnormal and to an undisguised anti-humanism.

A typology limited in this way to the *homme moyen*

sensuel and the idiot also opens the door to 'experimental' stylistic distortion. Distortion becomes as inseparable a part of the portrayal of reality as the recourse to the pathological. But literature must have a concept of the normal if it is to 'place' distortion correctly; that is to say, to see it *as* distortion. With such a typology this placing is impossible, since the normal is no longer a proper object of literary interest. Life under capitalism is, often rightly, presented as a distortion (a petrification or paralysis) of the human substance. But to present psychopathology as a way of escape from this distortion is itself a distortion. We are invited to measure one type of distortion against another and arrive, necessarily, at universal distortion. There is no principle to set against the general pattern, no standard by which the petty-bourgeois and the pathological can be seen in their social context. And these tendencies, far from being relativized with time, become ever more absolute. Distortion becomes the normal condition of human existence; the proper study, the formative principle, of art and literature.

I have demonstrated some of the literary implications of this ideology. Let us now pursue the argument further. It is clear, I think, that modernism must deprive literature of a sense of *perspective*. This would not be surprising; rigorous modernists such as Kafka, Benn and Musil have always indignantly refused to provide their readers with any such thing. I will return to the ideological implications of the idea of perspective later. Let me say here that, in any work of art, perspective is of overriding importance. It determines the course and content; it draws together the threads of the narration; it enables the artist to choose between the important and the superficial, the crucial and the episodic. The direction in which characters develop is determined by perspective, only those features being described which are material to their development. The more lucid the perspective – as in Molière or the Greeks – the more economical and striking the selection.

Modernism drops this selective principle. It asserts that it can dispense with it, or can replace it with its dogma of the *condition humaine*. A naturalistic style is bound to be the result. This state of affairs – which

to my mind characterizes all modernist art of the past fifty years – is disguised by critics who systematically glorify the modernist movement. By concentrating on formal criteria, by isolating technique from content and exaggerating its importance, these critics refrain from judgement on the social or artistic significance of subject matter. They are unable, in consequence, to make the aesthetic distinction between *realism* and *naturalism*. This distinction depends on the presence or absence in a work of art of a 'hierarchy of significance' in the situations and characters presented. Compared with this, formal categories are of secondary importance. That is why it is possible to speak of the basically *naturalistic* character of modernist literature – and to see here the literary expression of an ideological continuity. This is not to deny that variations in style reflect changes in society. But the particular form this principle of naturalistic arbitrariness, this lack of hierarchic structure, may take is not decisive. We encounter it in the all-determining 'social conditions' of naturalism, in symbolism's impressionist methods and its cultivation of the exotic, in the fragmentation of objective reality in futurism and constructivism and the German *Neue Sachlichkeit*, or, again, in surrealism's stream of consciousness.

These schools have in common a basically static approach to reality. This is closely related to their lack of perspective. Characteristically, Gottfried Benn actually incorporated this in his artistic programme. One of his volumes bears the title, *Static Poems*. The denial of history, of development, and thus of perspective, becomes the mark of true insight into the nature of reality.

> The wise man is ignorant
> of change and development
> his children and children's children
> are no part of his world.

The rejection of any concept of the future is for Benn the criterion of wisdom. But even those modernist writers who are less extreme in their rejection of history tend to present social and historical phenomena as static. It is, then, of small importance whether this condition is 'eternal', or only a transitional stage punctuated by sudden catastrophes (even in early naturalism the static presentation was often broken up by these catastrophes, without altering its basic character). Musil, for instance, writes in his essay *The Writer in Our Age*: 'One knows just as little about the present. Partly, this is because we are, as always, too close to the present. But it is also because the present into which we were plunged some two decades ago is of a particularly all-embracing and inescapable character.' Whether or not Musil knew of Heidegger's philosophy, the idea of *Geworfenheit* is clearly at work here. And the following reveals plainly how, for Musil, this static state was upset by the catastrophe of 1914: 'All of a sudden, the world was full of violence . . . In European civilization, there was a sudden rift.' In short: thus static apprehension of reality in modernist literature is no passing fashion; it is rooted in the ideology of modernism.

To establish the basic distinction between modernism and that realism which, from Homer to Thomas Mann and Gorky, has assumed change and development to be the proper subject of literature, we must go deeper into the underlying ideological problem. In *The House of the Dead* Dostoevsky gave an interesting account of the convict's attitude to work. He described how the prisoners, in spite of brutal discipline, loafed about, working badly or merely going through the motions of work until a new overseer arrived and allotted them a new project, after which they were allowed to go home. 'The work was hard,' Dostoevsky continues, 'but, Christ, with what energy they threw themselves into it! Gone was all their former indolence and pretended incompetence.' Later in the book Dostoevsky sums up his experiences: 'If a man loses hope and has no aim in view, sheer boredom can turn him into a beast.' I have said that the problem of perspective in literature is directly related to the principle of selection. Let me go further: underlying the problem is a profound ethical complex, reflected in the composition of the work itself. Every human action is based on a presupposition of its inherent meaningfulness, at least to the subject. Absence of meaning makes a mockery of action and reduces art to naturalistic description.

Clearly, there can be no literature without at least the appearance of change or development. This conclusion should not be interpreted in a narrowly metaphysical sense. We have already diagnosed the obsession with psychopathology in modernist literature as a desire to escape from the reality of capitalism. But this implies the absolute primacy of the *terminus a quo*, the condition from which it is desired to escape. Any movement towards a *terminus ad quem* is condemned to impotence. As the ideology of most modernist writers asserts the unalterability of outward reality (even if this is reduced to a mere state of consciousness) human activity is, *a priori*, rendered impotent and robbed of meaning.

The apprehension of reality to which this leads is most consistently and convincingly realized in the work of Kafka. Kafka remarks of Josef K., as he is being led to execution: 'He thought of flies, their tiny limbs breaking as they struggle away from the flypaper.' This mood of total impotence, of paralysis in the face of the unintelligible power of circumstances, informs all his work. Though the action of *The Castle* takes a different, even an opposite, direction to that of *The Trial*, this view of the world, from the perspective of a trapped and struggling fly, is all-pervasive. This experience, this vision of a world dominated by *Angst* and of man at the mercy of incomprehensible terrors, makes Kafka's work the very type of modernist art. Techniques, elsewhere of merely formal significance, are used here to evoke a primitive awe in the presence of an utterly strange and hostile reality. Kafka's *Angst* is the experience *par excellence* of modernism.

Two instances from musical criticism – which can afford to be both franker and more theoretical than literary criticism – show that it is indeed a universal experience with which we are dealing. The composer Hanns Eisler says of Schönberg: 'Long before the invention of the bomber, he expressed what people were to feel in the air raid shelters.' Even more characteristic – though seen from a modernist point of view – is Theodor W. Adorno's analysis (in *The Ageing of Modern Music*) of symptoms of decadence in modernist music: 'The sounds are still the same. But the experience of *Angst*, which made their originals great, has vanished.' Modernist music, he continues, has lost touch with the truth that was its *raison d'être*. Composers are no longer equal to the emotional presuppositions of their modernism. And that is why modernist music has failed. The diminution of the original *Angst*-obsessed vision of life (whether due, as Adorno thinks, to inability to respond to the magnitude of the horror or, as I believe, to the fact that this obsession with *Angst* among bourgeois intellectuals has already begun to recede) has brought about a loss of substance in modern music, and destroyed its authenticity as a modernist art-form.

This is a shrewd analysis of the paradoxical situation of the modernist artist, particularly where he is trying to express deep and genuine experience. The deeper the experience, the greater the damage to the artistic whole. But this tendency towards disintegration, this loss of artistic unity, cannot be written off as a mere fashion, the product of experimental gimmicks. Modern philosophy, after all, encountered these problems long before modern literature, painting, or music. A case in point is the problem of *time*. Subjective idealism had already separated time, abstractly conceived, from historical change and particularity of place. As if this separation were insufficient for the new age of imperialism, Bergson widened it further. Experienced time, subjective time, now became identical with real time; the rift between this time and that of the objective world was complete. Bergson and other philosophers who took up and varied this theme claimed that their concept of time alone afforded insight into authentic, i.e. subjective, reality. The same tendency soon made its appearance in literature.

The German left-wing critic and essayist of the 1920s, Walter Benjamin, has well described Proust's vision and the techniques he uses to present it in his great novel: 'We all know that Proust does not describe a man's life as it actually happens, but as it is remembered by a man who has lived through it. Yet this puts it far too crudely. For it is not actual experience that is important but the texture of reminiscence, the Penelope's tapestry of a man's memory.' The connection with Bergson's theories of time is obvious. But whereas with Bergson, in the abstraction of philosophy, the unity of perception is preserved, Benjamin shows that with Proust, as a result of the radical disintegration of the time-sequence, objectivity is eliminated: 'A lived event is finite, concluded at least on the level of experience. But a remembered event is infinite, a possible key to everything that preceded it and to everything that will follow it.'

It is the distinction between a philosophical and an artistic vision of the world. However hard philosophy, under the influence of idealism, tries to liberate the concepts of space and time from temporal and spatial particularity, literature continues to assume their unity. The fact that, nevertheless, the concept of subjective time cropped up in literature only shows how deeply subjectivism is rooted in the experience of the modern bourgeois intellectual. The individual, retreating into himself in despair at the cruelty of the age, may experience an intoxicated fascination with his forlorn condition. But then a new horror breaks through. If reality cannot be understood (or no effort is made to understand it), then the individual's subjectivity – alone in the universe, reflecting only itself – takes on an equally incomprehensible and horrific character. Hugo von Hofmannsthal was to experience this condition very early in his poetic career:

> It is a thing that no man cares to think on,
> And far too terrible for mere complaint,
> That all things slip from us and pass away,
>
> And that my ego, bound by no outward force –
> Once a small child's before it became mine –
> Should now be strange to me, like a strange dog.

By separating time from the outer world of objective reality, the inner world of the subject is transformed into a sinister, inexplicable flux and acquires – paradoxically, as it may seem – a static character.

On literature this tendency towards disintegration, of course, will have an even greater impact than on philosophy. When time is isolated in this way, the artist's world disintegrates into a multiplicity of partial worlds. The static view of the world, now combined with diminished objectivity, here rules unchallenged. The world of man – the only subject matter of literature – is shattered if a single component is removed. I have shown the consequences of isolating time and reducing it to a subjective category. But time is by no means the only component whose removal can lead to such disintegration. Here, again, Hofmannsthal anticipated later developments. His imaginary 'Lord Chandos' reflects: 'I have lost the ability to concentrate my thoughts or set them out coherently.' The result is a condition of apathy, punctuated by manic fits. The development towards a definitely pathological protest is here anticipated – admittedly in glamorous, romantic guise. But it is the same disintegration that is at work.

Previous realistic literature, however violent its criticism of reality, had always assumed the unity of the world it described and seen it as a living whole inseparable from man himself. But the major realists of our time deliberately introduce elements of disintegration into their work – for instance, the subjectivizing of time – and use them to portray the contemporary world more exactly. In this way, the once natural unity becomes a conscious, constructed unity (I have shown elsewhere that the device of the two temporal planes in Thomas Mann's *Doctor Faustus* serves to emphasize its historicity). But in modernist literature the disintegration of the world of man – and consequently the disintegration of personality – coincides with the ideological intention. Thus *Angst*, this basic modern experience, this by-product of *Geworfenheit*, has its emotional origin in the experience of a disintegrating society. But it attains its effects by evoking the disintegration of the world of man.

To complete our examination of modernist literature, we must consider for a moment the question of allegory. Allegory is that aesthetic genre which lends itself *par excellence* to a description of man's alienation from objective reality. Allegory is a problematic genre because it rejects that assumption of an immanent meaning to human existence which – however unconscious, however combined with religious concepts of transcendence – is the basis of traditional art. Thus in medieval art we observe a new secularity (in spite of the continued use of religious subjects) triumphing more and more, from the time of Giotto, over the allegorizing of an earlier period.

Certain reservations should be made at this point. First, we must distinguish between literature and the visual arts. In the latter, the limitations of allegory can be the more easily overcome in that transcendental, allegorical subjects can be clothed in an aesthetic immanence (even if of a merely decorative kind) and the rift in reality in some sense be eliminated – we have only to think of Byzantine mosaic art. This decorative element has no real equivalent in literature; it exists only in a figurative sense, and then only as a secondary component. Allegorical art of the quality of Byzantine mosaic is only rarely possible in literature. Secondly, we must bear in mind in examining allegory – and this is of great importance for our argument – a historical distinction: does the concept of transcendence in question contain within itself tendencies towards immanence (as in Byzantine art or Giotto), or is it the product precisely of a rejection of these tendencies?

Allegory, in modernist literature, is clearly of the latter kind. Transcendence implies here, more or less consciously, the negation of any meaning immanent in the world or the life of man. We have already examined the underlying ideological basis of this view and its stylistic consequences. To conclude our analysis, and to establish the allegorical character of modernist literature, I must refer again to the work of one of the finest theoreticians of modernism – to Walter Benjamin. Benjamin's examination of allegory was a product of his researches into German baroque drama. Benjamin made his analysis of these relatively minor plays the occasion for a general discussion of the aesthetics of allegory. He was asking, in effect, why it is that transcendence, which is the essence of allegory, cannot but destroy aesthetics itself.

Benjamin gives a very contemporary definition of allegory. He does not labour the analogies between modern art and the baroque (such analogies are tenuous at best, and were much overdone by the fashionable criticism of the time). Rather, he uses the baroque drama to criticize modernism, imputing the characteristics of the latter to the former. In so doing, Benjamin became the first critic to attempt a philosophical analysis of the aesthetic paradox underlying modernist art. He writes:

In Allegory, the *facies hippocratica* of history looks to the observer like a petrified primeval landscape. History, all the suffering and failure it contains, finds expression in the human face — or, rather, in the human skull. No sense of freedom, no classical proportion, no human emotion lives in its features — not only human existence in general, but the fate of every individual human being is symbolized in this most palpable token of mortality. This is the core of the allegorical vision, of the Baroque idea of history as the passion of the world; History is significant only in the stations of its corruption. Significance is a function of mortality — because it is death that marks the passage from corruptibility to meaningfulness.

Benjamin returns again and again to this link between allegory and the annihilation of history:

In the light of this vision history appears, not as the gradual realization of the eternal, but as a process of inevitable decay. Allegory thus goes beyond beauty. What ruins are in the physical world, allegories are in the world of the mind.

Benjamin points here to the aesthetic consequences of modernism — though projected into the baroque drama — more shrewdly and consistently than any of his contemporaries. He sees that the notion of objective time is essential to any understanding of history, and that the notion of subjective time is a product of a period of decline. 'A thorough knowledge of the problematic nature of art' thus becomes for him — correctly, from his point of view — one of the hall-marks of allegory in baroque drama. It is problematic, on the one hand, because it is an art intent on expressing absolute transcendence that fails to do so because of the means at its disposal. It is also problematic because it is an art reflecting the corruption of the world and bringing about its own dissolution in the process. Benjamin discovers 'an immense,

anti-aesthetic subjectivity' in baroque literature, associated with 'a theologically determined subjectivity'. (We shall presently show — a point I have discussed elsewhere in relation to Heidegger's philosophy — how in literature a 'religious atheism' of this kind can acquire a theological character.) Romantic — and, on a higher plane, baroque — writers were well aware of this problem, and gave their understanding, not only theoretical, but artistic — that is to say, allegorical — expression. 'The image', Benjamin remarks, 'becomes a rune in the sphere of allegorical intuition. When touched by the light of theology, its symbolic beauty is gone. The false appearance of totality vanishes. The image dies; the parable no longer holds true: the world it once contained disappears.'

The consequences for art are far-reaching, and Benjamin does not hesitate to point them out: 'Every person, every object, every relationship can stand for something else. This transferability constitutes a devastating, though just, judgement on the profane world — which is thereby branded as a world where such things are of small importance.' Benjamin knows, of course, that although details are 'transferable', and thus insignificant, they are not banished from art altogether. On the contrary. Precisely in modern art, with which he is ultimately concerned, descriptive detail is often of an extraordinary sensuous, suggestive power — we think again of Kafka. But this, as we showed in the case of Musil (a writer who does not consciously aim at allegory) does not prevent the materiality of the world from undergoing permanent alteration, from becoming transferable and arbitrary. Just this, modernist writers maintain, is typical of their own apprehension of reality. Yet presented in this way, the world becomes, as Benjamin puts it, 'exalted and depreciated at the same time'. For the conviction that phenomena are *not* ultimately transferable is rooted in a belief in the world's rationality and in man's ability to penetrate its secrets. In realistic literature each descriptive detail is both *individual* and *typical*. Modern allegory, and modernist ideology, however, deny the *typical*. By destroying the coherence of the world, they reduce detail to the level of mere particularity (once again, the connection between modernism and naturalism is plain). Detail, in its allegorical transferability, though brought into a direct, if paradoxical, connection with transcendence, becomes an abstract function of the transcendence to which it points. Modernist literature thus replaces concrete typicality with abstract particularity.

We are here applying Benjamin's paradox directly to aesthetics and criticism, and particularly to the aesthetics of modernism. And, though we have reversed his scale of values, we have not deviated from the course of his argument. Elsewhere, he speaks out even more plainly – as though the baroque mask had fallen, revealing the modernist skull underneath:

Allegory is left empty-handed. The forces of evil, lurking in its depths, owe their very existence to allegory. Evil is, precisely, the non-existence of that which allegory purports to represent.

The paradox Benjamin arrives at – his investigation of the aesthetics of baroque tragedy has culminated in a negation of aesthetics – sheds a good deal of light on modernist literature, and particularly on Kafka. In interpreting his writings allegorically I am not, of course, following Max Brod, who finds a specially religious allegory in Kafka's works. Kafka refuted any such interpretation in a remark he is said to have made to Brod himself: 'We are nihilistic figments, all of us; suicidal notions forming in God's mind.' Kafka rejected, too, the gnostic concept of God as an evil demiurge: 'The world is a cruel whim of God, an evil day's work.' When Brod attempted to give this an optimistic slant, Kafka shrugged off the attempt ironically: 'Oh, hope enough, hope without end – but not, alas, for us.' These remarks, quoted by Benjamin in his brilliant essay on Kafka, point to the general spiritual climate of his work: 'His profoundest experience is of the hopelessness, the utter meaninglessness of man's world, and particularly that of present-day bourgeois man.' Kafka, whether he says so openly or not, is an atheist. An atheist, though, of that modern species who regard God's removal from the scene not as a liberation – as did Epicurus and

the encyclopedists – but as a token of the 'God-forsakenness' of the world, its utter desolation and futility. Jacobsen's *Niels Lyhne* was the first novel to describe this state of mind of the atheistic bourgeois intelligentsia. Modern religious atheism is characterized, on the one hand, by the fact that unbelief has lost its revolutionary *élan* – the empty heavens are the projection of a world beyond hope of redemption. On the other hand, religious atheism shows that the desire for salvation lives on with undiminished force in a world without God, worshipping the void created by God's absence.

The supreme judges in *The Trial*, the castle administration in *The Castle*, represent transcendence in Kafka's allegories: the transcendence of Nothingness. Everything points to them, and they could give meaning to everything. Everybody believes in their existence and omnipotence; but nobody knows them, nobody knows how they can be reached. If there is a God here, it can only be the God of religious atheism: *atheos absconditus*. We become acquainted with a repellent host of subordinate authorities; brutal, corrupt, pedantic – and, at the same time, unreliable and irresponsible. It is a portrait of the bourgeois society Kafka knew, with a dash of Prague local colouring. But it is also allegorical in that the doings of this bureaucracy and of those dependent on it, its impotent victims, are not concrete and realistic, but a reflection of that Nothingness which governs existence. The hidden, non-existent God of Kafka's world derives his spectral character from the fact that his own non-existence is the ground of all existence; and the portrayed reality, uncannily accurate as it is, is spectral in the shadow of that dependence. The only purpose of transcendence – the intangible *nichtendes Nichts* – is to reveal the *facies hippocratica* of the world.

That abstract particularity which we saw to be the aesthetic consequence of allegory reaches its high mark in Kafka. He is a marvellous observer; the spectral character of reality affects him so deeply that the simplest episodes have an oppressive, nightmarish immediacy. As an artist, he is not content to evoke the surface of life. He is aware that individual detail must point to general significance. But how does he go about the business of abstraction? He has emptied everyday life of meaning by using the allegorical method; he has allowed detail to be annihilated by his transcendental Nothingness. This allegorical transcendence bars Kafka's way to realism, prevents him from investing observed detail with typical significance. Kafka is not able, in spite of his extraordinary evocative power, in spite of his unique sensibility, to achieve that fusion of the particular and the general which is the essence of realistic art. His aim is to raise the individual detail in its immediate particularity (without generalizing its content) to the level of abstraction. Kafka's method is typical, here, of modernism's allegorical approach. Specific subject matter and stylistic variation do not matter; what matters is the basic ideological determination of form and content. The particularity we find in Beckett and Joyce, in Musil and Benn, various as the treatment of it may be, is essentially of the same kind.

If we combine what we have up to now discussed separately we arrive at a consistent pattern. We see that modernism leads not only to the destruction of traditional literary forms; it leads to the destruction of literature as such. And this is true not only of Joyce, or of the literature of expressionism and surrealism. It was not André Gide's ambition, for instance, to bring about a revolution in literary style; it was his philosophy that compelled him to abandon conventional forms. He planned his *Faux-Monnayeurs* as a novel. But its structure suffered from a characteristically modernist schizophrenia: it was supposed to be written by the man who was also the hero of the novel. And, in practice, Gide was forced to admit that no novel, no work of literature, could be constructed in that way. We have here a practical demonstration that – as Benjamin showed in another context – modernism means not the enrichment, but the negation of art.

2

JEAN-PAUL SARTRE

The 'Situation' of Literature

Will anyone doubt that I am aware how incomplete and debatable these analyses are? Exceptions abound, and I know them, but it would take a big book to go into them. I have touched only the high spots. But above all, one should understand the spirit in which I have undertaken this work. If one were to see in it an attempt, even superficial, at sociological explanation, it would lose all significance. Just as for Spinoza, the idea of a line segment rotating about one of its extremities remains abstract and false if one considers it outside of the synthetic, concrete, and bounded idea of circumference which contains, completes, and justifies it, likewise here, the considerations remain arbitrary if they are not replaced in the perspective of a work of art, that is, of a free and unconditioned appeal to a freedom. One cannot write without a public and without a myth – without a *certain* public which historical circumstances have made, without a *certain* myth of literature which depends to a very great extent upon the demand of this public. In a word, the author is in a situation, like all other men. But his writings, like every human project, simultaneously enclose, specify, and surpass this situation, even explain it and set it up, just as the idea of a circle explains and sets up that of the rotation of a segment. *Being situated* is an essential and necessary characteristic of freedom. To describe the situation is not to cast aspersion on the freedom. The Jansenist ideology, the law of the three unities, and the rules of French prosody are not art; in regard to art they are even pure nothingness, since they can by no means produce, by a simple combination, a good tragedy, a good scene, or even a good line. But the art of Racine

had to be invented *on the basis* of these; not by conforming to them, as has been rather foolishly said, and by deriving exquisite difficulties and necessary constraints from them, but rather by reinventing them, by conferring a new and peculiarly Racinian function upon the division into acts, the cesura, rhyme, and the ethics of Port Royale, so that it is impossible to decide whether he poured his subject into a mould which his age imposed upon him or whether he really elected this *technique* because his subject required it. To understand what *Phèdre* could not be, it is necessary to appeal to all anthropology. To understand what it *is*, it is necessary only to read or listen, that is, to make oneself a pure freedom and to give one's confidence generously to a generosity. The examples we have chosen have served only to *situate* the freedom of the writer in different ages, to illuminate by the limits of the demands made upon him the limits of his appeal, to show by the idea of his role which the public fashions for itself the necessary boundaries of the idea which he invents of literature. And if it is true that the essence of the literary work is freedom totally disclosing and willing itself as an appeal to the freedom of other men, it is also true that the different forms of oppression, by hiding from men the fact that they were free, have screened all or part of this essence from authors. Thus, the opinions which they have formed about their profession are necessarily truncated. There is always some truth tucked away in them, but this partial and isolated truth becomes an error if one stops there, and the social movement permits us to conceive the fluctuations of the literary idea, although each particular work surpasses, in a certain way, all conceptions which one can have of art, because it is always, in a certain sense, unconditioned, because it comes out of nothingness and holds the world in suspense in nothingness. In addition, as our descriptions have permitted us to catch a glimpse of a sort of dialectic of the idea of literature, we can, without in the least pretending to give a history of belles-lettres, restore the movement of this dialectic in the last few centuries in order to discover at the end, be it as an ideal, the pure essence of the literary work and, conjointly, the type of public – that is, of society – which it requires.

I say that the literature of a given age is alienated when it has not arrived at the explicit consciousness of its autonomy and when it submits to temporal powers or to an ideology, in short, when it considers itself as a means and not as an unconditioned end. There is no doubt that literary works, in their particularity, surpass this servitude and that each one contains an unconditioned exigence, but only by implication. I say that a literature is abstract when it has not yet acquired the full view of its essence, when it has merely set up the principle of its formal autonomy and when it considers the subject of the work as indifferent. From this point of view the twelfth century offers us the image of a concrete and alienated literature. Concrete, because content and form are blended; one learns only to write about God; the book is the mirror of the world insofar as the world is his work; it is an inessential creation on the margin of a major Creation; it is praise, psalm, offering, a pure reflection. By the same token literature falls into alienation; that is, since it is, in any case, the reflectiveness of the social body, since it remains in the state of non-reflective reflectiveness, it mediatizes the Catholic universe; but for the clerk it remains the immediate; it retrieves the world, but by losing itself. But as the reflective idea must necessarily reflect *itself* on pain of annihilating itself with the whole reflected universe, the three examples which we have studied showed a movement of the retrieving of literature by itself, that is, its transition from the state of unreflective and immediate reflection to that of reflective mediation. At first concrete and alienated, it liberates itself by negativity and passes to abstraction; more

exactly, it passes in the eighteenth century to abstract negativity before becoming in the late nineteenth and early twentieth centuries absolute negation. At the end of this evolution it has cut all its bonds with society; it no longer even has a public. 'Every one knows', writes Paulhan, 'that there are two literatures in our time, the bad, which is really unreadable (it is widely read) and the good, which is not read.'

But even that is an advance; at the end of this lofty isolation, at the end of this scornful rejection of all efficacity there is the destruction of literature by itself; at first, the terrible 'it's *only* literature'; then, that literary phenomenon which the same Paulhan calls terrorism, which is born at about the same time as the idea of parasitic gratuity, and as its antithesis, and which runs all through the nineteenth century, contracting as it goes a thousand irrational marriages and which finally bursts forth shortly before the First World War. Terrorism, or rather the terrorist complex, for it is a tangle of vipers. One might distinguish, first, so deep a disgust with the sign of such that it leads in all cases to preferring the thing signified to the word, the act to the statement, the word conceived as object to the word-signification, that is, in the last analysis, poetry to prose, spontaneous disorder to composition; secondly, an effort to make literature one expression among others of life, instead of sacrificing life to literature; and thirdly, a crisis of the writer's moral conscience, that is, the sad collapse of parasitism. Thus, without for a moment conceiving the idea of losing its formal autonomy, literature makes itself a negation of formalism and comes to raise the question of its essential content. Today we are beyond terrorism and we can make use of its experience and the preceding analyses to set down the essential traits of a concrete and liberated literature.

We have said that, as a rule, the writer addressed all men. But immediately afterward we noted that he was read only by a few. As a result of the divergence between the real public and the ideal public, there arose the idea of abstract universality. That is, the author postulates the constant repetition in an indefinite future of the handful of readers which he has at present. Literary glory peculiarly resembles

Nietzsche's eternal recurrence; it is a struggle against history; here, as there, recourse to the infinity of time seeks to compensate for the failure in space (for the author of the seventeenth century, a recurrence *ad infinitum* of the gentleman; for the one of the nineteenth century, an extension *ad infinitum* of the club of writers and the public of specialists). But as it is self-evident that the effect of the projection into the future of the real and present public is to perpetuate, at least in the representation of the writer, the exclusion of the majority of men, as, in addition, this imagining of an infinity of unborn readers is tantamount to extending the actual public by a public made up of merely possible men, the universality which glory aims at is partial and abstract. And as the choice of the public conditions, to a certain extent, the choice of subject, the literature which has set up glory as its goal and its governing idea must also remain abstract.

The term 'concrete universality' must be understood, on the contrary, as the sum total of men living in a given society. If the writer's public could ever be extended to the point of embracing this totality, the result would not be that he would necessarily have to limit the reverberations of his work to the present time, but rather he would oppose to the abstract eternity of glory, which is an impossible and hollow dream of the absolute, a concrete and finite duration which he would determine by the very choice of his subjects, and which, far from uprooting him from history, would define his situation in social time. As a matter of fact, every human project outlines a certain future by its very motto: if I'm going to sow, I'm putting a whole year of waiting before me; if I get married, my venture suddenly causes my whole life to rise up before me; if I launch out into politics, I'm mortgaging a future which will extend beyond my death. The same with writing. Already, under the pretence of belaureled immortality, one discerns more modest and more concrete pretensions. The aim of *The Silence of the Sea* was to lead the French to reject the enemy's efforts to get them to collaborate. Its effectiveness and consequently its actual public could not extend beyond the time of the occupation. The books of Richard Wright will remain alive as long as the negro question is raised in the United States. Thus, there is no question as to the writer's renouncing the idea of survival; quite the contrary, he is the one who decides it; he will survive so long as he acts. Afterward, it's honorary membership, retirement. Today, for having wanted to escape from history, he begins his honorary membership the day after his death, sometimes even while he is alive.

Thus, the concrete public would be a tremendous feminine questioning, the waiting of a whole society which the writer would have to seduce and satisfy. But for that the public would have to be free to ask and the writer to answer. That means that in no case must the questions of one group or class cover up those of other milieux; otherwise, we would relapse into the abstract. In short, *actual* literature can only realize its full *essence* in a classless society. Only in this society could the writer be aware that there is no difference of any kind between his *subject* and his *public*. For the subject of literature has always been man in the world. However, as long as the virtual public remained like a dark sea around the sunny little beach of the real public, the writer risked confusing the interests and cares of man with those of a small and favored group. But, if the public were identified with the concrete universal, the writer would really have to write about the human totality. Not about the abstract man of all the ages and for a timeless reader, but about the whole man of his age and for his contemporaries. As a result, the literary antinomy of lyrical subjectivity and objective testimony would be left behind. Involved in the same adventure as his readers and situated like them in a society without cleavages, the writer, in speaking about them, would be speaking about himself, and in speaking about himself would be speaking about them. As no aristocratic pride would any longer force him to deny that he is in a situation, he would no longer seek to soar above his times and bear witness to it before eternity, but, as his situation would be universal, he would express the hopes and anger of all men, and would thereby express himself completely, that is, not as a metaphysical creature like the medieval clerk, nor as a psychological animal like our classical writers, nor even as a social entity, but as a totality emerging into the world from the void and containing within it all those structures in the indissoluble unity of the human condition; literature would really be anthropological, in the full sense of the term.

It is quite evident that in such a society there would be nothing which would even remotely recall the separation of the temporal and the spiritual. Indeed, we have seen that this division necessarily corresponds to an alienation of man and, therefore, of literature; our analyses have shown us that it always tends to oppose a public of professionals or, at least, of enlightened amateurs, to the undifferentiated masses. Whether he identifies himself with the Good and with divine Perfection, with the Beautiful or the True, a clerk is always on the side of the oppressors. A watchdog or a jester: it is up to him to choose. M. Benda has chosen the cap and bells and M. Marcel the kennel; they have the right to do so, but if literature is one day to be able to enjoy its essence, the writer, without class, without colleges, without salons, without excess of honors, and without indignity, will be thrown into the world, among men, and the very notion of clerkship will appear inconceivable. The spiritual, moreover, always rests upon an ideology, and ideologies are freedom when they make themselves and oppression when they are made. The writer who has attained full self-consciousness will therefore not make himself the guardian of any spiritual hero; he will no longer know the centrifugal movement whereby certain of his predecessors turned their eyes away from the world to contemplate the heaven of established values; he will know that his job is not adoration of the spiritual, but rather spiritualization.

Spiritualization, that is, *renewal*. And there is nothing else to spiritualize, nothing else to renew but this multicolored and concrete world with its weight, its opaqueness, its zones of generalization and its swarm of anecdotes, and that invincible Evil which gnaws at it without ever being able to destroy it. The writer will renew it as is, the raw, sweaty, smelly, everyday world, in order to submit it to freedoms on the foundation of a freedom. Literature in this classless society would thus be the world aware of itself, suspended in a free act, and offering itself to the free judgement of all men, the reflective self-awareness of a classless society. It is by means of the book that the members of this society would be able to get their bearings, to see themselves and see their situation. But as the portrait compromises the model, as the simple presentation is already the beginning of change, as the work of art, taken in the totality of its exigencies, is not a simple description of the present but a judgement of this present in the name of a future, finally, as every book contains an appeal, this awareness of self is a surpassing of self. The universe is not contested in the name of simple consumption, but in the name of the hopes and sufferings of those who inhabit it. Thus, concrete literature will be a synthesis of Negativity, as a power of uprooting from the given, and a Project, as an outline of a future order; it will be the Festival, the flaming mirror which burns everything reflected in it, and generosity, that is, a free invention, a gift. But if it is to be able to ally these two complementary aspects of freedom, it is not enough to accord the writer freedom to say everything; he must write for a public which has the freedom of changing everything; which means, besides suppression of classes, abolition of all dictatorship, constant renewal of frameworks, and the continuous overthrowing of order once it tends to congeal. In short, literature is, in essence, the subjectivity of a society in permanent revolution. In such a society it would go beyond the antinomy of word and action. Certainly in no case would it be regarded as an act; it is false to say that the author *acts* upon his readers; he merely makes an appeal to their freedom, and in order for his works to have any effect, it is necessary for the public to adopt them on their own account by an unconditioned decision. But in a collectivity which constantly corrects, judges, and metamorphoses itself, the written work can be an essential condition of action, that is, the moment of reflective consciousness.

Thus, in a society without classes, without dictatorship, and without stability, literature would end by becoming conscious of itself; it would understand that form and content, public and subject, are identical, that the formal freedom of saying and the material freedom of doing complete each other, and that one should be used to demand the other, that it best manifests the subjectivity of the person when it translates most deeply collective needs and, reciprocally, that its function is to express the concrete universal to the concrete universal and that its end is to appeal to the freedom of men so that they may realize and maintain the reign of human freedom. To be sure, this is utopian. It is possible to conceive this society, but we have no practical means at our disposal of realizing it. It has allowed us to perceive the conditions under which literature might manifest itself in its fullness and purity. Doubtless, these conditions are not fulfilled today; and it is today that we must write. But if the dialectic of literature has been pushed to the point where we have been able to perceive the essence of prose and of writing, perhaps we may at this time attempt to answer the only question which is urgent for us: what is the situation of the writer in 1947; what is his public; what are his myths; what does he want to write about; what can he and what ought he write about?

3

BERTOLT BRECHT

A Short Organum for the Theatre

Prologue

The following sets out to define an aesthetic drawn from a particular kind of theatrical performance which has been worked out in practice over the past few decades. In the theoretical statements, excursions, technical indications occasionally published in the form of notes to the writer's plays, aesthetics have only been touched on casually and with comparative lack of interest. There you saw a particular species of theatre extending or contracting its social functions, perfecting or sifting its artistic methods and establishing or maintaining its aesthetics − if the question arose − by rejecting or converting to its own use the dominant conventions of morality or taste according to its tactical needs. This theatre justified its inclination to social commitment by pointing to the social commitment in universally accepted works of art, which only fail to strike the eye because it was the accepted commitment. As for the products of our own time, it held that their lack of any worthwhile content was a sign of decadence: it accused these entertainment emporiums of having degenerated into branches of the bourgeois narcotics business. The stage's inaccurate representations of our social life, including those classed as so-called naturalism, led it to call for scientifically exact representations; the tasteless rehashing of empty visual or spiritual palliatives, for the noble logic of the multiplication table. The cult of beauty, conducted with hostility towards learning and contempt for the useful, was dismissed by it as itself contemptible,

especially as nothing beautiful resulted. The battle was for a theatre fit for the scientific age, and where its planners found it too hard to borrow or steal from the armoury of aesthetic concepts enough weapons to defend themselves against the aesthetics of the press they simply threatened 'to transform the means of enjoyment into an instrument of instruction, and to convert certain amusement establishments into organs of mass communication' ('Notes to the opera *Mahagonny*' − see No. 13): i.e. to emigrate from the realm of the merely enjoyable. Aesthetics, that heirloom of a by now depraved and parasitic class, was in such a lamentable state that a theatre would certainly have gained both in reputation and in elbowroom if it had rechristened itself thaëter. And yet what we achieved in the way of theatre for a scientific age was not science but theatre, and the accumulated innovations worked out during the Nazi period and the war − when practical demonstration was impossible − compel some attempt to set this species of theatre in its aesthetic background, or anyhow to sketch for it the outlines of a conceivable aesthetic. To explain the theory of theatrical alienation except within an aesthetic framework would be impossibly awkward.

Today one could go so far as to compile an aesthetics of the exact sciences. Galileo spoke of the elegance of certain formulae and the point of an experiment; Einstein suggests that the sense of beauty has a part to play in the making of scientific discoveries; while the atomic physicist R.

Oppenheimer praises the scientific attitude, which 'has its own kind of beauty and seems to suit mankind's position on earth'.

Let us therefore cause general dismay by revoking our decision to emigrate from the realm of the merely enjoyable, and even more general dismay by announcing our decision to take up lodging there. Let us treat the theatre as a place of entertainment, as is proper in an aesthetic discussion, and try to discover which type of entertainment suits us best.

1

'Theatre' consists in this: in making live representations of reported or invented happenings between human beings and doing so with a view to entertainment. At any rate that is what we shall mean when we speak of theatre, whether old or new.

2

To extend this definition we might add happenings between humans and gods, but as we are only seeking to establish the minimum we can leave such matters aside. Even if we did accept such an extension we should still have to say that the 'theatre' set-up's broadest function was to give pleasure. It is the noblest function that we have found for 'theatre'.

3

From the first it has been the theatre's business to entertain people, as it also has of all the other arts. It is this business which always gives it its particular dignity; it needs no other passport than fun, but this it has got to have. We should not by any means be giving it a higher status if we were to turn it e.g. into a purveyor of morality; it would on the contrary run the risk of being debased, and this would occur at once if it failed to make its moral lesson enjoyable, and enjoyable to the senses at that: a principle, admittedly, by which morality can only gain. Not even instruction can be demanded of it: at any rate, no more utilitarian lesson than how to move pleasurably, whether in the physical or in the spiritual sphere. The theatre must in fact remain something entirely superfluous, though this indeed means that it is the superfluous for which we live. Nothing needs less justification than pleasure.

4

Thus what the ancients, following Aristotle, demanded of tragedy is nothing higher or lower than that it should entertain people. Theatre may be said to be derived from ritual, but that is only to say that it becomes theatre once the two have separated; what it brought over from the mysteries was not its former ritual function, but purely and simply the pleasure which accompanied this. And the catharsis of which Aristotle writes − cleansing by fear and pity, or from fear and pity − is a purification which is performed not only in a pleasurable way, but precisely for the purpose of pleasure. To ask or to accept more of the theatre is to set one's own mark too low.

5

Even when people speak of higher and lower degrees of pleasure, art stares impassively back at them; for it wishes to fly high and low and to be left in peace, so long as it can give pleasure to people.

6

Yet there are weaker (simple) and stronger (complex) pleasures which the theatre can create. The last-named, which are what we are dealing with in great drama, attain their climaxes rather as cohabitation does through love: they are more intricate, richer in communication, more contradictory and more productive of results.

7

And different periods' pleasures varied naturally according to the system under which people lived in society at the time. The Greek *demos* (literally: the *demos* of the Greek circus) ruled by tyrants had to be entertained differently from the feudal court of Louis XIV. The theatre was required to deliver different representations of men's life together: not just representations of a different life, but also representations of a different sort.

8

According to the sort of entertainment which was possible and necessary under the given conditions of men's life together the characters had to be given varying proportions, the situations to be constructed according to varying points of view. Stories have to be narrated in various ways, so that these particular Greeks may be able to amuse themselves with the inevitability of divine laws where ignorance never mitigates the punishment; these French with the graceful self-discipline demanded of the great ones of this earth by a courtly code of duty; the Englishmen of the Elizabethan age with the self-awareness of the new individual personality which was then uncontrollably bursting out.

9

And we must always remember that the pleasure given by representations of such different sorts hardly ever depended on the representation's likeness to the thing portrayed. Incorrectness, or considerable improbability even, was hardly or not at all disturbing, so long as the incorrectness had a certain consistency and the improbability remained of a constant kind. All that mattered was the illusion of compelling momentum in the story told, and this was created by all sorts of poetic and theatrical means. Even today we are happy to overlook such inaccuracies if we can get something out of the spiritual purifications of Sophocles or the sacrificial acts of Racine or the unbridled frenzies of Shakespeare, by trying to grasp the immense or splendid feelings of the principal characters in these stories.

10

For of all the many sorts of representation of happenings between humans which the theatre has made since ancient times, and which have given entertainment despite their incorrectness and improbability, there are even today an astonishing number that also give entertainment to us.

11

In establishing the extent to which we can be satisfied by representations from so many different periods – something that can hardly have been possible to the children of those vigorous periods themselves – are we not at the same time creating the suspicion that we have failed to discover the special pleasures, the proper entertainment of our own time?

12

And our enjoyment of the theatre must have become weaker than that of the ancients, even if our way of living together is still sufficiently like theirs for it to be felt at all. We grasp the old works by a comparatively new method – empathy – on which they rely little. Thus the greater part of our enjoyment is drawn from other sources than those which our predecessors were able to exploit so fully. We are left safely dependent on beauty of language, on elegance of narration, on passages which stimulate our own private imaginations: in short, on the incidentals of the old works. These are precisely the poetical and theatrical means which hide the imprecisions of the story. Our theatres no longer have either the capacity or the wish to tell these stories, even the relatively recent ones of the great Shakespeare, at all clearly: i.e. to make the connection of events credible. And according to Aristotle – and we agree there – narrative is the soul of drama. We are more and more disturbed to see how crudely and carelessly men's life together is represented, and that not only in old works but also in contemporary ones constructed according to the old recipes. Our whole way of appreciation is starting to get out of date.

13

It is the inaccurate way in which happenings between human beings are represented that restricts our pleasure in the theatre. The reason: we and our fore-bears have a different relationship to what is being shown.

14

For when we look about us for an entertainment whose impact is immediate, for a comprehensive and penetrating pleasure such as our theatre could give us by representations of men's life together, we have to think of ourselves as children of a scientific age. Our life as human beings in society – i.e. our life – is determined by the sciences to a quite new extent.

15

A few hundred years ago a handful of people, working in different countries but in correspondence with one another, performed certain experiments by which they hoped to wring from Nature her secrets. Members of a class of craftsmen in the already power-ful cities, they transmitted their discoveries to people who made practical use of them, without expecting more from the new sciences than personal profit for themselves.

Crafts which had progressed by methods virtually unchanged during a thousand years now developed hugely; in many places, which became linked by competition, they gathered from all directions great masses of men, and these, adopting new forms of organization, started producing on a giant scale. Soon mankind was showing powers whose extent it would till that time scarcely have dared to dream of.

16

It was as if mankind for the first time now began a conscious and coordinated effort to make the planet that was its home fit to live on. Many of the earth's components, such as coal, water, oil, now became treasures. Steam was made to shift vehicles; a few small sparks and the twitching of frogs' legs revealed a natural force which produced light, carried sounds across continents, etc. In all directions man looked about himself with a new vision, to see how he could adapt to his convenience familiar but as yet unex-ploited objects. His surroundings changed increas-ingly from decade to decade, then from year to year, then almost from day to day. I who am writing this write it on a machine which at the time of my birth was unknown. I travel in the new vehicles with a rapidity that my grandfather could not imagine; in those days nothing moved so fast. And I rise in the air: a thing that my father was unable to do. With my father I already spoke across the width of a continent, but it was together with my son that I first saw the moving pictures of the explosion at Hiroshima.

17

The new sciences may have made possible this vast alteration and all-important alterability of our surroundings, yet it cannot be said that their spirit determines everything that we do. The reason why the new way of thinking and feeling has not yet pene-trated the great mass of men is that the sciences, for all their success in exploiting and dominating nature, have been stopped by the class which they brought to power – the bourgeoisie – from operating in another field where darkness still reigns, namely, that of the relations which people have to one another during the exploiting and dominating process. This business on which all alike depended was performed without the new intellectual methods that made it possible ever illuminating the mutual relationships of the people who carried it out. The new approach to nature was not applied to society.

18

In the event people's mutual relations have become harder to disentangle than ever before. The gigantic joint undertaking in which they are engaged seems more and more to split them into two groups; increases in production lead to increases in misery; only a minority gain from the exploitation of nature, and they only do so because they exploit men. What might be progress for all then becomes advancement for a few, and an ever-increasing part of the productive process gets applied to creating means of destruction for mighty wars. During these wars the mothers of every nation, with their children pressed to them, scan the skies in horror for the deadly inventions of science.

19

The same attitude as men once showed in face of unpredictable natural catastrophes they now adopt towards their own undertakings. The bourgeois class, which owes to science an advancement that it was able, by ensuring that it alone enjoyed the fruits, to convert into domination, knows very well that its rule would come to an end if the scientific eye were turned on its own undertakings. And so that new science which was founded about a hundred years ago and deals with the character of human society was born in the struggle between rulers and ruled. Since then a certain scientific spirit has developed at the bottom, among the new class of workers whose natural element is large-scale production; from down there the great catastrophes are spotted as undertakings by the rulers.

20

But science and art meet on this ground, that both are there to make men's life easier, the one setting out to maintain, the other to entertain us. In the age to come art will create entertainment from that new productivity which can so greatly improve our maintenance, and in itself, if only it is left unshackled, may prove to be the greatest pleasure of them all.

21

If we want now to surrender ourselves to this great passion for producing, what ought our representations of men's life together to look like? What is that productive attitude in face of nature and of society which we children of a scientific age would like to take up pleasurably in our theatre?

22

The attitude is a critical one. Faced with a river, it consists in regulating the river; faced with a fruit tree, in spraying the fruit tree; faced with movement, in constructing vehicles and aeroplanes; faced with society, in turning society upside down. Our representations of human social life are designed for river-dwellers, fruit farmers, builders of vehicles and upturners of society, whom we invite into our theatres and beg not to forget their cheerful occupations while we hand the world over to their minds and hearts, for them to change as they think fit.

23

The theatre can only adopt such a free attitude if it lets itself be carried along by the strongest currents in its society and associates itself with those who are necessarily most impatient to make great alterations there. The bare wish, if nothing else, to evolve an art fit for the times must drive our theatre of the scientific age straight out into the suburbs, where it can stand as it were wide open, at the disposal of those who live hard and produce much, so that they can be fruitfully entertained there with their great problems. They may find it hard to pay for our art, and immediately to grasp the new method of entertainment, and we shall have to learn in many respects what they need and how they need it; but we can be sure of their interest. For these men who seem so far apart from natural science are only apart from it because they are being forcibly kept apart; and before they can get their hands on it they have first to develop and put into effect a new science of society; so that these are the true children of the scientific age, who alone can get the theatre moving if it is to move at all. A theatre which makes productivity its main source of entertainment has also to take it for its theme, and with greater keenness than ever now that man is everywhere hampered by men from self-production: i.e. from maintaining himself, entertaining and being entertained. The theatre has to become geared into reality if it is to be in a position to turn out effective representations of reality, and to be allowed to do so.

24

But this makes it simpler for the theatre to edge as close as possible to the apparatus of education and mass communication. For although we cannot bother it with the raw material of knowledge in all its variety, which would stop it from being enjoyable, it is still free to find enjoyment in teaching and inquiring. It constructs its workable representations of society, which are then in a position to influence society, wholly and entirely as a game: for those who are constructing society it sets out society's experiences, past and present alike, in such a manner that the audience can 'appreciate' the feelings, insights and impulses which are distilled by the wisest, most active and most passionate among us from the events of the day or the century. They must be entertained with the wisdom that comes from the solution of problems, with the anger that is a practical expression of sympathy with the underdog, with the respect due to those who respect humanity, or rather whatever is kind to humanity; in short, with whatever delights those who are producing something. And this also means that the theatre can let its spectators enjoy the particular ethic of their age, which springs from productivity. A theatre which converts the critical approach – i.e. our great productive method – into pleasure finds nothing in the ethical field which it must do and a great deal that it can. Even the wholly anti-social can be a source of enjoyment to society so long as it is presented forcefully and on the grand scale. It then often proves to have considerable powers of understanding and other unusually valuable capacities, applied admittedly to a destructive end. Even the bursting flood of a vast catastrophe can be appreciated in all its majesty by society, if society knows how to master it; then we make it our own.

26

For such an operation as this we can hardly accept the theatre as we see it before us. Let us go into one of these houses and observe the effect which it has on the spectators. Looking about us, we see somewhat motionless figures in a peculiar condition: they seem strenuously to be tensing all their muscles, except where these are flabby and exhausted. They scarcely communicate with each other; their relations are those of a lot of sleepers, though of such as dream restlessly because, as is popularly said of those who have nightmares, they are lying on their backs. True, their eyes are open, but they stare rather than see, just as they listen rather than hear. They look at the stage as if in a trance: an expression which comes from the Middle Ages, the days of witches and priests. Seeing and hearing are activities, and can be pleasant ones, but these people seem relieved of activity and like men to whom something is being done. This detached state, where they seem to be given over to vague but profound sensations, grows deeper the better the work of the actors, and so we, as we do not approve of this situation, should like them to be as bad as possible.

27

As for the world portrayed there, the world from which slices are cut in order to produce these moods and movements of the emotions, its appearance is such, produced from such slight and wretched stuff as a few pieces of cardboard, a little miming, a bit of text, that one has to admire the theatre folk who, with so feeble a reflection of the real world, can move the feelings of their audience so much more strongly than does the world itself. In any case we should excuse these theatre folk, for the pleasures which they sell for money and fame could not be induced by an exacter representation of the world, nor could their inexact renderings be presented in a less magical way. Their capacity to represent people can be seen at work in various instances; it is especially the rogues and the minor figures who reveal their knowledge of humanity and differ one from the other, but the central figures have to be kept general, so that it is easier for the onlooker to identify himself with them, and at all costs each trait of character must be drawn from the narrow field within which everyone can say at once: that is how it is.

For the spectator wants to be put in possession of quite definite sensations, just as a child does when it climbs on to one of the horses on a roundabout: the sensation of pride that it can ride, and has a horse; the pleasure of being carried, and whirled past other children; the adventurous daydreams in which it pursues others or is pushed, etc. In leading the child to experience all this the degree to which its wooden seat resembles a horse counts little nor does it matter that the ride is confined to a small circle. The one important point for the spectators in these houses is that they should be able to swap a contradictory world for a consistent one, one that they scarcely know for one of which they can dream.

29

That is the sort of theatre which we face in our operations, and so far it has been fully able to transmute our optimistic friends, whom we have called the children of the scientific era, into a cowed, credulous, hypnotized mass.

30

True, for about half a century they have been able to see rather more faithful representations of human social life, as well as individual figures who were in revolt against certain social evils or even against the structure of society as a whole. They felt interested enough to put up with a temporary and exceptional restriction of language, plot and spiritual scope; for the fresh wind of the scientific spirit nearly withered the charms to which they had grown used. The sacrifice was not especially worthwhile. The greater subtlety of the representations subtracted from one pleasure without satisfying another. The field of human relationships came within our view, but not within our grasp. Our feelings, having been aroused in the old (magic) way, were bound themselves to remain unaltered.

31

For always and everywhere theatres were the amusement centres of a class which restricted the scientific spirit to the natural field, not daring to let it loose on the field of human relationships. The tiny proletarian section of the public, reinforced to a negligible and uncertain extent by renegade intellectuals, likewise still needed the old kind of entertainment, as a relief from its predetermined way of life.

32

So let us march ahead! Away with all obstacles! Since we seem to have landed in a battle, let us fight! Have we not seen how disbelief can move mountains? Is it not enough that we should have found that something is being kept from us? Before one thing and another there hangs a curtain: let us draw it up!

33

The theatre as we know it shows the structure of society (represented on the stage) as incapable of being influenced by society (in the auditorium). Oedipus, who offended against certain principles underlying the society of his time, is executed: the gods see to that; they are beyond criticism. Shakespeare's great solitary figures, bearing on their breast the star of their fate, carry through with irresistible force their futile and deadly outbursts; they prepare their own downfall; life, not death, becomes obscene as they collapse; the catastrophe is beyond criticism. Human sacrifices all round! Barbaric delights! We know that the barbarians have their art. Let us create another.

34

How much longer are our souls, leaving our 'mere' bodies under cover of the darkness, to plunge into those dreamlike figures up on the stage, there to take part in the crescendos and climaxes which 'normal' life denies us? What kind of release is it at the end of all these plays (which is a happy end only for the conventions of the period – suitable measures, the restoration of order), when we experience the dream-like executioner's axe which cuts short such crescendos as so many excesses? We slink into *Oedipus*; for taboos still exist and ignorance is no excuse before the law. Into *Othello*; for jealousy still causes us trouble and everything depends on possession. Into *Wallenstein*; for we need to be free for the competitive struggle and to observe the rules, or it would peter out. This deadweight of old habits is also needed for plays like *Ghosts* and *The Weavers*, although there the social structure, in the shape of a 'setting', presents itself as more open to question. The feelings, insights and impulses of the chief characters are forced on us, and so we learn nothing more about society than we can get from the 'setting'.

35

We need a type of theatre which not only releases the feelings, insights and impulses possible within the particular historical field of human relations in which the action takes place, but employs and encourages those thoughts and feelings which help transform the field itself.

36

The field has to be defined in historically relative terms. In other words we must drop our habit of taking the different social structures of past periods, then stripping them of everything that makes them different; so that they all look more or less like our own, which then acquires from this process a certain air of having been there all along, in other words of permanence pure and simple. Instead we must leave them their distinguishing marks and keep their impermanence always before our eyes, so that our own period can be seen to be impermanent too. (It is of course futile to make use of fancy colours and folklore for this, such as our theatres apply precisely in order to emphasize the similarities in human behaviour at different times. We shall indicate the theatrical methods below.)

37

If we ensure that our characters on the stage are moved by social impulses and that these differ according to the period, then we make it harder for our spectator to identify himself with them. He cannot simply feel: that's how I would act, but at most can say: if I had lived under those circumstances. And if we play works dealing with our own time as though they were historical, then perhaps the circumstances under which he himself acts will strike him as equally odd; and this is where the critical attitude begins.

38

The 'historical conditions' must of course not be imagined (nor will they be so constructed as mysterious Powers in the background); on the contrary, they are created and maintained by men (and will in due course be altered by them): it is the actions taking place before us that allow us to see what they are.

39

If a character responds in a manner historically in keeping with his period, and would respond otherwise in other periods, does that mean that he is not simply 'Everyman'? It is true that a man will respond differently according to his circumstances and his class; if he were living at another time, or in his youth, or on the darker side of life, he would infallibly give a different response, though one still determined by the same factors and like anyone else's response in that situation at that time. So should we not ask if there are any further differences of response? Where is the man himself, the living, unmistakable man, who is not quite identical with those identified with him? It is clear that his stage image must bring him to light, and this will come about if this particular contradiction is re-created in the image. The image that gives historical definition will retain something of the rough sketching which indicates traces of other movements and features all around the fully worked-out figure. Or imagine a man standing in a valley and making a speech in which he occasionally changes his views or simply utters sentences which contradict one another, so that the accompanying echo forces them into confrontation.

40

Such images certainly demand a way of acting which will leave the spectator's intellect free and highly mobile. He has again and again to make what one might call hypothetical adjustments to our structure, by mentally switching off the motive forces of our society or by substituting others for them: a process which leads real conduct to acquire an element of 'unnaturalness', thus allowing the real motive forces to be shorn of their naturalness and become capable of manipulation.

41

It is the same as when an irrigation expert looks at a river together with its former bed and various hypothetical courses which it might have followed if there had been a different tilt to the plateau or a different volume of water. And while he in his mind is looking at a new river, the socialist in him is hearing new kinds of talk from the labourers who work by it. And similarly in the theatre our spectator should find that the incidents set among such labourers are also accompanied by echoes and by traces of sketching.

42

The kind of acting which was tried out at the Schiffbauerdamm Theatre in Berlin between the First and Second World Wars, with the object of producing such images, is based on the 'alienation effect' (A-effect). A representation that alienates is one which allows us to recognize its subject, but at the same time makes it seem unfamiliar. The classical and medieval theatre alienated its characters by making them wear human or animal masks; the Asiatic theatre even today uses musical and pantomimic A-effects. Such devices were certainly a barrier to empathy, and yet this technique owed more, not less, to hypnotic suggestion than do those by which empathy is achieved. The social aims of these old devices were entirely different from our own.

43

The old A-effects quite remove the object represented from the spectator's grasp, turning it into something that cannot be altered; the new are not odd in themselves, though the unscientific eye stamps anything strange as odd. The new alienations are only designed to free socially conditioned phenomena from that stamp of familiarity which protects them against our grasp today.

44

For it seems impossible to alter what has long not been altered. We are always coming on things that are too obvious for us to understand them. What men experience among themselves they think of as 'the' human experience. A child, living in a world of old men, learns how things work there. He knows the run of things before he can walk. If anyone is bold enough to want something further, he only wants to have it as an exception. Even if he realizes that the arrangements made for him by 'Providence' are only what has been provided by society he is bound to see society, that vast collection of beings like himself, as a whole that is greater than the sum of its parts and therefore not in any way to be influenced. Moreover, he would be used to things that could not be influenced; and who mistrusts what he is used to? To transform himself from general passive acceptance to a corresponding state of suspicious inquiry he would need to develop that detached eye with which the great Galileo observed a swinging chandelier. He was amazed by this pendulum motion, as if he had not expected it and could not understand its occurring, and this enabled him to come on the rules by which it was governed. Here is the outlook, disconcerting but fruitful, which the theatre must provoke with its representations of human social life. It must amaze its public, and this can be achieved by a technique of alienating the familiar.

45

This technique allows the theatre to make use of its representations of the new social scientific method known as dialectical materialism. In order to unearth society's laws of motion this method treats social situations as processes, and traces out all their inconsistencies. It regards nothing as existing except insofar as it changes, in other words is in disharmony with itself. This also goes for those human feelings, opinions and attitudes through which at any time the form of men's life together finds its expression.

46

Our own period, which is transforming nature in so many and different ways, takes pleasure in understanding things so that we can interfere. There is a great deal to man, we say; so a great deal can be made out of him. He does not have to stay the way he is now, nor does he have to be seen only as he is now, but also as he might become. We must not start with him; we must start on him. This means, however, that I must not simply set myself in his place, but must set myself facing him, to represent us all. That is why the theatre must alienate what it shows.

74

So let us invite all the sister arts of the drama, not in order to create an 'integrated work of art' in which they all offer themselves up and are lost, but so that together with the drama they may further the common task in their different ways; and their relations with one another consists in this: that they lead to mutual alienation.

75

And here once again let us recall that their task is to entertain the children of the scientific age, and to do so with sensuousness and humour. This is something that we Germans cannot tell ourselves too often, for with us everything easily slips into the insubstantial and unapproachable, and we begin to talk of *Weltanschauung* when the world in question has already dissolved. Even materialism is little more than an idea with us. Sexual pleasure with us turns into marital obligations, the pleasures of art subserve general culture, and by learning we mean not an enjoyable process of finding out, but the forcible shoving of our nose into something. Our activity has none of the pleasure of exploration, and if we want to make an impression we do not say how much fun we have got out of something but how much effort it has cost us.

76

One more thing: the delivery to the audience of what has been built up in the rehearsals. Here it is essential that the actual playing should be infused with the gesture of handing over a finished article. What now comes before the spectator is the most frequently repeated of what has not been rejected, and so the finished representations have to be delivered with the eyes fully open, so that they may be received with the eyes open too.

77

That is to say, our representations must take second place to what is represented, men's life together in society; and the pleasure felt in their perfection must be converted into the higher pleasure felt when the rules emerging from this life in society are treated as imperfect and provisional. In this way the theatre leaves its spectators productively disposed even after the spectacle is over. Let us hope that their theatre may allow them to enjoy as entertainment that terrible and never-ending labour which should ensure their maintenance, together with the terror or their unceasing transformation. Let them here produce their own lives in the simplest way; for the simplest way of living is in art.

4

WALTER BENJAMIN

The Work of Art in the Age of Mechanical Reproduction

I

In principle a work of art has always been reproducible. Man-made artifacts could always be imitated by men. Replicas were made by pupils in practice of their craft, by masters for diffusing their works, and, finally, by third parties in the pursuit of gain. Mechanical reproduction of a work of art, however, represents something new. Historically, it advanced intermittently and in leaps at long intervals, but with accelerated intensity. The Greeks knew only two procedures of technically reproducing works of art: founding and stamping. Bronzes, terra cottas, and coins were the only art-works which they could produce in quantity. All others were unique and could not be mechanically reproduced. With the woodcut graphic art became mechanically reproducible for the first time, long before script became reproducible by print. The enormous changes which printing, the mechanical reproduction of writing, has brought about in literature are a familiar story. However, within the phenomenon which we are here examining from the perspective of world history, print is merely a special, though particularly important, case. During the Middle Ages engraving and etching were added to the woodcut; at the beginning of the nineteenth century lithography made its appearance.

With lithography the technique of reproduction reached an essentially new stage. This much more direct process was distinguished by the tracing of the design on a stone rather than its incision on a block of wood or its etching on a copperplate and permitted graphic art for the first time to put its products on the market, not only in large numbers as hitherto, but also in daily changing forms. Lithography enabled graphic art to illustrate everyday life, and it began to keep pace with printing. But only a few decades after its invention, lithography was surpassed by photography. For the first time in the process of pictorial reproduction, photography freed the hand of the most important artistic functions which henceforth devolved only upon the eye looking into a lens. Since the eye perceives more swiftly than the hand can draw, the process of pictorial reproduction was accelerated so enormously that it could keep pace with speech. A film operator shooting a scene in the studio captures the images at the speed of an actor's speech. Just as lithography virtually implied the illustrated newspaper, so did photography foreshadow the sound film. The technical reproduction of sound was tackled at the end of the last century. These convergent endeavours made predictable a situation which Paul Valéry pointed up in this sentence: 'Just as water, gas, and electricity are brought into our houses from far off to satisfy our needs in response to a minimal effort, so we shall be supplied with visual or auditory images, which will appear and disappear at a simple movement of the hand, hardly more than a sign'.[1] Around 1900 technical reproduction had reached a standard that not only permitted it to reproduce all transmitted works of art and thus to cause the most profound change in their impact upon the public; it also had captured a place of its own among the artistic processes. For the study of this standard nothing is more revealing than the nature of the repercussions that these two different manifestations – the reproduction of works of art and the art of the film – have had on art in its traditional form.

II

Even the most perfect reproduction of a work of art is lacking in one element: its presence in time and space, its unique existence at the place where it happens to be. This unique existence of the work of art determined the history to which it was subject throughout the time of its existence. This includes the changes which it may have suffered in physical condition over the years as well as the various changes in its ownership. The traces of the first can be revealed only by chemical or physical analyses which it is impossible to perform on a reproduction; changes of ownership are subject to a tradition which must be traced from the situation of the original.

The presence of the original is the prerequisite to the concept of authenticity. Chemical analyses of the patina of a bronze can help to establish this, as does the proof that a given manuscript of the Middle Ages stems from an archive of the fifteenth century. The whole sphere of authenticity is outside technical – and, of course, not only technical – reproducibility. Confronted with its manual reproduction, which was usually branded as a forgery, the original preserved all its authority; not so *vis-à-vis* technical reproduction. The reason is twofold. First, process reproduction is more independent of the original than manual reproduction. For example, in photography, process reproduction can bring out those aspects of the original that are unattainable to the naked eye yet accessible to the lens, which is adjustable and chooses its angle at will. And photographic reproduction,

with the aid of certain processes, such as enlargement or slow motion, can capture images which escape natural vision. Secondly, technical reproduction can put the copy of the original into situations which would be out of reach for the original itself. Above all, it enables the original to meet the beholder halfway, be it in the form of a photograph or a phonograph record. The cathedral leaves its locale to be received in the studio of a lover of art; the choral production, performed in an auditorium or in the open air, resounds in the drawing room.

The situations into which the product of mechanical reproduction can be brought may not touch the actual work of art, yet the quality of its presence is always depreciated. This holds not only for the art-work but also, for instance, for a landscape which passes in review before the spectator in a movie. In the case of the art-object, a most sensitive nucleus – namely, its authenticity – is interfered with whereas no natural object is vulnerable on that score. The authenticity of a thing is the essence of all that is transmissible from its beginning, ranging from its substantive duration to its testimony to the history which it has experienced. Since the historical testimony rests on the authenticity, the former, too, is jeopardized by reproduction when substantive duration ceases to matter. And what is really jeopardized when the historical testimony is affected is the authority of the object.

One might subsume the eliminated element in the term 'aura' and go on to say: that which withers in the age of mechanical reproduction is the aura of the work of art. This is a symptomatic process whose significance points beyond the realm of art. One might generalize by saying: the technique of reproduction detaches the reproduced object from the domain of tradition. By making many reproductions it substitutes a plurality of copies for a unique existence. And in permitting the reproduction to meet the beholder or listener in his own particular situation, it reactivates the object reproduced. These two processes lead to a tremendous shattering of tradition which is the obverse of the contemporary crisis and renewal of mankind. Both processes are intimately connected with the contemporary mass movements. Their most powerful agent is the film. Its social significance, particularly in its most positive form, is inconceivable without its destructive, cathartic aspect, that is, the liquidation of the traditional value of the cultural heritage. This phenomenon is most palpable in the great historical films. It extends to ever new positions. In 1927 Abel Gance exclaimed enthusiastically: 'Shakespeare, Rembrandt, Beethoven will make films . . . all legends, all mythologies and all myths, all founders of religion, and the very religions . . . await their exposed resurrection, and the heroes crowd each other at the gate.'[2] Presumably without intending it, he issues an invitation to a far-reaching liquidation.

III

During long periods of history, the mode of human sense perception changes with humanity's entire mode of existence. The manner in which human sense perception is organized, the medium in which it is accomplished, is determined not only by nature but by historical circumstances as well. The fifth century, with its great shifts of population, saw the birth of the late Roman art industry and the Vienna Genesis, and there developed not only an art different from that of antiquity but also a new kind of perception. The scholars of the Viennese school, Riegl and Wickhoff, who resisted the weight of classical tradition under which these later art-forms had been buried, were the first to draw conclusions from them concerning the organization of perception at the time. However far-reaching their insight, these scholars limited themselves to showing the significant, formal hall-mark which characterized perception in late Roman times. They did not attempt – and, perhaps, saw no way – to show the social transformations expressed by these changes of perception. The conditions for an analogous insight are more favorable in the present. And if changes in the medium of contemporary perception can be comprehended as decay of the aura, it is possible to show its social causes.

The concept of aura which was proposed above with reference to historical objects may usefully be illustrated with reference to the aura of natural ones. We define the aura of the latter as the unique phenomenon of a distance, however close it may be. If, while resting on a summer afternoon, you follow with your eyes a mountain range on the horizon or a branch which casts its shadow over you, you experience the aura of those mountains, of that branch. This image makes it easy to comprehend the social bases of the contemporary decay of the aura. It rests on two circumstances, both of which are related to the increasing significance of the masses in contemporary life. Namely, the desire of contemporary masses to bring things 'closer' spatially and humanly, which is just as ardent as their bent toward overcoming the uniqueness of every reality by accepting its reproduction. Every day the urge grows stronger to get hold of an object at very close range by way of its likeness, its reproduction. Unmistakably, reproduction as offered by picture magazines and newsreels differs from the image seen by the unarmed eye. Uniqueness and permanence are as closely linked in the latter as are transitoriness and reproducibility in the former. To pry an object from its shell, to destroy its aura, is the mark of a perception whose 'sense of the universal equality of things' has increased to such a degree that it extracts it even from a unique object by means of reproduction. Thus is manifested in the field of perception what in the theoretical sphere is noticeable in the increasing importance of statistics. The adjustment of reality to the masses and of the masses to reality is a process of unlimited scope, as much for thinking as for perception.

IV

The uniqueness of a work of art is inseparable from its being imbedded in the fabric of tradition. This tradition itself is thoroughly alive and extremely changeable. An ancient statue of Venus, for example, stood in a different traditional context with the Greeks, who made it an object of veneration, than with the clerics of the Middle Ages, who viewed it as an ominous idol. Both of them, however, were equally confronted with its uniqueness, that is, its aura. Originally the contextual integration of art in tradition found its expression in the cult. We know that the earliest art-works originated in the service of a ritual – first the magical, then the religious kind. It is significant that the existence of the work of art with reference to its aura is never entirely separated from its ritual function. In other words, the unique value of the 'authentic' work of art has its basis in ritual, the location of its original use value. This ritualistic basis, however remote, is still recognizable as secularized ritual even in the most profane forms of the cult of beauty. The secular cult of beauty, developed during the Renaissance and prevailing for three centuries, clearly showed that ritualistic basis in its decline and the first deep crisis which befell it. With the advent of the first truly revolutionary means of reproduction, photography, simultaneously with the rise of socialism, art sensed the approaching crisis which has become evident a century later. At the time, art reacted with the doctrine of *l'art pour l'art*, that is, with a theology of art. This gave rise to what might be called a negative theology in the form of the idea of 'pure' art, which not only denied any social function of art but also any categorizing by subject matter. (In poetry, Mallarmé was the first to take this position.)

An analysis of art in the age of mechanical reproduction must do justice to these relationships, for they lead us to an all-important insight: for the first time in world history, mechanical reproduction emancipates the work of art from its parasitical dependence on ritual. To an ever greater degree the work of art reproduced becomes the work of art designed for reproducibility. From a photographic negative, for example, one can make any number of prints; to ask for the 'authentic' print makes no sense. But the instant the criterion of authenticity ceases to be applicable to artistic production, the total function of art is reversed. Instead of being based on ritual, it begins to be based on another practice – politics.

V

Works of art are received and valued on different planes. Two polar types stand out: with one, the accent is on the cult value; with the other, on the exhibition value of the work. Artistic production begins with ceremonial objects destined to serve in a cult. One may assume that what mattered was their existence, not their being on view. The elk portrayed by the man of the Stone Age on the walls of his cave was an instrument of magic. He did expose it to his fellow men, but in the main it was meant for the spirits. Today the cult value would seem to demand that the work of art remain hidden. Certain statues of gods are accessible only to the priest in the cella; certain Madonnas remain covered nearly all year round; certain sculptures on medieval cathedrals are invisible to the spectator on ground level. With the emancipation of the various art practices from ritual go increasing opportunities for the exhibition of their products. It is easier to exhibit a portrait bust that can be sent here and there than to exhibit the statue of a divinity that has its fixed place in the interior of a temple. The same holds for the painting as against the mosaic or fresco that preceded it. And even though the public presentability of a mass originally may have been just as great as that of a symphony, the latter originated at the moment when its public presentability promised to surpass that of the mass.

With the different methods of technical reproduction of a work of art, its fitness for exhibition increased to such an extent that the quantitative shift between its two poles turned into a qualitative transformation of its nature. This is comparable to the situation of the work of art in prehistoric times when, by the absolute emphasis on its cult value, it was, first and foremost, an instrument of magic. Only later did it come to be recognized as a work of art. In the same way today, by the absolute emphasis on its exhibition value the work of art becomes a creation with entirely new functions, among which the one we are conscious of, the artistic function, later may be recognized as incidental. This much is certain: today photography and the film are the most serviceable exemplifications of this new function.

VI

In photography, exhibition value begins to displace cult value all along the line. But cult value does not give way without resistance. It retires into an ultimate retrenchment: the human countenance. It is no accident that the portrait was the focal point of early photography. The cult of remembrance of loved ones, absent or dead, offers a last refuge for the cult value of the picture. For the last time the aura emanates from the early photographs in the fleeting expression of a human face. This is what constitutes their melancholy, incomparable beauty. But as man withdraws from the photographic image, the exhibition value for the first time shows its superiority to the ritual value. To have pinpointed this new stage constitutes the incomparable significance of Atget, who, around 1900, took photographs of deserted Paris streets. It has quite justly been said of him that he photographed them like scenes of crime. The scene of a crime, too, is deserted; it is photographed for the purpose of establishing evidence. With Atget, photographs become standard evidence for historical occurrences, and acquire a hidden political significance. They demand a specific kind of approach; free-floating contemplation is not appropriate to them. They stir the viewer; he feels challenged by them in a new way. At the same time picture magazines begin to put up signposts for him, right ones or wrong ones, no matter. For the first time, captions have become obligatory. And it is clear that they have an altogether different character than the title of a painting. The directives which the captions give to those looking at pictures in illustrated magazines soon become even more explicit and more imperative in the film where the meaning of each single picture appears to be prescribed by the sequence of all preceding ones.

VII

The nineteenth-century dispute as to the artistic value of painting versus photography today seems devious and confused. This does not diminish its importance, however; if anything, it underlines it. The dispute was in fact the symptom of a historical transformation the universal impact of which was not realized by either of the rivals. When the age of mechanical reproduction separated art from its basis in cult, the semblance of its autonomy disappeared for ever. The resulting change in the function of art transcended the perspective of the century; for a long time it even escaped that of the twentieth century, which experienced the development of the film.

Earlier much futile thought had been devoted to the question of whether photography is an art. The primary question – whether the very invention of photography had not transformed the entire nature of art – was not raised. Soon the film theoreticians asked the same ill-considered question with regard to the film. But the difficulties which photography caused traditional aesthetics were mere child's play as compared to those raised by the film. Whence the insensitive and forced character of early theories of the film. Abel Gance, for instance, compares the film with hieroglyphs: 'Here, by a remarkable regression, we have come back to the level of expression of the Egyptians . . . Pictorial language has not yet matured because our eyes have not yet adjusted to it. There is as yet insufficient respect for, insufficient cult of, what it expresses.'[3] Or, in the words of Séverin-Mars: 'What art has been granted a dream more poetical and more real at the same time! Approached in this fashion the film might represent an incomparable means of expression. Only the most high-minded persons, in the most perfect and mysterious moments of their lives, should be allowed to enter its ambience.'[4] Alexandre Arnoux concludes his fantasy about the silent film with the question: 'Do not all the bold descriptions we have given amount to the definition of prayer?'[5] It is instructive to note how their desire to class the film among the 'arts' forces these theoreticians to read ritual elements into it – with a striking lack of discretion. Yet when these speculations were published, films like *L'Opinion publique* and *The Gold Rush* had already appeared. This, however, did not keep Abel Gance from adducing hieroglyphs for purposes of comparison, nor Séverin-Mars from speaking of the film as one might speak of paintings by Fra Angelico. Characteristically, even today ultra-reactionary authors give the film a similar contextual significance – if not an outright sacred one, then at least a supernatural one. Commenting on Max Reinhardt's film version of *A Midsummer*

Night's Dream, Werfel states that undoubtedly it was the sterile copying of the exterior world with its streets, interiors, railroad stations, restaurants, motorcars, and beaches which until now had obstructed the elevation of the film to the realm of art. 'The film has not yet realized its true meaning, its real possibilities . . . these consist in its unique faculty to express by natural means and with incomparable persuasiveness all that is fairylike, marvelous, supernatural.'[6]

VIII

The artistic performance of a stage actor is definitely presented to the public by the actor in person; that of the screen actor, however, is presented by a camera, with a twofold consequence. The camera that presents the performance of the film actor to the public need not respect the performance as an integral whole. Guided by the cameraman, the camera continually changes its position with respect to the performance. The sequence of positional views which the editor composes from the material supplied him constitutes the completed film. It comprises certain factors of movement which are in reality those of the camera, not to mention special camera angles, closeups, etc. Hence, the performance of the actor is subjected to a series of optical tests. This is the first consequence of the fact that the actor's performance is presented by means of a camera. Also, the film actor lacks the opportunity of the stage actor to adjust to the audience during his performance, since he does not present his performance to the audience in person. This permits the audience to take the position of a critic, without experiencing any personal contact with the actor. The audience's identification with the actor is really an identification with the camera. Consequently the audience takes the position of the camera; its approach is that of testing. This is not the approach to which cult values may be exposed.

IX

For the film, what matters primarily is that the actor represents himself to the public before the camera, rather than representing someone else. One of the first to sense the actor's metamorphosis by this form of testing was Pirandello. Though his remarks on the subject in his novel *Si Gira* were limited to the negative aspects of the question and to the silent film only, this hardly impairs their validity. For in this respect, the sound film did not change anything essential. What matters is that the part is acted not for an audience but for a mechanical contrivance – in the case of the sound film, for two of them. 'The film actor', wrote Pirandello, 'feels as if in exile – exiled not only from the stage but also from himself. With a vague sense of discomfort he feels inexplicable emptiness: his body loses its corporeality, it evaporates, it is deprived of reality, life, voice, and the noises caused by his moving about, in order to be changed into a mute image, flickering an instant on the screen, then vanishing into silence . . . The projector will play with his shadow before the public, and he himself must be content to play before the camera.'[7] This situation might also be characterized as follows: for the first time – and this is the effect of the film – man has to operate with his whole living person, yet forgoing its aura. For aura is tied to his presence; there can be no replica of it. The aura which, on the stage, emanates from Macbeth, cannot be separated for the spectators from that of the actor. However, the singularity of the shot in the studio is that the camera is substituted for the public. Consequently, the aura that envelops the actor vanishes, and with it the aura of the figure he portrays.

It is not surprising that it should be a dramatist such as Pirandello who, in characterizing the film, inadvertently touches on the very crisis in which we see the theater. Any thorough study proves that there is indeed no greater contrast than that of the stage play to a work of art that is completely subject to or, like the film, founded in, mechanical reproduction. Experts have long recognized that in the film 'the greatest effects are almost always obtained by "acting" as little as possible . . .' In 1932 Rudolf Arnheim saw 'the latest trend . . . in treating the actor as a stage prop chosen for its characteristics and . . . inserted at the proper place'.[8] With this idea something else is closely connected. The stage actor identifies himself with the character of his role. The film actor very often is denied this opportunity. His creation is by no means all of a piece; it is composed of many separate performances. Besides certain fortuitous considerations, such as cost of studio, availability of fellow players, décor, etc., there are elementary necessities of equipment that split the actor's work into a series of mountable episodes. In particular, lighting and its installation require the presentation of an event that, on the screen, unfolds as a rapid and unified scene, in a sequence of separate shootings which may take hours at the studio; not to mention more obvious montage. Thus a jump from the window can be shot in the studio as a jump from a scaffold, and the ensuing flight, if need be, can be shot weeks later when outdoor scenes are taken. Far more paradoxical cases can easily be construed. Let us assume that an actor is supposed to be startled by a knock at the door. If his reaction is not satisfactory, the director can resort to an expedient: when the actor happens to be at the studio again he has a shot fired behind him without his being forewarned of it. The frightened reaction can be shot now and be cut into the screen version. Nothing more strikingly shows that art has left the realm of the 'beautiful semblance' which, so far, had been taken to be the only sphere where art could thrive.

X

The feeling of strangeness that overcomes the actor before the camera, as Pirandello describes it, is basically of the same kind as the estrangement felt before one's own image in the mirror. But now the reflected image has become separable, transportable. And where is it transported? Before the public. Never for a moment does the screen actor cease to be conscious of this fact. While facing the camera he knows that ultimately he will face the public, the consumers who constitute the market. This market, where he offers not only his labor but also his whole self, his heart and soul, is beyond his reach. During the shooting he has as little contact with it as any article made in a factory. This may contribute to that oppression, that new anxiety which, according to

Pirandello, grips the actor before the camera. The film responds to the shriveling of the aura with an artificial build-up of the 'personality' outside the studio. The cult of the movie star, fostered by the money of the film industry, preserves not the unique aura of the person but the 'spell of the personality', the phony spell of a commodity. So long as the moviemakers' capital sets the fashion, as a rule no other revolutionary merit can be accredited to today's film than the promotion of a revolutionary criticism of traditional concepts of art. We do not deny that in some cases today's films can also promote revolutionary criticism of social conditions, even of the distribution of property. However, our present study is no more specifically concerned with this than is the film production of Western Europe.

It is inherent in the technique of the film as well as that of sports that everybody who witnesses its accomplishments is somewhat of an expert. This is obvious to anyone listening to a group of newspaper boys leaning on their bicycles and discussing the outcome of a bicycle race. It is not for nothing that newspaper publishers arrange races for their delivery boys. These arouse great interest among the participants, for the victor has an opportunity to rise from delivery boy to professional racer. Similarly, the newsreel offers everyone the opportunity to rise from passer-by to movie extra. In this way any man might even find himself part of a work of art, as witness Vertoff's *Three Songs About Lenin* or Ivens's *Borinage*. Any man today can lay claim to being filmed. This claim can best be elucidated by a comparative look at the historical situation of contemporary literature.

For centuries a small number of writers were confronted by many thousands of readers. This changed toward the end of the last century. With the increasing extension of the press, which kept placing new political, religious, scientific, professional, and local organs before the readers, an increasing number of readers became writers – at first, occasional ones. It began with the daily press opening to its readers space for 'letters to the editor'. And today there is hardly a gainfully employed European who could not, in principle, find an opportunity to publish somewhere or other comments on his work, grievances, documentary reports, or that sort of thing. Thus, the distinction between author and public is about to lose its basic character. The difference becomes merely functional; it may vary from case to case. At any moment the reader is ready to turn into a writer. As expert, which he had to become willy-nilly in an extremely specialized work process, even if only in some minor respect, the reader gains access to authorship. In the Soviet Union work itself is given a voice. To present it verbally is part of a man's ability to perform the work. Literary license is now founded on polytechnic rather than specialized training and thus becomes common property.

All this can easily be applied to the film, where transitions that in literature took centuries have come about in a decade. In cinematic practice, particularly in Russia, this change-over has partially become established reality. Some of the players whom we meet in Russian films are not actors in our sense but people who portray *themselves* – and primarily in their own work process. In Western Europe the capitalistic exploitation of the film denies consideration to modern man's legitimate claim to being reproduced. Under these circumstances the film industry is trying hard to spur the interest of the masses through illusion-promoting spectacles and dubious speculations.

XI

The shooting of a film, especially of a sound film, affords a spectacle unimaginable anywhere at any time before this. It presents a process in which it is impossible to assign to a spectator a viewpoint which would exclude from the actual scene such extraneous accessories as camera equipment, lighting machinery, staff assistants, etc. – unless his eye were on a line parallel with the lens. This circumstance, more than any other, renders superficial and insignificant any possible similarity between a scene in the studio and one on the stage. In the theater one is well aware of the place from which the play cannot immediately be detected as illusionary. There is no such place for the movie scene that is being shot. Its illusionary nature is that of the second degree, the result of cutting.

That is to say, in the studio the mechanical equipment has penetrated so deeply into reality that its pure aspect freed from the foreign substance of equipment is the result of a special procedure, namely, the shooting by the specially adjusted camera and the mounting of the shot together with other similar ones. The equipment-free aspect of reality here has become the height of artifice; the sight of immediate reality has become an orchid in the land of technology.

Even more revealing is the comparison of these circumstances, which differ so much from those of the theater, with the situation in painting. Here the question is: how does the cameraman compare with the painter? To answer this we take recourse to an analogy with a surgical operation. The surgeon represents the polar opposite of the magician. The magician heals a sick person by the laying on of hands; the surgeon cuts into the patient's body. The magician maintains the natural distance between the patient and himself; though he reduces it very slightly by the laying on of hands, he greatly increases it by virtue of his authority. The surgeon does exactly the reverse; he greatly diminishes the distance between himself and the patient by penetrating into the patient's body, and increases it but little by the caution with which his hand moves among the organs. In short, in contrast to the magician – who is still hidden in the medical practitioner – the surgeon at the decisive moment abstains from facing the patient man to man; rather, it is through the operation that he penetrates into him.

Magician and surgeon compare to painter and cameraman. The painter maintains in his work a natural distance from reality, the cameraman penetrates deeply into its web. There is a tremendous difference between the pictures they obtain. That of the painter is a total one, that of the cameraman consists of multiple fragments which are assembled under a new law. Thus, for contemporary man the representation of reality by the film is incomparably more significant than that of the painter, since it offers, precisely because of the thoroughgoing permeation of reality with mechanical equipment, an aspect of reality which is free of all equipment. And that is what one is entitled to ask from a work of art.

XII

Mechanical reproduction of art changes the reaction of the masses toward art. The reactionary attitude toward a Picasso painting changes into the progressive reaction toward a Chaplin movie. The progressive reaction is characterized by the direct, intimate fusion of visual and emotional enjoyment with the orientation of the expert. Such fusion is of great social significance. The greater the decrease in the social significance of an art-form, the sharper the distinction between criticism and enjoyment by the public. The conventional is uncritically enjoyed, and the truly new is criticized with aversion. With regard to the screen, the critical and the receptive attitudes of the public coincide. The decisive reason for this is that individual reactions are predetermined by the mass audience response they are about to produce, and this is nowhere more pronounced than in the film. The moment these responses become manifest they control each other. Again, the comparison with painting is fruitful. A painting has always had an excellent chance to be viewed by one person or by a few. The simultaneous contemplation of paintings by a large public, such as developed in the nineteenth century, is an early symptom of the crisis of painting, a crisis which was by no means occasioned exclusively by photography but rather in a relatively independent manner by the appeal of art-works to the masses.

Painting simply is in no position to present an object for simultaneous collective experience, as it was possible for architecture at all times, for the epic poem in the past, and for the movie today. Although this circumstance in itself should not lead one to conclusions about the social role of painting, it does constitute a serious threat as soon as painting, under special conditions and, as it were, against its nature, is confronted directly by the masses. In the churches and monasteries of the Middle Ages and at the princely courts up to the end of the eighteenth century, a collective reception of paintings did not occur simultaneously, but by graduated and hierarchized mediation. The change that has come about is an expression of the particular conflict in which painting was implicated by the mechanical reproducibility of paintings. Although paintings began to be publicly exhibited in galleries and salons, there was no way for the masses to organize and control themselves in their reception. Thus the same public which responds in a progressive manner toward a grotesque film is bound to respond in a reactionary manner to surrealism.

XIII

The characteristics of the film lie not only in the manner in which man presents himself to mechanical equipment but also in the manner in which, by means of this apparatus, man can represent his environment. A glance at occupational psychology illustrates the testing capacity of the equipment. Psychoanalysis illustrates it in a different perspective. The film has enriched our field of perception with methods which can be illustrated by those of Freudian theory. Fifty years ago, a slip of the tongue passed more or less unnoticed. Only exceptionally may such a slip have revealed dimensions of depth in a conversation which had seemed to be taking its course on the surface. Since *The Psychopathology of Everyday Life* things have changed. This book isolated and made analyzable things which had heretofore floated along unnoticed in the broad stream of perception. For the entire spectrum of optical, and now also acoustical, perception the film has brought about a similar deepening of apperception. It is only an obverse of this fact that behavior items shown in a movie can be analyzed much more precisely and from more points of view than those presented on paintings or on the stage. As compared with painting, filmed behavior lends itself more readily to analysis because of its incomparably more precise statements of the situation. In comparison with the stage scene, the filmed behavior item lends itself more readily to analysis because it can be isolated more easily. This circumstance derives its chief importance from its tendency to promote the mutual penetration of art and science. Actually, of a screened behavior item which is neatly brought out in a certain situation, like a muscle of a body, it is difficult to say which is more fascinating, its artistic value or its value for science. To demonstrate the identity of the artistic and scientific uses of photography which heretofore usually were separated will be one of the revolutionary functions of the film.

By close-ups of the things around us, by focusing on hidden details of familiar objects, by exploring commonplace mileux under the ingenious guidance of the camera, the film, on the one hand, extends our comprehension of the necessities which rule our lives; on the other hand, it manages to assure us of an immense and unexpected field of action. Our taverns and our metropolitan streets, our offices and furnished rooms, our railroad stations and our factories appeared to have us locked up hopelessly. Then came the film and burst this prison-world asunder by the dynamite of the tenth of a second, so that now, in the midst of its far-flung ruins and debris, we calmly and adventurously go traveling. With the close-up, space expands; with slow motion, movement is extended. The enlargement of a snapshot does not simply render more precise what in any case was visible, though unclear: it reveals entirely new structural formations of the subject. So, too, slow motion not only presents familiar qualities of movement but reveals in them entirely unknown ones 'which, far from looking like retarded rapid movements, give the effect of singularly gliding, floating, supernatural motions'.[9] Evidently a different nature opens itself to the camera than opens to the naked eye – if only because an unconsciously penetrated space is substituted for a space consciously explored by man. Even if one has a general knowledge of the way people walk, one knows nothing of a person's posture during the fractional second of a stride. The act of reaching for a lighter or a spoon is familiar routine, yet we hardly know what really goes on between hand and metal, not to mention how this fluctuates with our moods. Here the camera intervenes with the resources of its lowerings and liftings, its interruptions and isolations, its extensions and accelerations, its enlargements and reductions. The camera introduces us to unconscious optics as does psychoanalysis to unconscious impulses.

XIV

One of the foremost tasks of art has always been the creation of a demand which could be fully satisfied only later. The history of every art-form shows critical epochs in which a certain art-form aspires to effects which could be fully obtained only with a changed technical standard, that is to say, in a new art-form. The extravagances and crudities of art which thus appear, particularly in the so-called decadent epochs, actually arise from the nucleus of its richest historical energies. In recent years, such barbarisms were abundant in dadaism. It is only now that its impulse becomes discernible: dadaism attempted to create by pictorial – and literary – means the effects which the public today seeks in the film.

Every fundamentally new, pioneering creation of demands will carry beyond its goal. Dadaism did so to the extent that it sacrificed the market values which are so characteristic of the film in favor of higher ambitions – though of course it was not conscious of such intentions as here described. The dadaists attached much less importance to the sales value of their work than to its uselessness for contemplative immersion. The studied degradation of their material was not the least of their means to achieve this uselessness. Their poems are 'word salad' containing obscenities and every imaginable waste product of language. The same is true of their paintings, on which they mounted buttons and tickets. What they intended and achieved was a relentless destruction of the aura of their creations, which they branded as reproductions with the very means of production. Before a painting of Arp's or a poem by August Stramm it is impossible to take time for contemplation and evaluation as one would before a canvas of Derain's or a poem by Rilke. In the decline of middle-class society, contemplation became a school for asocial behavior; it was countered by distraction as a variant of social conduct. Dadaistic activities actually assured a rather vehement distraction by making works of art the center of scandal. One requirement was foremost: to outrage the public.

From an alluring appearance or persuasive

structure of sound the work of art of the dadaists became an instrument of ballistics. It hit the spectator like a bullet, it happened to him, thus acquiring a tactile quality. It promoted a demand for the film, the distracting element of which is also primarily tactile, being based on changes of place and focus which periodically assail the spectator. Let us compare the screen on which a film unfolds with the canvas of a painting. The painting invites the spectator to contemplation; before it the spectator can abandon himself to his associations. Before the movie frame he cannot do so. No sooner has his eye grasped a scene than it is already changed. It cannot be arrested. Duhamel, who detests the film and knows nothing of its significance, though something of its structure, notes this circumstance as follows: 'I can no longer think what I want to think. My thoughts have been replaced by moving images.'[10] The spectator's process of association in view of these images is indeed interrupted by their constant, sudden change. This constitutes the shock effect of the film, which, like all shocks, should be cushioned by heightened presence of mind. By means of its technical structure, the film has taken the physical shock effect out of the wrappers in which dadaism had, as it were, kept it inside the moral shock effect.

XV

The mass is a matrix from which all traditional behavior toward works of art issues today in a new form. Quantity has been transmuted into quality. The greatly increased mass of participants has produced a change in the mode of participation. The fact that the new mode of participation first appeared in a disreputable form must not confuse the spectator. Yet some people have launched spirited attacks against precisely this superficial aspect. Among these, Duhamel has expressed himself in the most radical manner. What he objects to most is the kind of participation which the movie elicits from the masses. Duhamel calls the movie 'a pastime for helots, a diversion for uneducated, wretched, worn-out creatures who are consumed by their worries . . . a spectacle which requires no concentration and presupposes no intelligence . . . which kindles no light in the heart and awakens no hope other than the ridiculous one of someday becoming a "star" in Los Angeles'.[11] Clearly, this is at bottom the same ancient lament that the masses seek distraction whereas art demands concentration from the spectator. That is a commonplace. The question remains whether it provides a platform for the analysis of the film. A closer look is needed here. Distraction and concentration form polar opposites which may be stated as follows. A man who concentrates before a work of art is absorbed by it. He enters into this work of art the way legend tells of the Chinese painter when he viewed his finished painting. In contrast, the distracted mass absorbs the work of art. This is most obvious with regard to buildings. Architecture has always represented the prototype of a work of art the reception of which is consummated by a collectivity in a state of distraction. The laws of its reception are most instructive.

Buildings have been man's companions since primeval times. Many art-forms have developed and perished. Tragedy begins with the Greeks, is extinguished with them, and after centuries its 'rules' only are revived. The epic poem, which had its origin in the youth of nations, expires in Europe at the end of the Renaissance. Panel painting is a creation of the Middle Ages, and nothing guarantees its uninterrupted existence. But the human need for shelter is lasting. Architecture has never been idle. Its history is more ancient than that of any other art, and its claim to being a living force has significance in every attempt to comprehend the relationship of the masses to art. Buildings are appropriated in a twofold manner: by use and by perception – or rather, by touch and sight. Such appropriation cannot be understood in terms of the attentive concentration of a tourist before a famous building. On the tactile side there is no counterpart to contemplation on the optical side. Tactile appropriation is accomplished not so much by attention as by habit. As regards architecture, habit determines to a large extent even optical reception. The latter, too, occurs much less through rapt attention than by noticing the object in incidental fashion. This mode of appropriation, developed with reference to architecture, in certain circumstances acquires canonical value. For the tasks which face the human apparatus of perception at the turning points of history cannot be solved by optical means, that is, by contemplation, alone. They are mastered gradually by habit, under the guidance of tactile appropriation.

The distracted person, too, can form habits. More, the ability to master certain tasks in a state of distraction proves that their solution has become a matter of habit. Distraction as provided by art presents a covert control of the extent to which new tasks have become soluble by apperception. Since, moreover, individuals are tempted to avoid such tasks, art will tackle the most difficult and most important ones where it is able to mobilize the masses. Today it does so in the film. Reception in a state of distraction, which is increasing noticeably in all fields of art and is symptomatic of profound changes in apperception, finds in the film its true means of exercise. The film with its shock effect meets this mode of reception halfway. The film makes the cult value recede into the background not only by putting the public in the position of the critic, but also by the fact that at the movies this position requires no attention. The public is an examiner, but an absent-minded one.

References: Chapter 4

1 Paul Valéry, *Aesthetics*, 'The conquest of ubiquity', tr. Ralph Mannheim (New York: Pantheon, 1964), p. 226.
2 Abel Gance, 'Le temps de l'image est venu', *L'Art cinématographique*, vol. 2, 1927, pp. 94 f.
3 ibid., pp. 100–1.
4 Séverin-Mars, quoted by Gance, op. cit., p. 100.
5 Alexandre Arnoux, *Cinéma pris*, 1929, p. 28.
6 Franz Werfel, 'Ein Sommernachstraum, Ein Film von Shakespeare und Reinhardt', *Neues Wiener Journal*, cited in *Lu*, vol. 15, November 1935.
7 Luigi Pirandello, *Si Gira*, quoted by Léon Pierre-Quint, 'Signification du cinéma', in *Gance*, op. cit., pp. 14–15.
8 Rudolf Arnheim, *loc. cit.*, p. 138.
9 ibid.
10 Georges Duhamel, *Scènes de la vie future* (Paris: Mercure de France, 1930), p. 52.
11 ibid., p. 58.

PART TWO

Cultural Criticism in Advanced Industrial Society

Introduction to Part Two

In the three-and-a-half decades since the end of the Second World War, after an initial period of reconstruction followed by rapid economic expansion and growth, Europe's old societies reached a stage of advanced industrial civilization in their social history. The challenges presented to the venerable cultural traditions of the old continent by the new sociological configurations shaping the collective destinies of its major nations have provided the main focus of postwar cultural criticism. The fundamental preoccupation underlying this mode of cultural criticism concerns the significance of cultural forms as outlets for the expression of an understanding of the human predicament in 'post-industrial' civilization. The prevailing tone of this conception is set by a sense of experiencing a uniquely new social reality pointing beyond the heritage of familiar modes of culture in the great European tradition.

Thus Lucien Goldmann interprets the continuing experimentation with modernist forms of cultural expression as a revolt against the sociological conditions of advanced industrialism, stressing the critical aspects of modernism in the arts and letters. The obverse side of this perception of the broad significance of modernism as criticism can be seen by taking into account the historical fact that modernism accompanied the rise of industrialism and, having become a cultural tradition itself, it has developed its own standards of acceptability determining artistic success. Thus it has become in a way the framework of a new conformity in cultural expression.

The dangers of cultural conformity and their political implications are hinted at in the context of their broadest social significance by Hans Magnus Enzensberger in his discussion of the 'industrialization of the mind'. His essay is one of the best statements of the concern that has been voiced by several European cultural critics regarding the effects of the new sophisticated technology of leisure, propaganda, and commercialism on the integrity of the human being as a thinking person. Enzensberger, while pointing at the dangers, does not relapse into a facile and conceited renunciation of the cultural realities of the new age, but insists on a full awareness and experience of the new configuration in order to make use of its possibilities in moving forward beyond the society of 'one-dimensional' men and women. In this acknowledgement of the contribution of the new culture, Enzensberger joins Goldmann in a message of hope that hints at a vision of a future humanized culture for which the resources of industrial society will be useful instruments rather than constraints.

Some of these problems and preoccupations emerge in a more specific form from the concrete cultural commentaries directed at the major industrial societies of contemporary Europe: Britain, France, and Germany. By putting his finger in such a detailed and well-informed way on the limitations of British culture and thought, Krishan Kumar in his original essay relates contemporary issues to the tradition of cultural criticism so brilliantly re-created by Raymond Williams.

Michel Crozier who, in an earlier essay, had spoken of a 'cultural revolution' caused by the reception of the imperatives of economic growth and technical efficiency in·

French culture, touches on the cultural anxieties and uneasiness that disturbed traditional cultural patterns as a consequence of the introduction of such changes under the Fifth Republic. Finally, Heinz Ludwig Arnold, in his essay, offers a lucid application of how to study cultural phenomena in their context by tracing the emergence of a new temper in contemporary German literature. The 'subjective pragmatism' marking the literature of present-day Germany is certainly a characteristic expression of the experience of post-industrial affluence that has replaced the uncertainties and soul-searching of the period of material and moral reconstruction immediately following the war.

5

LUCIEN GOLDMANN

The Revolt of Arts and Letters in Advanced Civilizations

I am still far from able to present an adequate synthesis of the 'revolt in the literature of advanced industrial societies'. But the subjects, writers, and film-makers I work with nonetheless pose precisely the problem of revolt against contemporary society. Thus I hope to address the fundamental problems by discussing only some concrete examples, which I will try to situate in the very general framework of the problematic of democracy and freedom in advanced industrial societies. It is better to analyze some texts or a writer's work in more or less depth than to conduct the sort of general survey in which only a few words are said about any particular work. Thus, I will first outline the sociological framework for reflection on contemporary cultural life and art.

If we deal with advanced industrial societies then clearly, at least in the West, we are dealing with a universe which sociology, economics, and even history still call the capitalist world (although at present this practice is changing somewhat). But that exact term is beginning to lose its precision, since capitalist society has endured a long time and has passed through different periods. Increased precision thus requires that distinctions be made in the form of a periodization. This must be done not only on the social and economic planes but also on the cultural, philosophical, literary, and artistic planes, which are intimately linked to the former. Cultural life is not separate from economic, social, and political realities;

any periodization (which is indispensable for comprehending the history of capitalism) must be, if not identified with, then at least related to, a complementary periodization of philosophical and cultural history. Thus I propose a periodization at the economic level, merely indicating what corresponds to it in philosophy and literature.

There are three distinct periods in the history of Western capitalism, the first of which, extending until about the 1910s, can be called 'liberal capitalism'. This is the individualist period in which the idea of the ensemble as totality (*l'idée d'ensemble de totalité*) tends to disappear from consciousness. On the plane of thought, this period was expressed above all by two forms of radical individualist philosophy, the two great currents of what we call classical philosophy: rationalism and empiricism. On the literary plane it was expressed by, among other things, the classical novel: the novel of the problematic character.

For sociologists a probem arises even at this level; I will only point it out in passing. On the whole, in the history of Western culture we almost always find a relation of rather strict homology between great philosophical currents and great literary creations;[1] and it is fairly easy to turn up homologous couples in the imaginary universes created by writers and in the conceptual systems elaborated by philosophers.

I merely point out in passing, for example, the

couples formed by the works of Pascal and Racine, Descartes and Corneille, Gassendi and Molière, Kant and Schiller, Schelling and the romantics. But in regard to Enlightenment philosophy, which despite everything is one of the liberal period's most important forms of philosophical thought, no writer can be found who rigorously corresponds to the rationalist current. There is of course the Descartes–Corneille example above; but it is rather unlike the other couples. Descartes's role and his influence in the history of Western culture are enormous, and extend beyond Enlightenment philosophy to contemporary rationalism; whereas only some of Corneille's plays, and not even his entire opus, are the only literary expression relatively akin to the Cartesian position. The disproportion seems obvious between the importance of rationalism in Western culture (especially in the history of Western philosophy) on the one hand, and the importance of Corneille's plays in the history of literature on the other.

The novel of the problematic character is the literary genre which, because of its importance, corresponds to the era of liberal capitalism. But this novel is not homologous to empiricism, to rationalism, or to Enlightenment philosophy. It is a critical literary form implying a positive element: the affirmation of the individual and of individual value implicit in the novels of this period, from *Don Quixote* to *The Red and the Black* to *Madame Bovary*. But, precisely in this primary affirmation of the individual's value, the novel is an extremely vigorous social critique. It shows that the society in which its heroes live, founded exclusively on the values of individualism and the development of personal character, does not permit the individual to develop or realize himself (I mention this problem only in passing, but obviously it is intimately linked to the problematic of critique and revolt in modern literature).

The second large period in the history of Western capitalism is that currently called the imperialist period. I have designated it the period of 'capitalism in crisis', which may indicate its link with literature. The Marxist thinkers who lived and wrote in that era believed a final crisis of capitalism was at hand, the great crisis which would lead to the fall of that order

and to the transition to socialism. Today we know that it was actually a period of very acute economic and social crisis, but a period of transition nonetheless. I cannot analyze it in detail, and will point out only the frequency of social and economic crises it evidences, especially as compared with the preceding period.

Historians of imperialism locate the transition from liberal capitalism to this second phase around 1910–11. Beginning from this date we find the First World War in 1914, a profound social and political crisis at the end of the war from 1917 to 1918, between 1929 and 1933 an economic crisis of proportions unprecedented in Western history, Hitler's seizure of power in 1933, and the Second World War between 1939 and 1945 (not to mention the events along the periphery of the advanced industrial world, in Spain and Italy). Evidently, during this entire period economic and social equilibrium was particularly difficult to establish, was realized only provisionally and very unstably, and was followed immediately by the outbreak of new crises.

From the economic viewpoint the explanation is primarily that the mechanism of regulation through the market, essential to the liberal economy, had been disrupted by the development of monopolies and trusts, while the new mechanisms of regulation which characterize the third period had not yet been established.

In any case, on the philosophical plane a specific, original philosophy corresponds to this period of capitalism in crisis. In some respects it conserved individualistic elements (Heidegger's *Dasein*, Sartre's *pour-soi* in *Being and Nothingness*, and the organic subject in *The Critique of Dialectical Reason*); but such elements were centered no longer on reason or perception – on the individual's possibilities – but instead on his limits, and on the limit *par excellence*: death. On the psychic plane this philosophy, existentialism, also gave a central position to the sensibility which developed out of the consciousness of limits and of death: anguish.

With Kafka, Musil, Sartre's *Nausea*, and Camus's *The Stranger*, there is in this period a novelistic literature which is much closer to philosophy, and especially to existentialist philosophy. This fact is easily explained insofar as this philosophy explicitly asserted the individual's difficulty in adapting to the surrounding world, a problem already at the center of the novel in the preceding period. It can also be mentioned in passing that from this time the novel collided with one of the most important of the problems which were to determine its subsequent evolution: the problem of the character. On the economic plane, the transition from liberal capitalism to the capitalism of monopolies and trusts had already been characterized by the individual's loss of economic and social importance. The writer can give form only to what is essential in the reality out of which he elaborates his work. With the individual's importance diminished by economic development, it would have been difficult to create a great literary work relating the story of a character – a biography which, on the plane of reality, had become merely anecdotal.

With the importance socialist thought had gained in the West, there were attempts to replace the character with the collectivity, and to write novels with collective characters: Martin du Gard's *The Thibaults*, for example; the other family novels, Mann's *Buddenbrooks* and Galsworthy's *The Forsyte Saga*; and the novel of the revolutionary community, Malraux's *Man's Fate* (*La Condition humaine*). But ultimately this was a transitional phase: the socialist revolution did not really transform Western society, the collectivity was not a force capable of changing it, nor did the novel of the collectivity become a predominant literary form.

Finally, the third stage, of special interest to us, is the one in which we live today. Sociologists use various terms to denote this period of capitalism: consumer society, mass society, organizational capitalism, technocratic society. Basically, each of these designations stresses a principal aspect of a society which, however, constitutes an overall structure. It is initially characterized by the appearance of conscious mechanisms of self-regulation (the market was a mechanism which did not penetrate consciousness, and the period of capitalism in crisis was marked precisely by the lack of effective mechanisms for regulating the economy and the society).

In the liberal period, men's everyday thought, like economics, sociology, and classical philosophy, had completely lost sight of the totality, the ensemble of social life (the overall history of society, production as a whole, etc.). They no longer saw anything but the individual: *homo economicus* in economics; the Cartesian *ego* in philosophy; the autonomy of individual consciousness, reason, and perception; and, in literature, the novel hero. On the contrary, in organizational capitalism the awareness of totality appears to be the fundamental phenomenon, at least on the level of the will and behavior of managers and directors.

Hardly twenty years ago I proposed a thesis on Quesnay's *Le Tableau économique* to a famous professor at the Paris Faculty of Law. He looked at me curiously and said: 'That subject is of no interest; it was just an amusement of the physiocrats.' Today one cannot enter a room where a course on political economy is being given without hearing about national accounts, the model of growth, etc. – in other words, about the overall structure of production which was precisely the subject of *Le Tableau économique* and was first studied by the physiocrats.

To summarize: Marxist thinkers believed capitalism could never integrate a vision of the ensemble of society and of production. But capitalism has survived crises which, according to the Marxists, had to be fatal to it; and its theoreticians have become aware of the problems of the overall organization of society and the economy.

Comparing capitalism in the crisis period between 1910–12 and 1945 with the preceding period, we find that between 1848 and 1912 there were essentially no important European crises, whereas between 1912 and the end of the Second World War they followed each other at very short intervals. On the other hand, since the end of that war there have been no more internal crises in Western societies. Of course there were the Algerian events, for example; but they were repercussions on an advanced industrial society from its break with developing countries and with old colonies. Such events are entirely unlike the internal crises of the intermediate era.

These transformations are extremely important and have had considerable consequences. The conscious self-regulation mechanisms developed since the end of the Second World War have ended up reinforcing a tendency which existed even earlier, but which sociologists had hardly noticed: the integration of the whole society through a rise in the standard of living which, although slow at first, is much greater today (and, in the United States, considerable).

The traditional Marxist schema of the pauperization of the middle classes has lost its validity in Western industrial societies. Of course to a great extent it still applies to developing countries, where differences in the standard of living are extremely marked and poverty is even increasing. But in the industrial societies, in Western capitalism, not only do self-regulation mechanisms lead to a much more rapid rise in the standard of living for the majority of the population; also, one of the psychological consequences of this fact is constituted by the integration of society and the considerable weakening of traditional oppositional forces. This last process is especially important, and it is what those who speak of the affluent society or the consumer society have in mind.

A third and final phenomenon is at once the result of and the precondition for these transformations: the considerable concentration of decision-making power in the hands of a relatively small group (several thousand people) which I will call *technocrats*.[2] For the functioning of their mechanisms, however, advanced industrial societies need an increasing number of professionals with a very high level of knowledge in their specialties. These specialists, whose competence is increasing, who must be highly skilled in their own domains in order to be able to execute the decisions made elsewhere, can be called *technicians*. It must never be forgotten that the greatest part of the lives of these technicians takes place only at the level of execution, the power of decision being reserved to the members of that relatively narrow social stratum which I have called the technocrats.

In these societies where the competence of the social body's members rises considerably, the problem of extreme concentration of decision-making

power becomes fundamental: the rise in competence does not lead the great majority of individuals to participate in essential decisions. This fact has extremely serious psychic consequences. Here I will not analyze it psychologically or sociologically in depth; but clearly the most important result of this phenomenon is the considerable reduction of the psychic life of individuals.

It is not true that the rising level of knowledge and professional skill necessarily and implicitly entails expanded freedom, intensified psychic and intellectual life, or strengthened possibilities of comprehension. What I once called 'the illiterate specialist' is a danger which threatens to grow considerably in organizational society. Herbert Marcuse has posed this question strikingly in *One-Dimensional Man*, although in my judgement his conclusions are too pessimistic.

Traditionally, during the entire history preceding our contemporary societies (and probably also in the present and the future, although there things are not as clear), man has defined himself in terms of two fundamental dimensions in which his psychic life and his behavior develop: the tendency to adapt to the real, and the tendency to overcome the real toward the possible – toward a beyond which men must create by their behavior.

Adaptation to the real is an essential function for the individual as much as for social groups. Such adaptation, however, tends to create equilibria which threaten to become static. Until now society always changed due not only to the action of the individuals and groups composing it but also to external influences. Thus, well before it was attained (usually as it was only being approached), equilibration was no longer adapted to the real problems of social life; and men came to be oriented toward a different and often higher equilibrium.

Although I cannot pursue the point here – I have written a book on the subject[3] – I will say that the *possible* is the fundamental category for comprehending human history. The great difference between positivist and dialectical sociology consists precisely in the fact that whereas the former is content to develop the most exact and meticulous possible photography of the existing society, the latter tries to isolate the potential consciousness in the society it studies: the potential (*virtuelles*), developing tendencies oriented toward overcoming that society. In short, the first tries to give an account of the functioning of the existing structuration, and the second centers on the possibilities of varying and transforming social consciousness and reality.

Pascal grasped this phenomenon early, saying that man cannot be defined without self-contradiction because the only valid definition of man is that he is infinitely more than what he is. In a dialectical perspective which is not Pascal's, I would add that man is greater than what he is because he is always making himself and making a new world.

But the fundamental problematic of modern capitalist societies is no longer located at the level of poverty – although, I repeat, poverty remains even in the most advanced industrial countries – or even at the level of a freedom directly limited by law or external constraint. Instead, it lies entirely in the contraction of the level of consciousness and in the concomitant tendency to reduce the fundamental human dimension of the possible. As Marcuse says, if social evolution does not change direction, man will live and act increasingly only in the single dimension of adaptation to reality, and not in the other, the dimension of transcendence.

The contraction of personal character and individuality is a disquieting phenomenon even in the transitional period in which we are living. It threatens to become increasingly serious if social evolution is actually oriented toward men's perfect adaptation to a society where most of them become mere well-paid functionaries with a high standard of living and long vacations, living better and better – but with a restricted consciousness – as specialized technicians. This, I believe, is the fundamental problem of technocratic society.

Nonetheless, in opposition to Marcuse I believe there are tendencies toward overcoming this situation. One-dimensional man (to use the singularly well-chosen formulation he originated) represents only one of the alternatives facing contemporary industrial societies. Here I will not enter into this large problem, but will restrict myself to analyzing the types of reactions produced out of this situation at the level of literary and cultural creation, and especially the revolt within that creation.

This revolt can be comprised and described under two different, complementary aspects. There is the formal revolt of an art which, not accepting a society, refuses it by finding new forms of expression unlike those which that society has created and in which it has traditionally seen itself. I believe it necessary to comprehend the first manifestations of the 'new novel', and a whole series of today's literary works, on the basis of this extremely important phenomenon. The other aspect is the theme of revolt itself in the work of certain writers and artists.

Despite the intimate link uniting these two aspects of negation, there is nonetheless a fundamental difference between them. In one case it is a matter of refusing society, a revolt expressed through the invention of new forms; in the other, the problem of men's revolt in and against the society they refuse is treated in the work itself and forms its subject, theme, central concern, and structuration. I will deal very quickly with the first of these two aspects of revolt in order to move on to a brief analysis of the work of the greatest writer of the revolt in French literature today, Jean Genet, in his theater from *The Maids* to *The Screens*.

It goes without saying that I begin with the idea that a great writer cannot write a valid work at any time or in any place. In the first place, he can write only in an overall perspective which he has not invented and which must exist in society so that he can subsequently transpose it in a coherent imaginary universe. Secondly, this imaginary universe will constitute a valid work only insofar as it centers on the essential aspects of the social reality which has helped to elaborate the categories structuring it. I will not dwell on this undeniably difficult business; I will merely say that this is the translation of a central idea of Hegelian philosophy, the identity of subject and object, into the language of the sociology of culture.

But in contemporary society the important phenomenon is the loss and progressive disappearance of the individual's importance and of the meaning of what is immediately lived on one hand, and the tendency to constrict consciousness on the other. Writers' resistance to this rising and developing society thus encounters a double obstacle. On the one hand it is in fact no longer possible to address the great problems of modern society, of man in today's world, at the level of an immediately perceived story. The biography of a character has become merely anecdotal. Narration restricted to things and events at the immediately lived level risks remaining in miscellaneous fact with no essential meaning. Inversely, if the writer tries to address the overall problems he must place himself at a level which, although not conceptual (no great work of art is conceptual), nonetheless becomes totalizing and increasingly loses relation with the perceived and the immediately lived. And this occurs at a time when, because of the psychic and intellectual constriction I have described, the consciousness of the individuals living in society (of the great majority of readers) becomes less and less suited to grasping phenomena at this level of abstraction and generality. Two examples will clarify these observations.

One of the best-known studies of Robbe-Grillet has been published by an American professor.[4] In this extremely intelligent, penetrating study he has demonstrated that each of this author's narratives contains a narrated story which, with some ability to follow the text very closely, can be extracted; and that in certain respects this story ultimately resembles those narrated in the novels of the liberal capitalist era. From this he concludes that Robbe-Grillet's originality lies primarily in the fact that his way of narrating the story is different from that of earlier writers.

In the course of a long discussion with this critic I tried to maintain that if a writer narrates things differently it is because things themselves have become essentially different, and therefore he can no longer say them in the accepted way. The discussion ended with the analysis of a passage from *Jealousy*: 'The light, rubber-soled shoes make no sound on the hallway tiles.'[5] The critic said: 'Clearly, this involves a jealous man who walks very softly so as not to make noise and surprise his wife.' I replied: 'Perhaps what is essential is simply that Robbe-Grillet wrote not "a man walks very softly" but instead "the light . . . shoes . . . make no sound", probably because what was essential was the fact that in today's world the shoes carry the man: the motor of events is no longer man but inert objects.'

The reply, of course, was: 'This is no doubt an amusing, ingenious witticism, but nevertheless a witticism.' Then I asked my interlocutor to choose between two statements which I would present and tell me which he found more accurate, understanding that the answer to the problem at issue would depend on this choice. One could say that every year between July and August some millions of people in advanced industrial countries take vacations, carrying cameras and taking photographs which they then show to their friends and family. Or one could say that every year, in rarely explicit, usually implicit, accord with certain travel agencies, the boards of directors of Kodak and the major camera firms decide to produce a certain number of cameras which will travel around the world, while a certain number of other cameras sold in previous years will remain in circulation. These decisions once made, the cameras set out on their travels with a corresponding number of people to operate them. Which of these formulations gives the best account of the phenomenon's essential reality?

Any serious sociologist, I think, will choose the second. And insofar as it permits the more exact comprehension of reality it is also chosen in the literary transposition which leads Robbe-Grillet to say 'the soles move forward' rather than 'the man moves forward'. But this is a fundamental change and the writer can express it only at this level of abstraction, which makes him seem paradoxical to most people who read his text. Men live at the level of immediate perceptions and thus, confronted with a text of this sort, they say 'This is absurd' and return to the immediately grasped and lived viewpoint which remains superficial and does not touch the essence of the phenomenon. But consciously or unconsciously, the great writer tries precisely to reach this essence and to say what is essential. The story of a jealous man is only a miscellaneous fact whereas, whether or not we are conscious of it, the soles which carry the man have on the whole become the central phenomenon of our everyday life.

Another example: I made a test by asking a certain number of people who had seen Godard's film *Contempt* to tell me its subject. So far, the responses have been almost unfailingly of the same type: 'A couple falls apart because the woman begins to scorn the man.' Just once, I believe, someone answered: 'It's about a book; the *Odyssey*, I think.' But the film's apparent subject is the impossibility of being loved in a world where one cannot film the *Odyssey*. It can now be comprehended in only two ways: the dying, cultivated, traditional humanism of Fritz Lang, who knows that the gods appear in the *Odyssey* and have disappeared from the world in which he finds himself; or Prokosch's view, which does not even recognize that there were gods in the *Odyssey*. Although the problem of the *Odyssey* and its cinematic transposition is present almost constantly in the film, most spectators have not even noticed it.

Godard's film attempts to circumscribe the Lang–Prokosch opposition. Becoming aware of the problem, the woman comes to scorn her husband, who understands nothing of the world around him and lives in total unconsciousness. Love is impossible in a world where there are no more gods, where adapted men do not even know what 'god' or 'love' might mean or what meaning those words might give their existence. The film ends with collision and death between two stationary vehicles, symbolically prolonging the opposition between Lang and Prokosch as the former continues to film a caricatural *Odyssey* in front of a hopelessly empty sea.

Although the *Odyssey* is in the background, Godard gives the problems of film, the discussions of the *Odyssey*, and the Lang–Prokosch opposition materially greater room than he gives the rest of the story. But if you try the experiment you will see the extent to which spectators have not even perceived this essential aspect of the film.

This is the central problem for literary creation today. The writer wants to express the problematic of the gods' absence in the modern world (the gods signify fundamental values and the possibilities of individual realization). But access to this problematic is difficult or impossible for most of his readers; they are hardly aware that the soles are really what move the man forward and carry him . . . Taking a whole series of important modern books and films, one can find the same problematic, which film-makers and writers cannot address on the immediate level of Pierre's or Jean's life-story because that has become a mere anecdote. A film like *Contempt* addresses it at the level of a couple's story. But to do so, it must overcome that story and thus become incomprehensible in a society where reading is increasingly oriented toward professional problems and immediate life, and where the very possibility of comprehending the problematic of the gods' existence (what Marcuse called man's dimension of the possible) is considerably reduced. This situation gives rise to a difficult art which no longer seems to speak immediately to the reader, although every great writer – and there are still several of them – does everything he can to make himself understood (I am speaking not of epigones but of truly creative works). For this reason, criticism today is assuming an increasingly important role.

I have mentioned only two examples, *Jealousy* and *Contempt*, but I could reconsider the problem by analyzing about twenty literary works and films. Almost all contemporary art is an art of refusal which inquires into man's existence in the modern world and which, in order to do so, must take place on an abstract level. It can no longer speak with the aid of the story of an individual or even an account of a lived event, because the individual himself is no longer an essential element of contemporary society as he was in the age of Stendhal, Balzac, and Flaubert. Thus results what I call the revolt on the formal plane, which is necessary in order to remain at the level of essentials and of authentic creation. An art which refuses this society, a humanist art signalling the dangers it presents for man, must necessarily speak this new language.

This leads to the problem of the public's comprehension of contemporary literature and art. Godard's films enjoy a relative success; but when you try to ask spectators what the films are saying you discover the extent to which the message fails to come across despite the success. Let me recall another anecdote. One day after a showing of Godard's film *La Chinoise* I was in a cafe, next to respectable people who were discussing the film they had seen. They tried to outdo each other with statements like 'The film is absurd, ridiculous; it doesn't make sense and doesn't mean anything', 'It makes fun of us, it takes us for idiots', and so forth. The conversation continued in this vein for about ten minutes until one lady, in a peremptory tone and with the air of making the most negative possible statement about the film, concluded it: 'In a word, it's like Picasso.'

A single process obliges writers to speak less and less at the level of immediate perception and prevents the public, except in exceptional cases and by special efforts, from understanding them and overcoming the immediately perceived. In such a society, how can this art convey its meaning? That is the problem.

The other side of the problematic is oppositional thought and the theme of revolt in literature. So far, industrial societies seem solidly integrated at the level of their external and more or less visible manifestations. In a book written three or four years ago[6] I said that the forces of transformation in contemporary technocratic society may not be as weak as they might seem on the manifest perceptual level. These forces would have to be studied sociologically in depth; but in fact, literature has been written until now in a society where the forces of contestation seem to be growing increasingly weaker. Therefore, exactly as writers can no longer relate the story of an individual in a universe where this individual no longer has any essential reality, neither can they relate the story of forces of contestation which no longer exist or are disappearing. For this reason the literature of revolt has gained only a relatively secondary place in the recent development of contemporary literature.

Nonetheless, a very great writer, Jean Genet, has placed this problem at the center of his work in his last four plays: *The Maids, The Balcony, The Blacks,* and *The Screens*. Moreover, the study of these texts raises a rather important problem of aesthetic sociology which I will only note in passing. In my seminar we are studying existentialism and, although we cannot explain it at this point, we find that at the

very moments Genet and Sartre tackled the themes of class struggle, revolt, and revolution, they both moved from prose and the novel to the theater.

The great existentialist works of the first period are clearly *The Wall* and *Nausea*, but in them Sartre does not address the problem of history and revolution at all. When he did engage that problematic he still tried to write a novel, *Roads to Freedom*, which had enormous success at the time. But whereas *The Wall* and *Nausea* are still read today, to most serious critics *Roads to Freedom* appears to be a failed novel (and Sartre himself never finished it). He was subsequently to address the new problematic in a series of plays, from *The Flies* to *The Condemned of Altona*. To a great extent the problems of revolution form the theme of these plays; but the author still addresses them in the perspective of classical philosophy: the relation between the individual and external social reality (Orestes and revolution, Goetz and history, Frantz and torture). In short, as opposed to the theme of his novels the question in almost all of Sartre's plays is the conflict between the ethical and the historical.

Almost exactly the same thing occurred in Genet's work. He begins as a novelist. He writes a play, *Deathwatch*, which is rather average since it is still centered on the old problematic. Then the conflict between dominated and dominators appears in his work, and he writes his four great plays. This judgement does not express a merely personal opinion; objectively, it suffices to ascertain the frequencies of performance: *Deathwatch* is rarely performed whereas *The Maids, The Balcony, The Blacks,* and *The Screens* play throughout the world. Above all, the public perceives Genet's plays as 'poetic': if that means anything, it usually means simply: 'They are very beautiful; I like them, but I don't know why.' But these are complex plays whose structure is not grasped at first and which, in analysis, appear extremely rigorous, to the point that there is a reason for almost every phrase being exactly where it is. These four plays also have a common basic structure, which I will now try to outline.

A first common element distinguishes them from all the rest of contemporary literature: the characters are collective. There are no individual characters except, to some extent, Said in *The Screens*; but he is defined in relation to collective forces and, in addition, is not entirely individual in that he is part of the group formed by himself, his mother, and his wife Leila. In *The Maids* there are Monsieur and Madame on the one hand, Solange and Claire on the other; in *The Balcony* there are the characters of the balcony on the one hand, and on the other the rebels and the populace who come to the house of illusions; in *The Blacks* there are the Blacks and the Whites; in *The Screens* there are the colonists, the rebels, and the dead, not to mention the army and the prostitutes.

Clearly, insofar as historical action forms the theme and problematic of a work, the forces acting are not individuals but groups, since individual time is only biographical whereas historical time is that of groups. But after Malraux, whose literary work already dates from a number of years ago, Genet has been the only important writer of contemporary literature who has presented the conflict of collective forces.

What are the relations between these collective characters? At least for the first three of these plays and to some extent for the fourth, the subject is the opposition, the conflict between dominated and dominators, with the dominated assuming a different face each time (the maids, the Blacks, the populace and the rebels in *The Balcony*, and the colonized people; to whom are opposed Monsieur and Madame, the Whites, the powers of the balcony, the colonists or the victorious group of colonial rebels in *The Screens*).

Conflict in these four plays also presents certain common traits. In the first place, the dominated people's feelings toward their dominators are complex, comprising two contradictory elements: hate and fascination. Hate and fascination are justified in the plays and create the coherence of their universe because all attempts by the dominated to destroy the dominators end in failure. The maids want to kill Madame but cannot succeed; in *The Balcony* the rebels cannot destroy the established order (this problem will be seen to be posed somewhat differently in *The Blacks* and especially in *The Screens*). This failure justifies the fascination of the

dominated with the dominators' power.

The dominated can realize only ritual in this universe. Ritual comprises two elements which, although they do not always have the same proportions or weight in each play, are nonetheless present in each. In *The Maids*, *The Balcony*, and *The Blacks*, the dominated play at destroying – killing – the dominators, and as well at being the dominators. In this ritual, hate inspires the destructive aspect, fascination the identification. The maids play at being Madame and at killing Madame. In *The Balcony* the populace play at being the powerful and at destroying them by revolution. We find the same situation in *The Blacks* and also, partially, in *The Screens*.

A final element of this universe: the real is always deceptive, inauthentic, and even odious; whereas on the contrary the only authentic, profound values are unquestionably those of the ritual. Nothing is true but appearance; nothing is human but the imaginary, even if it never succeeds in transforming reality.

In their reception, however, these plays have encountered a fundamental misunderstanding on this point. Certain critics (especially the particularly intelligent American critic Lionel Abel, but also many others) have presented Genet as the poet of appearance. Abel, moreover, has drawn all the consequences of this analysis, remarking that Genet, a very great writer in the beginnings of his plays, becomes much weaker in his endings. In fact, such a view cannot see why the plays do not end in the perspective in which they begin; why the maids finally commit suicide or why Roger mutilates or kills himself at the end of *The Balcony*. If the appearance is marvellous and the imaginary alone is valid, the characters would have to delight in that; one cannot see what leads them to despair. Faced with this discrepancy the critics – instead of asking 'Isn't Genet saying something else? Haven't I made a mistake?' – stick by their interpretation at the risk of failing to understand the work in its entirety. Even if ritual is the only valid thing in this universe, it is not satisfactory. Each play leads to the problematic of passage from the imaginary to the real; the impossibility of this passage creates despair: the maids' suicide, Roger's self-mutilation, and, in a more complex way which will be discussed shortly, the ending of *The Screens*.

This, then, is the universe of the four plays. I will now try to address their differences, starting with the first two.

Genet did everything he could to make *The Maids* clear. A passage which seems to me absolutely central is the one where the maids and Madame say the same things (that they love Monsieur and will follow him even to the penal colony). But when the maids say this it is authentic, dramatic, and human; whereas coming from Madame it becomes ridiculous and odious. In fact, every evening the maids play at being Madame and killing Madame; every evening they resume a ritual in which Claire plays at being Madame and Solange at being Claire. They have tried to kill Madame in reality as in the ritual, but have never succeeded. In addition, they have testified falsely against Monsieur, who has been imprisoned.

When the curtain rises we witness one of these soirées. Imagining they are Madame, Claire and Solange tell us how much they love Monsieur with an authentic love – Monsieur who may be convicted. At this point Madame arrives. With only some slight stylistic variations, she says the same thing, and it becomes absolutely odious. It is odious because, in the first place, Madame speaks in the conditional: she explains that Monsieur will make an agreement and will never be deported but that, if he were deported, she would follow him even to the penal colony. It is odious because, although she has declared that nothing interests her any longer, that she is going to give away her furs, and that she no longer wants to check the accounts, learning that Monsieur will be freed is enough to make her ask for the accounts and reclaim her furs: we understand that she had never stopped thinking about them. Finally, it is odious when in the final phrase of her great tirade she exclaims: 'Solange, give me a cigarette.'

Thus from beginning to end the play centers on the authenticity of the imaginary as opposed to the sordidness of real life; on the human and dramatic – although humbled – maids as opposed to the deceitful and ridiculous Madame. But Monsieur is freed. It becomes clear that the maids will be arrested

for false testimony, will not be able to continue their daily ritual, and will have to acknowledge defeat. They try anew to poison Madame but, as the text says, objects themselves conspire in her favor: Madame cannot be destroyed, she is too strong. To triumph in the imaginary the maids can only destroy themselves. At the end, Madame is magnanimous as always. Believing the maids adore her, she will pity the poor Claire killed by the evil Solange; but Solange will respond: 'I am no longer the maid: I am Mademoiselle Solange.' The play ends with an evocation of Holy Communion which is not at all parodic: Claire drinks the poison from a precious vessel, in accord with Solange.[7]

We find the same schema in the next play, *The Balcony*, whose action is otherwise the literary transposition of the great transformations of contemporary Western society. In the balcony are the powerful, the chief of police and the proprietress, Madame Irma; below is the populace which comes to the house of illusions to play at being powerful. In fact, they play at being what everyone imagines to be powerful – at being general, bishop, or judge – whereas society was transformed long ago, and the truly powerful are the chief of police and Madame Irma, the proprietress of the house of illusions. The play's subject is the series of events (at the level of a poetic transposition) which has made society conscious of these transformations, and which creates the situation at the end of the play in which people come to the house of illusions no longer to play judge or general, but to play chief of police. As related in the play, this evolution corresponds rigorously to the history of Western society, in which awareness has resulted to a very great extent from the revolutionary threat during the post-Second World War years and from the defeat of the forces favorable to revolution.[8]

The way of formulating the problem of ritual here is homologous to that in *The Maids*: identification and desire for destruction in the imaginary. I will restrict myself to the first three scenes in the house of illusions. The first tells us precisely that the real bishop cannot be a true bishop: he cannot realize the essence of a bishop because it is incompatible with reality. A real bishop is obliged to accept innumerable compromises and deceptions; whereas the essence of the bishop, who must refuse every compromise, can be found only in the imaginary: in the house of illusions. The second scene tells us that the imaginary judge, who realizes the essence of the judge, depends on the criminal's existence and essence. Finally the third of these scenes, involving the general, shows us the extent to which imaginary essence constitutes the only poetic and authentic value. Of course these three aspects coexist in the three scenes, but with a different accent in each.

Then there is the revolt, during which the populace gains awareness of the power held by the chief of police and the proprietress of the house of illusions. Madame Irma. The real bishop, judge, and general having been killed in the course of the struggle, the powers of the balcony replace them with the populace in the house of illusions: they are made bishop, judge, and general in reality. Of course, this transformation deprives them of all pathetic, dramatic character, and returns them to the level of mere caricatures.

Roger, the revolutionary leader, understood the importance of organization, demanded it, and opposed whoever defended dream, spontaneity, or authenticity. After the defeat he comes to the house of illusions and asks to play the chief of police. This is the great event which everyone has long awaited. But very soon he explains it himself: he is chief of police only in appearance, whereas he would have liked to be the chief of the executive in reality. As the maids killed themselves, he will mutilate himself (a way of telling us that he will kill himself). Having thus entered the imagination of the entire society, the chief of police will reign there for two thousand years.

In *The Blacks* we find the same problem. Moreover the powers, the dominators, the Whites in the balcony are the same characters as in the preceding play: soldier, magistrate, cleric, queen, and servant (who corresponds to the queen's messenger in *The Balcony*). Nothing could better underline the link between the two plays; but the critics have almost never perceived it. Genet has again done everything to be clear; certainly it is not his fault if he has not been understood.

But a new aesthetic problem arises in the analysis of this play. The Whites cannot be played by white actors and the Blacks by blacks. As in the preceding play, the central theme is the radical opposition between dominated and dominators (here, Blacks and Whites); and this theme would be contradicted in the course of a performance involving collaboration between them. Thus the Whites must be played by Blacks who carry white masks, while constantly letting it be seen that they are masks. And at a certain moment Genet has the masks raised in order to make them actors again and to explain their solidarity with those playing the role of the dominated.

The play is constructed on the same schema as the two preceding ones. At the beginning the Blacks perform the periodic ritual of assassinating a white woman, a ritual in which they must be condemned by the Whites at the end. And just as the maids can only kill themselves, just as Roger ends up mutilating himself, only outside the play's action do the Blacks kill another Black who, the whole play suggests, has betrayed them. At a certain point, however, the action is transformed. Ville de Saint-Nazaire, who establishes the link with the outside, returns to the stage to say that after this execution a new chief will come, who perhaps will lead the Blacks to victory. At this point the ritual's aim seems to change, and the play ends with the imaginary destruction of the Whites. Victory still exists only on the plane of ritual, of the imaginary; but it exists nonetheless, and replaces defeat.

The play's problematic is especially clear in a repeated scene, with which I will stop. The ritual centers on a murder, but the various participants do not want to join in the scheme. Archibald, the game's ringleader, always has to collect them and recall them to the roles they must play. Vertu and Village, a pair of lovers, explain that their love for each other suffices them and that they do not need to participate in the ritual. Archibald's response, which in part provides the key to the play, is substantially this: 'You cannot love, because you can do so only with white words. But to be able to use them you have to be not on the stage but in the drawing-room, among the Whites who don't accept you. You are Blacks; and love between Blacks, between the dominated, is impossible in the world of those who dominate you, and impossible with words not your own. First a new world must be created and, corresponding to that world, a new language: then you could really engage in a love that would be yours, a black love.' Less clearly expressed, this theme has already been encountered in *The Maids*. Solange and Claire's love for the milkman can only be sordid: the sole authentic love is their love for Monsieur; identifying with Madame, they imagine they will follow him even to the penal colony the day he is convicted. This is why at the end of *The Blacks*, when the play's action is practically finished, the ritual accomplished, and the Whites executed, as the other actors retire from the stage we see Vertu and Village remaining and restating the same problem. Village wants to hug Vertu in his arms:

VERTU: All men are like you: they imitate. Can't you invent something else?
VILLAGE: For you I could invent anything: fruits, brighter words, a two-wheeled wheelbarrow, cherries without pits, a bed for three, a needle that doesn't prick. But gestures of love, that's harder . . . Still, if you really want me to . . .
VERTU: I'll help you. At least, there's one thing: you won't be able to wind your fingers in my long golden hair . . .[9]

This ending accords with the fact that the situation outside it is no longer the same. There is a new black leader, and the ritual enters a struggle which may lead to freedom. Without moving from the defeat of the dominated to their real victory and the defeat of the dominators, the play shows at least the possibility or hope of it. And, on the plane of Vertu and Village's love, this change is also the reason that hope of finding words which would permit their love's realization can appear.

Finally, Genet has written a fourth play, *The Screens*, which is much more complex but begins with a universe whose schema is analogous to the one we are already acquainted with: the opposition of dominated and dominators. But this time the play's subject is the victory of the dominated. In the course

of the action three social orders appear: the order of the dominated and the dominators, of colonized and colonists, which we have already encountered; then the order of the victorious rebels; and finally the order of the dead.

As a sociologist I will point out that these three orders correspond to three concepts of the group held by the radical left, whose vision Genet has transposed in his entire theater. There is the society of exploitation constituted by the dominated–dominator opposition; the not yet ideal society in which the victorious dominated take power but maintain the state; and finally the dreamed-of society which abolishes all contradictions and reconciles everyone, where all the contradictions which placed men in opposition during their lives on Earth have disappeared and where, leaving aside all that formerly separated them, old enemies understand each other.

But there is a group opposed to these three orders. This opposition could have been an individual's, Said's; but we have already seen that at his side Said has his wife Leila and his mother. These three characters are not identical, since there is a hierarchization until the end of the play (Said is much more anarchic and oppositional than Leila or his mother); but they form a group opposing all the orders it encounters in the course of the action.

In addition to this fundamental theme of the relations between the three orders and Said, his wife, and his mother, there are two other parts of this particularly complex play which are transformed in a parallel way in the unfolding of the main action: the brothel and the army.

The story of the brothel, which I will outline very quickly, parallels the transformation and succession of the three orders. Moreover, there are three prostitutes corresponding to the three orders and to the two transformations constituting the passages from one to another. At the outset the brothel is the imaginary universe, the universe of ritual where the colonized come to find authenticity and essence. And as I have already said, as in all four plays, this is the only authenticity which can exist in a world where the colonists, the dominators, are odious or ridiculous and where the colonized find themselves in the same situation as the maids, the populace, or the Blacks. In the brothel the perfect prostitute, Warda, represents this authentic universe of the imaginary.

In the second episode the prostitutes themselves say that they have been integrated into the society and the struggle. They now have a function in revolutionary combat. They are respected, saluted, received, and accepted by the others as members of society. Their function, having become real, has replaced the imaginary one; their activity has become part of life. This situation is incarnated in Malika, the prostitute who from the beginning had relations with the resistance.

Finally there is the place of the third order, of the revolutionaries' victory and, somewhere in the distance, the appearance of the order of the dead. Here we see the society born of the victory of the dominated depriving the brothel of all value. Warda is killed; Malika moves to the second plane; and another prostitute who arrives from the north and no longer has any valid social function will replace them. In fact one of the play's central problems, or perhaps even its central problem, is that the rebels' victory has created a universe which denies both nonconformity and the imaginary: the latter no longer has a place in this new world (and the rebels' view is the same as that of the soldiers who once fought in defense of the dominators). Precisely for this reason, Said cannot accept this world. It can be seen how rigorously homologous, functional, and meaningful these transformations of the brothel are in relation to the succession of the three.orders which forms the play's main subject.

Now a word about the army, since this aspect of the play has provoked all the trouble and has been least understood by the public. Here I will address a fundamental problem of literary criticism. A rather questionable practice in criticism consists of relating all the events and problems it encounters in a writer's work to his personality and his deep aspirations.[10] But criticism agrees on this, particularly on the existence of a connection between the homosexuality it finds in Genet's writing and the deep yearnings of his personality, to such an extent that at the Venice Biennial a well-known critic seriously stated that the Living Theater had had men perform *The Maids*, 'as Genet wished'. But Genet's preface to the play says explicitly that it must be played by women. For this critic and his audience, it was so obvious that homosexuality is fundamental in Genet's work that they unquestioningly accepted the idea that the women in *The Maids* must be played by men.

Actually, the homosexuality which is constant in the novels and in the first play, *Deathwatch*, disappears in Genet's other plays or can be found there only through highly questionable interpretations. The important loves are all heterosexual: the love of the maids for Monsieur or the milkman, of Village for Vertu, of Roger for Chantal, of Said for Leila. Homosexuality disappears from this theater, reappearing only in the single relation of the lieutenant and the sergeant in the army of *The Screens*. If it wants to be taken seriously, any scientific attempt to relate homosexuality in Genet's work to his biography or personality must account for this disappearance and reappearance. Why does homosexuality vanish in the passage from the novel to theater? Why does it reappear in this single part of *The Screens*?

Formulating the problem at the level of structural analysis clarifies matters. Nonconformity, the refusal of the existing world, is an essential element in the structure of Genet's work. But in his novels, from *The Thief's Journal* to the first play, *Deathwatch*, Genet structures his universe only with values definitively recognized by society. The attempt to extract the elements constituting this universe uncovers an ensemble of mature relations, especially those of love, friendship, and courage. Limited to their relations at the level of their immediate assertion, these elements can provide the material for a very beautiful romantic book, but not at all for a nonconformist work. Since the anticonformist element was essential to the meaning and message of the writer's universe, he had only a single possibility of obtaining it: to the structure formed by these elements he had to add a second dimension which renders them nonconformist and is, if you wish, oblique. For this reason Genet added the second aspect to all the constitutive values of his pre-theatrical work, making those values unacceptable to the existing society: love, no doubt, but homosexual love; courage, but courage in crime; friendship, but friendship in vice and in socially condemned behavior; etc.

When Genet joins the radical left, primarily the group around Sartre and *Les Temps Modernes*, discovering the universe of class struggle and transposing it in his work, he no longer needs this second, oblique dimension to make the work nonconformist and to introduce social criticism into it. Also apparent is the abrupt disappearance of everything which was connected with that dimension, especially homosexuality. The question thus involves not a problem of personal expression but an aesthetic problem.

But then why does homosexuality reappear precisely in the army of *The Screens*? There is a very analogous reason, which is not in the least a mere desire to denigrate or caricature. In the first part, the colonists are drawn very caricaturally; otherwise Genet would have to resort to the oblique dimension. In the case of the army, the reason involved seems exactly the reverse, since in *The Screens* the army no longer struggles for victory. This army has already lost the war and no longer does anything but celebrate a ritual, conducting an imaginary war. But in Genet's universe, where reality appears unacceptable, this situation gives the army an essential, positive value.

The problem arose before in *The Blacks*: 'Grief, sir, is another of their adornments', says Snow,[11] and Archibald explains that this risk had to be run if the Whites were to be fought. And it was for this reason that some actors in the ritual, especially Snow, did not want to participate in this destruction.

That is to say that Genet again encounters a problem analogous to that of his first works. In fact, by valorizing the army because in the play it is situated in ritual and the imaginary, he risks apologizing for an institution which still really exists in society. In the effort to avoid this misunderstanding, all the old oblique dimensions reappear.

To go to the center of the problem we should analyze the scene which, more than any other, has provoked scandal. To consider only what it says in substance, it can first be analyzed leaving the oblique dimension aside. This army is no longer struggling for victory, its combat has therefore become essential

and authentic. It is important to each of its members not to die alone in an alien world, and to preserve the familiar surroundings of its native land to the maximum extent. When the lieutenant dies, all the others sacrifice to give his more trivial death the values which they have conserved in order to guarantee themselves less woeful deaths.

If we remain at this level, where the dying lieutenant's comrades join together to help him and to make his death less solitary, the scene is pathetic and romantic. To avoid this valorization, Genet has added the coarseness which provoked scandal. But it has been said before in *The Blacks*: when the dominators are conquered they become authentic and acceptable. The problematic is clear, as is the reason why we must not stop at the coarseness but must try to comprehend the play's structural ensemble and the problematic which has given rise to this aspect of it, which in fact seems to me aesthetically questionable.

Thus, the main action is framed by two parallel actions: the brothel on one side, the army on the other. This action itself is perfectly coherent and precise. First there is the order of oppression, where authenticity exists only in the imaginary. Then there is the revolt, begun by Said, who rejects it at the very instant when it becomes general (when the others say to him and his mother 'You were right; we join you' he will refuse to join forces with them and will remain isolated to preserve his nonconformity and individual autonomy). Finally there is the victory; and at that moment the problem of Said's status in the new order arises. To those previously dominated who, since the victory, have become dominators, the collective symbolic figure Ommu will explain that, now that they have replaced the old powers,[12] their revolt can be justified only to the extent that it can build a free world where nonconformity is not only possible but has a sanction and a recognized function: a universe with a place for singing and for Said's values. The new masters do not understand this perspective: with the struggle ended, they are at most disposed to pardon Said, accepting him and expunging the past. But Ommu replies that the question is one not of pardoning but of the very nature of the order they are creating, which cannot be justified so long as it must merely pardon nonconformity. The play ends when one of the new masters fires the gunshot which kills Said.

Despite the appearance of a fortuitous accident which she had wanted to create, the mother in fact participated in the revolt and the resistance; therefore she has entered the kingdom of the dead. There she awaits Leila and her son. But, less radical than Said, Leila does not accept the order of the dead: she will not enter it, but will nonetheless send her veil. Said, the nonconformist who remains alive until the end, is probably the first positive character in contemporary *avant-garde* literature; he neither accepts the order of the dead nor will he send any sign or trace there, and instead will pass directly into nothingness. He has remained alive from the beginning to the end of the play. For the first time in the modern universe, the world of freedom is affirmed, through him, as something which can open up a hope for the future.

Genet seems alone among great contemporary authors in having written a play whose axis is primarily the dimension of the possible and of transcendence, and in having centered it on the problem of freedom, revolt, and nonconformity.

This paper deals only with some of the aspects of modern art and literature. It goes without saying that a series of specific and rather precise sociological and aesthetic inquiries in depth must be developed. It might then be possible to establish a synthesis. And much more important, perhaps someday a society will arise where the problem of authentic art will no longer be merely the problem of refusal, but also that of acceptance: of men's entrance into a truly human society which can open the doors to hope.

Notes and References: Chapter 5

Written in 1968, this essay was first published in *Liberté et organisation dans le monde actuel* (Brussels: Desclées de Brouwer, Collection du Centre d'Etude de la Civilisation Contemporaine, 1969).

1 It would of course be necessary to try to verify at the level of positive science whether this parallelism, this homology, can also be extended to the history of painting and the other plastic arts.

2 To avoid any misunderstanding it should be stressed that the term 'technocrat' used in this sense by no means signifies a superior technical cadre specifically concerned with the production process, but denotes a member of that stratum which participates in the important, basic decisions concerning the life of society. Thus there are technocrats of education, politics, the economy, cultural life, etc., in addition, of course, to technocrats of production.

3 Lucien Goldmann, *The Human Sciences and Philosophy*, tr. Hayden V. White and Robert Anchor (London: Cape, 1969).

4 Bruce Morrissette, *Les Romans de Robbe-Grillet* (Paris: Editions de Minuit, 1963, 1965, 1971).

5 *Jealousy*, in *Two Novels by Robbe-Grillet*, tr. Richard Howard (New York: Grove Press, 1965), p. 58.

6 Lucien Goldmann, *Pour une sociologie du roman* (Paris: Gallimard, 1964).

7 For a more detailed analysis of these four plays see Lucien Goldmann, 'La théâtre de Genet. Essai d'étude sociologique', in *Structures mentales et création culturelle* (Paris: Editions Anthropos, 1970).

8 From the side of Eastern society, moreover, there is a homological transposition in Witold Gombrowicz's play *The Marriage*, which shows how technocratic society and the predominance of the executive arose out of revolutionary victory.

9 Jean Genet, *The Blacks*, tr. Bernard Frechtman (New York: Grove Press, 1960), p. 128.

10 I add that, on the contrary, all my work tends to show that the only problems posed by a valid work are aesthetic problems linked with the coherent expression of a world view, which most often have relatively little to do with the author's personality.

11 Genet, op. cit., p. 11.

12 They are less ridiculous than the colonists because, perhaps contrary to the play's deep coherence, Genet wants to maintain the difference in value between the old and new orders by not putting both on the same plane.

6

HANS MAGNUS ENZENSBERGER

The Industrialization of the Mind

All of us, no matter how irresolute we are, like to think that we reign supreme in our own consciousness, that we are masters of what our minds accept or reject. Since the soul is not much mentioned any more, except by priests, poets, and pop musicians, the last refuge a man can take from the catastrophic world at large seems to be his own mind. Where else can he expect to withstand the daily siege, if not within himself? Even under the conditions of totalitarian rule, where no one can fancy any more that his home is his castle, the mind of the individual is considered a kind of last citadel and hotly defended, though this imaginary fortress may have been long since taken over by an ingenious enemy.

No illusion is more stubbornly upheld than the sovereignty of the mind. It is a good example of the impact of philosophy on people who ignore it; for the idea that men can 'make up their minds' individually and by themselves is essentially derived from the tenets of bourgeois philosophy: second-hand Descartes, run-down Husserl, armchair idealism; and all it amounts to is a sort of metaphysical do-it-yourself.

We might do worse, I think, than dust off the admirably laconic statement which one of our classics made more than a century ago: 'What is going on in our minds has always been, and will always be, a product of society.' This is a comparatively recent insight. Though it is valid for all human history ever since the division of labor came into being, it could not be formulated before the time of Karl Marx. In a society where communication was largely oral, the dependence of the pupil on the teacher, the disciple on the master, the flock on the priest was taken for granted. That the few thought and judged and decided for the many was a matter of course and not a matter for investigation. Medieval man was probably other-directed to an extent which our sociology would be at a loss to fathom. His mind was, to an enormous degree, fashioned and processed from 'without'. But the business of teaching and of indoctrination was perfectly straightforward and transparent – so transparent indeed that it became invisible as a problem. Only when the processes which shape our minds became opaque, enigmatic, inscrutable for the common man, only with the advent of industrialization, did the question of how our minds are shaped arise in earnest.

The mind-making industry is really a product of the last hundred years. It has developed at such a pace, and assumed such varied forms, that it has outgrown our understanding and our control. Our current discussion of the 'media' seems to suffer from severe theoretical limitations. Newsprint, films, television, public relations tend to be evaluated separately, in terms of their specific technologies, conditions, and possibilities. Every new branch of the industry starts off a new crop of theories. Hardly anyone seems to be aware of the phenomenon as a whole: the industrialization of the human mind. This is a process which cannot be understood by a mere examination of its machinery.

Equally inadequate is the term *cultural industry*, which has become common usage in Europe since the Second World War. It reflects, more than the scope of the phenomenon itself, the social status of those who have tried to analyze it: university professors and academic writers, people whom the power elite has relegated to the reservations of what passes as 'cultural life' and who consequently have resigned themselves to bear the unfortunate name of cultural critics. In other words, they are certified as harmless; they are supposed to think in terms of *Kultur* and not in terms of power.

Yet the vague and insufficient name *cultural industry* serves to remind us of a paradox inherent in all media work. Consciousness, however false, can be induced and reproduced by industrial means, but it cannot be industrially produced. It is a 'social product' made up by people: its origin is the dialogue. No industrial process can replace the persons who generate it. And it is precisely this truism of which the archaic term *culture* tries, however vainly, to remind us. The mind industry is monstrous and difficult to understand because it does not, strictly speaking, produce anything. It is an intermediary, engaged only in production's secondary and tertiary derivatives, in transmission and infiltration, in the fungible aspect of what it multiplies and delivers to the customer.

The mind industry can take on anything, digest it, reproduce it, and pour it out. Whatever our minds can conceive of is grist to its mill; nothing will leave it unadulterated: it is capable of turning any idea into a slogan and any work of the imagination into a hit. This is its overwhelming power, yet it is also its most vulnerable spot: it thrives on a stuff which it cannot manufacture by itself. It depends on the very substance it must fear most, and must suppress what it feeds on: the creative productivity of people. Hence the ambiguity of the term *cultural industry*, which takes at face value the claims of culture, in the ancient sense of the word, and the claims of an industrial process which has all but eaten it up. To insist on these claims would be naive; to criticize the industry from the vantage point of a 'liberal education' and to raise comfortable outcries against its vulgarity will neither change it nor revive the dead souls of culture: it will merely help to fortify the ghettos of educational programs and to fill the backward, highbrow section of the Sunday papers. At the same time, the indictment of the mind industry on purely aesthetic grounds will tend to obscure its larger social and political meaning.

At the other extreme we find the ideological critics of the mind industry. Their attention is usually limited to its role as an instrument of straightforward or hidden political propaganda, and from the messages reproduced by it they try to distill the political content. More often than not, the underlying understanding of politics is extremely narrow, as if it were just a matter of taking sides in everyday contests of power. Just as in the case of the 'cultural critic', this attitude cannot hope to catch up with the far-reaching effects of the industrialization of the mind, since it is a process which will abolish the distinction between private and public consciousness.

Thus, while radio, cinema, television, recording, advertising and public relations, new techniques of manipulation and propaganda are being keenly discussed, each on its own terms, the mind industry, taken as a whole, is disregarded. Newsprint and publishing, its oldest and in many respects still its more interesting branch, hardly comes up for serious comment any longer, presumably because it lacks the appeal of technological novelty. Yet much of the analysis provided in Balzac's *Illusions perdues* is as pertinent today as it was a hundred years ago, as any copywriter from Hollywood who happens to know the book will testify. Other, more recent branches of the industry still remain largely unexplored: fashion and industrial design, the propagation of established religions and of esoteric cults, opinion polls, simulation, and, last but not least, tourism, which can be considered a mass medium in its own right.

Above all, however, we are not sufficiently aware of the fact that the full deployment of the mind industry still lies ahead. Up to now it has not managed to seize control of its most essential sphere, which is education. The industrialization of instruction, on all levels, has barely begun. While we still indulge in controversies over curricula, school systems, college and university reforms, and shortages in the teaching professions, technological systems are being perfected which will make nonsense of all the adjustments we are now considering. The language laboratory and the closed-circuit TV are only the forerunners of a fully industrialized educational system which will make use of increasingly centralized programming and of recent advances in the study of learning. In that process, education will become a mass medium, the most powerful of all, and a billion-dollar business.

Whether we realize it or not, the mind industry is growing faster than any other, not excluding armament. It has become the key industry of the twentieth century. Those who are concerned in the power game of today, political leaders, intelligence men, and revolutionaries, have very well grasped this crucial fact. Whenever an industrially developed country is occupied or liberated today, whenever there is a *coup d'état*, a revolution, or a counter-revolution, the crack police units, the paratroopers, the guerrilla fighters do not any longer descend on the main squares of the city or seize the centers of heavy industry, as in the nineteenth century, or symbolic sites like the royal palace; the new regime will instead take over, first of all, the radio and television stations, the telephone and telex exchanges, and the printing presses. And after having entrenched itself, it will, by and large, leave alone those who manage the public services and the manufacturing industries, at least in the beginning, while all the functionaries who run the mind industry will be immediately replaced. In such extreme situations the industry's key position becomes quite clear.

There are four conditions which are necessary to its existence; briefly, they are as follows.

(1) Enlightenment, in the broadest sense, is the philosophical prerequisite of the industrialization of the mind. It cannot get under way until the rule of theocracy, and with it people's faith in revelation and inspiration, in the Holy Book or the Holy Ghost as taught by the priesthood, is broken. The mind industry presupposes independent minds, even when it is out to deprive them of their independence; this is another of its paradoxes. The last theocracy to vanish was Tibet; ever since, the philosophical condition is met with throughout the world.

(2) Politically, the industrialization of the mind presupposes the proclamation of human rights, of equality and liberty in particular. In Europe, this threshold has been passed by the French Revolution; in the communist world, by the October Revolution; and in America, Asia, and Africa, by the wars of liberation from colonial rule. Obviously, the industry does not depend on the realization of these rights; for most people, they have never been more than a pretense, or at best, a distant promise. On the contrary, it is just the margin between fiction and reality which provides the mind industry with its theater of operations. Consciousness, both individual and social, has become a political issue only from the moment when the conviction arose in people's minds that everyone should have a say in his own destiny as well as in that of society at large. From the same moment any authority has to justify itself in the eyes of those it would govern; coercion alone would no longer do the trick; he who ruled must persuade, lay claim to people's minds and change them, in an industrial age, by every industrial means at hand.

(3) Economically, the mind industry cannot come of age unless a measure of primary accumulation has been achieved. A society which cannot provide the necessary surplus capital neither needs it nor can afford it. During the first half of the nineteenth century in Western Europe, and under similar conditions in other parts of the world, which prevailed until fairly recently, peasants and workers lived at a level of bare subsistence. During this stage of economic development the fiction that the working class is able to determine the conditions of its own existence is meaningless; the proletariat is subjected by physical constraint and undisguised force. Archaic methods of manipulation, as used by the school and by the church, the law and the army, together with old customs and conventions, are quite sufficient for the ruling minority to maintain its position during the earlier stages of industrial development. As soon as the basic industries have been firmly established and the mass production of consumer goods is beginning to reach out to the majority of the population, the ruling classes will face a dilemma. More sophisticated methods of production demand a constantly rising standard of education, not only for the privileged but also for the masses. The immediate compulsion which kept the working class 'in their place' will

slowly decrease. Working hours are reduced, and the standard of living rises. Inevitably, people will become aware of their own situation; they can now afford the luxury of having a mind of their own. For the first time, they become conscious of themselves in more than the most primitive and hazy sense of the word. In this process, enormous human energies are released, energies which inevitably threaten the established political and economic order. Today this revolutionary process can be seen at work in a great number of emergent nations, where it has long been artificially retarded by imperialist powers; in these countries the political, if not the economic conditions for the development of mind industries can be realized overnight.

(4) Given a certain level of economic development, industrialization brings with it the last condition for the rise of a mind industry: the technology on which it depends. The first industrial uses of electricity were concerned with power and not with communications: the dynamo and the electrical motor preceded the amplifying valve and the film camera. There are economic reasons for this time-lag: the foundations of radio, film, recording, television, and computing techniques could not be laid before the advent of the mass production of commodities and the general availability of electrical power.

In our time the technological conditions for the industrialization of the mind exist anywhere on the planet. The same cannot be said for the political and economic prerequisites; however, it is only a matter of time until they will be met. The process is irreversible. Therefore, all criticism of the mind industry which is abolitionist in its essence is inept and beside the point, since the idea of arresting and liquidating industrialization itself (which such criticism implies) is suicidal. There is a macabre irony to any such proposal, for it is indeed no longer a technical problem for our civilization to abolish itself. However, this is hardly what conservative critics have in mind when they complain about the loss of 'values', the depravity of mass civilization, and the degeneration of traditional culture by the media. The idea is, rather, to do away with all these nasty things, and to survive, as an elite of happy pundits, in the nicer comforts offered by a country house.

Nonetheless, the workings of the mind industry have been analyzed, in part, over and over again, sometimes with great ingenuity and insight. So far as the capitalist countries are concerned, the critics have leveled their attacks mainly against the newer media and commercial advertising. Conservatives and Marxists alike have been all too ready to deplore their venal side. It is an objection which hardly touches the heart of the matter. Apart from the fact that it is perhaps no more immoral to profit from the mass production of news or symphonies than from the mass production of soap and tires, objections of this kind overlook the very characteristics of the mind industry. Its more advanced sectors have long since ceased to sell any goods at all. With increasing technological maturity, the material substrata, paper or plastic or celluloid, tend to vanish. Only in the more old-fashioned offshoots of the business, as for example in the book trade, does the commodity aspect of the product play an important economic role. In this respect, a radio station has nothing in common with a match factory. With the disappearance of the material substratum the product becomes more and more abstract, and the industry depends less and less on selling it to its customers. If you buy a book, you pay for it in terms of its real cost of production; if you pick up a magazine, you pay only a fraction thereof; if you tune in on a radio or television program, you get it virtually free; direct advertising and political propaganda is something nobody buys − on the contrary, it is crammed down our throats. The products of the mind industry can no longer be understood in terms of a sellers' and buyers' market, or in terms of production costs: they are, as it were, priceless. The capitalist exploitation of the media is accidental and not intrinsic; to concentrate on their commercialization is to miss the point and to overlook the specific service which the mind industry performs for modern societies. This service is essentially the same all over the world, no matter how the industry is operated: under state, public, or private management, within a capitalist or a socialist economy, on a profit or non-profit basis. The mind industry's main business and concern is not to sell its product: it is to 'sell' the existing order, to perpetuate the prevailing pattern of man's domination by man, no matter who runs the society, and by what means. Its main task is to expand and train our consciousness – in order to exploit it.

Since 'immaterial exploitation' is not a familiar concept, it might be as well to explain its meaning. Classical Marxism has defined very clearly the material exploitation to which the working classes have been subjected ever since the industrial revolution. In its crudest form, it is characteristic of the period of the primary accumulation of capital. This holds true even for socialist countries, as is evident from the example of Stalinist Russia and the early stages of the development of Red China. As soon as the bases of industrialization are laid, however, it becomes clear that material exploitation alone is insufficient to guarantee the continuity of the system. When the production of goods expands beyond the most immediate needs, the old proclamations of human rights, however watered down by the rhetoric of the establishment and however eclipsed by decades of hardship, famine, crises, forced labor, and political terror, will now unfold their potential strength. It is in their very nature that, once proclaimed, they cannot be revoked. Again and again, people will try to take them at their face value and, eventually, to fight for their realization. Thus, ever since the great declarations of the eighteenth century, every rule of the few over the many, however organized, has faced the threat of revolution. Real democracy, as opposed to the formal facades of parliamentary democracy, does not exist anywhere in the world, but its ghost haunts every existing regime. Consequently, all the existing power structures must seek to obtain the consent, however passive, of their subjects. Even regimes which depend on the force of arms for their survival feel the need to justify themselves in the eyes of the world. Control of capital, of the means of production, and of the armed forces is therefore no longer enough. The self-appointed elites who run modern societies must try to control people's minds. What each of us accepts or rejects, what we think and decide, is now, here as well as in Vietnam, a matter of prime political concern: it would be too dangerous to leave these matters to ourselves. Material exploitation must camouflage itself in order to survive; immaterial exploitation has become its necessary corollary. The few cannot go on accumulating wealth unless they accumulate the power to manipulate the minds of the many. To expropriate manpower they have to expropriate the brain. What is being abolished in today's affluent societies, from Moscow to Los Angeles, is not exploitation, but our awareness of it.

It takes quite a lot of effort to maintain this state of affairs. There are alternatives to it. But since all of them would inevitably overthrow the prevailing powers, an entire industry is engaged in doing away with such alternatives, eliminating possible futures and reinforcing the present pattern of domination. There are several ways to achieve this end: on the one hand we find downright censorship, bans, and a state monopoly on all the means of production of the mind industry; on the other hand, economic pressures, systematic distribution of 'punishment and reward', and human engineering can do the job just as well and much more smoothly. The material pauperization of the last century is followed and replaced by the immaterial pauperization of today. Its most obvious manifestation is the decline in political options available to the citizens of the most advanced nations: a mass of political nobodies, over whose heads even collective suicide can be decreed, is opposed by an ever-decreasing number of political moguls. That this state of affairs is readily accepted and voluntarily endured by the majority is the greatest achievement of the mind industry.

To describe the effects of the mind industry on present-day society is not, however, to describe its essence. The emergence of the textile industry has ruined the craftsman of India and caused widespread child labor in England, but these consequences do not necessarily follow from the existence of the mechanical loom. There is no more reason to suppose that the industrialization of the human mind must produce immaterial exploitation. It would even be fair to say that it will eventually, by its own logic, do away with the very results it has today. For this is the most fundamental of all its contradictions: in order to obtain consent, you have to grant a choice, no matter how marginal and deceptive; in order to harness the faculties of the human mind, you have to develop them, no matter how narrowly and in how deformed a fashion. It may be a measure of the overwhelming power of the mind industry that none of us can escape its influence. Whether we like it or not, it enlists our participation in the system as a whole. But this participation may well veer, one day, from the passive to the active, and turn out to threaten the very order it was supposed to uphold. The mind industry has a dynamic of its own which it cannot arrest, and it is not by chance but by necessity that in this movement there are currents which run contrary to its present mission of stabilizing the status quo. A corollary of its dialectical progress is that the mind industry, however closely supervised in its individual operations, is never completely controllable as a whole. There are always leaks in it, cracks in the armor; no administration will ever trust it all the way.

In order to exploit people's intellectual, moral, and political faculties, you have got to develop them first. This is, as we have seen, the basic dilemma faced by today's media. When we turn our attention from the industry's consumers to its producers, the intellectuals, we find this dilemma aggravated and intensified. In terms of power, of course, there can be no question as to who runs the business. Certainly it is not the intellectuals who control the industrial establishment, but the establishment which controls them. There is precious little chance for the people who are productive to take over their means of production: this is just what the present structure is designed to prevent. However, even under present circumstances, the relationship is not without a certain ambiguity, since there is no way of running the mind industry without enlisting the services of at least a minority of men who can create something. To exclude them would be self-defeating. Of course, it is perfectly possible to use the whole stock of accumulated original work and have it adapted, diluted, and processed for media use, and it may be well to remember that much of what purports to be new is in fact derivative. If we examine the harmonic and melodic structure of any popular song hit, it will most likely turn out to employ inventions of serious composers centuries ago. The same is true of the dramaturgical cliches of mediocre screenplays: watered down beyond recognition, they repeat traditional patterns taken from the drama and the novel of the past. In the long run, however, the parasitic use of inherited work is not sufficient to nourish the industry. However large a stock, you cannot sell out for ever without replenishment; hence the need 'to make it new', the media's dependence on men capable of innovation, in other words, on potential troublemakers. It is inherent in the process of creation that there is no way to predict its results. Consequently, intellectuals are, from the point of view of any power structure bent on its own perpetuation, a security risk. It takes consummate skill to 'handle' them and to neutralize their subversive influence. All sorts of techniques, from the crudest to the most sophisticated, have been developed to this end: physical threat, blacklisting, moral and economic pressure on the one hand, overexposure, star-cult, co-optation into the power elite on the other, are the extremes of a whole gamut of manipulation. It would be worthwhile to write a manual analyzing these techniques. They have one thing in common, and that is that they offer short-term, tactical answers to a problem which, in principle, cannot be resolved. This is an industry which has to rely, as its primary source, on the very minorities with whose elimination it is entrusted: those whose aim it is to invent and produce *alternatives*. Unless it succeeds in exploiting and manipulating its producers, the mind industry cannot hope to exploit and manipulate its consumers. On the level of production, even more than on the level of consumption, it has to deal with partners who are potential enemies. Engaged in the proliferation of human consciousness, the media proliferate their own contradictions.

Criticism of the mind industry which fails to recognize its central ambiguities is either idle or dangerous. It is a measure of their limitations that many media critics never seem to reflect on their own position, just as if their work were not itself a part of what it criticizes. The truth is that no one can nowadays express any opinion at all without making use of the industry, or rather, without being used by it.

Anyone incapable of dialectical thinking is doomed as soon as he starts grappling with this subject. He will be trapped to a point where even retreat is no longer possible. There are many who feel revolted at the thought of entering a studio or negotiating with the slick executives who run the networks. They detest, or profess to detest, the very machinery of the industry, and would like to withdraw into some abode of refinement. Of course, no such refuge really exists. The seemingly exclusive is just another, slightly more expensive line of styling within the same giant industrial combine.

Let us rather try to draw the line between intellectual integrity and defeatism. To opt out of the mind industry, to refuse any dealings with it may well turn out to be a reactionary course. There is no hermitage left for those whose job is to speak out and to seek innovation. Retreat from the media will not even save the intellectual's precious soul from corruption. It might be a better idea to enter the dangerous game, to take and calculate our risks. Instead of innocence, we need determination. We must know very precisely the monster we are dealing with, and we must be continually on our guard to resist the overt or subtle pressures which are brought to bear on us.

The rapid development of the mind industry, its rise to a key position in modern society, has profoundly changed the role of the intellectual. He finds himself confronted with new threats and new opportunities. Whether he knows it or not, whether he likes it or not, he has become the accomplice of a huge industrial complex which depends for its survival on him, as he depends on it for his own. He must try, at any cost, to use it for his own purposes, which are incompatible with the purposes of the mind machine. What it upholds he must subvert. He may play it crooked or straight, he may win or lose the game; but he would do well to remember that there is more at stake than his own fortune.

Translated by the author

7

MICHEL CROZIER

France's Cultural Anxieties under Gaullism: The Cultural Revolution Revisited

(1) An Unexpected Story

For those readers who might be misled, the cultural revolution I am referring to is not the thundering radical hope of the Maoists but the title of a modest article this writer contributed to the journal *Daedalus* in 1963 (Michel Crozier, 'The cultural revolution in the new Europe', *Daedalus*, Winter 1963).

The thesis of my article could be summarized in the following manner. The intellectual as torchbearer of humanity had been the hero of the late 1940s and early 1950s. But one should not have any illusions about the alleged radicalism of the intellectual of this period. In manner and in mode of reasoning he was an aristocrat who suddenly found himself out of pace with the changing social patterns. The intellectual establishment was already in process of being displaced because of the very success of the knowledge which was its product. At the same time this was due to the liberalization of social relations and social hierarchies for which these individuals fought. Such painful displacement was at the root of diverse intellectual upheavals and disarray. It had greater impact in France where the intellectual establishment has a considerable stake in a very conservative hierarchical society. But France – like other European countries at that time – was about to come of age. And her tumultuous ordeal might even have led to new social and intellectual discoveries.

In this regard the period 1958–78 hardly lived up to these expectations. To be sure, there was turmoil. Admittedly this had been an ordeal that had little to do with the peaceful end of ideology contemplated by Daniel Bell and many other Americans, yet there was no sign of a coming of age. Worse, and what was particularly dismaying, the traditional intellectual leftist establishment not only resisted but conquered the media, exerted a tremendous influence on the public consciousness, and became a form of parallel power under Gaullism.

In a sense these facts may only hold true as far as appearances are concerned. One should inquire about what kind of practical relations underlie successive intellectual modes. May not something be salvaged from the old thesis? Indeed, could a new thesis be drawn up to meet the actual state of affairs? These will be the questions to which I shall address myself in a paper which is, I hasten to admit, quite speculative.

In order to further our understanding of the problem, I shall attempt to tell the story – at least as I perceive it – in a very rough sketch. At the same time I shall try to relate it to my thesis of 1963. Finally I shall attempt to speculate on the more basic questions. But before entering the complexity of this chaotic period, I should like to present a few general remarks.

(1) This was an unusual period as regards the tempo of change and the radicalism of the successive intellectual fashions. These fashions not only succeeded one another more rapidly than ever, they were also in opposition to one another as much as they attacked the conventional world view.

(2) Successive intellectual fashions were intertwined with another parallel rhythm, the rhythm of political activism: periods such as 1945–50, 1956–61, 1967–70, 1975–8 had been periods of political activism. In between there had been (similar to the present) temporary lulls. Throughout these interwoven trends nevertheless there was an overwhelming dominance of the left in French culture which can be contrasted with the reign of the Gaullists and moderates in politics.

(3) Although the leftist cultural drift was overwhelming during this twenty-year period, there was a rapid left-wing acceleration crowned by May 1968. After the climax of 1968 the period was one of deceleration.

(4) May 1968 was the major cultural event which divided the period sharply. Prior to this singular event we were still in an era of cultural optimism; after 1968 pessimism became dominant tempered only by millenarist hysteria.

(5) The failure of the left in the 1978 elections may in the future be considered as another major event. It was preceded by a gradual disenchantment with millenarism and may even come to be viewed as an important step in the coming-of-age process.

I will divide this period into sections which exemplify the dominance of one or another of the prevailing intellectual fashions. This is necessarily arbitrary, especially since intellectual actors require a lengthy time of latency and work. Moreover, contributions have often become obsolete once they have made their major impact. Contributions of an opposing nature may also coexist while only one fashion dominates in the trend-making intellectual set.

The dominance of a fashion nevertheless is an important element for understanding the intellectual debate, the pressure on intellectuals themselves, the impact on students and on the public. Finally, it should be remarked that the media played an important role in promoting the fashion. In contrast with the past, ideas were brought to public attention much more rapidly. This in turn had an impact on politics.

(2)   The Golden Years *Malentendu*

The years of the liberation had been dominated by political activism. Sartre and Camus were its heroes. Economic and social issues were translated into lofty intellectual debates. France's powerlessness could be transfigured by its intellectual prominence. The great powers could claim financial and military strength. Gallic supremacy, however, was moral and intellectual.

This came to an end when France's recovery made it possible to take responsibility for substantive issues. Mendès France's prodigious success in 1954 was a sign of this aforementioned change.

The Algerian War years only partially marked a revival of old-style intellectual activism. This era can be viewed as the last glow of Sartre's intellectual magnetism. The manifesto of the 121 was one of the major instances of the prowess of the intelligentsia. But this cultural exploit did not have any impact on politics or on social events. It soon became clear that the battle to be waged was not in this arena. Problems were too serious to be left to intellectuals. Even Algerian nationalists did not trust their cumbersome allies and they were all too happy to hold talks and subsequently negotiations with the more responsible French leaders. The last years of the Algerian War marked a period of political and cultural lull.

The younger generation which then came to the forefront was a mixed breed of student union leaders, journalists, civil servants, and non-committed members of political clubs. The past had periodically witnessed similar gatherings. This one was to be especially crucial because of the demise of political parties during the early years of the Gaullist regime. It was also a product of the breakdown of social barriers and social relations, as exemplified by the disappearance of hostility between Catholic and anticlerical forces which was subsequently very influential in the building of the socialist party. They associated not only with the liberal wing of the Gaullist government but also with the trade unions, young farmers, and junior businessmen's associations.

The rather surprising non-catastrophic end of the Algerian War and the very successful repatriation of the European minority from Algeria may be attributed to these aforementioned groups as well as to de Gaulle. And when instead of the chaos and fascism predicted by the radicals of the left (without mentioning, of course, the disaster for Western civilization announced by the radical right) France peacefully absorbed one million former colonists not only to her own benefit but to the benefit of this group, the political and cultural climate was bound to change.

These were the golden years of the new intellectuals of the 1960s (I borrowed the term from Diana Pinto, whose remarkable thesis on the comparative development of sociology in France and Italy is essentially based upon such a diagnosis). Clearly from 1962 to 1966 cultural fashion tended to be represented by the moderate left. These were the years of a successful modernization of 'French ways' in the liberal 'American pattern'. The United States of JFK and the 'Best and the Brightest' was at a high point. These were the years of the John XXIII Catholic *aggiornamento*. France did not merely imitate and follow, but made contributions of her own. This was the heyday of democratic planning that was to be imitated in the United Kingdom and highly praised in the United States. A strong liberal democratic breeze was blowing, but there was no warning to announce the on-coming storm.

In the cultural world, the social sciences were the great beneficiaries of the change. There was now time to rethink old problems, away from the agitation and hysteria of impending doom. For the first time in years, day-to-day political events did not dominate. Political parties were out. Old-style rhetoric was out. New thinking was very much in demand. Moreover this time the elites seemed open to a new discourse.

To these demands the cultural answers were still very moderate. French 'new wave' movies will seem now hopelessly conventional. Democratic planning was a very moderate literal version of traditional establishment patterns. It was understood at the time that the social sciences were a tool for pointing out the more basic problems and realities of everyday life.

The misunderstanding was deep. Leaders of French society were searching for better relations with the public and not for challenging ideas. Change was slow, at least at the political, administrative, and organizational levels. New social science jargon was used to replace the Marxist and radical phraseology but with no more than cosmetic consequences.

The cultural revolution I was discussing at that time did not take place in the manner I had hoped. Certainly there was an acceleration in the displacement of old-style intellectuals and the enlargement of the intellectual community, but only to bring about a political and moral crisis within society, not to impose new ways of thinking and governing our own behavior.

(3) The Fascination with Structuralism

The end of this period of the conservative golden years (pre-1968) must be set apart not only because one can already identify during these years the first themes that were to become the main arguments of the crisis: the conditioning of man by organization, workers' alienation, existential drama of youth and middle-aged executive spleen, but also, and much more important, I think, because it was dominated by a new and specifically French craze: structuralism.

Structuralism can be viewed as the extreme and radical formalization of social scientific arrogance. As such it came as a complete surprise on the French scene. Since French intellectuals had been especially reluctant to accept modern social sciences in the same way as they had been to accept psychoanalysis, how is it that they became the most arrogant exponents of structuralism?

If one does not think in terms of cultural traits, or in terms of linear history, it makes a good deal of sense. New converts are usually more fanatical. Misunderstandings in science and especially in the social sciences may lead to new discoveries or at least to impressive new theories. The French intellectual tradition is sufficiently strong to respond to outside challenges with new contributions. One can find at the same time in French structuralism an accommodation to the vanguard of the social sciences, an original answer to the challenging problems of those sciences and a special French logical and even absolutist trend that tends to push the basic paradigm to its utmost limit. But fashion is not consciously made by intellectual leaders, it depends on public response. Why did the French intelligentsia react so wildly to people like Lévi-Straus, Foucault, and Barthès? Why did a whole literary school (the *nouveau roman*) develop around a structuralist paradigm? (Admittedly the first major novels of the *noveau roman* antedate the success of structuralism. The success of the *noveau roman*, however, occurred virtually in the same years. Literary critics as well as authors themselves were soon advocating the structural point of view in a very open manner.)

Let me venture to say that it is still part of the basic misunderstanding. French society was and still is frightened by change. Intellectual change is more important for France than for other societies because intellectual mechanisms are more basic to its social fabric. The success of the social sciences, therefore, could be experienced as a challenge to the predominant modes of thought of our humanistic societies. The structuralist craze was in a way a sort of exorcism. With structuralism one could at the same time reach the *avant-garde* of the social sciences and practically reject its consequences since structuralism could not deal with present-day problems. Or, at least, this seemed to be the case. Lévi-Straus himself made a point of insisting that structuralism could only deal with 'cold societies' where change did not take place.

Curiously, the *nouveau roman* went further, although nobody seemed to notice at first. The absence of man, i.e. the impossibility of meaninglessness of man's personal decision and free will, could not be read as social science but as a romantic call for help. At that point, we were not that far from the May Revolution to which of course literary ivory tower characters as well as arrogant scientists rallied in due time in the most extreme romantic confusion.

(4)   The Thunderstorm of May 1968

To most Frenchmen, and certainly to most intellectuals, the May 1968 Revolution was a thunderstorm out of a clear blue sky. Later, of course, it was understood that all the warning signs had been there. But who could have paid attention to those signs in the existing cultural climate? That a fashionable movie-maker like Godard made a success out of a provocative story of Nanterre radical students would not disturb any seasoned analyst of French mores and politics.

Many very good and convincing explanations have been offered to explain the crisis. In a sense they are all true since every crisis – that is, breakdown or rupture – has the characteristic of developing only because of the conjuncture of a number of unrelated and possibly contradictory elements. I would add, however, that for me the specific characteristic of May 1968 was that it happened without reason, i.e. without conventional social or political reasons.

Especially from this distance, in 1978, it seems that the events of ten years ago should be understood first of all as a cultural event, a crisis about the content of the culture and even more about the human relationships associated with it. This crisis has developed in all Western countries and has had an impact even on the Communist East. It is the coming to life of the problems I had discussed in my 1963 paper. Men need a new culture, new intellectual instruments. Our economic progress, our social developments have already disturbed our nineteenth-century bourgeois culture. But culture has always been a conservative field, and the change of cultures may become a revolutionary one. I had used the term as a figure of speech and it turned out to be almost a reality.

What is specifically French about May 1968 is its climactic quality. Everything was well arranged and played within six weeks: 'unité de temps', 'unité de lieu', an extraordinarily neat clinical tragedy, and at the same time an immediate association between culture and politics. In no other country has the play-acting of culture become the central event not only of politics but even of national consciousness.

But even if the events of May 1968 revealed the problems of a society in search of a new, more useful culture, if it gave vent to its cultural anxieties, it was not of direct assistance in obtaining realistic solutions, or constructive steps leading to solutions. It raised problems in such a climactic way that no one could escape listening. It offered a dream-like stage on which utopian solutions could be played out. But when the dreamers awoke the problems remained.

Thunderstorms, of course, always provide a sort of necessary relief. This one did not fail to do so, though it was in a deep and subtle way. It imposed on our social establishment some degree of modesty. To some extent, it changed the human relations game. It became possible for young people to assert their freedom to take initiatives. It made it possible for more people to communicate more openly across traditional boundaries of professional logic and ideology. Furthermore, it substantially weakened the old cultural establishment.

Yet as a structuring event in the field of culture and politics, its basic impact has been essentially regressive: it artificially brought back to life a ghost that had disappeared in the late 1950s, the intellectual as a torchbearer. The story of the next ten years was to be mainly the tale of the gradual recovery from the blow it represented for culture. This is, I think, why the cultural climate has been pessimistic for all these years.

What did May 1968 bring us?

First of all the return of an old hero – the revolutionary. But in a different way. No Winter Palace was to be stormed. Instead of the professional revolutionary, the new hero expressed revolution as a way of life. His appearance was much more cultural than political. Secondly, a strong association has been established between culture and revolution. Revolution is a way of culture, it is even a culture itself. And culture cannot be anything but revolution.

Of course, the majority of intellectuals did not subscribe to such dreams, but their logic led to such reasoning. Most left-wing intellectuals, that is, most

intellectuals at the time, insisted that politics was everywhere, that everything was political, and that culture was the main battlefield.

A third basic trait is of a completely different nature. This was the colonization of the media by *avant-garde* culture. Media that had been ignoring the universities and the social sciences seized upon the event and created the new fashion. They did not do so by intention although the response was both good and profitable. But journalists, traders in ideas, were themselves deeply perturbed by the crisis. They were the target of attacks and possible actors in the movement. A cause, a real cause for justifying one's own calling, was now at hand, while at the same time traditional constraints could not be enforced.

This change in the media had very far-reaching consequences. First, it gave the cultural world a much broader platform. It temporarily unified the cultural universe and gave intellectuals a wide audience. A new public was born. Secondly, it had a decisive impact on politics. From 1968 on, the logic of French politics has been a leftist logic according to which you always could beat your competitor by outflanking him on the left. This logic was not concocted by the media. But it dominated only because the media made it possible.

(5)   The Mad Years of Anti-Psychiatry

From 1968 to 1972 French politics can best be understood as a slow and difficult but constant process of returning to normalcy. The basic pattern of social control had been deeply shaken and the traditional social bards could no longer be trusted as they had been. Any day might find some group of hard-headed skilled machinists in some remote town refusing to listen to their union leaders. Because they happened to occupy their plant at the right moment, the whole industrial system might collapse again. The rank and file would not trust their leaders, who in turn could not afford to take risks. Bargaining was not possible, for its result might be immediately challenged. Industrial relations were, of course, not the only hazardous problem. Churches, universities, schools, in fact all cultural institutions were equally vulnerable.

In order to restore normalcy throughout the country, authority became very cautious, patient, at times even understanding. Liberals often had their own way, for they were ideally suited for such tasks. They tried to exploit their situation in order to promote their own ideas, but usually to little avail. They were not supported by the cultural and political wave and the establishment used them as sparingly as possible.

Culture took, however, an entirely different course. While politics in this period was the politics of cautious liberalization, even the major left-wing parties, both socialist and communist, made many attempts to seem respectable. Culture was dominated by a radical hysteria even stronger than the slogans of May 1968. Rarely was there so deep a divorce between political and social action on the one hand and the intellectuals on the other. Not that intellectuals retreated to their own ivory tower. On the contrary, the more they became part of the action the more estranged their problems became from the world of politics and social and economic life.

If there was to be found in politics a longing for an immediate return to normalcy, to be achieved with the overall complicity of all parties, culture was deliberately lagging behind. Or, if one leaves aside such considerations, it was fighting its own battle for its own stakes.

Seen at the distance of a decade this is what remains for me as the mad years of anti-psychiatry. The leftist logic, which was the dominant logic of the period, went ahead unchecked by constraints. Anti-psychiatry was only one of its aspects but it was most flamboyant, especially in a country which had always been cautious if not backward in this domain.

Basically, the mad years were dominated by a highly unusual and disorderly mixture of institutional fights over, and radical fashions in, the contents of culture.

These years, following the shake-up of 1968, marked the disintegration of a number of key cultural institutions. Not only were churches, universities, and secondary schools affected, but research institutes as well as public and semi-public agencies (this especially held true in the area of urban problems). Psychiatric institutions were perhaps the hottest battleground, possibly due to the fact that the problems being dealt with run the deepest in modern consciousness. To these should be added jails and legal institutions.

As far as content was concerned, the intellectual fashions were only partially convergent. Superficially, the main feature was the triumphant comeback of Marxism. This took several forms: the humanist approach of Henri Lefebvre whose triumph was absolute but limited to the period of revolution itself; the austere approach of Louis Althusser, whose rigor was supposed to be a proof of scientificity; the many nonconformist varieties, whose so-called openness did not prevent them from esotericism. Poulantzas was the new star of these diverse trends.

But behind the lip-service paid to Marxism, the real driving force of the period was a general, almost hysterical revolt against authority, which took several forms and exploded in the most varied domains but always eclipsed the more traditional political rhetoric.

Lacan was the first guru of all these trends, but here again those of his works which predated 1968 were more revered than used practically. There was a triumphant return to Freudianism, but the new heroes of the period, especially Deleuze and Guattari, were more in line with far-out educators, encounter group gurus, adamant opponents of authority, than they were students of Freud. (Although this is not the place, the story of the Ecole Normale vagaries should be carefully related and the *normalien* complex analyzed. Most of the above-mentioned disputes raged between these *normaliens* among whom Bourdieu was another guru.)

A place apart should be given to Michel Foucault, whose influence may prove to be the most lasting because it was more complex, although not esoteric and much more open to evolution and change. Foucault, who was more solidly rooted and scholarly in history, was the first intellectual leader in the fight against asylums and prisons. But he already possessed a more sophisticated view of contemporary and human relationships and was to develop in increasingly realistic terms.

During these years two views prevailed whose overwhelming dominance could be found in intellectual bookshops not only in Paris but everywhere in France.

(1) Authority is the problem and power is intrinsically evil.
(2) Progress is only achieved by the gaining of new rights of the individual against authority.

Not only were they written about in countless books and brochures but they were also debated in innumerable educational groups.

When viewed from this distance, one is impressed by the tremendous upsurge of intellectual activity during this period. This was, in a way, a general *aggiornamento* of French culture, at least inasmuch as it dealt with human relations. These were also the years of sexual liberation. Culture was understood to be providing answers – admittedly in a simplistic way – to all these new anxieties and queries of a modern man overwhelmed by his new-found freedom.

Yet if one compares France with other countries, it must be admitted that in the final analysis this difficult period of coming of age was achieved at a rather low social cost. Italy was to reveal much more disorder in the adjustment to a similar challenge of modernity. France seems to have followed a much more puritanical and restrained course. Hysteria was restricted to cultural argument. The acting out was limited and kept under control in the intelligentsia's labs under the tolerant benevolence of a lofty state.

Fashion not rooted in experience brings conformism more rapidly. This was the price paid by French society. But one wonders which is worse: the tamed aspect of intellectual hysteria turning to conformist or the risks of such hysteria turned loose for lack of social control.

In any case, whether viewed from an institutional or cultural bias, the lessons learned during the period do not seem to respond in any way either to the aims of the movement or to the demands of society or even to scientific possibilities.

(6) 'Waiting for Godot' and the Return to Normalcy

Only a few years later, everything seems to have faded away. Culture is no more a battleground. The equation culture equals revolution appears strange if not absurd. *Avant-garde* theaters have returned to Shakespeare and universities to scholarship. Progressive TV directors are promoting a fashionable revolt against the Communist Party.

The latest craze has been the new philosophers, i.e. a group of the 'sixty-eighters who have come the full circle from radical revolution to a harsh questioning of all that revolution stands for. Certainly culture has not become dominated by a political right wing or even by moderates but the leftward drift has stopped and the pendulum has begun to swing to the other direction.

This is all the more surprising since the years 1975–8 were the years during which an impending victory of the left was anticipated. This was to ultimately bring about in France, if not the millennium, at least the beginning of a new era. Never had there been such serious enthusiasm for change. It was if virtually all the promises and cherished goals of 1968 were finally to be fulfilled. Yet even prior to the final failure, the cultural movement was shifting to the other side of the spectrum.

What happened?

Two movements can be analyzed whose unpredictable conjunction made this fundamental reversal of the trend possible. First of all, the 'recuperation' by the establishment. Secondly, the internal collapse of the New Left in whom the last hopes of the 'sixty-eighters had dwelt.

A continuous theme of the students of 1968 was their fear of being 'recuperated'. However naive this obsession, they were quite right. For they were to succumb to the much-contested system – at least according to their own definition, and quite rapidly. Precisely because they refused to understand a world they pretended to deny, they could not resist very long. But the co-opting process was unexpected and it might be worthwhile to analyze it in depth, since this may offer clues in understanding the significance of the movement while being decisive in restructuring the period to come.

The 1967 perspective was no more enlightened than the preceding ones. Indeed, because of the complexity and turmoil of the time, it was bound to be much less consistent and even less resilient. Political gullibility had been a sort of second nature of the 'sixty-eighters.

Very few of this generation could maintain uncompromising radical positions. Their obsession with concrete practical deeds which had been the source of their strength very soon became their weakness. The outside world did frustrate them most effectively from this reality. The reality they were supposed to rediscover became more and more trapped in rhetoric.

In the first place, they were co-opted by the Communist Party. Radicals were superb at triggering agitation. But they could not exploit the events they provoked. Communist Party militants gradually discovered how useful these potential allies could be when handled properly. Conversely, the communist militants became attractive to the 'sixty-eighters because they were getting things done. Further, they seemed to have a principle of reality in this disturbed world. Despite the fact that one of the main and earliest targets of the students revolt had been the Communist Party, it became the first pole of attraction for the disenchanted radicals. Indeed the party found in them a new source of vigor that helped it to modernize itself and become a force for its latest drive for power.

But the socialist movement three and four years later was to become an even more powerful recuperating agency. This time it was not a party or a church which imposed a ritual together with behavioral constraints. Rather it was a very general undifferentiated hope which did not oblige one to abjure one's own faith. The Programme Commun was a prodigious solution for maintaining the May spirit. It was ostensibly practical and realistic, yet it was supposed to be a rupture. It could be interpreted in all possible ways. Moreover, it had enough ideological appeal to

be protected against the stigma of politics. The great majority of the French intelligentsia awaited the victory of the Programme Commun like the two tramps waiting for Godot. Not only did the 'sixty-eighters find a place in the fold, they were its driving spirit. Life was to be finally changed. Whatever the shortcomings of politicians the movement would carry them through.

Meanwhile other struggles also played a 'recuperating' role. The ecology movement which began much later than in the United States also represented an opportunity, a way of life, a satisfactory answer to the existential dilemma. The women's movement played a similar role. Both movements could be as radical as possible and yet had the virtue of being concrete 'here and now' fights, but at the same time they were socializing ventures forcing people to interact, to negotiate, to compromise.

If 'recuperation' seems to be a reasonable adjustment process whose theoretical difficulty originated with the young Frenchmen's obsessions with ideological purity, why did it not bring about a victory of the left and a new deal in French politics?

This is not the place to speculate about the reasons for the political failure of the Programme Commun. But what should be explained is the change in the trend which antedated the election by at least two years.

Why did the existing consensus of all the hopes and dreams for which people had fought so hard begin to lose its appeal? How is it that people could so quickly reject − without really giving it a try − the solution which they had professed to be the only possible substitute for revolution, and yet without reverting to their former radical position?

Two successive events exemplify the change which we will try to analyze. First, consider the resounding response to the publication of Solzhenitsyn and the discovery of Soviet dissent. Secondly, there was the astounding success of an unprecedented fashion: the new philosophers.

Solzhenitsyn's final victory was to force the Western world to face up to the repressive and sadistic nature of the Soviet regime. This was not in itself a French event. But it was to play a major role in the French context. Solzhenitsyn's appeal to the French intellectuals and especially to the 'sixty-eighters was felt deeply. It exposed in extremely concrete terms the contemporary drama of freedom and anti-authoritarianism. According to many studies on individual motivation, the preoccupation with this issue is a major and enduring issue with most Frenchmen. Therefore, again, the left was forced to face the impossible choice of freedom versus revolution. And despite all the efforts of the leftist leaders, this appeal finally made counter-revolution possible as a decent way of life. Following a spate of disillusionments – Cuba, Vietnam, Cambodia, Portugal – here was a new cause which could be understood as really pure. Not only was it counter-revolutionary as regards dogma but in non-romantic, even physical terms, as regards the arch-hero Lenin.

The new philosophers' success is the logical outcome of Solzhenitsyn's break-through. There is very little substance to be found in their rhetoric and prose. The contribution of this group has only been important inasmuch as it contradicts most of the stereotypes of the 'mad years'. What seems to me decisive and yet extremely puzzling is the reason for their success within the left. Solzhenitsyn had a hard time breaking through. *Le Monde* consistently tried to minimize his appeal. Only one year later this was not at all the case with the new philosophers, whose access to the influential public was immediate. Although they were quickly adopted by the Giscard clique, not only were they not denied access by the powerful gatekeepers of *Le Monde* and *Le Nouvel Observateur*, but they were launched in what can be viewed with hindsight as a major press campaign.

Why did the media change? Why did the public jump on the bandwagon?

I would only answer simply, because of a combination of the following: internal weakness, fear, anxiety. The risk of seeing the Communist Party coming to power was actually felt. France's existential drama seems to be the impossibility of acting out revolutionary dreams. As in Pagnol's famous play of the 1930s, the infuriated radical who is the hero looks to his companion who could stop him from going too far. The 1968 Revolution was a perfectly pure one whose only flaw was that it did not take place. Finally, so was the Programme Commun. It was waiting for Godot to the extent that Godot did not come.

To return to the media, the gatekeepers were internally divided, fearful of the Communist Party and feeling guilty because of their constant compromise. In 1977 this group of 1968 youngsters (the new philosophers) were not a threat; they looked like insiders rather than enemies. And the public cheered because it was tired of the left-wing revolutionary stance, because it had had second thoughts about the possible outcome of political change. A new era of realism was at hand. Props were no longer necessary. The 1968 movement was socialized more in keeping with the traditional values of French society than with the naive hopes of the movement.

(7) The State of the Union

Curiously enough, if we compare our cultural world in 1978 with the early 1960s we are not struck by the extent of change. The professional establishment has resisted extremely well. The engineering and professional schools still train a small elite through harsh selective processes. The influence of the Ecole Nationale d'Administration is greater than ever. On the other hand, philosophy, as the rallying cry of the cultural pundits, has almost recovered its former significance. What is more, the Ecole Normale Supérieure boarders do not feel guilty about enjoying their cultural primacy.

Everything is more or less back to normal. True enough the churches, the universities, even secondary education have not regained their equilibrium. But again, even among them the mood is temporarily at least one of restoration. And the legacy of 1968 seems to be in the long run only a singular disturbing and revealing accident.

Cultural life is beginning to be replenished at its source. The novel may even flourish once more. Stories and plots are in demand, and writers may even enjoy writing. Social sciences have only very partially come of age. History has kept its promises. The international success of the new French school of historians, its institutional expansion with the Ecole Pratique des Hautes Etudes, have made it the temporary leader and standard-bearer of all social sciences.

But its leadership is quite partial in this chaotic field. Sociology and political science are basically hampered by their own institutional weaknesses and paralyzed by their incapacity to accept minimum standards of scientific evidence. Economists have been very much stirred by the vigor of the political debate. But they too have gone from one misunderstanding to another, and have not gone substantially beyond skillful rhetoric. As in sociology, there are few contributions and they are not yet supported by the intellectual milieu.

Something has changed, nevertheless, in the cultural climate if one takes the long view. First, parochialism has decreased along with the inferiority complex counterbalancing it. This is, of course, especially noticeable as regards the United States. French intellectuals feel perfectly at ease with American approaches and fashions. There is less emphasis on a French tradition or some specific French knowhow. Left-wingers no longer use Marxism or radicalism as a protection against North American or Anglo-Saxon capitalist fashions. In counterpart one does not find very many zealots of the new American managerial creed. The American giant has fallen down. Its moral crisis has been stamped out, at least for the immediate present.

Secondly, taboos, especially sexual taboos, are gone. Intellectuals felt they were on fire in the early 1960s, but they had to learn the difference between the freedom of the happy few and the general exposure of the great many. They had to learn to express themselves and to remain 'cool'. The disappearance of all traditional restraints has forced people to change their behavior and learn coolness.

Thirdly, human relations have become more direct. Coolness as regards words and feelings may have brought more warmth in concrete relationships. The main regulator of behavior now is a growing sense of humor of which Claire Bretecher, the cartoonist of *Le Nouvel Observateur*, is the best example. Bretecher's mission for the last four years has been to teach her public to consider its own rituals, illusions, and fancies from a distance. Her tremendous success has been a sort of cultural counterpoint to the waiting-for-Godot years. Its nice and silly pretentious left-wing types, especially women, argue loftily and ponderously the radical creed but behave as much as ever in the bourgeois manner. They do not even have to be *recuperated* because they never quit.

(8)   What about Gaullism?

At this stage, I am beginning to worry because I have managed to discuss all these twenty years without either mentioning the name of de Gaulle or referring to Gaullism or to Gaullist institutions. Yet everything took place during those Gaullist years. They were in many ways *the Gaullist years*. Moreover, the regime was not neglecting the cultural milieu; on the contrary, it certainly placed culture high on the list of its ambitions of grandeur. Yet it seems to have made little impact. The regime had little influence on culture. The new crop of cultural fashions had no influence on politics. Indirectly, of course, the manner in which intellectuals behave may be important for politics and the guidance of society.

In any case, Gaullism does not seem to be relevant for an understanding of this period, at least from a cultural point of view.

Why? The fact is again puzzling. How is it that such a powerful state with an impressive father figure did not bring its influence to bear in the cultural world?

Estrangement and aloofness may be partial answers. De Gaulle's strategy was primarily to maintain himself as an aloof figure, to impress people by his distance from events and problems. Respect and estrangement may be two sides of the same coin. By forcing people to respect him and to respect the state, de Gaulle obliged French intellectuals to keep their distance. Frenchmen already had been accustomed to the divorce between culture and practical politics. They managed quite well in freely discussing existential problems while being well protected by a benevolent state. (The long fight of Sartre trying hard and yet failing to be put in prison is a good case in point.)

Tolerance may finally have been the General's contribution to French culture. To be sure his tolerance bore the mark of a lofty Gallic disdain. Yet it was very welcome in this country of religious and ideological warfare.

(9) The Cultural Revolution Revisited

When one now tries to assess the meaning of this long period of intense intellectual activity and controversy, it seems that what emerges is a feeling of chaos. It is a story of sound and fury. Radical fashions not only succeeded one another but coexisted without rhyme or reason in a senseless confrontation. All the contradictory tendencies I had pointed out in my 1963 article have seen the light of day. All the possible attitudes have been worn and discarded in facing up to the contradictions of the situation. The diagnosis of a crisis was well borne out. Reality, however, has gone far beyond revolution, i.e. there has been no passage from an earlier equilibrium to a new one.

Another remark comes to mind which qualifies what has just been said. That the crisis was serious is certain. But in another sense it was rather well managed. More specifically, society has been able to withstand this crisis without apparent loss. The cultural crisis erupted, was recognized, deeply shook the fabric of society briefly. It prompted a number of moral readjustments but society has not yet been basically affected. Moreover, if one compares France with other Western societies, the French experience has not been the worst, as many had earlier predicted. A tremendous spectacle was made out of the contradictions of modern times but people did not kill each other. Violence had been kept to minimum. No wild risks had been taken and altogether it seems that Frenchmen – even French intellectuals – have behaved quite properly according to a civilized tradition.

But what has been achieved through the crisis? The balance sheet here too is not clear. In 1963 I argued that we were engaged in a decisive learning process. Some learning has indeed taken place in human relations. Frenchmen are somewhat less tense, more open, even cooler in their debates. Young people may be more prepared to talk to one another and even to adults. But it is difficult to argue now that this learning process has been ended or that it has even been accelerated. The diagnosis, however, should be more qualified if one moves from the area of human relations to intellectual culture.

True enough, let me reiterate that without abandoning its own parochialism the French cultural milieu has learned to accommodate itself to the international environment where it is again active and well at ease. It has not progressed in a decisive way as regards modes of reasoning but more sophistication is now possible or even required when discussing complex human problems, and some sensible gains have been made in intellectual relationships. They have become simpler and more direct. Intellectuals may not have recognized the challenge of their increased numbers and the concomitant necessary loss of status, but they tend to adjust to it intuitively.

Curiously enough, what has finally survived more strongly than ever is what has been most strongly attacked, and what I had diagnosed as the weakest point – the institutions. I have pointed out the resilience of the strong cultural power centers which may have changed partially but basically so as to reinforce themselves.

If I was correct in 1963 this sturdy resistance may herald more problems and a revival of crisis in the future. If one could venture a prediction, however, it seems that we now come to the quiet part of the cycle after years of activism, i.e. that we may expect a period of respite analogous to the period of the golden years. But the basic problems have not been solved. Not only does the opposition between moral arrogance and short-term technocracy remain crystallized in the old institutions but it is now re-enacted and expanded on a broader scale in the basic opposition between the world of communication expertise and the world of action, responsibility, and scientific endeavor. Both worlds need each other, although they work on their own with completely independent regulations. The world of communications just emancipated in France during the crisis and its unregulated freedom are bound to exacerbate confrontations.

In this respect an important change may have been achieved but one which was unexpected and undesired. As in the United States the communication experts – the media people – are presently the most important influence in the cultural world. More and more they are going to be central in the process of change and they will be key actors in any new crisis. But new thinking is required to understand this other game.

8

KRISHAN KUMAR

The Nationalization of British Culture

Manchester is the centre of the modern life of the country.

William Ewart Gladstone, 1870

A yell followed this demonstration – a rioter's yell – a North of England – a Yorkshire – a West Riding – a West-Riding-clothing-district-of-Yorkshire rioter's yell.

Charlotte Brontë, *Shirley*, 1849

Among the most powerful forces in national life today are the centripetal forces making for centralization and uniformity in government, in education, in amusement, and in standards of taste.

Royal Commission on the Press, 1947–9

Judgements in cultural matters are, notoriously, as uncertain as they are inevitable. But in the case before us there is fortunately not much of a problem on that score. To compare British[1] culture in the nineteenth century with that of today is to be struck by a history of such manifest decline as to silence all dispute on the matter. In the last century British names and cultural influences ran worldwide. There was no more influential school of social thought than that of the British political economists, Adam Smith, Malthus, Ricardo. In political theory Bentham and John Stuart Mill, building on the foundations laid by Locke, provided the key constituents of the dominant theory of liberalism. British empirical philosophy,

continuing in the tradition of Bacon, Locke, and Hume, contended with German idealism for the intellectual mastery of Europe. Even in sociology, as a formal discipline never Britain's strong point, Herbert Spencer's achievement was considered sufficiently imposing for Durkheim to devote a good part of *The Division of Labour* to refuting him; while the pioneering Scottish school of sociology, founded by Adam Smith, Adam Ferguson, and John Millar, continued to command the admiration of such thinkers as Hegel and Marx. Framing and penetrating all these contributions in social and political theory was a powerful strand of cultural criticism, developed in the writings of Coleridge, Carlyle, Arnold, Ruskin, and Morris. It was perhaps above all in the profound critique of industrial civilization offered by these writers[2] – the new industrial society reflecting on itself – that the strength and vitality of English nineteenth-century culture were best displayed.

In the more specific fields of the arts and sciences the achievements are even more familiar and in some ways even more impressive. Poetry continued to flourish with Wordsworth, Keats, Byron, Shelley, Tennyson. The novel, an English invention, rose to unsurpassed heights in Jane Austen, Charles Dickens, George Eliot, the Brontë sisters, Thomas Hardy, Joseph Conrad. Priestly and Davy in chemistry, Dalton, Faraday, Kelvin, and Clerk-Maxwell in physics, maintained the level of British contributions in a field in which Britain was already exceptionally strong. In technology and engineering the accomplishments of Arkwright, Wilkinson, Watt, Boulton, Stephenson, and Brunel were a legend in their own time. In geology and biology the work of Lyell and Darwin revolutionized the whole conception of man's relation to nature.

Dazzled by such gold, it is easy to write off the whole of the present century as a failure. That is not part of the argument here. Britain has continued to make contributions of enormous importance in many fields – Russell and Whitehead in mathematics, Keynes in economics, Rutherford and Cockcroft in physics, Haldane and Fisher in biology. Englishmen invented the jet engine, radar, the hovercraft. There has even been a revival of certain art-forms in which Britain had not excelled for a century or more – as in the music of Elgar, Vaughan Williams, and Britten, and the sculpture of Moore and Hepworth. Moreover, if there has been a decline in Britain, it is paralleled in most other European societies, compared with the recent past.

So much can be argued, and admitted. What remains, however, is a clear sense first of the relative poverty of British contributions when set against the achievements of the last century; and, more to the point of this essay, of a decisive weakening of the general intellectual culture, the absence of significant centers of cultural and intellectual life capable of animating the society in new and creative ways. Within specialized fields there are still many impressive things done. But the impression remains confined to that field, and to the specialists within it. In searching for contributions to the culture at large, with the scope of significance comparable to the ideas of a Coleridge or an Arnold, we embark upon a fairly hopeless enterprise. Perhaps only Keynes in this century has made such a contribution, as suggested by the influence he has had throughout the industrial world; but it is an impulse generated from an uncomfortably narrow base.

It is beyond the scope of this essay even to attempt a complete explanation of this cultural decline, supposing such a thing were possible. Such an account would certainly have to emphasize factors common to all industrial societies, and not simply applicable to Britain. One would want to point especially to the immense extension and complication of the division of labor, leading to a 'Taylorization' of intellectual life, side by side with the Taylorization of economic life. Then there is the increasing concentration and centralization of economic, political, and cultural activities, closing off the 'gaps' in society where creative groups once flourished. The tendency to make the world safe for bureaucracy has had the similar effect of narrowing the lines of cultural communication. The products of culture now carry the stamp of their institutional original and institutional destination: books are written from and on behalf of one institutional base, the academic department, for transmission and storage within another institutional base, the academic library. The process is overseen by the good offices of the publisher, but whether any individual reader actually breaks the pure circuit of communication seems largely a matter of indifference to writer, publisher, and library. At the less elevated levels of culture there is the familiar fact of the extension of the market and of commerce to ever-increasing sectors of society, creating and then incorporating areas of 'leisure' and 'mass entertainment' according to the dictates of economic logic, to the displacement of other criteria of value.[3] Over and above all these tendencies, one would probably need to consider the evolution of the industrial system as a whole, its growth on a world scale, and within that development the dwarfing and 'de-industrialization' of Britain, the pioneer industrial nation.

These factors will not be ignored in the following account – indeed they are central to it. But I want to consider them within a more limited context: limited, that is, not simply by the fact that they are expressed within the confines of one society, Britain, but also by the particular coloring and direction given to them by the nature of British history and British society. I want, in particular, to see how far the general decline of British culture can be traced to one main process: the process of centralization, as part of a larger movement of change which I am loosely calling the 'nationalization of British culture'. This has been taking place over the past century and a half, but it has accelerated dramatically within the present century. It has involved, as a subsidiary theme, the institution-alization of cultural life as well: the displacement of the independent 'man of letters' by the salaried intel-lectual of the large cultural bureaucracies, whether in the mass media, the universities, or research insti-tutes. But that is a theme I shall leave for another occasion.[4]

One of the outstanding facts about nineteenth-century British society was its *provinciality*. We cannot, nowadays, easily remove the stigma of the second-best and the undercooked that attaches to the term. But, if we can set those associations aside for the time being, we will see more clearly how much the strength of Victorian society depended on this fact. It was in the peculiar tension between the metropolis – London – and the other great cities of the kingdom that, in all the activities that concerned its health and vitality, Victorian society found its greatest resources of creativity and growth.

It is important to recognize that the provincial character of British society was a new thing. It did not really exist before the end of the eighteenth century. Before that time there was simply 'town' and 'country'. To be 'out of town' was to be away from London and 'in the country'. Given the total pre-dominance of London at this time in the political, economic, and cultural life of the country, to go outside it really was to consign oneself to the 'idiocy of rural life', to live something of the life, and in the company, of types like Squire Weston in Fielding's *Tom Jones*.

The rise of 'the provinces' – a term derived from the French distinction between the old 'provinces' of France and the Ile de France with its capital, Paris – was a consequence of the industrial revolution. And it expressed itself principally in the growth of pro-vincial cities. In 1760, Bristol, with 60,000 inhabi-tants, was the only city of any real size outside London. By 1801 the quickening of economic life in the midlands and north had added six more cities with populations over 50,000: Manchester, Liverpool, Birmingham, Leeds, Edinburgh, and Glasgow. The unprecedentedly rapid increase in urban population in the early decades of the nine-teenth century soon added Sheffield and Bradford to this list; while many other towns in the industrial area – Leicester, Middlesbrough, Nottingham, Coventry, Salford – also grew to a considerable size.[5] From the 1780s the contrast between London and 'the provinces' became a familiar one. It is a contrast, expressed often enough as conflict, which provided nineteenth-century England with the staple of a good part of its economic, political, and cultural life.

The shift in emphasis is clearly illustrated in the political realm. Up to the late eighteenth century political activity took place almost entirely within the confines of the capital. This was still true, for instance, of the Wilkes affair of the 1760s. By 1830, at the time of the agitation over parliamentary reform, a dramatic change had occurred. It was from the provinces that the strongest pressure for reform came; and it was the provinces which took the lead in organizing and orchestrating the campaign. The new provincial press, especially the *Leeds Mercury* and the *Manchester Guardian*, played a key role, thus heralding the important political function they were to perform throughout the nineteenth century. Pro-vincial politicians, above all Thomas Attwood and his Birmingham Political Union, dominated the reform agitation, to the extent that 'Birmingham led the country in 1831–2'.[6]

Attwood's Political Union indeed had a signifi-cance that went well beyond the immediate aim of parliamentary reform. It signaled the shift away from 'influence', or coterie politics, and the rise of 'public opinion' in British politics. The rise of the provinces and the rise of public opinion as a political force are part of the same movement; and the creation of public opinion as an element of the 'political culture' of the nation is in many ways the most enduring contribu-tion of the English provinces in the nineteenth century. Contemporaries were aware of the funda-mentally regional nature of public opinion. As Joseph Parkes, one of the leaders of the Birmingham Political Union, said in 1832: 'In the Metropolis, in its present undivided chaos of men, the demonstration of public opinion (however intensely it may exist) cannot be compared with the expression and force of public opinion in the Country.' The provincial character of public opinion was a matter of need as much as of opportunity and superior effectiveness. Public opinion was the expression of organized and articulated opinion outside London, outside, that is, the customary centre of intrigue, privilege, and monopoly. It was the counterbalance to the traditional institutions and wielders of power. It was the means of 'the people', remote from the centers of decision-making, and largely unfranchised, to exercise some measure of control over the actions of the ruling groups at Westminster.

The economic contribution of the English provinces is a matter of world history, and too familiar to need repetition here. What is less often appreciated is how much of the political and cultural history of Britain in the nineteenth century can be written in terms of provincial initiatives and institutions. The major social movements, and a good deal of the social philosophy of the nineteenth century, had an unequivocally provincial origin.

Merely to list the names makes this abundantly clear. There was the Ten Hours factory movement, successfully led by the northern 'Tory Radicals' Richard Oastler and Michael Sadler from Yorkshire. There was Feargus O'Connor's domination of the Chartist movement from his northern base in Leeds, operating through his immensely influential newspaper the *Northern Star*. There was the brilliant success of the Anti-Corn Law League, under the leadership of Richard Cobden and John Bright in Manchester. Later in the century came the phenomenon of Joseph Chamberlain from Birmingham. Chamberlain's Birmingham organized the National Education League, which realized at least some of its aims in the 1870 Education Act. It also virtually founded the Liberal Party, through the establishment of the Birmingham 'caucus'. And not so very long after this the provinces were responsible for the revival of working-class politics in the founding of the Independent Labour Party at Bradford, with the notable backing of Robert Blatchford's paper, the *Clarion*, published in Manchester.

So important were the provincial towns in the life of Victorian England that historians have been able to chart the social changes of the century through the successive domination of individual cities. 'In many ways', G. M. Young has written, 'the change from Early to Late-Victorian England is symbolized in the names of two great cities: Manchester, solid, uniform, pacific, the native home of the great economic creed on which aristocratic England has always looked, and educated England was beginning to look, with some aversion and contempt: Birmingham, experimental, adventurous, diverse, where old Radicalism might in one decade flower into lavish Socialism, in another into pugnacious Imperialism.'[7]

It hardly needs to be stressed how unreal it would be to try to separate this vigorous political life from the more particular cultural and intellectual developments in the provinces. The ties between culture and politics were exceptionally strong during the course of the whole century, as was perhaps inevitable given the novelty and the challenge of the situation. Industrialism and democracy were momentous new forces, and Britain was the first society in the world to have to struggle simultaneously with both. British society was remade in the course of the nineteenth century, and in this remaking the provinces played a crucial part. It would have been surprising, given the dimensions of the problem, if politics and culture had pursued entirely separate paths, responding idiosyncratically in isolation from each other. In fact the development of cultural life closely reflected and paralleled the rise of the provinces as a political and economic force. That is, it both reacted against metropolitan domination, and aided the movement of the provinces toward relative autonomy and influence.

We have already seen, at various points, the involvement of the provincial press with provincial movements. A particularly close relationship was established by certain editors and newspapers with the political and social life of their cities: the two Edward Bainses, father and son, successive editors of the *Leeds Mercury*; J. E. Taylor and C. P. Scott, editors of the *Manchester Guardian*; Joseph Cowen, editor of the *Newcastle Chronicle*; R. K. Douglas, editor of the *Birmingham Journal*, and J. T. Bunce, editor of the *Birmingham Post*, and longstanding supporter of Chamberlain. The big provincial papers reached circulations of 20,000–40,000 readers; and, in their mid-Victorian heyday, only the London *Times* could rival these papers in quality and influence, an influence that extended well beyond the regional and even beyond the national. The development of the electric telegraph in the 1840s worked greatly to their advantage, allowing them to receive national and international news at virtually the same moment as the London press. It appears, too, that much of the vitality of these newspapers sprang from the need to educate the nation about the new industrial cities, to offset the metropolitan bias reflected in such papers as the London *Times* and *Telegraph*.[8]

A revulsion against a metropolitan monopoly also lay behind the movement for the foundation of 'civic' universities in the nineteenth century: although here that domination was geographically displaced to Oxford and Cambridge, and one had the curious spectacle of the first 'provincial' university being established in London, in the founding of University College by a group of Benthamites in 1828. But the impulse was clear. University College, writes Brian Simon, 'owed nothing to the example of the ancient universities of England [and] constituted a direct challenge to their monopoly of learning and higher education'. It drew its inspiration from the Scottish universities, especially Edinburgh, and also from the new or reformed German universities, such as Berlin. A conscious break was made with the traditional curriculum of Oxford and Cambridge – until well into the nineteenth century, still dominated by classics, mathematics, and theology – as well as with the traditional conception of the function of the university. Science and technology, medicine and the law, modern languages and the arts, all found a place at the new university, together with new methods of teaching, such as laboratory work. In one respect London, because of its size and complexity, could not do what the later civic universities were to attempt with a good deal of success: maintain a close tie between the university and the life of the town, to prevent the growth of the 'ivory tower' detachment characteristic of the old universities. But in most

ways, as Simon says, 'University College was the prototype for the modern universities initiated in the industrial cities in the latter half of the century'.[9] Of these the greatest was Owen's College, founded in 1851, which became in 1880 the Victoria University of Manchester; there followed Birmingham (1900), and, in 1903–5, Leeds, Liverpool, and Sheffield, originally colleges under the umbrella of the Victoria University.

Education, in the most general sense, was indeed one of the greatest achievements of provincial culture. Many of the outstanding intellectual and scientific contributions of nineteenth-century Britain came out of the activities of the societies and institutes set up in the provincial cities. Birmingham had early taken the lead with the famous Lunar Society, set up in 1766, where men such as Matthew Boulton, James Watt, Joseph Priestly, and Erasmus Darwin met to exchange ideas on everything from the steam engine to poetry and politics. Later came the first of the Literary and Philosophical Societies, established in Manchester in 1781, and involving such luminaries as Thomas Walker, Thomas Percival, and John Dalton. The Manchester 'Lit. and Phil.' achieved an international reputation – it was especially admired in France – and many of its members were active in stimulating Literary and Philosophical Societies in other towns: Liverpool (1812), Leeds (1820), Sheffield (1822). These societies, in close touch with each other and with scholars and scientists all over Europe and America, formed a network of intellectual activity that was unexampled in its brilliance, and which was a power-house of ideas in the establishment of new scientific, technical, and educational practices.

Faced with this picture of cultural efflorescence in the provinces, it is small wonder that a writer in the *Cornhill Magazine* in 1881 should reflect on how London, once 'the very focus of national thought and industry, surrounded on every side by the most flourishing parts of the country', had become 'isolated in the midst of the agricultural south . . . divorced from the feelings of the industrial centres'. But it would of course be wrong, and absurd, to think that London remained politically and culturally barren during this period. It was always the political center of the nation, where political questions had ultimately to be resolved in parliamentary decisions. It had a thriving literary and journalistic life, based on the great reviews and quarterlies of the period. And it was the home of some of the greatest poets and novelists. What was important in the nineteenth century was not the predominance of the provinces, or the eclipse of London, neither of which happened to any great extent. It was essentially the balance between the two which was the basis of the cultural achievements of both. A point was reached, roughly and temporarily, where the economic strength of the provinces gave them the means to assert themselves, politically and culturally, against the historic domination of London, the seat of the court, Parliament, and the law. Technology contributed to this balance: better roads, the railway, the telegraph, all allowed the provinces to be in sufficient contact with the metropolis, without being overwhelmed by it. Not to be in touch with the metropolis would have been to reduce themselves to a provinciality of culture as well as of geography; too much contact had the same, or worse, effect. For a while both London and the provinces shared in the explosion of energy released by the balance between them. But even as the gentleman of the *Cornhill Magazine* was reflecting on the change of London's fortunes, that balance was again being upset. London once more began to swallow up the economic, political, and cultural life of the nation. 'The story of Victorian cities in the nineteenth century', says Asa Briggs, 'is the story of the development of separate provincial cultures which during the last ten years of Queen Victoria's reign were increasingly "nationalised".'

The contrast between the provinces in the nineteenth century and in the twentieth could scarcely be more stark. Decline and decay is written on the face of every provincial institution and activity. And it is a decline which seems plausibly-related to the loss of vitality in British culture as a whole – although which is cause and which is effect is difficult to decide.

Economically, the provinces have decayed with the decline of British manufacturing power. This has been a long-drawn-out affair, lasting nearly a century. But at any time after about 1870 an astute observer might have seen the way things were going. From about that time, Britain ceased to be the 'workshop of the world' and became increasingly the 'banker to the world' – and shipper, and insurer, and provider of a host of other financial and commercial services. London, especially the City of London, was the heart of this service sector, as it has always been, a fact which gave it economic pre-eminence up to the time that the industrial revolution deflected the country's economic center northwards. In the course of this century other marketable services have been added to the traditional services of the City of London. These have to do with culture, the mass media, education, medical care, fashion, popular music, and tourism. All have been centered on London, and all have therefore tended to confirm, once more, the primacy of London in the economic life of the nation.

Politically, centralization has been the effect of two world wars, together with the increasing role of the state in planning and welfare. It has also been strengthened by the rise of organized mass political parties. Party control of the House of Commons has both elevated the executive power and nullified the independent power of the individual Members of Parliament and the local constituencies that they represent. Local government, too, largely dependent on central finance, has increasingly become merely the local agency of the state.

The centralization of culture has partly been the consequence of these other developments. Toward the end of the nineteenth century a 'communications revolution' took place, and its center was London. In 1896 Alfred Harmsworth, later Lord Northcliffe, founded the *Daily Mail*, the first of the mass national daily newspapers. In the same year the young Marconi arrived in London to sell his wireless inventions to the Post Office; and in the same year too the first cinema show was presented in the West End of London.[10] Given the renewed political and economic importance of London, it was inevitable that new developments in culture and communications would base themselves there. But they were no longer content to serve only the metropolis. The economics of the modern age demanded a national and an international market. Belief in 'economies of scale' promoted large enterprises, intent on 'horizontal' and 'vertical integration', that is, toward absorbing within the enterprise its main competitors, suppliers, and distributors. The result was the swamping of local and provincial markets by cheap, centrally produced, mass cultural products.

The effect was clearest in the case of the provincial press, the chief glory of the nineteenth-century provinces. Northcliffe had from the start set out to undercut the provincial newspapers by making a bid for their mainly middle- and lower-middle-class readership – the 'shopocracy'. The aim of the *Mail*, declared Northcliffe's chief assistant Kennedy Jones, was to build up a national readership 'centering on London and looking to London for its news and opinions'. A later Northcliffe initiative, the *Daily Mirror*, founded in 1903, was designed to do the same thing for the working class. The papers were to be kept cheap – the *Mail* sold at a half-penny – by relying heavily on advertising, responding to the need of manufacturers and retailers to reach out to a new mass market of consumers. The strategy was a great success. In 1921 forty-one newspapers were produced in provincial England, Scotland, and Wales, and thirteen cities outside London had more than one local daily paper. By 1970 only twenty provincial dailies survived, and no English provincial city had more than one local daily paper. The numbers have remained fairly steady since then, but what has gone on relentlessly is the even more ominous process of the concentration of ownership. By the late 1970s five large chains accounted for over half of the provincial daily and evening press.

Concentration is indeed the other side of centralization. The big companies that dominate the provincial press are mostly the same companies that dominate the national press even more completely. Five companies – Reed International, News International, Beaverbrook Newspapers, Associated Newspapers, and the Thompson Organization – between them account for nearly 90 per cent of the total circulation of both the national daily and the national Sunday newspapers.[11] If we take other media sectors – such as network television, paperback publishing, long-playing records, cinema exhibition – in each case we find that the five leading companies in the sector account for 70 per cent or more of the market. Moreover the companies do not restrict themselves to particular media sectors, but become multi-media conglomerates (such as EMI, Granada, the Thompson Organization), or extend even further out into the financial and industrial world. So, for instance, Pearson Longman not only controls the leading local newspaper group (the Westminster Press – which also publishes the national daily the *Financial Times*), the leading paperback house (Penguin Books), and a top hardback publishing group (Longman), but it also owns Lazards, the merchant bank, and has extensive industrial interests in glass and ceramics. And as with most other large corporations, a complex network of interlocking shareholdings and membership of each other's boards of directors link the companies of the culture industry.[12]

All this is by now a fairly familiar story, with fairly predictable consequences: the transformation of quality into quantity, of discrete audiences and readers into homogeneous masses, of activities pursued on behalf of specific cultural values or purposes into ventures undertaken on marketing criteria alone. It has happened similarly in all industrial countries, although the degree of centralization and concentration in Britain appears to be exceptional. What is less often noticed is the fact that in Britain this centralization was promoted, not simply by the external forces of economics and politics, but by an important strand of thinking within the sphere of culture itself. It has meant that the triumph of cultural centralization in Britain has been more than the regrettable side-effect of movements in other parts of the society. In certain important respects, it represents the honorable intention of some of the most gifted intellectuals of the day.

The villain of the piece is Matthew Arnold. Arnold, like many other intellectuals in the last third of the nineteenth century, was alarmed at what he took to be a growing spirit of anarchy among the English people. But unlike those, such as Walter Bagehot, who tended to see the solution in purely political terms, Arnold analyzed the problem as a profound deficiency in English *culture*. Arnold was not above reacting in a standard, class-bound way to the political events of his time. His remarks on what should be done to the working men who broke the railing in Hyde Park during a reform demonstration are treasured by all radicals. But the somewhat crude nature of his authoritarianism in politics was transmuted into a far subtler shape when it came to his cultural analysis.

In an essay on 'The literary influence of academies' (1864), Arnold compared the literary cultures of England and France, to the advantage of the latter. The higher general standard of French culture was attributed to the existence of a literary establishment, specifically the French Academy. This acted as a healthy check on the idiosyncrasies and propensity to waywardness of individual writers, a natural tendency however strong their native talent. All cultures, Arnold declared, require 'a recognized authority, imposing on us a high standard in matters of intellect and taste'. The want of a 'cultural authority representing high culture and sound judgement' had led in England to a literature 'full of hap-hazard, crudeness, provincialism, eccentricity, violence, blundering . . . In the bulk of the intellectual work of a nation which has no centre, no intellectual metropolis, like an academy . . . there is observable a *note of provinciality* [Arnold's emphasis] . . . The less a literature has felt the influence of a supposed centre of correct information, correct judgement, correct taste, the more we shall find in it this note of provinciality.'

In *Culture and Anarchy* (1869) Arnold gave this purely cultural analysis a more general social and political context. The want of authority in literature was part of a want of authority in society at large. The British, Arnold decided, suffered from an excess of 'Hebraism', and insufficient 'Hellenism'. Roughly this meant a proclivity to too much, and too swift, action, and not enough thought. Fortified by certain historical developments, such as the rise of Protestant

nonconformity, industrialism, and liberalism, it had led to a national tendency to assert the right of each individual 'to do what he pleases', so long as he respects the like right of others. This was a tendency, as Arnold saw it, destructive both of an ordered polity and of a high-minded culture, striving for perfection. The lack of a literary establishment was indeed paralleled by a more serious deficiency. The Englishman, says Arnold, 'has no idea of a *State*, of the nation in its collective and corporate character controlling, as government, the free swing of this or that one of its members in the name of the higher reason of all of them, his own as well as that of others'. Again and again Arnold reverts, in sonorous Hegelian terms, to England's need to develop a conception and a practice of the state as 'the organ of our collective best self, of our national right reason'. There is a glowing tribute to Wilhelm von Humboldt, the enlightened Prussian Minister of Education, and architect of the Prussian system of state education.

Arnold's wrath is especially directed at the English nonconformists, with their opposition to state education, and their general championing of the provinces against the center, the parts against the whole. He remarks on 'the undeniable provincialism' of the nonconformists, their narrowness of preoccupation and inability to rise to a sense of the whole – the whole man, or the whole culture. Why is this? 'Surely the reason is, that the Nonconformist is not in contact with the main currents of national life, like the member of an Establishment . . . While a national establishment of religion favours totality, *hole-and-corner* forms of religion . . . inevitably favour provincialism.' In a general paean to establishments, Arnold writes: 'The great works by which, not only in literature, art, and science generally, but in religion itself, the human spirit has manifested its approaches to totality and to a full, harmonious perfection, and by which its stimulates and helps forward the world's general perfection, come, not from Nonconformists, but from men who either belong to Establishments or have been trained in them.' The specific reference here is to religious establishments; but Arnold makes it clear that the need is for establishments in all the relevant areas of society, in church, state, education, and culture.

Arnold despaired of finding a lead to this end in any of the three main classes of society, the aristocracy (the 'Barbarians'), the middle class (the 'Philistines'), and the workers (the 'Populace'). All were too tainted by the predominant Hebraic spirit. He put his faith, such as it was, in men of culture and understanding drawn from all the classes – men, such as himself, who might form something akin to Coleridge's 'clerisy', a disinterested, guiding, cultural elite. Nothing of the sort has really emerged, of course. But there has been over the past century a development in the national culture which can, without stretching things too far, fairly be called the victory of Arnoldism. It has involved the creation of a number of central, public, national cultural institutions, staffed and administered by professionals in all the main spheres of culture and education. While these men and women can scarcely be said to represent the best of *all* classes, and indeed show their largely middle-class origin only too clearly, they do add up to a quite formidable cultural establishment, exercising considerable control over the cultural life of the whole society.

One part of this development has been brilliantly explored by Noel Annan, in his account of the rise of a new 'intellectual aristocracy' in late Victorian England. Annan writes:

Among all the changes in the structure of Victorian society few are so interesting as the emergence of an intellectual aristocracy which has profoundly influenced English politics, education and literature during the past hundred years. Certain families establish an intellectual ascendancy and begin to share the spoils of the professional and academic worlds between their children. These children intermarry and form a class of able men and women who draw into that circle people of intellectual distinction. The same blood can be found appearing among the headmasters of the public schools and the Fellows of Oxford and Cambridge colleges; the same tone of voice can be heard criticizing, teaching and leading middle class

opinion in the periodicals; and the same families fill the vacancies among the senior permanent officials in a Civil Service open to talent.[13]

These are the families whose names appear and reappear across the entire spectrum of intellectual and cultural life in Victorian and post-Victorian England: the Wedgwoods, Darwins, Huxleys, Macaulays, Trevelyans, Arnolds, Galtons; the Stephens, Wilberforces, Venns, Diceys, Thackerays, Fishers, Russells, Stracheys; the Vaughans, Haldanes, Hodgkins, Keyneses, and Butlers.[14] While the members of these families were not especially strong in the fine arts, they were responsible for re-creating and regenerating much of the institutional structure of contemporary cultural life in Britain.

They rescued the colleges of Oxford and Cambridge from the intellectually ramshackle and disreputable state in which they had lain for over a century, and made once more the pre-eminent bodies of learning in the land. They reformed the English public schools, establishing a virtually uniform system of education across the country, and thereby enabled the descendants of the new industrial middle class to aspire to the ranks of the new aristocracy of intellect. They revitalized the old scientific societies, such as the Royal Society, and were active in the new scientific and professional institutes established in the late nineteenth century. They were heads of colleges of art and of education. They became school inspectors, museum curators, secretaries of cultural and philanthropic societies. They joined the staff of *The Times*. 'Thus', says Annan, 'they gradually spread over the length and breadth of English intellectual life, criticizing the assumptions of the ruling class above them and forming the opinions of the upper-middle class to which they belonged.' Both as a class and as a body of opinion, they have as yet received no serious challenge from any area of English society.

In the course of this century new fields have opened up for this intellectual aristocracy to conquer and to colonize. A host of new public bodies have come into being, involving the state, directly or indirectly, in a wide range of cultural and educational activities. The

Royal Commission on Fine Arts came into being in 1924, the British Broadcasting Corporation received its charter in 1926, the British Film Institute was set up in 1933, and the British Council – for promoting the language and culture of Britain overseas – in 1934. After the war came the Arts Council in 1946, the Press Council in 1953, and, in 1955, the Independent Television Authority, to supervise the operations of the new commercial television stations. Then in the 1960s came the massive expansion of higher education, with the founding of eight universities: Sussex, Essex, Kent, East Anglia, Warwick, York, Lancaster, and Stirling (four in the south-east, one in the midlands, two in the north, one in Scotland – not a bad haul for the southern homelands of the cultural mandarins). All these new cultural institutions demanded new professionals, active in the arts and sciences, to man them. A new cultural intelligentsia, highly centralized and institutionalized by comparison with its Victorian predecessors, came into being, realizing at least partly Arnold's dream.

Probably the institution which would have pleased Arnold most was the BBC. Here was a public corporation holding a monopoly of broadcasting over the country, operating under a license which enjoined it to 'inform, educate, and entertain' – and in that order. It is a cultural establishment if ever there was one. The first director-general, Lord Reith, conceived his mission in essentially Arnoldian terms: the raising of the general culture of the country to new heights of seriousness and sensitivity.[15] Reith eschewed politics, in the narrow sense of parties, parliaments, and 'current affairs'. But he was quite aware that by putting all the emphasis on the cultural role of the BBC – on its talks, plays, features, poetry, and music – he was creating a new kind of politics, and a political role for the BBC. Over the years of Reith's guidance the BBC built itself into an extraordinarily central place in British society. As A. J. P. Taylor has said, 'in no time at all, the monopolistic corporation came to be regarded as an essential element in "the British way of life" '.[16] The Second World War set the seal on this development. During the war years the BBC was more or less identified, both at home and abroad, with the nation, and its struggle for survival. 'The nation at prayer' was how one observer described the atmosphere surrounding the BBC's nightly news bulletins. When in the 1950s commercial broadcasting was at last allowed, it was clear to all that it would not simply be given its head, on the American model. The BBC had established broadcasting as something different, something higher, and the Independent Television Authority was established to see that commercial television aimed at the same level.

The evidence of the involvement of Annan's 'intellectual aristocracy' in the new cultural bureaucracies is sometimes very direct. John Maynard Keynes, for instance, was the leading figure in the setting-up of the Arts Council. From 1942 he was chairman of the Committee for the Encouragement of Music and the Arts, a voluntary initiative of 1939 that was the direct predecessor of the Arts Council. Throughout the war Keynes was active in preparing the way for a properly centrally funded body, which came in 1946. Keynes, who had already been made chairman of the new Covent Garden Opera Trust, was designated as the first chairman of the Arts Council but died before he could take office. But his work was not wasted. The Arts Council, under the general direction of the Department of Education and Science, has become easily the most powerful patron of the arts in British society. It disburses over £10 million annually in grants. But the pattern of that disbursement is revealing. A full half of it goes to London: in the support of the Royal Opera House (which gets over 17 per cent of the Council's total budget), the English National Opera, the Royal Ballet, the National Theatre, the Royal Shakespeare Company, the London orchestras, the Festival Hall, the Wigmore Hall, and the Hayward Gallery. When one has mentioned these one has mentioned almost all that is significant in British artistic life today (adding other London cultural institutions, such as the National Gallery and the Tate Gallery, would complete the picture). Moreover, an examination of the membership of the Arts Council reveals the same feature of metropolitan concentration. A review of the members between 1946 and 1970 shows the predominance of the familiar London-based cultural elite. The Oxbridge provenance shows through even more clearly. 'The role played by the University of London and the provincial universities was insignificant, and, surprisingly, contributions by professional schools of art, music, and drama were modest.'[17]

It would be absurd to think that the members of a few charmed families have absorbed all the important positions in the nation's cultural life. The sheer limitation of numbers is fortunately a barrier to that. But what the intellectual aristocracy seems to have done, with an extraordinary degree of success, is to fix the basic pattern according to which future developments would take place. Twentieth-century British culture has been poured into a mold fashioned largely according to the social and intellectual contours of that group. It is middle, more precisely upper-middle, class. It is urban and metropolitan. Its members do not, except when on official visits, venture far outside the small triangle of London, Oxford, and Cambridge, although they have many links with the southern county families. Although they have no longer all been to public schools, they hold attitudes and values which are clearly public school. This has been made easier by the fact that the grammar schools have increasingly come to imitate the ethos, organization, and curriculum of the public schools. Finally, it is a highly centralized culture, with a marked public aspect to it. The centralizing drive here clearly has a different motive from that which has produced centralization in mass culture and communication. Its prophet is Arnold rather than Northcliffe. But the net result has been the same: to base the cultural life of the nation firmly in London, the economic and political center.

The result is that new cultural initiatives rapidly fall back into the old mold. The creation of the new field of broadcasting, for instance, especially with the great expansion of television in the 1950s and 1960s, generated an influx of hundreds of graduates as producers, editors, and directors. But right from the start, in the recruiting practice of the young BBC, arts graduates from Oxford and Cambridge pre-

dominated. In the 'general trainees' scheme, which was for long the BBC's main way of recruiting future producers and senior administrators, candidates from Oxford and Cambridge regularly claimed 80–90 per cent of the traineeships. The pattern was repeated with the new independent television companies, despite their commercial basis and more obviously popular orientation. Similarly with the new universities of the 1960s. These started with many brave flourishes about radical departures in teaching, subject areas, and social organization. But more to the point it was the senior common rooms of Oxford and Cambridge which provided most of the new professors, and it was graduates from the same universities who were most successful in securing the junior posts. This had an effect far greater than formal statements of intent. 'Oxbridge' styles became prevalent at many of the new universities – three of which, in conscious imitation of the old universities, were in any case collegiate. It became clear in fact that the main tendency in the new 'plateglass' universities was to counter, not Oxford and Cambridge, but the large provincial 'redbrick' universities of the midlands and the north. In this too there was an irony, not without its pathos. For in the course of this century, as A. J. P. Taylor remarks, 'the civic universities, which had started in aggressive repudiation of Oxford and Cambridge, now strove to resemble them, and increasingly offered an imitation or echo of upper-class education'.[18] The wheel had come full circle.

It is not in the least my intention to denigrate the contribution of the metropolitan intelligentsia. It has done much to prevent the rampant forces of commercialism from invading every cultural nook and cranny in the society. It has also, because of its privileged economic and social position, been relatively resistant to political blandishments and threats. It is, as Annan says, a civilized and humane aristocracy – 'secure, established, and, like the rest of English society, accustomed to responsible and judicious utterances and sceptical of iconoclastic speculation'.

But that too suggests a weakness, one indicated

better by Gertrude Himmelfarb in an essay on Victorian intellectuals. Noting that the Victorian intellectual in retrospect appears as the very type of the intellectual, moving freely and easily as if by 'unimpeachable right' through all the spheres of Victorian society, she comments:

> And yet the very quality of legitimacy which confers upon the Victorian the title of the perfect intellectual also, paradoxically, deprives him of the claim to it. For if to be an intellectual is as natural as breathing, it can be no more remarkable than breathing. If it has the status of an ordinary vocation it does not enjoy the extraordinary status of an avocation. If it is no special distinction which the individual must laboriously learn, if it comes to him as a right rather than a reward, if it is an incidental by-product of class and family rather than the result of application and dedication, then the much acclaimed Victorian intellectual may not be an intellectual at all, but rather a cultured gentleman whose occupation happens to be writing.[19]

This is a fitting comment on the whole metropolitan intelligentsia. There is an ordinariness and a blandness about it, which may make for humane cultural administration, but hardly for a living and thriving culture. This probably would not matter so much if its influence were not so exclusive and pervasive, if there were other centers of culture in society. But there are not. This has been the great loss: the decline of those vigorous provincial centers of culture which in the last century offset the metropolitan influence, and indeed spurred it on to better itself. The nationalization of culture has also meant a flattening and emptying of it. It represents the victory of what A. Alvarez has called 'the gentility principle' in British culture. This explains – at least partly – the vapidity, ephemerality, and superficiality of much post-1945 artistic culture. At best there develops a kind of feverish, neurasthenic energy. Typical of contemporary metropolitan culture are the plays of Harold Pinter (*The Caretaker, The Homecoming*) and Tom Stoppard (*Rosencrantz and Guildenstern Are Dead, Jumpers*). These are, in Stoppard's case, verbally corruscating, clever, full of witty tricks and paradoxes; in Pinter's, disconcerting and often unnerving. But they share the same qualities of negativeness and cynicism. Emotionally and intellectually they move within a very limited range, and morally they are empty.

What Gilbert Phelps says about fiction since 1945 seems an apt comment on the generality of postwar British culture:

> When we remember the scope and variety of English fiction at the beginning of the century in the hands of such writers as Henry James, Joseph Conrad, E. M. Forster, D. H. Lawrence, James Joyce, and Virginia Woolf, it is difficult not to feel that there has been a steady decline. The trend of the English novel since the war has been analogous to that of the poetry of the period – a turning aside from the mainstream of European literature, a complacent rejection of the culture of the past, and a retreat into parochialism.[20]

That this is not simply a nostalgic judgement can be illustrated by the fate of the one artistic movement since the war that seemed to contemporaries to carry hope: the movement of the 'Angry Young Men' of the 1950s and early 1960s. This included several plays first staged in London at the Royal Court Theatre and Joan Littlewood's Theatre Workshop in Stratford East: John Osborne's *Look Back in Anger* (1956) and *The Entertainer* (1957), Shelagh Delaney's *A Taste of Honey* (1958), Willis Hall's *The Long and the Short and the Tall* (1958), Arnold Wesker's trilogy, *Chicken Soup with Barley* (1958), *Roots* (1959), and *I'm Talking about Jerusalem* (1960), and a number of plays by John Arden, N. F. Simpson, and Ann Jellicoe. Among novels there were John Wain's *Hurry on Down* (1953), Kingsley Amis's *Lucky Jim* (1954), John Braine's *Room at the Top* (1957), and Alan Sillitoe's *Saturday Night and Sunday Morning* (1958). There was also a parallel movement in the English cinema. This however was largely a 'spin-off' from the movement in the theater and the novel, since many of the films made were of the 'Angry' plays and books, and the people who made them, such as

Lindsay Anderson and Tony Richardson, often also had theatrical backgrounds.[21]

Merely to state the names is to point to the problem. For where are they now? What came next? The answer is, practically nothing. The movement had nothing to sustain it beyond the first short burst of protest. As Raymond Williams says, 'the new feelings of the middle 1950s were not in themselves creative; they were a stage of dissent from old formulations, and contempt, sickness and anger were the predominant impressions'.[22] These are not emotions to sustain a movement for long. Some of the dramatists and writers continued to produce works in the 1960s and 1970s, but to all intents and purposes they were 'one-work' artists. The anger and contempt remained, but it was now expressed in more conventional, tired ways. Many of them, such as Amis, Braine, and Osborne, swung over to the right, and continued to vent their spleen in the more traditional tones of the ultra-conservatives. Braine sought Reds under every bed. Amis denounced the expansion of higher education. Young Jimmy Porter, the original angry young man of Osborne's *Look Back in Anger*, reappeared as the grouchy middle-aged solicitor, Bill Maitland, of his *Inadmissible Evidence*, railing away against motorways, miniskirts, and all things modern. The ranting tirade against modernity, offered by some faded figure from the past, became a standard feature of every Osborne play. It soon appeared that what he was really nostalgic for was the society of Edwardian England – Edwardian music-hall, Edwardian army officers, Edwardian gentlemen – where notions like honor and duty meant something, and men were truly men.

There was an aspect to the movement that pointed up its poverty even more. Many of its members were provincials – Arden, Delaney, Hall, Wain, Braine, Sillitoe. The derelict slag-heaps of the north, the run-down townscapes of Manchester and Salford, industrial Nottingham, provided the dramatic backdrop to much of the action. There was a lot of talk of fresh winds of change blowing from the provinces, of a revitalization, as of old, of the jaded metropolitan culture by raw provincial energy.

That provincial experience provided many of the works with what vitality they had is undeniable. But merely to compare them with the literature produced by the provinces in the past, in their great days, is to see what a shadow they are of their former selves, and how thin is the life that sustains them. In the nineteenth century an important part of the history of the novel can be written in terms of the provincial contribution. Dickens may have made only the routine journalist's trip to Preston to obtain copy for *Hard Times*; but Elizabeth Gaskell knew her Manchester, and made powerful use of this knowledge in *Mary Barton* and *North and South*. George Eliot went on to become almost the type of the cosmopolitan London intellectual; but no one can miss the importance in her work of the midlands counties where she spent her childhood and youth. In at least *Adam Bede, The Mill on the Floss*, and *Silas Marner*, the regional setting – Staffordshire, Lincolnshire, Warwickshire – is central to the whole tenor and emotional structure of the novels; while the midlands settings of both *Felix Holt* and *Middlemarch* adds an important dimension to both works (the latter is, after all, subtitled 'A Novel of Provincial Life'). The role of the moors of the West Riding of Yorkshire in the works of the Brontë sisters – *Wuthering Heights, Shirley* – is too well known to need elaboration. Then there is Hardy and the 'Wessex' countryside; and Arnold Bennett's series of novels – such as *Anna of the Five Towns* – set in the pottery district around Stroke-on-Trent. One might almost say that the whole concept of realism in the nineteenth-century novel, as developed by Eliot and Hardy, related intrinsically to the life of the provinces, where could best be seen, as George Eliot put it in *Adam Bede*, 'the dusty streets and the common green fields and the breathing men and women of England'.[23] Here was an achievement of an imposing kind, sustained over the course of a century. It drew on a social experience that was still growing and developing. The provincialism of the 'Angry Young Men', by comparison, seems paltry, a slight on what was genuinely carried out under that banner.

Toward the end of the nineteenth century a new phenomenon began to appear. Now it was not so much the English provinces as the realms of English-speaking cultures outside England which began to make a major contribution to British culture. There was Ireland, with Wilde, Shaw, Yeats, Joyce. There was America, with Henry James and T. S. Eliot; and there were such 'outsiders' as Conrad. This observation introduces a new theme, of a new kind of 'provincialism', which it is impossible to pursue any further here.[24] But it may allow us to make one final comment on contemporary British culture. Some of the most creative writing of the post-1945 era has come from British novelists who were born, or lived for many years, in the old British colonies. The pioneer of all these was Jean Rhys, who drew on her West Indian background to powerful effect in a series of novels of the 1920s and 1930s (*Voyage in the Dark, Good Morning, Midnight*), culminating in her magnificent last novel, *Wide Sargasso Sea* (1966). Then there is Doris Lessing, whose African experience was not only used directly in several of her novels (*The Grass Is Singing*), but seemed to provide a fresh and original perspective in her novels of English life, such as *The Golden Notebook* and the 'Children of Violence' sequence (*Martha Quest*, and others). Paul Scott, who spent much of his life in India, produced a splendid series of novels under the general title *The Raj Quartet*. India, too, has been the inspiration for Ruth Prawer Jhabvala (married to an Indian and long-time resident in India), in such novels as *Heat and Dust*, and in a very creative collaboration with the film director James Ivory (e.g. *Shakespeare Wallah*). And there is V. S. Naipaul, Trinidadian-born, perhaps the most interesting novelist currently writing in England, who draws upon his life and travels in the West Indies and Africa to create a sombre but exceptionally powerful image of the contemporary human condition (*The Mimic Man, In a Free State, Guerrillas, The Bend in the River*).

In an otherwise bleak scene, these are hopeful signs. British culture has for long not been confined to the shores of Britain. With the expansion of trade and the Empire, it increasingly became the possession of many regions of the globe, not forgetting that first region – America – that was the product of the first bout of imperialism. The possibility is there that increasingly in the future the vitality of British culture will turn on contributions deriving from that experience, contributions by people from those former British territories, as well as by native Britons reflecting on that vast theme – a fit subject, if there ever was one, for epic treatment. In a new and more extended form, a creative tension will have been established between the original center – Britain – and the parts, the English-speaking world. In no sense, any more than in nineteenth-century Britain, will the parts be dependent or subordinate, economically, politically, or culturally. But the cultural loss to all, if each goes its own way in isolation from the others, will be great. At the moment, the most urgent need is Britain's. George Canning, justifying British aid to the Latin American rebels at the beginning of the nineteenth century, declared that he had called the New World into existence to redress the balance of the Old. This time the boot is on the other foot: it is the New World which will have to reinvent and regenerate the Old.

NOTES AND REFERENCES: Chapter 8

1 'British culture' is an ugly and somewhat inaccurate term, more used in foreign texts about Britain than by native Britons. 'British industry', yes, but 'English culture', 'Scottish culture', and so on. This essay is in fact mainly about English culture and politics. But I have kept the wider term because some of the people and places discussed are not English, even though their main point of reference and theater of activities has usually been England.

2 The outstanding discussion – not to say definition – of this tradition remains Raymond Williams, *Culture and Society 1780–1950* (Harmondsworth: Penguin, 1963).

3 For a good account of this process as it affected Britain, see T. Burns, 'Leisure in industrial society', in M. A. Smith, S. Parker, and C. S. Smith (eds), *Leisure and Society in Britain* (London: Allen Lane, 1973).

4 For a discussion of this theme, see John Gross, *The Rise and Fall of the Man of Letters* (London: Weidenfeld & Nicolson, 1969), and Malcolm Bradbury, *The Social Context of Modern English Literature* (Oxford: Blackwell, 1971).

5 For the account of this growth, with vivid portraits of the individual cities, see Asa Briggs, *Victorian Cities*

(London: Odhams Press, 1963). For a varied collection of views on the life and culture of Victorian cities, see H. J. Dyos and M. Wolff (eds), *The Victorian City: Images and Realities*, 2 vols (London: Routledge & Kegan Paul, 1973).

6 Donald Read, *The English Provinces, c.1760–1960: A Study in Influence* (London: Edward Arnold, 1964), p. 90. Read's book is an excellent survey of the role of the provinces in the nineteenth century, although the concentration is mostly on politics.

7 G. M. Young, *Victorian England: Portrait of an Age* (London: 1936).

8 For a detailed study of the relationship between one provincial city and its press, see Asa Briggs, *Press and Public in Early Nineteenth Century Birmingham* (Oxford: The Dugdale Society, 1949).

9 Brian Simon, *The Two Nations and the Educational Structure 1780–1870* (London: Lawrence & Wishart, 1974), pp. 118–25.

10 On these developments see Raymond Williams, *The Long Revolution* (Harmondsworth: Penguin, 1965).

11 In terms of the newspapers read, this means that the readership of the whole country is more or less accounted for by seven daily newspapers: four popular ones – the *Mirror*, the *Sun*, the *Express*, the *Mail*; and (well down in numerical terms) three 'quality' dailies – *The Times*, the *Telegraph*, the *Guardian*. The Sunday national press is also dominated by seven newspapers: four popular – the *People*, the *Sunday Mirror*, the *News of the World*, the *Sunday Express*; and three 'quality' – the *Sunday Times*, the *Observer*, the *Sunday Telegraph*.

It is significant that the one provincial newspaper that continued to have national influence in the twentieth century – the *Manchester Guardian* – dropped the 'Manchester' from its title in 1959, and completed the process of 'nationalization' in 1964 by moving its editorial staff to London.

12 For the figures and their significance, see G. Murdock and P. Golding, 'For a political economy of mass communications', in R. Miliband and J. Saville (eds), *The Socialist Register 1973* (London: Merlin Press, 1974), pp. 205–34; Murdock and Golding, 'Capitalism, communication and class relations', in James Curran, Michael Gurevich, and Janet Woollacott (eds), *Mass Communication and Society* (London:

Edward Arnold, 1977), pp. 12–43; Raymond Williams, *Communications* (Harmondsworth: Penguin, 1968); Richard Hoggart, 'Mass communications in Britain', in B. Ford (ed.), *The Modern Age* (London: Cassell, 1964), pp. 442–57.

13 Noel Annan, *Leslie Stephen: His Thought and Character in Relation to his Time* (Cambridge, Mass.: Harvard University Press, 1952), p. 1.

14 For the relevant kinship charts, see Noel Annan, 'The intellectual aristocracy', in J. H. Plumb (ed.), *Studies in Social History* (London: Longman, 1955), pp. 241–87.

15 For a good biography, see Andrew Boyle, *Only the Wind Will Listen: Reith of the BBC* (London: Hutchinson, 1972).

16 A. J. P. Taylor, *English History 1914–1945* (Oxford: Clarendon Press, 1965), p. 233.

17 John S. Harris, *Government Patronage of the Arts in Great Britain* (Chicago: University of Chicago Press, 1970), pp. 39–89.

18 Taylor, op. cit., p. 309.

19 Gertrude Himmelfarb, 'Mr. Stephen and Mr. Ramsay: the Victorian as intellectual', *Twentieth Century*, December 1952, p. 515.

20 Gilbert Phelps, 'The novel today', in Ford (ed.), *The Modern Age*, op. cit., p. 475.

21 It should be pointed out that – apart from the fact that the 'Angry Young Men' included some young women – many of these writers did not recognize any 'movement', and did not see themselves as sharing a community of theme or purpose. For a general survey, see Kenneth Allsop, *The Angry Decade: A Survey of the Cultural Revolt of the Fifties* (London: Peter Owen, 1958); and John Russell Taylor, *Anger and After: A Guide to the New British Theatre*, 2nd edn (London: Methuen, 1969).

22 Williams, *The Long Revolution*, op. cit., p. 380. For a more extended treatment, see Raymond Williams, 'Recent English drama', in Ford (ed.), *The Modern Age*, op. cit., pp. 496–508.

23 See Phyllis Bentley, *The English Regional Novel* (London: Allen & Unwin, 1941).

24 There are some stimulating remarks on this theme in the literary essays by Rayner Heppenstall, *The Fourfold Tradition* (London: Barrie & Rockcliff, 1961).

9

HEINZ LUDWIG ARNOLD

From Moral Affirmation to Subjective Pragmatism: The Transformation of German Literature since 1947

When Thomas Mann stated at the time of his emigration from Nazi Germany 'Where I am is where German culture is' he may have regarded himself as the representative of a bourgeois society that had in the past been intact. Yet his society had already begun its process of disintegration during the Weimar Republic, and its remnants collapsed with the accession of the Nazis to power. Thus Thomas Mann's ironic self-evaluation may simply have expressed his yearning for a different and better Germany and his opposition to the cultural barbarism of the Nazis.

In the post-Second World War period a statement like Thomas Mann's is totally inappropriate, whether applied to an individual writer or to a literary group. German culture is not represented by Heinrich Böll, who explicitly rejected such a notion, nor by Günter Grass, who might possibly be more sympathetic to the idea. And not even Gruppe 47 (the literary group) encompassed German culture or even German literature. Gruppe 47 became 'representative', if at all, only to the extent that it mirrored the most important expressions of creative writing in West Germany.

1

The new literature continued its growth without disruption until the early 1960s and developed a certain universally accepted concept of its function. It is possible to make this statement today since at the pinnacle of its success, between 1960 and 1963, this literature experienced an identity crisis: its rather inflexible self-image was challenged with sound arguments by a new generation of writers. At the onset of the cultural-revolutionary phase, initiated by the student rebellion of 1966, this literature was even dismissed as completely outdated: bourgeois literature was declared dead.

It has become increasingly clear that the hopes of the first generation of postwar writers for the ability of literature to achieve a moral and intellectual renewal of society were a illusion. What was the historical basis for this hope?

This society had been found guilty because it had participated in the unprecedented terror of National Socialism. Drawing on this historical experience, a number of young writers whom the war had spared considered it their moral duty to promote a strong anti-fascist and anti-Stalinist, but nevertheless passionately socialist, message. Based on their historical experience, these writers developed an image of themselves as the moral *avant-garde* that would mold the character of a new society and new state.

Wolfdietrich Schnurre first formulated this elitist image of a literature in 1947 in the *Ruf*, shortly before this important journal of the new Germany was prohibited by the Americans for its liberal leanings. The publishers of the *Ruf*, Hans Werner Richter and Alfred Andersch, together with Schnurre, Walter Jens, and other writers, later founded Gruppe 47. Schnurre wrote:

We who believe ourselves called upon to announce the future and explain the present, we have the duty, more than anyone else, not to let the old wounds heal. Let those who want to hide their faces hide them when they learn our history. We did not survive the collapse of a sham world only to create another world of illusions on the ruins of this one. Only he whose knowledge of the most recent past has burdened him has the right today to write and to come before the public.

It is this type of literary moralistic confession directed against any kind of social totalitarianism or ideology that the writers of Gruppe 47 were identified with for years. In that way they developed a political-literary self-image that gave the effect of homogeneity, and which corresponded to their literary output, notwithstanding the variety of literary styles.

Yet West German society moved away from the historical origin of the moral impulse that had motivated its leading literary group. It had done so in spirit, simply by repressing the intolerable inhumanity of the Third Reich rather than trying to come to terms with it. Furthermore the growing economic prosperity began to implant a strong anti-socialist feeling into the consciousness of West German society, a feeling that was publicly reinforced by the government and the media, aided by the developments in the communist part of Germany, which provided irrefutable evidence for anti-socialist propaganda.

The unwillingness of the Germans to look critically at their past and present became obvious in the public opposition to nearly all criticism: not only that of the organized political left (the Communist Party was banned in 1956), but also that of the morally committed writers, who denounced society's growing materialism and uniformity as 'the fouling of their own nest'. In the meantime, the morally engaged writers were no longer satisfied to work on the past but had begun confronting the past with their experiences in the present, thereby creating more parallels between past and present than would appeal to a materialistically interested public. Moralizing idealism was considered a disturbance in the frenzy of material success. A literature bound by its historical experience to humanism and morality was confronted by a society that refused to face its past.

2

It is really paradoxical that this literature met with success at all in the 1960s; but then what do we mean by success? Isolated from the society whose renewal it advocated and whose materialistic emptiness it denounced in vain, this literature, fifteen years after the end of a moral and spiritual *Kahlschlag*, achieved a sense of assertiveness which no longer looked for society's acceptance of its self-appointed mission. This literature mistook its media success for having social impact.

The conservative climate of the Federal Republic and the recognition by the media of the marketability of this oppositional phenomenon opened up the German market for a nonconformist literature: meetings of Gruppe 47 in the late 1950s assumed the atmosphere of a media event that absolutely demanded the presence of journalists, publishers, and TV commentators on a scale equal to that of the Frankfurt Book Fair. Any young writer who could gain entrance, and was able to present a halfway acceptable manuscript, could count on establishing his career – provided he bowed to the required rituals of the group. In 1966, then still unknown, Peter Handke attacked what he called the descriptive impotence of Gruppe 47 authors. By that he meant not only their threadbare realism but also the elitist pretensions of many writers who by then had achieved prominence and gloried in their own importance. The group reacted with amusement and concern: but it failed to understand this attack, since it was no longer flexible enough to accept criticism of its ritual nor able to renege on its hard-won self-image. The young writers used Gruppe 47 the way a nephew uses a rich uncle: they used the publicity of Gruppe 47 for their own successes, but would not be swayed from their own moral and political credos. The last meeting of Gruppe 47 took place in 1967, when young leftist students demonstrated against its failing political involvement, as in the case of the Vietnam War. Most of its authors were not even ready to discuss these matters with the students. The openness which most writers of Gruppe 47 still practiced in their writings did not carry over into political and social reality. 'We did not survive the collapse of a sham world only to create another world of illusions.' Schnurre's warning of 1947 became fact twenty years later: the belief in the ability of literature to bring about the moral and spiritual regeneration of society had proved itself an illusion. Not only did the politically committed, oppositional literature fail to achieve a position of societal leadership but, paradoxically, with its success it ensured that it became increasingly isolated from that society.

It was not the political commitment of the writers that was responsible for the change of opinion in West German society, but the sum total of political failures generally: from the construction of the wall in 1961 until the first recession of 1966, events multiplied that bore witness to the inflexible politics of conservatism characterized by the slogan 'No Experiments' which could not create a productive policy of reform. What eventually triggered the first change in a German government in seventeen years was not the moral indignation of the people but their overpowering fear of losing through recession what they had achieved in the years of the miraculous economic recovery before this change – not even the direct campaign support extended by the leading literary personalities to the SPD in 1961 and 1965 could prevent an overwhelming victory by the CDU/CSU in 1965. Two events show clearly the extent to which the belief in a spiritual, moral, and political guidance through literature was based on self-delusion: Willy Brandt's refusal in 1965 publicly to denounce the Vietnam policy of the United States – which had already caused Martin Walser to cease his support of the SPD – and the willingness of the SPD in 1966 to join the great coalition under a chancellor who had once been a member of the Nazi Party. Thus the SPD on which the writers had pinned their hopes for the realization of their moral principles instead opted for *Realpolitik*. At the same time a new generation of writers began to look for a new direction, recognizing that the self-image of Gruppe 47 had become obsolete.

Thus literature at the peak of its public success soon lost the oppositional stance. Instead, it now became a consumer item, a market phenomenon in a politically and economically stable society which viewed that literature's critical character as welcome evidence of its liberalism. The nonconformist literature stagnated, because it lost its commitment to the historical past and its specific intellectual component, which was to be a productive opposition to any social status quo. Now it had become part of that status quo.

3

Documentary literature radically attempted to overcome the limitations of conventional literature, asserting that it was closer to reality than fiction and, therefore, also closer to the truth. What was to act on the reader or spectator was not the inverted, structured, manipulated morality of the author – not his so-called 'fictional authenticity' (as Martin Walser said) – but rather the historical document, that is, history itself, was to have its effect on the reader or spectator. Of course even documentary material had to be organized and arranged, but the elements of this arrangement were original. Thus Heinar Kipphardt's play *In the Matter of J. R. Oppenheimer* is based on the stenographic records of the American investigatory committee; Peter Weiss's *The Investigation* uses the newspaper accounts of the Auschwitz trial in Frankfurt; and in the interview transcriptions by Erika Runge, although they, too, were rearranged, workers, employees, housewives, and so on voiced their problems in their own language. Even Rolf

Hochhuths's dramas *The Deputy* and *Soldiers* – very conventional pieces – based their claim to truth on the authenticity of historical documents. Of course the reality, which documentary literature wanted to present, could be shown only in small segments. Consequently, all documentary material was chosen by the author and in effect preselected and organized by him.

Nevertheless this documentary procedure nullifies the literary autonomy of the 'old' realism: the apparently objective work or the 'fictional authenticity' is replaced by actual materials, the arrangement of which furthers rational understanding of a specific situation. The author, working with facts in order to increase the perceptive abilities of the reader or spectator, invites him to participate, stimulating his individual imagination. In other words the reader is given the opportunity to take part in history which has now become a concrete experience. While documentary literature through its own poetical practice questioned the literary convention from a point of view of reality, another literary concept emerged, one which questioned literary convention through a critical approach to language: the 'concrete poetry' of Helmut Heissenbüttel, Franz Mon, and others.

What was its original premiss? Helmut Heissenbüttel mistrusts the possibility of subjective language in principle. Not the person who speaks, but the objective conditions of the language used by the speaker, determine what he says, because language is limited by a preconceived reality. There is no longer a subjective language because we do not possess language, but it possesses us. What follows from this, in its extreme form, is that the individual can no longer create by himself an autonomous artistry of language.

'Concrete poetry' therefore uses a variety of methods: it destroys the traditional sentence structure, as stated by Heissenbüttel, 'to destroy the prejudices and obduracy that are preserved in the traditional usage of language'. It paints words acoustically and visually in order to let us experience their meaning in a completely new sense, or in order to demonstrate the insufficiency of the traditional language system. This variety of methods is not intended, as its opponents maintain, to be elitist and self-serving, but rather to evince a changed experience in a changing environment (Heissenbüttel) and to provide, within this environment, opportunities for new linguistic orientation.

Just as documentary literature had disrupted literary convention by turning the reader or spectator into a literary and thus also a politically active subject, through a confrontation with a largely unformed reality, so does 'concrete poetry' demonstrate to the reader the linguistic and therefore also substantive questionability of this tradition, through the destruction of the common language and through the extension of acoustic as well as visual possibilities. 'Concrete poetry' also wants to transform the passive reader into an active individual. This intention, common to both approaches, had some effect, although neither documentary literature nor 'concrete poetry' became lasting literary movements. And whatever influence they had was not as spectacular as the discussion about the 'death of bourgeois literature' – a discussion which started from a quite different premiss.

4

In 1962 Hans Magnus Enzensberger wrote in a postscript to his critical cultural essays entitled *Einzlheiten*: 'Criticism as it is used here does not want to liquidate or dispatch its objects but it wants to expose them to an alternative view: revision – not revolution – is its purpose.' Five years later, in 1967, Enzensberger wrote in the *Times Literary Supplement* as follows: 'Today we are not engaged in confrontation with Communism but with Revolution. The political system of the Federal Republic is beyond repair. We either live with it or we find a new one to replace it . . . Not the writers but the students were first confronted by this alternative, and they carry their scars.' This was no longer a symptom of an identity crisis of a nonconformist writer, it was a warning and farewell by a writer who had been one of the leading figures.

Thus Enzensberger became the spokesman for the student left which, following the Grand Coalition in 1966, established itself as the extra-parliamentary opposition, since a true and effective parliamentary opposition no longer existed in the *Bundestag*.

In the view of the young left, all literary opposition had really had no effect and this was especially true of Gruppe 47: no matter how 'committed' or 'critical' literary realism was, it could not, in their opinion, transform moral convictions into political action, and it could not mobilize the now-needed resistance against a powerful government operating without opposition. The nonconformist literature had also lost touch with the daily existence of the people. These writers, Peter Schneider stated in 1968, 'silently hoped that the reader, through the portrayal of his personal misery, would be brought to political rage, a rage, which they – the writers – preferred to invest in the sensual literary presentation of that misery'. But: 'Whatever it is that would make the reader react has to be triggered through action.' Schneider, after this, demanded solidarity from the writers instead of individualism, political analyses instead of moralizing; he also required an individualism that grew out of this concrete experience rather than an abstract objectivism striving for literary autonomy. He thus formulated the criticism of literary convention exercised by the practitioners of documentary literature and of 'concrete poetry'; however, in actuality this criticism began to assume a different outlook.

In *The Timetable* (1968) Enzensberger wrote: 'if the most intelligent minds between the ages of 20 and 30 are more concerned with agitation than with experimental texts, if they prefer data collection to picaresque novels, if they no longer care to create fiction or to buy it – these are indeed good signs; but these signs must be understood'. However, West German society did not wish to understand these signs. There was no reaction to the agitation models or to the data collections as offered by the *Timetable* to a predominantly left intelligentsia and to many groups of politicized students.

Rather the mass audience, the workers, who were supposed to be influenced by these positive signs, did not understand them. The whole program of the left was marked for many years by a 'verbose speechlessness', because it could not successfully convey its vague sociopolitical concepts nor did it engage in an accurate description of social reality. The new left became fragmented in its spontaneous activism and assumed sectarian characteristics. Its rebellion, due to its impatience, emerged merely as the revolt of a radical bourgeois minority.

Still, in the long run, the fundamental democratic concepts of the new left had their effects: in the many initiatives and referenda found today at the level of German local government we can see the continuation, in a much less aggressive form, of what the student movement once practiced.

The cultural-revolutionary phase had a more immediate impact on literature than on society or government: by de-literizing literature. To that extent Enzensberger was right: the generation of 20- to 30-year-olds could no longer cope with the old literature, because it neither dealt with that generation's problems *vis-à-vis* the state and society, nor satisfied its secret longings for a world free of conservative materialism. Consequently, its ahistorical radicalism objected to literature in the most abstract manner. Instead of traditional literature, action programs as well as political, psychological, and sociological theories became the substance of literary texts. Next to Marx, Marcuse, and Reich, only Brecht could hold his own as a literary illustrator of theory: he became an idol as did the Marxist theoreticians.

But the ideas of the left did not achieve a new literature. However, they *did* prepare the way for a new literary consciousness: the left forced this literature from the exceptional to everyday life, a development to which many a writer of Gruppe 47 resigned himself.

Thus it was the highly individualistic and nonconformist writer Heinrich Böll, and not an author of the new left, who in 1974 published a book which accurately described the social situation in the Federal Republic: *The Lost Honor of Katherine Blum, How Violence Begins and Where It Can Lead To.* This book and later the film effectively demonstrated the new reflexes of a society which had become insecure due to the dogmatism of the new left and which had been disturbed by the terrorism of a few misguided leftists. It now appeared as if the process of domestic reforms and external détente with East Europe initiated by the Brandt administration in 1969 only covered over the authoritarian social structure which had developed during the first twenty years of the Federal Republic, and was unable to bring about any deep-seated changes. The experience with terrorism made the old patterns of thinking in German society appear stronger than they actually were. Nevertheless, a comparison between the conservative 1950s and the more relaxed 1970s shows that the liberalization triggered by the anti-authoritarian student movement and consolidated in the Brandt era did succeed. At any rate, Böll's story describes accurately a government and a media which perceived themselves as pluralist, and yet were unable to differentiate between groups within society and evaluate them individually. The story conveys the prevalent climate of coldness, alienation, terror, and impersonality.

5

In 1973 Ingeborg Drewitz wrote in the first issue of *Literaturmagazin*: 'The literary output in the Federal Republic today is even more diverse than ten years ago.' Indeed, today's literature is not characterized by a homogeneity such as that found in the early Gruppe 47. And what should such a homogeneous self-image consist of? After so much destruction, after so much denunciation of literature by the new left, as well as by a public made insecure by that left, and after this literature had become separated from certain individuals whose output no longer coincided with reality or who denied it the character of literature because it had wanted to be the pure reality – was it not obvious that even the writers needed to start afresh after such fundamental soul-searching? Did they not need to start with their own experiences, their own immediate environment?

Hiltrud Gnüg's remarks concerning poetry today

applied as well to the general literary scene: 'Every belief in the transcendental powers of the poetic work has disappeared, withdrawal into metaphysics is blocked, what remains is the acceptance of reality as it exists and this reality is characterized by the domination of political pragmatism, a combination of technological, economic, and political rationalism.' This is the reality of a cold world in which the absence of literature and culture shows a great lack of opportunities for the creation of identity. 'Renunciation of culture also means renouncing those aids that help the individual shape the world and himself in it' wrote Hazel E. Hazel in *Literaturmagazin* no. 4 of 1975, devoted to the topic 'Literature after the death of literature'.

In reaction to the times a trend toward subjectivism now appears in the literature of the 1970s. This subjectivism is tied closely to a pronounced autobiographical orientation. Thus in Peter Handke's writings, including *The Hour of Recognition*, we find an increasing preoccupation with private perceptions similar to Hubert Fichte's prose of the late 1960s, which confronted a standard public reality with a repressed reality of the social outsiders. This autobiographical subjectivism also appears in Karin Struck's novel *Class Love*, although *there* it is still searching, untouched by literary standardization of individuality, and it is enthusiastically endorsed as the first sign of a new literary expressiveness. Somewhat less efficacious publicly but even more radical that Karin Struck, Herbert Achternbusch is gaining recognition as an individualist in both his books and his films.

There are more names that can be added: Nicolas and F. C. Delius, Peter Schneider, Jürgen Theobaldy, Hugo Dittberner, and so on. Each of these authors has a special message, with the common denominator that they want to subject the reader to the very same level of subjective consciousness from which they have obtained their own unique social identity. By communicating in this way these writers want to obtain a warmth and closeness beyond their own private domain, rejecting a literature clothed in the aura of the exceptional, since that kind of literature only serves to obscure reality. Instead, they want to make the reader the subject, that is, to help him find his identity which has been left behind in the coldness of social reality. Literature in this new sense remains tied to reality – as a sphere of experience and a potential for protest. 'The poem', Theobaldy once said, 'has to divorce itself from poetic prophecy – the poets should bring the poems back to the level of everyday life, which most of them know best; they should make their poems relate again to the seemingly profane problems of life and deal with the ordinary objects that surround them day and night . . . The poet puts himself on the line, he opens up the sensual experience needed for social change which, after all, does not occur just to provide empirical evidence for a few Marxist–Leninist ideas.'

Theobaldy's statement is applicable not only to poetry or internationally recognized literature. It has, in fact, already been realized – in the form of a second literature. We now have a women's literature, a prison literature, a homosexual literature, and so on. This is target group literature which addresses itself to the problems of specific groups. It is not theory, but literature itself, that will raise the consciousness of individuals not belonging to the accepted groups of society. It appears that young people have at last become more receptive to literature – not to a literature that floats in splendid isolation above society, but to a literature that immerses itself in everyday life, in the trials and tribulations of that society.

Hence a new literary concept does exist, and it has a name: new subjectivity. The writers who are thus classified have only made a beginning. And they are individuals, notwithstanding attempts to group them under a common term.

In 1977 Helmut Heissenbüttel coined the term 'open literature' (in *TEXT + KRITIK-Yearbook* for 1977). His definition also encompasses the 'new subjectivity':

Openness, first of all, means recognition of alternatives and an unbiased attitude toward them. Openness also means not to be committed to only one point of view. Openness means keeping open the channels for discussion.

In literature, to be open means unconditional self-discovery and, with regard to social-political discussion, unrestrained, uncensored writing. Openness demands that literature should not be written according to prescribed, traditional patterns but rather must experimentally explore the limits of contemporary language and communication. 'Open literature' – this term does not want to be a new slogan, but it wants to characterize a situation.

One facet of this situation is to acknowledge the historical fact that the era of representative styles and programs, the era of linear development, in which one fashion unfolds from another, is over.

I gladly accept this definition of literature. I consider it to be realistic. As a consequence, my own attempt to explain the disintegration of a representative literature as resulting from specific literary and political developments could be only partially successful. It also had to be rather unfair, because the attempt to chart currents in litetarure necessitates systematization. This method, in trying to define certain literary trends, often fails to mention those names which have not yet become part of the literary canon.

Therefore, in the final analysis, writing about literature proves to be just another subjective approach within the subjective diversity of literary expression.

PART THREE

Culture and Change

Introduction to Part Three

The concern with the nature, pattern, and effects of social and cultural change that surfaced in the commentaries on the civilization of advanced industrialism provides the central theme of cultural criticism in the societies of Mediterranean Europe as well. The structural reason for this orientation of cultural thought is obvious: the societies of the Iberian peninsula, Italy, and Greece have undergone with intensity and strain, in the postwar period, the pains of profound changes in several spheres of their collective experience. While their more socioeconomically advanced neighbors to the north-west were making the transition to post-industrial society and its culture of leisure, the societies of Mediterranean Europe lived through the changes that displaced the timeless vestiges of medieval culture, transformed the traditional agrarian traits marking their larger segments, and introduced in their bosom the structural and cultural characteristics of modernity. The most dramatic expression of the strains of this transformation in southern Europe came, of course, in politics. The perennial crisis of the Italian parliamentary system, the troubles of democratic government in Greece, and the struggle against the dictatorships which for several decades attempted to pre-empt or to arrest the political effects of social change in Spain and Portugal represent so many signs of this interrelationship.

Within this context, cultural life was faced with several conflicting options. It could dilute the impact of the pressures for change by flying from the problems of the real world and retreating into an idealist aestheticism that ultimately bordered on irrelevance; or it could accomplish the same effect by reducing to transient fashions the substantive claims for cultural innovation stirring a changing society. Alternatively, culture in its various forms could respond directly to the experiences of its social environment by registering pressing social concerns and by recasting into the language of symbolic expression the aspirations and vicissitudes of the struggle for political change. In this case ideological conflict with those espousing opposing causes became an integral part of the cultural experience. Out of this engagement, however, emerged a real possibility of cultural revitalization, the opening of new horizons of creativity and a sense of new strength deriving from the feeling of relevance and belonging to one's community and sharing in its destinies.

The temper of cultural life in Spain and Greece as discussed in the essays by Antonio Bar and Dimitris Maronites was shaped in the three decades from the mid-1940s to the mid-1970s by the experiences of the struggle against political and social oppression in its many forms. Direct involvement in political action in which the representatives of cultural creation often found themselves, as Maronites points out in interpreting the political ethic of postwar Greek poetry, provided a decisive precondition of cultural creation. In the cases of both Greece and Spain, cultural creativity and cultural criticism registered the alteration of feelings of expectancy and disappointment generated by the struggle for democratic politics.

The clear-cut issues of freedom versus oppression and traditionalist reaction versus human progress that demarcated the parameters of cultural choice in Spain and Greece – and, of course, in Portugal – were and remain more complicated in Italy where the needs of social and cultural change have been felt with equal intensity but the practice of liberal democratic politics obscured, in many instances, the targets of cultural criticism. It is true that the inadequate responsiveness of Italian liberalism to the country's basic needs and the consequent persisting pressures of unresolved social and cultural problems have fueled a remarkable tradition of radical social and cultural criticism which, inspired by the theoretical legacy of Antonio Gramsci, has distinguished itself with its originality, sophistication, and lucidity. These traits, which are due to the concrete practical problems that inform Italian theoretical explorations, clearly mark out this tradition of criticism from its counterparts elsewhere in Europe.

This achievement, however, itself a response to certain basic problems in Italian culture and thought, has not remedied a basic problem in Italy's cultural temper discussed here by Umberto Eco. He is concerned with the dilution of cultural issues and outlooks, with their reduction to fashionable trends that stir for a while the surface of cultural life but after their disappearance leave things as they were before. In thus directing attention to the problem of transient trends in Italian cultural fashions, Eco is essentially pointing to the issue of substantive cultural innovation and the obstacles it encounters in Italian society. He thus returns to the persisting problematic of change typical of progressive Mediterranean social thought.

10

UMBERTO ECO

The Modes of Cultural Fashion in Italy

The national game of cultivated Italians is composed of three moves, played by 'Dottor Bianchi' against 'Dottor Neri' (for maximum precision on the dynamic of the 'games' see Eric Berne, *Games People Play*; you will understand shortly why I rush to cite my source of inspiration: otherwise, as Neri, the author, I would be victim to the second move of Bianchi, the reader.

First move
Neri: 'People like that should be killed!'
Bianchi: 'The usual Italian provincialism. In England, it is at least ten years since homicide was proven useless. If you would read . . .'
Second move
Neri: 'I have reconsidered. I believe that no human being should be killed.'
Bianchi: 'What you say is no big deal. Gandhi has already said it.'
Third move
Neri: 'Very well, I think Gandhi was right.'
Bianchi: 'I knew it. Now we have the fashion of pacifism.'

There is an endless number of variations on this theme. (1) 'Children should not read comic books.' 'You are mistaken, if you were up on recent American sociological research . . .' (2) 'OK. I have read them myself and don't find them so bad.' 'It doesn't seem to be such a great discovery: forty years ago Gilbert Seldes in *Seven Lively Arts* . . .' (3) 'Very well, I agree with Seldes . . .' 'I knew it! Now we have the fashion of comics!

Or: (1) 'In *Promessi Sposi* lyric openings are kept in check by an unpoetical structure.' 'You are mistaken: if you read the American studies on narrative structure . . .' (2) 'I have reconsidered. Plot has poetic value.' 'That we know: Aristotle (already) knew that.' (3) 'Agreed. Did you know that he was right?' 'I knew it! Now everyone is an Aristotelian.'

This game is not a fiction. If there is anything that strikes the foreign speaker in one of our cultural circles it is the objection that that which he is saying was already said by someone else. Usually the foreigner does not understand why this should bother him. What he does not know is that as soon as he has left anyone who agrees with his opinions will be accused of conformism. After three attempts, any Italian fan of his will be unable to cite him again.

There is no escape from this game, insofar as it is based upon three indisputable logical-anthropological principles, namely, (1) for every statement made in one place one can find a contrary statement made previously elsewhere; (2) for every statement made in any given era there exists a piece of pre-Socratic work that preceded it; (3) any statement of agreement with a thesis expressed by others renders their opinions definable as 'derivative' or 'conformist'.

The national game that we have just defined makes Italians particularly sensitive to that danger commonly called 'cultural fashion'. Anxious to be up to date and severe with those who are not, Italians tend to regard as pathetic any idea springing from other people's updating and to condemn as mere fashion the very updating that they themselves strive for. Since the anxiety of updating exposes them to the risk of fashion, their severity towards others' updating acts as a corrective, rendering these updatings rapid and transitory, and therefore 'fashion'. As a consequence, it is difficult to create cultural currents and movements because the Bianchis scrutinize the Neris, stimulating the rotation of their choices, each Bianchi becoming in his turn a Neri for someone else who was a Neri in his time. The anxiety of updating unites in fear of fashion and thereby neutralizes the updating and encourages fashion.

This situation would have a tightrope-walking quality, and the not ignoble grace of a permanent ballet of critical intelligence, were it not for the fact that the development of mass media has introduced a new element into the game: the presence of Italians who follow soccer.

Stimulated by the rapid and popular circulation of pictorial magazines and daily newspapers, Italians interested in soccer have come to know the game played by the upper class. Of this game they play only some, and not all of the positions, so that they perform the cycle of ignorance-information-consensus-fashion-rejection only in part. In a certain sense they enter the game only at move number 3, when player Neri agrees with a dominant thesis expressed by others, and they focus on this discovery, losing view of the fact that the scene player, acted by Bianchi, repentantly abandons the thesis and plays another game. As a consequence, in the lower classes fashions last longer (for example, linguistic trends, idiomatic expressions, and topics of argument) than in the ruling classes (it still being true that the divisions between the ruling class and the proletariat follow along lines that do not necessarily correspond with economic reality).

This is why it could be interesting to follow, along the arc of a decade, the birth, the life, the decomposition of a series of cultural fashions. Their permanence is demonstrated by frivolities, quotations, and journalistic aberrations of various kinds; their death demonstrates the volubility of the learned players, their unfortunate incapacity to stimulate suggestions and ideas, lines of research, topics, and problems.

Of particular interest, then, will be to follow this adventure, as we are doing, along a decade, that (to use the by now famous formula of Arbastivo) of the outing to Chiasso. A provincial Italian culture, that during fascism rationalized its own timidity by accusing the dictator who restricted contact with what was happening outside (and we update: it is not even necessary to arrive at Chiasso to know what has been published abroad. Gramsci in prison managed to read plenty), in the first ten years after the liberation continues to cultivate its own guilt feelings, but as it approaches the 1960s suddenly immerses itself in its own updating and forces its own children, from the columns of its own cultural pages, with the printing presses of its hard-cover editions, in its news-stands bloated with paperbacks. Discoveries become excitements, excitements linguistic habits, linguistic habits idioms, idioms absurdities.

The dark episode of the word 'alienation' demonstrates our point: a venerable term, a terrible reality, a cultural datum that the scholars manipulate among themselves without difficulty, suddenly becomes popular currency. Usage develops the muscle, but it weakens the word. The word that we are examining was abused, but it is good that someone pointed out the excess. But the fear of excess has also closed the mouths of those who could use the term calmly and wisely. I know a student of philosophy who for some years had been working on a thesis on Marx's concept of alienation, and who between 1961 and 1962 was forced to change the title of his own research in order to be taken seriously. But in other cases someone decisively changed not only the title but the argument. This is what is sad.

I don't know if we will succeed in correcting our behavior. Here is another example that occurs to me as I re-read this essay.

A lengthy conversation with a friend whom I had not seen for a long time, now a professor at a small provincial university, absorbed in problems of classical philology but aware of 'fashionable' cultural events – with detachment, naturally, a shade of irony, but always with intellectual tension. I tell him that I have met Roman Jakobson in America. Smiling he says, 'Too late. Just now that they are destroying him . . .' 'Who is destroying him?' 'But everyone. He is over the hill, isn't he?'

OK. Jakobson was born in the last century. He participated in the Moscow Circle, passed through the revolution, arrived in Prague, lived through the 1930s, survived Nazism, initiated the American adventure, survived the war, confronted the new structuralist generation and was acclaimed a master, survived the youngest of the new generation, survived well into his seventies, survived the new school of Slavic, French, and American semiotics of which he remains a leader, leaving each experience with the unanimous recognition of international culture. He made mistakes − to be sure − but survived them all. Alas, cited in Italy in 1964, read in 1965, translated in 1966, the decline of 1967 failed to survive the erosion of Italian intelligence. *Quod non fecerunt barbari etcetera.* Three years of renown in Italy ripped him apart. In order to still believe the validity of his words one must be very young, very ingenuous, very secluded, and very non-Italian. Now we must try to make Chomsky old-fashioned as fast as we can, possibly before he is translated (if the game is played right the blow will succeed, in time). These are difficult tasks, but well worth the personal satisfaction.

One need not be a high priest of knowledge to recognize that the birth and diffusion of a cultural fashion lead to misinterpretation, confusion, and illegitimate use. We deplore cultural fashion. All who have seriously confronted an argument that then became a fashion have felt the uneasiness deriving from the fact that every word that they would have used would not have been interpreted according to the context in which it appeared, but rather waved like a flag, a label, a road sign.

It is absolutely and sadly true that today not even a scientist of construction can speak of structure without passing as a structuralist *à la page*. It is nevertheless in the indignation over fashion that there is something so immodest and snobbish (move number 3 of the proposed game) as to be as destructive as fashion itself.

'Fashions' are not born when there is a rigorous class culture or a rigorously specialized one. A class culture permits themes and problems to circulate at a level unattainable to most: the tastes of the Duke of Berry are not fashion, but for the fact that they appear at the top of a unique manuscript copy; no one will think to print the images of the months on *foulards* for miniskirt-wearers.

A specialized culture defends itself by its impenetrability. The word 'relativity' could have induced a certain fad, but the equations of Maxwell could not.

The problem of fashion is born therefore when, for various reasons, a cultural idea travels from the top to the bottom (meaning every popularizing technique, from the wallposter to the weekly to television). Popularization drafts new users into the culture, bringing them closer to it, but paying for this draft with waste and conscription. The terms and concepts that circulate pass through too many hands to be able to return to the summit of the pyramid from which they left − intact as they were.

Contemporaneously, the excess of specialization imposes a tendency toward interdisciplinarity. Interdiciplinarity means contact and comprehension among men who work in diverse sectors of specialization. This contact is performed in two ways. First of all the technician of one sector needs to make clear to the technician of another the sense of his own discourse, and the borders of his own universe of discourse; in the second place, both must attempt to translate the valid elements of their own discourse into terms that can be assimilated into the universe of discourse elsewhere. In this 'pouring off' (in which the entire culture collaborates) much is spilled on the ground. The attempts to translate generate hurried, misunderstood, strained metaphors in the apparent updating. As in the popularization from the summit to the base, so does this spreading from sector to sector of the same level produce inflation.

But if this is true, cultural fashions are the consequences of a dynamism of culture. To the degree to which it is vital, allowing a revision and continued communication between its various levels, a culture produces a fashion for each of the aspects which it exhibits. It is not that fashion is only the chaff or waste on the fringes of an authentic cultural process, but it forms at the same time the dung, the fertile ground. Since delivery and dispersion of knowledge do not come by absolutely pure means, he who learns or translates in terms for learning elsewhere often passes first across the territory of cultural fashion, seeing a problem in aberrant form before grasping it in its exact form; cultural fashion is so essential to the process of a culture that often it is only through the recall of fashion that a culture recruits its future leaders.

Therefore, in the face of fashions that it generates, a culture need not so much seek to repress them as to control them. The function of a culture is to produce both specialized knowledge and spontaneous and diffuse knowledge; and – in criticizing the excesses of spontaneous knowledge – not only to repress it but to allow it to generate connections, opportunities, other specialized knowledge, in a more or less coordinated movement in which misunderstanding often becomes serendipity. Of one thing we can be sure, that a culture that does not generate fashion is a static culture. There were not and are not fashions in Hopi or Alorese culture. Because there is no creative process. Cultural fashion is the teenage acne of the cultural process. When it is repressed too violently, it merely accelerates the coming of a new fashion. Thus, cultural fashion as a permanent model becomes the most visible aspect of that culture, which becomes the Culture of Alternating Fashions. This is our problem today. We should not worry because we have cultural fashions, but because they change too quickly.

French culture, which is more mature than ours, has been supporting the structuralist fashion for ten years, and is not ashamed of it, though aware of its excesses. That which is disturbing in Italian culture is not the thousands of imbeciles who fill their mouths with the word 'structure' in the most irrelevant circumstances, but rather the knowledge that these imbeciles will be massacred so soon and so viciously. Undervaluing the bacterial function (in the botanical sense) of these imbeciles is a sign of cultural immaturity.

On the other hand, if a culture that does not generate fashions is a static culture, a culture that represses fashions is a reactionary one. The first move of the conservative is to label any novelty 'fashion': Aristofani with Socratism, Cicero with the *cantones Euphorionis*, and so forth until the indignation of the *omini salvatici* (wildmen) of Papinian and Giuliottian memory.

Provided that it is long, a fashion returns the rigor that it had taken in another form. The danger is when it is short.

11

D. N. MARONITES

The Poetic and Political Ethic of Postwar Greek Poetry

I Post War Poetry: Poetic Praxis and Political Participation

The day after tomorrow marks the second anniversary of the events at the Athens Polytechnic,* which automatically became myth in order to avoid the tentacles of easy history. In the meantime, the culprits mock the spilled blood and the tardy allies sermonize, while the voice of those killed whistles in the air with a wrathful silence. However, all these incongruous happenings do not abolish the practical debt. The following piece of writing wishes to be an indirect contribution to such an offering, in order to keep alive the memory of a massacre that has stamped the forehead of today's student generation.

Sometimes we forget that today's student generation are the children of another generation (perhaps the most sorely tried one of twentieth-century Greece), those who survived the Second World War, the occupation, and the civil carnage. This earlier generation is weighed down by its enthusiasms and struggles, hopes and illusions, killings, and a voice that became murky seeking literalness. These essays wish to comment upon this

---

*This essay was first published in the Athens daily *To Vema* on 15 November 1975. The anniversary to which it refers commemorates the bloody suppression of the student rising at the Athens Polytechnic by the tanks of the military junta on 17 November 1973. [*Eds*]

coarse voice, whose pulse was taken by poetic praxis in the midst of political participation.

I am talking about our postwar poetry, positing a conventional starting point in the year 1939, when the Second World War broke out. It is not easy to review such a recent poetical period, about which our critics are so summary, even when they dare devote a few lines to it. However, the attempt is worth the effort, both for the reasons stated in my introduction as well as for the following additional ones.

Without the support of established criticism, we are obliged to draw upon our own personal taste, our own poetic inclination. And this axiological daring, no matter how subjective, measures our judgement more definitively than our agreement with, or opposition to, established opinion concerning an already known poet. It is precisely for this reason that poets who continue to write today but earned their critical reputations in the prewar period, such as Seferis, Elytis, Engonopoulos, Embeirikos, even Ritsos, fall outside the framework of this essay.

Further, with the postwar poets we find ourselves extremely close to our personal experiences. In their case, the relation between poetry and current life is immediate, and not second-hand. The same holds true for the poets themselves: they are circulating among us, some of them are friends of ours, and this compression of distances prevents the growth of a mythical influence, which the prewar poets still exert upon us. How, then, does our critical judgement function when the poetic material is the stuff of our personal experience, and the poets sheltered in the same house as we? I proceed.

Postwar poetry is differentiated from the previous poetic generation in a number of ways. I have selected the following distinguishing characteristics, whose combination leads perhaps to the recognition of a poetic form.

(1) There is a larger volume of poetry in the postwar than in the previous period.

(2) The postwar poets have a different scale of values. In the postwar period nobody asks who is first, second, or third in the poetical generation, whether Anagnostakis surpasses Sachtouris, or Sinopoulos Anagnostakis. Schematically I would say that in place of an aristocratic scale of values the laws of an incipient poetic democracy have been established.

(3) The preceding proposition implies a third characteristic of our postwar poetry. The reading public refers now much less to the poets themselves and more to their poems. It distinguishes mature poems, and not mature poets. It makes a selection of poems, and not a choice of poets.

(4) Most of the postwar poets have been more deeply involved in the political affairs of the country than their predecessors. A result of this political (often even partisan) participation is the abolition of the aesthetic dilemma of the previous generation: engaged or non-engaged art. The most important postwar poets are directly or indirectly political poets, and the majority inhabit the territory of the modern Greek left: they are following its adventures and vacillations from the inside. Very often, indeed, our postwar political poets are forced to make a connection between their personal poetic sensibility and the partisan orthodoxy of the environment they defend politically. And this connection is not at all simple. Sonetimes it becomes truly dramatic; at the least it implies new and difficult problems for poetry as well as politics. This is how, I believe, the deeper nature of postwar poetry emerged: in other words its particular poetic and political ethic. It is precisely this poetic-political ethic that I would like to approach: its style, its means of expression, its dimensions, the political and poetic problems it creates, its poetic allusions.

Indeed, this last subject (the poetic allusions of our postwar poetry) can be broken down into some questions of general interest.

(1) If didacticism is an inevitable, basic element of political poetry, it is valuable to investigate the references our postwar poets use to exercise their didactic role. I mean, to which older, Greek or foreign, poetical examples do they refer? I do not believe that it is by chance that the clearest allusion in this respect is to Cavafy, of course to the didactic Cavafy (cf. the later Ritsos, the later Alexandrou, etc.). However, in other poets, such as Anagnostakis or Sinopoulos, what is the origin of their didactic allusions, when they exist?

(2) A similar question can be asked about a second element of political poetry – that which could be called poetic rhetoric. From where do our postwar poets borrow poetic rhetoric, and how do they transform it? From Palamas? From Sikelianos? From Varnalis?

(3) Finally, in order to complete the trinity: a third basic ingredient of political poetry is, I think, critical satire, muted or overt. On this level, what are the reference points of our postwar poets? The satirical Karyotakis? The satirical Cavafy? The satirical Varnalis?

Here we must end the introduction to a difficult but timely subject: for sometimes responsible discourse is required even more than responsible action.

II The Ancestors and the New Generation of Postwar Poetry

I brought up the subject of the postwar poetical generation underlining, primarily, two of its most salient features: (*a*) the participation of its chief representatives in the politics of the era in which they came of age (war, occupation, resistance, liberation, civil war); (*b*) the hatching of a new poetic ethic resulting from the intertwining of poetic praxis and political activity. The functional blending of poetry and politics brings forth new problems for poetry as well as politics – and these comments wish to register these problems. In the meantime, we need to retrace postwar poetry in its opening moves.

In a lecture in January 1970 Alekos Argyriou tried to summarize the relevant matter and his conclusions under the revealing title 'Our first postwar poetic generation'. His information and assessments support to a great degree my own observations and proposals.

(1) The year 1939, the outbreak of the Second World War, can be considered the beginning of our postwar poetry. Its first landmark is 1946, a critical transitional stage from liberation and the events of December 1944 toward the civil war, and a signpost for the already public presence of the first postwar group of poets.

(2) By 1939 the generation of the 1930s has completed its first cycle based on French metasymbolism, French surrealism, and Anglo-Saxon modernistic poetry (Eliot, Pound). At the same time the upcoming postwar generation, despite its youth, constitutes the most awakened and supportive – as well as critical – reading public of these poems. And yet interwar criticism still stood embarrassed and conservative.

(3) Neither in its beginning movements nor in its mature moments was postwar poetry granted critical assessment commensurate with its form and material. It never had to answer in a syllogistic manner rather than by dictum the question: are we talking about poets of the postwar era who are the mere descendants of the generation of the 1930s and who moreover tend to be absorbed by their prolific forerunner, Yiannis Ritsos? Or perhaps their physiognomy exhibits such distinctive genealogical characteristics that they constitute a new current in the history of our poetry?

This question will remain unanswered until preliminary work is completed and thus permits its definitive answer – the fragmentary essays of Argyriou, Dallas, Thasites, Nora Anagnostakis, and others younger than the above constitute only the beginning of this preliminary work. For now, therefore, it is indispensable at least to question in good faith and to collect information.

Argyriou's lecture, to which I referred above, lists about twenty names that appear between 1939 and 1946 forming the early framework of postwar poetry. Fifteen survive, and among them one recognizes easily the strong and creative forerunners. In order of appearance the fifteen poets are: Andreas Kambas, Nanos Valaorites, and G. Dallas (1939), Manolis Anagnostakis and Ares Alexandrou (1941), Takis Sinopoulos (1943), Helen Vakalo, Miltos Sachtouris, Dimitris Papaditsas, Hector Kaknavatos, and A. Nikolaides (1944), Th. Frangopoulos, George Gavalas, Michael Katsaros, and Tasos Lavadites (1946).

Eight of these fifteen poets appear immediately or very early on as conduits of extremely political poetry. The other seven attempt a poetic manner that comments upon the concrete political juncture with the measures of a local existential agony, thus creating a special climate of domestic political existentialism.

A characteristic of this poetic group is the early age at which its poets are first published: on average 20 years, ranging from 18 to 26. We have to deal, therefore, with a poetic generation in a hurry to express itself – events and its own experiences are pressing upon it.

In the matter of style, free verse and the free system of stanzas dominate for the entire group. Wherever the traditional system of stanzas and rhyme survives (in the first writings of Anagnostakis, Dallas, Nikolaides) we have to deal with their clear satirical abuse.

Furthermore, the renunciation by this group of the associations of pure surrealism and formalistic acrobatics is impressive. The seriousness of empirical matter dictates, obviously, a more solid poetic form, which is expressed basically through the poetic vocabulary of Seferis. It is intensely imbued with Cavafian and Karyotakian memories as well as new personal tones: realistic literalness, poetic prosaism, paranoid clarity.

In all these cases we have to cope with early efforts which, if not innocent of looseness and often paratactic articulation, do consciously avoid lyrical sentimentality and above all change, I would say, the focal distance between the poet and the empirical stuff on its way to become a poem. We are no longer dealing with the distance of observation that dominated in interwar poetry and even in the generation of the 1930s. Now this distance of observation has been abolished and its place is taken by a painful participation of the poet in a concrete event. From this change issues forth the intense character of familiarity that these poetical early writings exude.

In almost no case among these early efforts do we certify an elevated militant or heroic tone. On the contrary, all of them or almost all of them are characterized by a latent or manifest dynamic pessimism, sometimes coordinated with satirical rage, at other times with political thoughtfulness, and in rarer cases with muted *Angst*.

III Epilogue and Prologue of a Puzzlement

Researching the era of our postwar poetry (the first postwar generation) and recognizing as its basic characteristic the weaving of political praxis and poetic participation (what I called a poetic and political ethic), it was my ambition to pinpoint in brief, in the thirty-year period between 1940 and 1970, at least the most important laborers who provoked me into this task.

I do not claim that the material I commented upon corroborated in full the characteristics which early on I had ascribed to the first postwar poetic generation, that is, democratic prolixity, sapping of the personal hierarchy, the significance of poetry as an X-ray with regard to our postwar leftist movement, and so on. Nor that some crucial questions were answered definitively, such as the status of successors pertaining or not to this generation, the weight of their predecessor Ritsos, Greek and foreign sources of their didacticism, oratory, satirical criticism, and so forth. However, I do hope that something fell on both these scales. In any case, what interests me more now at the end of this essay is the unanticipated harvest from this political and poetic ethic which I tried to define: the trial of time, which in this case begins with a foreshadowing movement, then hovers somewhere in the middle over a political or partisan void,

and finally oscillates back to the search for a lost geography of the human; the establishment of a scale from the individual to the circle of friends and from the circle of friends to the organized whole, a scale that makes possible the critical interpolation of the specific personal adventure into the cold space of historical conformism; the transformation of the erotic into a political pathology and vice versa; the clear agony about the closure of the poetic triangle, whose base is formed by the commands of a specific political praxis and the ethos of a specific poem; the function of a communal banquet table of lines and motifs; the collection finally of all these elements into a series of poetic signs. I give an account of all this material with the regret that I did not work with it as long and in the manner that I should have.

I like the idea of this epilogue's becoming simultaneously the prologue for a new search. To account for the paradox, let us say that the new puzzlement grew like a tail on the rear of a disappearing animal, or turned into horns that the animal rubs until they bleed. Leaving aside metaphors and similes, I proceed with its first very provisional formulation, which concerns precisely the relations among plain language, metaphor, and simile in the language of our poetry. My curiosity grew out of a recent study of our postwar political poetry and its ties to what is called realism, giving to the term its widest significance. It would take me too far afield to define here scientifically and with examples the concepts and the functions of 'plain language–metaphor–simile' as factors of poetic language, when this distinction is controversial and incomprehensible even in common linguistic usage. I proceed therefore to the hasty presentation of my suspicion, taking for granted that *grosso modo* we understand one another to mean concerning the conceptual and functional content of these three crucial terms.

I do not know if it is solely the Greek version of the romanticism of the Athenian school which bequeaths to Palamas the habit (*a*) of seeking the precise word in its rarest and most unused form while avoiding the hackneyed expression; (*b*) of taking for granted the confessed latent or silenced precise term in a given poem, and of joining to this the metaphor or simile as a lingustic element that is unexpected but, in the final analysis, ornamental; in other words, not directly endowing with name, which means: the metaphor or the simile does not in the first instance name things that we do not yet know, that lack therefore their precise term, but supplants, complements, or decorates an already invented precise name.

If I am right that this linguistic tactic is consolidated in Palamas, then it is, I think, worth the pains to ask (a) which poets continue this tactic and in which developmental stage do we recognize it in our postwar political poetry? (b) which poets combat the first time this functional schema of poetic language, what counter-proposals do they make, and what influence do their proposals have up until our own day?

Of course I cannot here give extensive answers to all these difficult questions. I am stimulated, however, and I hope to stimulate, by proposing as a possible continuation of the Palamaic linguistic tactic in this respect the line Sikelianos–Elytis–Ritsos (partially), to mention only major names of our poetry, thus bridging the interwar and the postwar periods. As far as the second question is concerned, I am almost certain that the person who, consciously or unconsciously, subverts the Palamaic function of precision-metaphor-simile in our modern poetry is Cavafy, and that his most consistent successor in this direction is Seferis. Why Seferis must be considered the perpetuator of Cavafy in this respect, and which post-war poets inherit this inverted scale, may for the time

being remain open questions. As regards Cavafy, however, I owe an elementary explanation, so that the working hypothesis I propose may not be hanging in the void.

It is not only trite precision that strikes us in Cavafy; nor the quantitatively extremely limited use of metaphor and simile. In my opinion, what is of greater interest is when and how Cavafy uses, and indeed in a limiting manner, the system of metaphor and simile. I believe that this happens where we come across real gaps of precision. In other words: when Cavafy transposes or compares meanings; this he does in order to name experimentally things that still lack titles and relations that have not yet been accounted for. Which means that, in Cavafy, metaphor as well as simile functions in the area of poetic expression, as long as the precise term has not yet been invented. And to construct a further paradox: the metaphoric and analogical use of poetic language in Cavafy has as its final goal the sought-for precise term.

I stop here. I promised to stimulate, not to begin describing, a new thematic cycle. Only a final question-proposal: does not the realistic exactness of our postwar poetry depend in the end on whether it follows the Cavafian or Palamaic tradition?*

*The Palamaic tradition refers to the stylistic heritage and influence of the Greek poet Kostes Palamas (1859–1943) on modern Greek poetry, from which the Alexandrian Constantine Cavafy was the first to depart. The modernist school, broadly speaking, has attempted to emancipate the Greek poetic tradition from the Palamaic heritage. [Eds]

12

ANTONIO BAR

Spain: A Culture in Transition

If present-day Spanish culture had to be defined in one word, then that word would be crisis. An awareness of crisis, a lack of orientation, a certain inferiority complex in the face of some foreign intellectual production, and even an identity crisis, which causes many to wonder whether an authentic Spanish culture really does exist, are all phenomena that are clearly perceived in the intellectual work of many Spanish thinkers and writers.[1] Without necessarily accepting or rejecting the premiss that today's Spanish culture really is in such a prostrate and void situation, what can now be said is that this situation is not new. On the contrary, one could say that the crisis of Spanish culture is, in fact, in its final moment, for now there can be perceived an obvious recuperation from the traumas inflicted by General Franco's long and harsh dictatorship, the main cause of this crisis.

Indeed, to make a valid analysis of present-day Spanish culture one must refer back to Francoism and consider the impact that the three years of bloody civil war and almost forty years of absolute dictatorship had upon the natural development of all the intellectual and artistic production of the Spanish people.[2]

The end of the Spanish Civil War and the consequent establishment of the Francoist regime signified the virtual decapitation of Spanish culture, driving not only the country's elite, but also what could be considered culture's middle sectors, into exile, if not to their deaths; that is, Francoism severely affected not only the creation of culture but also its propagation. Without attempting to formulate a list of names, which would unfortunately be too long, one can give examples of the most notable cases of those persons who already enjoyed a certain amount of international renown when they had to leave Spain, or who acquired it during their exile in countries that allowed them to develop and flourish intellectually. Such are the cases of the poets Juan Ramón Jiménez, Antonio Machado, or Rafael Alberti, the novelists Max Aub or Ramón J. Sender, the philosophers José Gaos, Juán García Bacca, or José Ferrater Mora, the scientists José Trueta or Severo Ochoa, musicians such as Pablo Casals, architects such as José L. Sert, and many others from all fields of culture.[3] It has been calculated that at the end of the civil war, in 1939, some 118 university professors, 200 secondary education teachers, and 2,000 general school teachers had to flee Spain,[4] which meant a loss of virtually 90 per cent of the country's intelligentsia.

But to this problem of external exile one should also add what has been referred to in Spain as 'internal' exile, which was suffered by that small group of intellectuals who were not resolute sympathizers of the new regime, but who either did not leave the country at the end of the civil war, or, having left it, soon returned home. Such were the cases of the philosopher José Ortega y Gasset, the writer Dámaso Alonso, or the painter Juan Miró, to mention only three intellectuals from very different fields, all of whom suffered to different extents from the ostracism that independent creativity was subjected to by the Francoist regime, above all during its first period. In general, one senses that the Francoist regime merely fulfilled the premisses that lay deep within the ominous cry that the rebel General Millán Astray uttered in the old University of Salamanca in October 1936, following an intervention by the rector, Miguel de Unamuno: *'¡Muera la inteligencia!'* ('Let intelligence die!').[5]

After this terrible blow, the history of the last forty years of Spanish culture is solely the history of a colossal attempt to refill a virtually unfillable void. It is the history of a tremendously slow recuperation along a path pitted with almost unsurmountable obstacles, such as the burden of the official 'culture' and ideology, the total lack of means, and a censorship that controlled everything: sex, religion, and politics. Only after General Franco's death and the definitive establishment of democracy and basic liberties could that recuperation process intensify. And it is still in progress today.

But, on this difficult path of cultural recuperation, Spain had to go through different stages, determined by the political, social, and economic events in the country, which had a decisive influence upon the intellectual and artistic work of those Spaniards living there.[6] For this reason, I feel it is necessary to break this process down into different periods in which we can relate the cultural phenomena to the social, political, and economic conditions in which they are found in such a way that those phenomena may be more comprehensible and explicable. Using the sociopolitical and economic events as a guide, I would divide the history of Spain in the last forty years into the following periods:

(1) 1939–51. This is the postwar period, as much civil (1939–45) as world (1945–51), when Spain lives, especially from 1945 onwards, in real and absolute isolation. It is the period that has been termed autarchic.

(2) 1951–6. This is the period in which, following the outbreak of the Cold War, the Spanish authorities try to take advantage of their role as leaders of anti-communism to break out of their isolation and seek economic advantages from joining the reconstruction process taking place in Europe.

(3) 1957–62. This is the period determined by a certain recomposition of the dominant political forces within the regime, which resulted in the rise of integrist Catholicism and the establishment of the necessary bases for Spain's rapid economic growth in a later period.

(4) 1962–73. This period covers what has been called the 'economic development period' in Spain. It is a development that is accompanied by an institutional perfection of the regime and by an accentuation of its repressive policies, especially in the later years of this period.

(5) 1974–6. The decomposition of the Francoist regime occurs at this time, brought about more quickly by the death of the dictator himself and by the economic crisis which followed the radical rise of oil prices in 1973 and 1974. The failure of reformist Francoism in its attempt to somehow extend the authoritarian system beyond Franco's death caused the Francoist dictatorship finally to disappear in 1976, after forty years of existence.

(6) 1977–today. The beginning of this period can be considered to be in December 1976, when, by means of popular referendum, the Law for Political Reform, which was to establish the bases for the formal construction of democracy in Spain, was approved. But the period's zenith is really June 1977, when the first general elections in forty-one years were held. It is at this point that Spain finally starts to live under a democratic system.

(1) 1939–51

As I have already stated at the beginning of this essay, the end of the civil war signified, from a strictly cultural point of view, a severe trauma for Spain. And that was not only due to the cultural decapitation resulting from the exile of the vast majority of the country's intelligentsia, but also because of the grave wound inflicted upon the Spanish people, which would take many years to heal and which would influence all their activities throughout that whole time.

Death, hunger, devastation were ills all too evident to be evaded through speculation or lyrics. But, just in case there remained some small chink through which free thought could enter in a way inopportune for the interests of the new regime, this latter took the corresponding repressive measures to prevent it from happening: prior censorship, political purging of the organs of cultural diffusion,[7] and systematic imposition at all levels of the ideology of the civil war's victorious forces. In general terms, education, especially at primary and secondary levels, remained virtually under the control of the Catholic Church, while information and, to some extent, higher education and cultural affairs went over to the hands of the Falange. The Catholic Church took charge of ridding education as best it could of the slightest trace of laicism and imposing, on the contrary, the most militant and integrist of catholicisms.[8] The Falange, under the guise of supposed modernity, not only strove to eliminate all intimations of Marxist thought, but also acted with similar intensity against liberal thought, which was considered both harmful to national interests and decadent.

This oppressive atmosphere, intensified by the immediate consequences of the civil war, was to darken even more with the end of the Second World War and the victory of the Western powers, which embodied all the values against which the Francoist forces had fought: freedom, pluralism, democracy. In December 1946, following UN recommendations, the Western powers withdrew their ambassadors from Madrid, and Spain started to live in total international isolation.

In such a situation there was no place for any kind of cultural activity which did not emanate from the regime itself. It is for this reason that the cultural dynamics and diffusion of this period were virtually reduced to the publications subordinate to official organizations or to ideological sectors close to the regime. The *Revista de Estudios Politicos* (1941), edited by the Instituto de Estudios Politicos (Institute of Political Studies, created in September 1939 with the basic idea of giving the regime a juridical-political and ideological support), served as an organ of expression for the more intellectualized sectors of Falangism; whereas *Arbor*, published by the Consejo Superior de Investigaciones Científicas (Higher Council of Scientific Research, created in November 1939 with the intention of promoting scientific and humanistic research of an orthodox nature, following the patterns of the newly established ideology), became the mouthpiece for the integrist Catholic sectors of the regime. There were also other publications in this period that dealt more specifically with literary subjects, poetry, and so on, the majority of which were also controlled by the Falangists. In this sense, the cases of *El Español* (1942–7), *Garcilaso* (1943–6), or *Escorial* (1940–50) can be cited. But perhaps the review that deserves to stand out over all these is *Insula* (1946), which, concentrating very specifically upon literary subjects, managed to maintain great independence and to rely upon the most famous pens of the day.[9]

In all truth, very little else could be done and, to a certain extent, that very minimum of cultural activity occurring in this period was due to the decision of the more 'liberal' sectors of Falangism, among which were persons such as Dionisio Ridruejo already known for their earlier literary activity. They were, of course, the only ones allowed to engage freely in some kind of cultural activity, but they should be given credit, anyhow, for having attempted an intellectual-literary recuperation in the bleakness of the post-civil war period.[10]

Independent of the official culture, and insofar as literary creativity at that time could be independent, there appeared some isolated products which represent milestones in the evolution of Spanish culture. Works such as *La familia de Pascual Duarte* (1942) by Camilo J. Cela, or *Nada* (1945) by Carmen Laforet, which somehow reflect the anguish and misery of the Spain of that time – in which the characters moved and their authors wrote – are totally different from the novels insulting those who had lost the civil war, which then abounded, and from those of pure escapism which were at that time written by some members of the 1898 generation who had remained in Spain (*Laura*, 1941, by Pio Baroja, *La isla sin aurora*, 1944, by Azorín, etc.). Although these works are not of outstanding quality, they did set an important precedent for literary creativity in the following years, when social realism was to assert itself as forcefully as it could as a way of denouncing an injust and oppressive situation. Cela's *La Colmena*

(1951) about postwar Madrid was to appear totally within this trend. In a similar sense and with the force that is to be found in verse, the realist poetry of Dámaso Alonso (*Hijos de la ira*, 1944) or Blas de Otero (*Angel fieramente humano*, 1950) ended up causing the cold and affected Garcilasist poetry of the wooden sonnets by the Falangist poets who wrote for such reviews as *Escorial* or *Garilaso* to disappear.

However, the balance for this first period could not be more desolate. Totalitarianism, imperialist nationalism, elitism, traditionalism, and the religiosity of the official ideology and culture were a cumbersome burden that weighed too heavily upon the breaking backs of a hungry and repressed people. More favorable circumstances would have to be awaited for a greater cultural revitalization and a better quality in cultural production to occur.

(2)   1951–6

The period commencing in 1951 constituted the first opportunity to return to a minimally acceptable level of cultural activity. A series of circumstances of different kinds contributed to this possibility. First there was the international situation. In 1950 the UN withdrew the sanctions imposed upon Spain and at around the same time the tension between the two great powers – the United States and the Soviet Union – caused the start of the Cold War. That made it possible for Spain to break out of its international isolation and to go to seek economic aid from the United States. International isolation had kept Spain from access to the important aid for the reconstruction of Europe embodied in the Marshall Plan, and for that reason, while all the other European countries had already begun economic recovery, in 1951 Spain was still in a state of complete underdevelopment and still suffered the economic consequences of the civil war. But in order to attain that international backing, Spain had to offer something more than its anti-communism in return. However, the blatantly integrist government that had led Spain during the autarchic period had barely anything to show for its efforts; not the slightest step toward an internal reconciliation had been taken, nor had there been much improvement in the postwar economic situation. Consequently, on 18 July 1951, the commemoration of the fifteenth anniversary of the military uprising, Franco made a change in his government, which allowed for the first time the inclusion of more open-minded sectors of Catholicism as was the case of Joaquin Ruiz Giménez who was then named Minister of Education.

Spain's opening to the outside world was to materialize with the return of the ambassadors to Madrid (the return of the American ambassador in 1951 being the most significant), with the signing of the Concordat with the Vatican (1953), with the signing of the defense and economic aid treaties with the United States (1953), and with its own entry into the UN (1955).

In the midst of this relatively favorable situation, the first since the civil war, to which even a slight improvement in the economic situation – which permitted the abolition of ration books – seemed to be contributing, the presence of Mr Ruiz Giménez in the government allowed an important step forward to be taken toward the country's cultural recuperation. During this period neo-liberal and ortegan thought, which had already begun to spread during the previous period, especially from the end of the Second World War, was, to some extent, accepted and became part of what the philosopher Aranguren was to later call the 'established culture'.[11] That is to say, although not the official culture of the regime, ortegan thought, along with other liberal-conservative intellectual trends, became the cultural common property of a certain elite which caused very little trouble to the Francoist system and thus was tolerated.

However, besides the official culture and what was becoming the 'established culture', the slight opening-out in this period allowed an outburst of other stylistic forms totally independent from the establishment's official neo-classicism. Social realism, which had some slight precedents in the previous period, now spread rapidly, and the authors' unemotional, sometimes cruel, stories described Spanish social reality, with the serious economic and social problems of the times. The protagonist was collective; it was the Spanish people that were behind every story, and there was no fervor in the author, who sought to penetrate reality objectively, presenting it as it was and hoping, by doing that, to make his story as effective as possible. It was also the time of the forceful poetry of Gabriel Celaya, and of Blas de Otero who published his *Redoble de conciencia (Drumming of the Conscience)* in 1951. Novels of this period, such as *El Jarama* (1956) by Rafael Sánchez Ferlosio, or *Los Bravos* (1954) by Jesús Fernández Santos, have left their mark upon the Spanish novelistic tradition. And what better evocation could be found of the anxiety with which the Spanish people awaited the end of international isolation and the arrival of foreign economic aid to help them to escape from their economic penury, and of the frustration they felt at the meagreness of what they received, than the film *Bienvenido Mr Marshall* (1953), by the then young director Luis G. Berlanga.

But, logically, this slight aperturist attitude did not last too long and the social conflicts that were to occur at that time (in 1956 the first important protest movement occurred within the university), and the struggle among the different political 'families' of Francoism for the hegemony within the power bloc, caused Franco to carry out fresh changes in his government and to put an end to this 'moderate' experiment.[12]

(3)   1957–62

The period 1957 to 1962 signified an intermediate era of changes in Spain's economic dynamics, changes that were to establish the necessary bases for what was later to become its rapid economic growth. American aid had been minimal and, of course, insufficient to bring about the country's economic recovery. Other more efficient measures and people able to carry them out at that moment had to be found. That was how Catholic integrism, which had criticized harshly the previous period's aperturist experiment, returned to power, this time in the form of the Opus Dei, a religious organization which was just now beginning

to put its first men into the government, but which was gradually to increase its influence within the key institutions of the country. The plan for economic stabilization that was started in 1959, and which had been preceded by other measures, was to attempt to put the Spanish economy in order, so that it could attain definitive international recognition and adequate economic assistance, and to facilitate the integration of Spain's economy with Europe's. The economic readjustments involved affected above all the country's working class, and its clandestine organizations began to proliferate (the first workers' commission, the origin of Spain's largest syndical organization today, was founded in Asturias in 1962).

This period's difficult social and economic situation prolonged the forms of expression that had been successful during the previous period, with hardly any important changes taking place in this sense. Social realism continued to be prevalent and was even going along far more militant and politically compromising lines, scathingly criticizing both the economic situation of the popular classes and the bourgeoisie that was involved with Francoism. Novels such as *Central eléctrica* (*Electric Power Station*), 1958, by Jesús López Pacheco, *La piqueta* (*The Pick*),1959, by Antonio Ferrés, or *La mina* (*The Mine*), 1961, by Armando López Salinas, though not in any sense masterpieces, are blatant examples, meaningful even down to their titles, of this style and this period.

However, it was in a field very different from literature that Spanish culture was, during this period, first internationally recognized: that of the fine arts and in the persons of such important artists as the sculptors Jorge de Oteiza – Grand Award for Sculpture in the Fourth Biennial of São Paulo, in 1957 – and Eduardo Chillida – Grand Award for Sculpture in the Thirtieth Biennial of Venice, in 1958 – and the painter Antonio Tapies, who received the David Bright Foundation prize in 1958.

Art in Francoist Spain was totally ignored, for in the first years the presence in the country of such outstanding painters as Juan Miró or Dalí was merely tolerated, while no mention whatsoever was made of those who remained abroad, such as Picasso, just to name those who were already recognized masters before the civil war. However, and despite all the difficulties, from the early postwar years onwards young Spanish artists did a great deal toward keeping Spanish fine art at the high level at which historically it has always stood. The creation of such groups as the Barcelona Dau-al-Set (1948), which was made up in part of painters who today are of international renown, such as A. Tapies, M. Cuixart, and J. Tharrats; or the Madrilenian El Paso (1957), with such painters as Rafael Canogar, Luis Feito, Manuel Millares, and Antonio Saura; or Equipo 57 (Cordoba, 1957), with painters like Agustin Ibarrola; or the *Grupo Parpalló* (Valencia, 1956), with painters such as Juan Genovés; or the Galician painters Lugrís, Xeoane, Laxeiro, and so on, whose styles cover virtually all the modern pictorial schools, ranging from vanguard surrealism to realist formalism, are all a vivid example of Spanish art's refusal to be subjected to the cultural penury that Spain itself had to go through during these years, with levels of quality being reached that would be hard enough to attain in more settled cultural spheres.[13]

It was not a good time for intellectual life, which tended to confine itself to its own circles. However, the definitive emptying of the intellectual content of Francoism was to take place in this period, when intellectual figures who had originally played a decisive role in the regime's early days were now won over to the opposition. Such are the cases of persons like Pedro Laín Entralgo (*La espera y la esperanza*, 1957), Dionisio Ridruejo (*Escrito en España*, 1961), or even Ruíz Giménez himself, after having left his post as Minister for Education. They were now to reveal themselves as explicitly opposed to the dictatorial form of the Spanish government.

And alongside the neo-liberalism enclosed within its ivory tower, there was Marxism. It was, in fact, during this period that the first papers and essays on Marxist theory were to appear, and although they were confined to intellectual and university environments, they were restricted in publication, and were not even of particular quality; they did, however, gradually open a door toward the creation of a real revolution in Spanish intellectual life in the 1960s

and 1970s.[14] Marxism, of course, although not as an intellectual trend, but rather as a political militancy, was already acquiring in this period (and virtually from the time of the previous one) a great reputation among certain sectors of the country's intelligentsia. A great number of intellectuals from the most diverse fields committed themselves at this time to political militancy against Francoism and gathered beneath the flags of different clandestine political groups, most of them of Marxist inspiration. Especially benefited by this new tendency was the Spanish Communist Party, which changed its political strategy in 1956 and launched the slogan of 'national reconciliation' in which there was submersed the idea of the alliance of cultural and work forces, as a revolutionary bloc that would prompt social change; a strategy that caused it to acquire a large audience in Spanish intellectual circles.

(4)   1962–73

The decade spanning 1962–73, that is to say, from the time of the World Bank's favorable report on the Spanish economy and the creation of the Development Plan Commissariat in 1962 until the first radical rises in oil prices in late 1973 and early 1974, was the peak period of the Francoist regime. It was during this period that Spain acquired a prodigious economic growth, the rate of which was superior to those of some European countries,[15] and became an industrial power in the following years. At the same time the Francoist regime tried to perfect its institutionalization and to assure its continuance, in the event, becoming more and more possible, of the disappearance of its mainstay, General Franco. The totalitarian attempts of the early years were completely abandoned and a way to give the system a more constitutional appearance was sought. The middle of the period is, then, the most important in this sense. After having celebrated the so-called *25 años de Paz* (25 Years of Peace) in glorious fashion in 1964, the year when the First Development Plan was also introduced, by late 1966 the Ley Orgánica del Estado (State Organic Law) was approved by referendum. This was a law that regulated the functions of state organs with greater precision and which already looked ahead to how they would function at that moment when the head of state, General Franco, was to disappear. According to the regime, Spain was already an *organic democracy* (in contrast to the individualist one) and in order to comply with that appearance the regime had to act in a more permissive fashion.[16] It was thought that economic development would act as a silencer to the opposition and that repression would not be necessary, therefore, except when a certain limit was exceeded.

Thus, from the point of view of cultural expansion, the passing of the Press Law (1966), which abolished prior censorship in exchange for a system of control and sanctions *a posteriori*, and lowered the levels of restriction slightly, allowed an indubitable increase in the possibilities of free expression, not only in the means of communication, but in all kinds of publications. However, the application of this law was full of ambivalences and it caused new press organs to appear as much as others to disappear on account of the heavy sanctions.[17]

It was during this time that the first periodical publications of a critical nature of some kind appeared (*Triunfo, Cuadernos para el Diálogo*, 1963), and some newspapers started to publish editorials and articles containing opinions critical of the regime, which all coincided in trying to provoke it to open up further, although they were written in such a cryptic language and convoluted style that often they were unintelligible to the reader who was not aware of the situation. But in fact the most important phenomenon to occur in this period was the publishing boom.[18] Better economic conditions, increased purchasing power, greater leeway on censorship, and the need and wish to fill in the cultural void caused by years of isolation and strict censorship were the decisive elements contributing to this boom. Not only were more works by Spanish authors published, but there was also an increase in the number of translations of foreign works, the majority of which were already classics in their original languages. The subjects covered also increased tremendously. In fact,

along with this boom, there was also a flourishing of the social sciences. Publications on history, politics, sociology, economy, and philosophy literally filled bookshop windows and replaced the escapist literature both in the stores and on students' desks. The university student and the Spanish reader of this time both wanted to recoup their own history and to be reinstated in the Spanish and European cultural trends and tradition, violently severed in 1939. This offers a clear explanation for the publishing boom, which was further helped along by the appearance of pocket-sized paperbacks which were both inexpensive and accessible to wider sectors of the population.

Needless to say, within this essayistic literature the most significant development was that of the critical essay and, specifically, those works of a Marxist nature, and even those of Marx himself – published for the first time since the civil war. Thus, as social criticism turned to its specific environment, the social essay, it abandoned the field of escapist literature. Indeed, during those years of the evolving Spain, the realist novel was to lose all its force, for literature was now heading along totally different paths. The novel *Tiempo de silencio* (1962) by Luis Martín Santos represents the peak of this break with the realism that characterized the literary output of the preceding periods. It was this very novel that opened up a certain period of reflection and of genuine silence in Spanish literature, after which, and as a product of a profound catharsis, there emerged a new kind of novel of extremely high quality, with a new aesthetic outlook.[19] Juan Goytisolo (*Señas de identidad*, 1966, and *Reivindicación del Conde Don Julián*, 1970, both published first in Mexico and then again years later in Spain); Juan Marsé (*Ultimas tardes con Teresa*, 1966); Miguel Delibes (*Cinco horas con Mario*, 1967, and *Parábola del náufrago*, 1969); and Juan Benet (*Volverás a Región*, 1968) are the most famous examples of authors of the new Spanish narrative technique which emerged at that time. The parallel phenomenon of the Latin American narrative, which then started to reach Spain in force, also had to be of great influence in the Spanish novel, bringing a freshness, a color, and a dynamism that had no connection with the moving realism of the 1950s.

Camilo J. Cela himself, already a classic author of the Spanish novel, was to reveal the change of perspective in his novel *San Camilo 1936* (1969), with which he tried to become part of the new trend.

A similar radical inflexion took place in Spanish poetry, clearly evident in the anthology published in 1970 by José M. Castellet (*Nueve novísimos poetas españoles*), which brings together examples of the poetry of this period by nine poets of distinct styles, but all of whom are characterized by their break with the old realism and their incursions along new aesthetic lines more in accord with the historic moment. In short, as Castellet said referring to the poets in his anthology, though the comment could also be extended to other writers starting to publish in this period, they were the first not to have been educated in *literary humanism*, basic to the intellectual formation of the preceding generations, but rather under the influence of the mass media and, I would add, of the ideologization and cultural deformation of the first years of Francoism.[20] That, along with Spain's new social reality of the 1960s and early 1970s, had necessarily to create a new sensibility and a different conceptual and aesthetic response. This generational break was, however, to become even greater, more violent and obvious, in the later generations that cropped up in the 1970s, to which the young 1960s writers are only a mild precedent.

But perhaps the theater was the medium where the most radical changes of the moment occurred. After a long, long time of darkness, in which Spanish theater was nothing but a mockery of what dramatic work ought to be, in the 1960s there began a real revival of theatrical activity, brought into motion not only by the proliferation of independent groups, originating for the most part in universities, which performed an endless number of plays by the most famous Spanish and foreign dramatists, but also by the performance of some fairly good plays by young authors, such as José Martín Recuerda, Antonio Gala, and Alfonso Sastre, whose plays took their place alongside those of the new 'classic' dramatists such as Antonio Buero Vallejo or Miguel Mihura. But the changes occurring here were, more than in any other area of Spanish culture, influenced by foreign drama which, excepting the revitalization of modernism's classic molds by Valle Inclán, found one of its principal sources of inspiration in Brecht. Of course, as always happened during the Francoist period, the best material remained outside; and thus plays of great quality such as Fernando Arrabal's vanguard theater, already a success on European stages, and others by the aforementioned Sastre, by the Galician Eduardo Blanco Amor, or by Francisco Nieva were banned by the censors.[21]

Similarly, the cinema underwent a great expansion in this period, due to some official help which caused it to get out of the ghetto in which it had been isolated following the slight revival that had come about in earlier periods, particularly in the middle of the neorealist wave.[22] The first productions of the new directors to emerge then were still affected by neorealism, into which trend they fitted perfectly; but soon, as their films became more mature, they forsook critical realism and joined the new aesthetic trend that was to be found in the European cinema of that time. Standing out above all are the films of Carlos Saura whose success ranges from his first great film *La caza* (which received an award in the Berlin Film Festival in 1968), to *La prima Angélica* (which won a Cannes Film Festival award in 1974). It is an intellectual and symbolic style of cinema, not always easy to understand by a foreign audience (despite its indubitable success abroad), which reflects the traumas of a repressive and insufficient education suffered by youth under Francoism, and the defects of a compliant bourgeoisie, such as the Spanish one was and is. Luis Buñuel, who had made most of his films outside Spain, except for the significant case of *Viridiana* (1961), which was condemned by the Catholic Church and consequently banned by the Spanish authorities, made a second attempt in 1969, taking advantage of that aperturist moment, with *Tristana*, which was based upon a nineteenth-century novel by Benito Pérez Galdós. In both cases the iconoclastic tradition of Spanish critical intellectuality, so typical in Buñuel's work, crops up, and Catholicism and society, church and bourgeoisie, are the subjects of his sharp criticism. On a similar line, although with a more sentimental vision of the history and frustrations of the Spanish people during the Franco years, one can also mention films such as *Canciones para después de una guerra* (1971), by Basilio Martín Patiño, which moved deeply all those who had lived through the terrible moments of the Spanish postwar period and those who knew nothing more about it than what their parents had told them; *Mi querida señorita* (1971) by Jaime de Armiñán; or *El espíritu de la colmena* (1973) by Victor Erice. The opening in 1967 of special theaters, called Salas de Arte y Ensayo (Art and Essay Cinemas), was especially important at this time for they allowed the Spanish cinema-lover to see a great many of the good foreign productions previously banned, and also old films in their original versions, without their being dubbed or distorted by this same system, as had often occurred.[23]

But due to an ever-increasing tourist trade, Spain was fast becoming the most important tourist center in Europe, managing to welcome as many tourists a year as the whole country had inhabitants. And so it could not remain apart from the undeniable socio-logical consequences of this phenomenon, which came to transform radically different parts of the Mediterranean coast and the southern area of the country, precisely the poorest and most under-developed parts. Tourism brought in different fashions, habits, and attitudes, but, above all, it brought in cultural communication, in the widest sense of the word, which broke down the wall of isolation and psychologically paved the way for cultural reintegration into Europe, just starting in this period. This reintegration was, of course, also favored by another human displacement of a very different kind: the forced departure of thousands of Spanish workers who, from the previous period onwards, had been moving into the different industrialized countries of Europe in search of work, just as the intellectuals had followed the same path seeking a creative freedom which did not exist in Spain. Indeed, in this period, as the cultural framework expanded, the tendency to criticize the dictatorship also increased, and it spread through different intellectual circles at the same time as political opposition to the system grew. University movements, strikes, clandestine political militancy,

and other milder forms of criticism of the regime resulted in a new wave of repression, which cast so many intellectuals, writers, and artists into exile that it could be said that it was in this period that the second great Spanish intellectual exile provoked by the Francoist dictatorship was to start; and it would not cease until the regime finally disappeared.

(5) 1974–6

The assassination of the president of the government, Luis Carrero Blanco, by the Basque separatist organization ETA, in December 1973, and the first radical rise in oil prices which also occurred at the end of that year, marked the beginning of the end of the Francoist regime. Carrero Blanco's murder deprived Franco of one of his most resolute and loyal supporters, in whom he had placed all his hopes for the continuation of the regime. It was, without any doubt, a very severe blow from which Francoism never managed to recover, though it still took almost three years to collapse completely. But, while this political blow was of decisive importance, there is no doubt that it would not have been so significant had the Spanish economic situation not also entered into a deep crisis at this time, caused by the tremendous increase in oil prices after the Arab-Israeli War in 1973. Carrero Blanco's death and an aging Franco provoked a confrontation between the different political families and groups of Francoism, which could not agree among themselves on what would be the best formula to make the system continue, and this set the regime's decomposition into motion. The pseudo-aperturism initiated by the new president of the government, Carlos Arias Navarro, was soon rejected both by the most extremist sectors of Francoism and by the democratic opposition itself, whose political forces, still in clandestinity, did not cease to harass the regime and press harder for a real democratization of the country's political life. General Franco's death, on 20 November 1975, merely accelerated the regime's decomposition and brought it to its final consequences. Finally, the attempts to prolong the Francoist system beyond the death of its founder, giving the dictatorship a new air, were to fail in the face of the Spanish people's resolute opposition and they came to an end with Arias Navarro being removed from office in July 1976.[24]

At the same time, the rocketing oil prices of 1973, 1974, and the following years caused energy sources to become more expensive and provoked a general economic crisis in the Western world – one which was to affect Spain especially hard. This, though, was not only because Spain's economic development in the previous period had been partially based upon a lack of equilibrium and of homogeneity, which made her especially weak, but was also due to problems of an external origin. Of that nature were, in fact, problems such as the return of the emigrant workers from countries also hard-hit by the economic crisis, which caused a considerable rise in unemployment figures; the drop in foreign exchange, caused by a falling-off of tourism and the return of the emigrants; the rise in price of imported goods; the drop in investment, caused by the flight of capital (both foreign and national) in the face of the country's political insecurity; and so on. Along with the considerable increase in inflation these economic problems made the country's social situation clearly unstable.[25]

In this highly conflictive situation Spanish cultural production was obviously affected. The intensity of the moment called for nothing less. They were difficult moments characterized by great violence, where official repression (just two months prior to his death General Franco signed the order for five activists to be executed, and they were immediately shot) was to be joined by the activity of the fascist bands, tolerated by those in power, and of the terrorist groups ETA, FRAP, and GRAPO. An ever-growing spiral of violence seemed ready to destroy everything. Thus, the struggle for the democratization of the country and against Francoism led by the principal democratic political parties, which were still in hiding, required the collaboration of all the progressive social forces, and, naturally enough, the cultural world took full part in it.

The result of all this was a great politicization of all fields of cultural production, ranging from the novel to painting, passing through the cinema, the theater, and so on. And the more that the regime's own crisis, in its tremendous fluctuations from repression to permissiveness, was allowed to become apparent, the greater and more perceptible this politicization was. The criticism, of course, was not always directed toward the present, but rather it often took the form of an analysis of the historic past, of the early years of Francoism and of all the values and ideas that the dictatorship tried to impose upon the Spanish people. And the Catholic Church, which had been of such great importance in the ideological justification of the Francoist military coup – which it qualified as a new *crusade* against the impious[26] – and in the obscurantist education of the new generations, was also the object of this criticism. In many cases this looking back, this delving anew into the past years when the dictatorship was thriving, was not so much a direct criticism of the regime as a melancholic review, a search of the past, in order to discover the origin of the present-day frustrations and thereby to recover one's own identity. It was almost a form of psychoanalysis, a casting-off of the past and the reconstruction of a future felt to be near and full of hope. But that process was still to take quite some time and it was a task that could not be finished in that period, and which is not finished even today, though the process of recovery is evident.

This search back into the past is to be found in films such as *La prima Angélica* (1973) by Carlos Saura, and in novels like *Si te dicen que caí* (1974) by Juan Marsé, which reflect, from different perspectives, the effects of the civil war upon postwar youth. From a less critical and far more poetical point of view there were also other important works at that time, such as José L. Borau's film *Furtivos* (1975) which became the biggest Spanish box-office success of all time. This fact is a symbol of the Spanish cinema's quality and audience, which until then had never managed to enjoy the complete favor of the Spanish public, who had been more fond of showy foreign superproductions. At this time, Juan Goytisolo also published his *Juan Sin Tierra* (1974) which, along with his earlier *Señas de identidad* (1966) and *Reivindicación del Conde Don Julián* (1970), was to complete the trilogy that introduced a novelistic style based upon meditation over past historic events, a technique that was to be used in later years by other authors. Yet there was still the need to rediscover one's own identity, what was real, seeking it out from beneath the deformations and misrepresentations of the triumphalist history of Francoism and the old Catholic and imperial orthodoxy. In the theater the group La Cuadra had a great success at this time with its play *Quejío* (1975), which in using the vehicle of the Spanish gypsies' aesthetic notions expressed that same search for authenticity.

At the other end of the scale, and expressing the maximum of politicization, there were introduced into Spain the same social, political, and philosophical debates then taking place in Europe between the different schools of philosophy. The exponents of these different theories tried to have an influence upon the collective conscience, often in justification of the varying political alternatives of the different parties that, in hiding, were fighting a tough battle for the democratization of the country. It would be too long and tedious a task to give a list of authors' names, but some of the periodical publications that, from then on, reflected the ideological debate taking place in Spain, which still could not be altogether freely expressed, can be cited: *Sistema* (1973), *Zona Abierta* (1974), *Materiales* (1976), *Nagaciones* (1976), and others.

Politics made use of art, but not so much from a merely partisan point of view as with the noble intention of putting the message of freedom, which could scarcely be heard through other channels closed by the dictatorship, across to the people. It was in this way that the concerts by singers such as Raimon from Valencia, the Catalonian Lluis Llach, or the Galicians Bibiano and Benedicto became real political acts where the thousands and thousands of people present all sang together those songs alluding to the regime and lit matches in the darkness of the concert halls symbolizing, thereby, the flame that was being kindled and which would put an end to the long dark night of Francoism. Political too was Tapies's work, when he painted posters for the PSUC (Catalonia's Unified Socialist Party), and that of Juan Genovés,

when he painted his famous picture *El abrazo*, which soon became a propaganda poster crying out for amnesty and for the release of political prisoners, and which was to cost him a short time in prison.

It was, in short, a time of struggle and of the destruction of a regime and its out-of-date forms. But it was also a time of creation, of searching for what was real, authentic, which would allow a new society to be built according to new political patterns which would result in a new culture free of the past's traumas and impediments. It is logical then that the cultural contribution of this short but difficult and important period was clearly militant and that, in many cases, it was committed not only politically, but in a partisan way as well.[27]

(6)   1977 – Today

Finally, in December 1976, the Spanish people, although still suffering some political restrictions, approved by referendum the Law for Political Reform, which was to pave the way for the dismantling of the Francoist regime; and in June 1977 the first general elections were held, which effectively set the democratic transformation of the country's political structures in motion. At the time of writing not three years have yet gone by. Thus it could be rather premature to evaluate the evolution of Spain's cultural production since June 1977. What can be said, however, is that the political and partisan content observed in the period of the Francoist regime's decline and death is clearly subsiding. However, there is still ample criticism of the previous regime, but this criticism has evolved from a simple condemnation of the regime itself to an attempt to analyze specific aspects of it which directly affected the lives of citizens during its existence, such as the social and personal relations at that time, which were burdened by prejudices and restrictions, the political and social oppression, the moral and religious repression, and so on. There is, then, in this respect, an obvious continuity with the previous period, which is shown through the use of the same subject matter and, even, of the same aesthetic molds, although these objects are used much more freely and openly today.[28]

The history of the civil war, on which there is now an abundant objective bibliography, is being gone over once again; it is also a subject that has invaded recent Spanish cinema, with such films as *La vieja memoria* (1978) by Jaime Camino or *En el corazón del bosque* (1979) by Manuel Gutiérrez Aragón, the latter dealing with the immediate postwar period and the presence of guerrillas in the woods, being two of the best known. Nor has the theater ignored this question, for plays such as Rafael Alberti's *Noche en el Museo del Prado* which, although written long before, was first performed in Madrid in 1978, have reached the Spanish stage. The history of the Francoist period also appears not only in films of a semi-documentary nature, such as Juan A. Bardem's *Siete días de enero* (1978), dealing with the murder of five labor lawyers in Madrid by a fascist group in January 1977, or Imanol Uribe's *El proceso de Burgos* (1979), reporting the famous trial which was held in Burgos in 1970 against several militants of the Basque separatist group ETA, but also in critical films of great quality such as Gutiérrez Aragón's *Camada negra* (1976), which was an interesting study of the fascist groups that acted with a complete impunity in the last years of the Francoist regime.

The frustrations of a personal or collective nature experienced in the previous period had been analyzed (*Asignatura pendiente*, 1977, by José L. Garci) and the members of the Francoist political class have been criticized and ridiculed (*La escopeta nacional*, 1978, by Luis G. Berlanga), as have been those who, once having belonged to that class, now try to appear as if they have been 'democrats all their lives' (*Jueces en la noche*, 1979, by Buero Vallejo).

Up to now I have quoted only film or play titles since I consider them to be more representative, due to their ability to reach a wider audience, of what Spanish cultural production has been over the last two or three years. It can also be said, however, that literature has now taken a very different course, tending to go beyond Francoism and its period as subject matter. A concentration on history as a source of Spanish identity continues to be a major question. It is for this reason that Fernando Sánchez Dragó's *Gárgoris y Habidis* (1978) – awarded the National Essay Prize in 1979 – has been so successful, for it is a book which does not try to be a rigorous historical study, but rather, as the author himself subtitles his work, *a magic history of Spain*. Beyond this historical field, the world of fiction has already produced some works of outstanding quality which show how this evident process of cultural recuperation, started back in the 1960s, is now taking giant steps towards its culmination. One such case is that of *Extramuros* (1978), by Jesús Fernández Santos, which received the 1979 National Literature Prize.

Similarly, art and poetry have reached a period of total creative freedom where styles, subject matter, and forms mix and blend together, overcoming the old disputes between schools, in a pluralism where validity and modernity are not argued over and the only matter at issue is the work's quality and the artist's authenticity. It should be noted that it is those who are already 'classics' who are better known, though many of them are only just now beginning to be known by the public at large due to the difficulties that existed in the previous periods for the diffusion of cultural work. Indeed, it is in poetry where Spanish culture of today has first achieved international recognition of note, when Vicente Aleixandre, a 'classic' of the 1927 generation, was awarded the Nobel Prize for Literature in 1977.

This prize, awarded at this moment and to this author, is the perfect symbol of acknowledgement of those who under Francoism managed to keep the torch of culture burning and who have made it possible for the cultural reconstruction process to continue without having to start from scratch again. But it is also an acknowledgement of that very process that is taking place right now.

In short, it could be concluded that Spanish culture has, from the time of the civil war on, been undergoing a mere transition. The non-existence of an enormous and radical change once democracy was established should not, then, be too much of a surprise to those who had expected it. But neither should such a confirmation cause frustration. Things had, in fact, already been evolving for several years prior to the change in the political system, and it would be a serious mistake to regard Spanish culture as a totally paralysed entity throughout the forty years of Francoist dictatorship. It has not been like that at all, as I have tried to show in this essay. The Spanish people's creative ability, if not in all the fields of purely cultural activity then at least in many of them, managed to expand and gradually break down the barriers and obstacles that the Francoist regime had imposed. For that reason the cultural phenomenon in Spain can only be considered as a phenomenon in transition, from the very beginnings of the dictatorship until today. It is a transition that goes from the establishment of the minimal bases necessary for cultural activity to take place to the integration into European and Western trends of thought, of which Spanish culture has always been part and from which at one moment in its life it was violently separated.

One should not, then, in the search for Spanish cultural identity, which today is the concern of many Spanish intellectuals, try to find it in total originality. Identity must not be confused with originality. This has never occurred, but it is, of course, even less probable today, when modern means of transportation and communication bring us to a maximum integration of cultures. However, the fact that Spain, due to its inferior level of economic development, may well be technically dependent upon other, better-developed countries, and the fact that it may well have accepted cultural influences from these same countries as a price for that dependence, does not mean in any way the total disappearance of its own creativity and, hence, of its own identity, which remains and is revealed at least in its own interpretation of those cultural phenomena shared with other countries and people.

This consideration of a generic nature does not stop me from finding the question asked by some Spanish intellectuals in the last years of the dictatorship about whether a Spanish culture really did exist to be justified at times. What they wanted, in so doing, was to emphasize the tremendous difficulty with which cultural phenomena occurred and developed under Francoism, to the extent that few things worthy of consideration existed. Even from this point of view,

though, it would be more valid to ask ourselves whether in Franco's Spain there existed *culture* and not a Spanish culture, for that would be tantamount to admitting the possibility of the existence of another culture that was not the proper Spanish one (perhaps the official one?), something which did not, of course, exist.

But what would the general definitional characteristics of this Spanish culture be? I do not propose to emphasize here the positive elements, which are precisely those which I have tried to detail in this essay, for I think it more opportune to conclude by pointing out those elements of a negative nature. In this sense, the following notes, already detailed by the Spanish literary critic José M. Castellet,[29] seem to me to be very adequate: (1) the *loss of the contemporary tradition*, due to the Francoist regime's attempt to bring about a radical change in the country's cultural trajectory, breaking away from the cultural tradition of the pre-civil war period and imposing orthodox molds of a *démodé* classicism; (2) the *collective memory block*, which logically derived from the imposed ignorance, or from the revilement, of the historico-cultural contribution from the preceding periods in Spain's history; (3) the *spontaneity of the cultural recuperation*, which gradually occurred, despite official restraints, and sometimes copying foreign trends inadequately;[30] (4) the *osmosis or involuntary complicity with Francoism*, as the new cultural process developed, in most cases, precisely out of the premises of Francoist society; (5) the *aesthetic regression of the language*, which can be observed in a literature that, up until the 1960s, lived apart from any modernist vanguard; (6) the *pathology of expression* caused by the difficulties in expressing one's own thought clearly, which made it necessary to use a cryptic language, full of strange turns of expression and nuances, barely intelligible to the person not versed in it, and which came to cause a deformation of the language (especially evident in journalistic language, but elsewhere too).

But to these negative characteristics I would also add the oppression and the contempt with which regional cultures were treated during the Francoist regime. In this sense, I have up till now always spoken of *Spanish culture*, but, as far as its written production is concerned, I have referred only to what is written in Castilian. It should be made clear, then, that the term Spanish culture (at least when it is referring to Spain and not to Latin America) has also to include the cultural production written in Galician, Basque, or Catalonian. In short, Spanish culture is made up of the different regional cultures of the country. However, I have referred – when it has been a question of written culture – only to what is written in Castilian, since this is the common language of the Spanish people and because it has been the predominant language throughout the period under analysis, so the country's cultural evolution can be perfectly well reflected through the work produced in Castilian. Still on this question, one can add that under Francoism the Galician, Basque, and Catalonian cultures were dealt the worst blow in their history, since, apart from the general limitations that the Francoist system imposed on the free development of the culture, there was also a total ban on the use of these languages and an attempt to destroy any evidence of their regional identity, which has gone to the ridiculous extreme of changing the names of towns and places for a Castilian version. But an analysis of Spain's regional cultures would, due to their importance, require special attention and a specific treatment that the framework of this essay cannot undertake. Let it suffice to point out their existence, as part of the overall Spanish culture, and to say that nowadays new legislation in the Spanish state both permits and advocates the use of regional languages, even in official instances.

To sum up, Spanish culture is today on the way to an evident recovery and overcoming of the critical period; a recovery which even affects – though to a lesser extent – the Galician, Basque, and Catalonian regional cultures.[31] But this qualitative recovery does not yet mean that culture has become far more widespread, and there is still a long way to go in this sense. Spanish society reads very little and there is a large sector of the population which has not even completed its primary education.[32] Nevertheless, one can say that this recovery is a consequence of the change undergone in the country's political structures. And

perhaps the most obvious example of the new official attitude toward cultural development can be found in the government's recent acquisition, for the Madrid Museum of Contemporary Art, of Juán Genovés's picture *El abrazo*, which was in the Marlborough Gallery of New York, and which became in the last months of the dictatorship a real symbol of the struggle for national reconciliation and the overcoming of the traumas inflicted by Francoism.

Notes and References: Chapter 12

1 The review *Cuadernos para el Diálogo* brought out an extra issue (no. 42) in August 1974, entitled '¿Existe una cultura española?', in which several authors analyzed this question, but without giving a definitive answer. After Franco's death the same question is posed by J. M. Castellet *et al.*, *La cultura bajo el franquismo* (Barcelona: Ediciones de Bolsillo, 1977). About the Spanish culture in general after the civil war, see Equipo Reseña, *La cultura española durante el franquismo* (Bilbao: Mensajero, 1977); J. L. Abellán, *La cultura en España* (Madrid: Edicusa, 1975): J. C. Clemente, *Una cultura en crisis* (Barcelona: Plaza y Janés, 1973); J. L. Aranguren, *La cultura española y la cultura establecida* (Madrid: Taurus, 1975); 'La cultura en la España del siglo XX', *Triunfo*, no. 507, 17 June 1972.

2 I understand by 'culture' the sum total of scientific, literary, and artistic knowledge of a person, a people, or a period; however, here for obvious reasons of space I shall refer solely and exclusively to part of the latter two aspects of Spanish culture.

3 There has been a considerable amount of works published recently on the Spanish intellectual exile. See, for example, J. L. Abellán, *Filosofía española en América, 1936–1966* (Madrid: Guadarrama, 1967) and *Panorama de la filosofía española actual* (Madrid: Espasa Calpe, 1978); Carlos Martínez, *Crónica de una emigración: la de los republicanos españoles en 1939* (Mexico: Libro Mex, 1969); Alberto Fernández, *La emigración republicana española (1939–1945)* (Madrid: Zero, 1972); Juan Marichal, *El nuevo pensamiento político español* (Mexico: Finisterre, 1974); Elías Díaz, *Notas para una historia del pensamiento español actual 1939–1973* (Madrid: Edicusa, 1974); Aurora de Albornoz, 'La España peregrina', *Triunfo*, no. 507, 17 June 1972.

4 Dario Puccini, *Romancero della resistenza spagnola, 1936–1965* (Roma: Editori Riuniti, 1965), p. 60.

5 Luis Portillo, *Vida y martirio de Don Miguel de Unamuno*, in Ricardo de la Cierva, *Historia ilustrada de la guerra civil española* (Barcelona: Danae, 1970).

6 Without ignoring the importance of the Spanish exiles and the quality of their cultural contributions, I shall not refer to them in great detail for I feel that their influence upon the cultural evolution taking place within the country was not excessively important, given the limitations that the dictatorship imposed; and, on the other hand, because they are not symbols of the evolution of the Spanish culture of the interior since they were the product of an entirely free elaboration and were not subjected to those same limitations.

7 The application of the Political Responsibilities and the Repression of Masonry and Communism Laws (9 February 1939 and 9 March 1940 respectively) and other similar ones meant that a great number of teachers and professors suspected of liberal or laic thought were driven out of their jobs.

8 On the important role of the Catholic Church in the francoist regime, see Rafel Gómez Pérez, *Política y Religión en el régimen de Franco* (Barcelona: Dopesa, 1976); X. Chao Rego, *La Iglesia en el Franquismo* (Madrid: Ediciones Felmar, 1976); J. J. Ruíz, *El papel político de la Iglesia católica en la España de Franco (1936–1971)* (Madrid: Tecnos, 1977); R. Belda *et al.*, *Iglesia y sociedad en España: 1939–1975* (Madrid: Editorial Popular, 1977).

9 On some of the periodical publications of this period, see Manuel Ramírez *et al.*, *Las fuentes ideológicas de un régimen: España 1939–1945* (Zaragoza: Pórtico, 1978); J. C. Mainer, *Literatura y pequeña burguesía en España (Notas 1890–1950)* (Madrid: Edicusa, 1972), and *Falange y literatura* (Barcelona: Labor, 1971); Elena de Jongh Rossel, 'La revista "Insula" y la cultura de posguerra', *El País*, 6 January 1980.

10 Pedro Laín Entralgo, a well-known member at this time of these culturally advanced sectors of the Falange, did not consider exaggerated the use of the epithet 'intellectual liberalism' when referring to those same sectors (P. Laín Entralgo, *El problema de la Universidad*, Madrid: Edicusa, 1968, pp. 88–9). On this intellectual Falangism see also M. Rubio Cabeza, *Los intelectuales españoles y el 18 de Julio* (Barcelona: Acervo, 1975), pp. 116–49.

11 José L. Aranguren, *La cultura española y la cultura establecida* (Madrid: Taurus, 1975), p. 14.

12 For a Marxist interpretation of the Francoist regime's evolution, from the point of view of the struggle for hegemony among the different sectors of the dominant bloc, see Valeriano Bozal, 'Cambio ideológico en España, 1939–1975', *Zona Abierta*, no. 5, 1975.

13 On recent Spanish art, see J. Camón Aznar, *XXV años de arte español* (Madrid, 1964); Carlos Areán, *Treinta años del arte español* (Madrid: Guadarrama, 1972); V. Aguilera Cerni, *Iniciación al arte español de la postguerra* (Madrid: Península, 1972); Valeriano Bozal, *Historia del arte en España* (Madrid: Itsmo, 1972); V. Bozal *et al.*, *Vanguardia artística y realidad social, 1936–1976* (Barcelona: Gustavo Gili, 1976).

14 On the introduction of Marxism and the modern trends of philosophical and social thought in Spain, see E. Díaz, *Notas . . .*, op. cit., pp. 161–291; J. L. Abellán, *Panorama . . .*, op. cit., pp. 92–101.

15 Spain's was 6 per cent, while France's and Italy's were 5·5 and 5·6 per cent respectively.

16 Manuel Fraga Iribarne's entry into the government as Minister for Information and Tourism in July 1962 played an important role in that opening out that was then occurring, as had happened ten years previously with Ruíz Giménez. On the institutionalization of the Francoist regime, see R. Fernandez Carvajal, *La Constitución española* (Madrid: Editora Nacional, 1969); J. Solé Tura, *Introducción al régimen político español* (Barcelona: Ariel, 1971). On its ideological content, see Manuel Ramírez, *España 1939–1975. Régimen político e ideología* (Madrid: Guardarrama, 1978).

17 The banning of the daily newspaper *Madrid* which had upheld a somewhat critical attitude during this period is a good example of this.

18 From the 13,041 titles published in 1969, with a total output of 165,202,000 copies, it went up to 21,595 titles and an output of 189,665,000 copies in 1973. Data from the Instituto Nacional del Libro Español and the Instituto Nacional de Estadística. On this subject, see J. L. Abellán, *La industria . . .*, op. cit., pp. 11–22.

19 Pere Gimferrer considers the qualitative level of this new Spanish novel to be one of the highest in Western literature; see P. Gimferrer, 'El pensamiento literario 1939–1976', in J. M. Castellet *et al.*, *La cultura . . .*, op. cit., p. 125.

20 J. M. Castellet, *Nueve novísimos poetas españoles* (Barcelona: Barral, 1970), p. 20.

21 On modern Spanish theatre, see José Monléon, *Treinta años de teatro de la derecha* (Barcelona: Tusquets, 1971); F. Ruíz Ramón, *Historia del teatro español. Siglo XX* (Madrid: Alianza, 1971); Alfonso Sastre, *La revolución y la crítica de la cultura* (Barcelona: Grijalbo, 1970); M. A. Medina, *El teatro español en el banquillo* (Valencia: F. Torres, 1976); L. Molero Manglano, *Teatro español contemporáneo* (Madrid: Editora Nacional, 1974).

22 In 1962, J. M. García Escudero was named Director General of Cinematography, and it was he who gave a certain amount of economic assistance to the cinema, as well as introducing special regulations for it, both of which led to the expansion of this Spanish industry. He was removed from office in 1969.

23 On modern Spanish cinema, see A. Pérez Gómez and J. Martínez Montalbán, *Cine español 1951–1978* (Bilbao: Mensajero, 1979); César Santos Fontenla, *Cine español en la encrucijada* (Madrid: Ciencia Nueva, 1966); M. Revuelta and M. Hernández, *Treinta años de cine al alcance de todos los españoles* (Madrid: Zero, 1976); Román Gubern, 'Cine y comunicación de masas', in J. M. Castellet *et al.*, *La cultura* . . ., op. cit., pp. 189–201, and 'La oscuridad del cine', in *Cuadernos para el Diálogo*, XLII, 1974, pp. 54–6.

24 On the crisis and decomposition of the Francoist regime, see J. de Esteban and L. López Guerra, *La crisis del Estado franquista* (Barcelona: Labor, 1977); Nicos Poulantzas, *The Crisis of the Dictatorships. Portugal, Greece, Spain* (London: New Left Books, 1976); P. Preston (ed.), *Spain in Crisis: The Evolution and Decline of the Franco Regime* (Hassocks, Sussex: Harvester Press, 1976); R. Carr and J. P. Fusi, *España, de la Dictadura a la Democracia* (Barcelona: Planeta, 1979).

25 In 1976 alone 36,979 strikes were registered in Spain, out of which 17,371 took place in the first three months of the year (R. Carr and J. P. Fusi, *España* . . ., op. cit., p. 273.

26 It seems that the term 'crusade' referring to the Spanish Civil War was first used by Cardinal Plà i Deniel in his pastoral letter *Las dos ciudades* of 30 September 1936, in which he said that the conflict 'has the external form of a civil war, but it is really a Crusade', and, he added later, 'a real Crusade for God, for Religion and for Civilization'; cf. note 8.

27 This momentary politicization of Spanish culture aroused the logical opposition of the most purist sector of intellectuality, which in exaggerated cases like that of Fernando Arrabal, and given the left-wing tone of this politicization, even spoke of a 'sovietization' of Spanish culture (see, for example, F. Arrabal, '¿Sovietización de la cultura española?', *El País*, 2 November 1979, p. 9).

28 Official censorship was abolished in November 1977. Today a work can only be banned by judicial ruling, after it has been denounced.

29 J. M. Castellet, '¿Existe hoy una cultura española?' in J. M. Castellet *et al.*, *La cultura* . . ., op. cit., p. 15.

30 On foreign influences in the Spanish culture of the Francoist period, see Rafael Conte, 'Aires del exterior', *Cuadernos para el Diálogo*, XLII, 1974, pp. 62–4.

31 In 1974, the year before Franco's death, 18,720 titles were published in Spain, of which 48 were in Galician, 92 in Basque, and 577 in Catalonian, which means that only 3·8 per cent of all the titles were in languages different from Castilian. In 1978 of the 24,447 titles published 129 were in Galician, 156 in Basque, and 1,132 in Catalonian, which means that the percentage of books written in a regional language had risen to 5·8 per cent (Instituto Nacional del Libro Español, *El Libro Español*, Madrid, 1979).

32 Recent surveys show that in Spain there are very few public libraries (1,435 in contrast to Italy's 8,886) and that 63·6 per cent of the Spanish population never read books; 92·5 per cent never go to a library; 37·4 per cent have fewer than six books at home, and 21·8 per cent have none. In Madrid, for example, 53·7 per cent of the population have not finished their primary education, and 2·9 per cent of those are completely illiterate (Data from *El País*, 7 October 1979, and from the Gabinete de Estudios y Asesoramiento, Madrid, 1979).

PART FOUR

Culture and Protest

Introduction to Part Four

Eastern Europe, geographically distant and linguistically isolated from the rest of the continent, has traditionally remained outside the mainstream of European culture. Its creative achievements – with the exception of the works of the major Russian creative geniuses of the nineteenth and twentieth centuries – have remained unknown and its cultural personality and potentialities have traditionally been obscured in the eyes of Western Europeans by stereotypes concerning Slavdom. Although the Cold War did not do much to improve this situation, it is a significant indication of the contemporary climate of European culture that Eastern Europe and its experiences constitute now an integral part of general European cultural preoccupations. The incorporation of the Eastern European experience into the general culture of the continent constitutes in itself an acknowledgement that the messages it conveyed were directly relevant to the yearnings for a new humanism, for a culture responsive to human needs as visualized by postwar cultural reconstruction.

The concerns of the Eastern half of European culture were voiced through the literature of protest and dissent that provided the primary medium of political criticism in the socialist regimes that emerged from the upheavals of the war. It was precisely the failures of these regimes to realize the human promise of socialism that motivated the literature of dissent. Hence the yearning for a socialist humanism emerged as the common imprint of cultural criticism and political protest in Eastern Europe. The whole movement began with the famous underground literature of the *samizdat* in Russia in the 1950s and was intensified with the cultural 'thaw' following the end of the Stalinist era. Criticism and the vision of a humanized socialism were not limited to the allusions or direct indictments presented in creative literature. They also influenced developments in philosophy and social theory. In these fields, as well as in works of the creative imagination, Eastern Europe made substantial contributions to contemporary European culture.

The literature of the *samizdat* is well known and does not need to be represented here. But the achievements of cultural criticism elsewhere in Eastern Europe deserve the serious attention of all students of European culture. Wolf Biermann's imaginative reconstruction of political criticism into poetry has enriched the literature of East Germany with a sensitivity and vision beyond all possible achievements of regimented 'socialist realism'. Thus Biermann emerged as the truest heir of Brecht's humanism to whose vision and hopes he appeals in one of his poems.

The story of the Praxis Group in Yugoslavia here recorded by one of its most distinguished exponents, Mihailo Marković, is a famous case in the universe of East European cultural criticism. In the attempt to bring out the humanist dimensions of Marxism through receptivity to existentialist and phenomenological influence, the Praxis Group strove to break the ossification imposed by Stalinist dogmatism on their culture. These efforts represented the finest hour in the history of Yugoslav philosophy and their reverberations were felt throughout East European thought. A less well-known, but equally remarkable in intellectual courage, group of philosophers and social theorists has been active in Hungary where the research of the Budapest school continues a tradition inaugurated by Georg Lukács.

The arduous course ahead for the efforts to translate the yearning for socialist humanism into practice are most eloquently expressed in the restrained drama of the Czechoslovak documents which demarcate a decade of desperate protests against the brutal disappointment of the hopes that accompanied the one serious attempt to make socialist humanism a reality in the Prague Spring of 1968. The increased responsiveness in the West to the achievements and predicaments of the culture of Eastern Europe as witnessed, among other instances, by the widespread support elicited in the West by the signers of Charter '77, indicate clearly the intimate cultural dialogue in which the formerly isolated two halves of Europe are now engaged. The universe of humanist concerns that the Eastern perspective has introduced in contemporary European culture sustains the temper of cosmopolitan humanism that constitutes its most constructive dimension.

13

MIHAILO MARKOVIĆ

Marxist Philosophy in Yugoslavia: The Praxis Group

I The Significance of the Praxis Group

Yugoslav philosophy in the 1960s and the beginning of the 1970s has been a curious social phenomenon.

Public lectures on philosophy have attracted unusually wide audiences; philosophical books and articles are read in all social strata; some issues of the journals *Praxis* and *Filosofija*, as well as some philosophical debates, are spoken of as most important cultural and, in a certain sense, political events.

It is a commonplace that philosophy is divorced from concrete social life and actual practical social needs. As a matter of fact, philosophy is often uncommitted, it is often apologetic or very abstract, and sometimes it lags considerably behind the social processes whose deeper meaning it tries to reveal. Minerva's owl flies only at dusk, when things have already taken place, when the necessary experience is already there. By contrast a characteristic feature of the philosophy which has been developing in Yugoslavia during the last two decades is its tendency to anticipate social processes, to reflect critically and in very concrete terms on the present, not only in the light of the past but also of a possible future.

Concrete, critical thinking is always a challenge to some existing authority, the more so if the ability of that authority to direct things and to realize its projects depends upon its full ideological control of the field. That is why Marxist theoreticians have difficulties not only with bourgeois power (the legitimacy of which they tend to destroy) but even more with past revolutionary power (which they legally support) as soon as they begin to really think, that is, begin to think freely. The Yugoslav Praxis Group has taken the risk of asserting its complete freedom in analysing the present-day world and its own society. This fact accounts for both its unusual vitality and its becoming the target of official ideological attacks over the last ten years.

The fate of the group is not an exceptional event. There is a long line of predecessors and contemporaries, indeed the most creative Marxist philosophers in this century, who have been rebuffed and occasionally persecuted by their own parties: Lukács, Bloch, Korsch, Kolakovsky, Kosik, Fischer, Marek, Ilyenkov, Lefebvre, Garaudy, Schaff, Heller, Marcuse and many others. What is nevertheless exceptional about the Praxis Group is that it has managed to resist so long while never giving up any of its principles and convictions: whereas the party bureaucracies have been able, in all the preceding cases, either to compel their theoretical *enfants terribles* to self-criticism (Lukács, Schaff) or else to isolate them completely from the labour movement (Kolakovsky, Lefebvre, Garaudy) or sometimes to silence them for long periods (Korsch, Kosik, Ilyenkov). That none of this has happened in

Yugoslavia is due to a fortunate constellation of factors, to be analysed later. Praxis philosophers still teach in universities, although the authorities have repeatedly been demanding, since 1968, that some of them must be eliminated. They continue to publish their books even though the doors of most publishing houses are closed to them. They continue to publish their journals, *Praxis* and *Filosofija*, with little money and much enthusiasm. They keep up lively links with many important figures in Yugoslav cultural life and enjoy strong support within their communities, although the establishment has made great efforts to isolate them and confine them within the narrow walls of an intellectual reservation. In order to cut off their international links the authorities have at times revoked some of their passports, but a spirit need not travel in space in order to touch another spirit.

Most Yugoslavs naturally do not understand what the whole fuss over philosophers is about. Some watch with amusement as Goliath fails once more against little David. But an enlightened minority which is likely to play a key role in the future development of Yugoslav socialism expects from the outcome of this conflict to obtain answers to some crucial questions – are Marxist intellectuals, under socialism, ever able to preserve their right to free, independent, critical thought when they find themselves under pressure from political power? Is the *avant-garde* of the socialist movement ever ready to tolerate true, creative, non-dogmatic, non-apologetic Marxism (let alone other forms of critical thought) after the seizure of political power? Consequently, is the nature of socialist bureaucracy merely that of a 'deformed' vanguard which is pathologically self-assured but not yet totally alienated from the mass movement, and therefore perhaps able to overcome its arrogant and authoritarian style of management when offered firm revolutionary resistance? Or is such bureaucracy a new oppressive class which tries to utilize isolated fragments from Marx's writings for the purpose of ideologically mystifying reality, but otherwise must regard every true Marxist revolutionary as its natural enemy? In any case, what is the possibility of preserving certain basic liberties in socialism after

they have been enjoyed on a mass scale for more than two decades? What are the chances of preserving the principle of self-management (even in its initial limited form) after it has become the ideological backbone of the whole political system?

The destiny of the Praxis Group is of such crucial importance because there are reasons for optimism if it survives. The historic lesson of this unique experiment would be that no matter how much bureaucracy in socialism may desire to rule in an easy way, without facing any public challenge, it can be compelled to accept the existence of criticism and to live with it. Intellectuals must take the liberty of critical thinking instead of waiting for an enlightened power that will kindly invite them to think freely. In the relation between a bureaucrat's arrogance and an intellectual's cowardice it is the latter that reinforces the former. Furthermore, one of the decisive factors that contributes to the transformation of the revolutionary vanguard into a bureaucratic elite is a general readiness to surrender, to escape, to accept the role of an object. Perhaps the only way to preserve a revolutionary socialist movement is to reduce the authority of the vanguard immediately after the abolition of the old power, and to oppose energetically every symptom of arbitrariness, autocracy and aggressiveness toward those who think differently.

If the Praxis Group perishes, that would mean simply that the intrinsic conflict between revolutionary Marxism and the ruling bureaucracy is so deep and antagonistic that a peaceful resolution is not possible, even under the most favourable conditions. The conditions in this case are indeed exceptionally favourable – Yugoslavia is still the most democratic socialist country. Its leadership, very early after the revolution and while still very young, was compelled to see in its adversary, in *the other* – Stalinism – what it might become itself. In a genuine effort to avoid bureaucratization it introduced initial forms of self-management and a considerable measure of political and academic freedom. Those democratic forms must be preserved if the country is to continue to enjoy its self-respect and a special economic and political status among non-socialist countries. On the other hand by any standard the Praxis Group is not a victim to be dealt with easily. Most of its members participated in the partisan war and have spotless backgrounds. Their scholarly reputation ranks high. They have not committed any illegal act – everyone knows the reason they are persecuted is that they have publicly expressed certain truths about their own society. If, in spite of all these obstacles, the bureaucracy decides that it must effectively silence this voice by force, that would be a proof that the interest of the bureaucracy in preserving its full unquestioned authority is incompatible with the interest of all progressive forces in further developing Marxist theory and in experiencing all the practical consequences of its basic philosophical ideas.

II Development of Marxist Philosophy in Yugoslavia, 1945–64; Formation of the Praxis Group

Marxist philosophy in Yugoslavia emerged with the rise of the socialist revolutionary movement before and during the Second World War. All the preceding history of Yugoslav philosophy is in an insignificant measure relevant for contemporary philosophical thought. Two important spiritual sources in the past however are: (1) a very old tradition of resistance to sheer force, expressed especially in beautiful epic poems about struggles for liberation against the Turks and other foreign invaders and (2) nineteenth-century socialist thought which combined a general revolutionary orientation with a concrete approach to existing backward, rural society in the south Slavic countries of that time.

School philosophy was not very attractive to the young generation that took part in the liberation war and struggle against Stalinism after 1948. With few exceptions professors of philosophy in Yougoslav universities were mere followers, epigones of influential European trends. Socially committed philosophical thought was needed, yielding a capacity to deal with, and settle, grave social issues. Marxism seemed the only existing philosophy that was likely to satisfy that need.

For a brief time, until 1947, the only interpretation of Marxism that was available was 'dialectical materialism' in the form elaborated by Soviet philosophers. But very soon, even before the conflict with Stalinism in 1948, the most gifted students of philosophy in the universities of Belgrade and Zagreb began to doubt whether what they found in the fourth chapter of *The History of the Communist Party of the Soviet Union (Bolsheviks)* was really the last word in revolutionary philosophy. It sounded superficial, simplified and dogmatic: and it altogether lacked any criticism of the existing forms of socialist society.

This very beginning throws considerable light on what followed. Those students who were later to constitute the core of the Praxis Group were mature people – they had held a range of responsible offices in the partisan army before they came to study. An attitude of inferiority and awe before Soviet achievements was entirely lacking. 'We made our own revolution and have the right to behave and to be treated as equals.' But the job of a revolutionary theory is to anticipate further development rather than to glorify the past. If socialist revolution requires a whole epoch, the initial episode of which is the overthrow of bourgeois power, then Marxist theory cannot be construed as something ready-made and fixed: rather it must gain a new form with each important practical step.

The year 1948 signified a great turning point. The fall of such an overwhelming authority as Stalin, the fourth classic, cleared the ground for a much freer, more independent and critical approach to all problems. For a generation which actively fought Stalinist dogmatism, realizing how it damaged Soviet philosophy, the basic motive for all subsequent work would remain the relentless search for truth rather than loyalty to any established authorities or institutions. The principle that 'the progressive is true' was transformed into 'the true is progressive'. For these people, Marxism lost the character of an ideology: no single individual and no organization would again have the right to determine and impose an official interpretation of the thought of the classics of Marxism. Accusations of 'revisionism' became pointless as the essential task ceased to be the *defence* of a sacrosanct classical heritage but its further *development*, involving the principle of revisability or of transcendence. The fall of the fourth classic could not occur without repercussions for the three preceding ones – their texts could no longer be regarded as ultimate truths only to be interpreted, commented upon, or confirmed by new data, but rather as more or less fruitful guidelines for further inquiry.

The most important ethical experience of 1948 was the realization that all means cannot be justified by the mere fact that they serve to attain a supposedly revolutionary goal. The old Jesuit doctrine was widely used by many pragmatically minded revolutionaries and was not questioned while it meant that violence was often necessary to achieve radical social change, or that a revolutionary must not tell the truth about his organization's activities in front of the class enemy. But socialists came to use the most absurd lies and threats of physical force against other socialists in order to subordinate them 'in the interests of the international workers' movement'. It turned out that to decide what really was a revolutionary goal presented a much greater problem than had hitherto been suspected. And even if a goal were not controversial in its abstract conceptual form, it might be profoundly deformed in the process of its practical realization if unsuitable means were chosen in its pursuit. Use of inhuman, unjust means deforms their agents profoundly and makes them deviate utterly from what they believed was their end. It has become clear that if one wants to avoid being caught up in myths and hypocritical ideological justifications of stupid or tyrannical actions one has to apply the same ethical criteria both to ends and to means, and to evaluate each action according to both consequences and to motives.

A major change in political philosophy has been the revaluation of demands for unity of all revolutionaries, both in theory and in practice. Unity (even 'monolithic' unity) used always to be highly esteemed by Marxists. Since the days of the *Communist Manifesto* it was believed that united proletarians were the only social force able to topple an extremely powerful and firmly entrenched capitalist elite. However, the issue of unity appeared in 1948 in an entirely new context. It became obvious that an abstract demand for unity was purely formal; the concrete problem was unity on the basis of certain principles and policies. Now, these principles and policies are either imposed by one central authority or reached by agreement among several equal partners. Only the latter alternative leads to an increase of freedom, initiative and self-determination of all the parts of a united whole. The differences that may be generated in this way, due to specific life-conditions of particular social groups and nations, do not necessarily lead to a disintegration of the whole: rather they enrich it, increase total creativity and accelerate the rate of development. This synthesis of monism and pluralism, of the principles of unity and individuality will remain one of the basic constitutive principles in various spheres of Yugoslav social life, and in particular in the information and development of the Praxis Group itself.

The 1950s was a period of reinterpretation of Marx's philosophy and modern science, a period of building up the theoretical foundations of a new philosophy which, while remaining in the tradition of Marx, was sharply opposed to rigid, dogmatic schemes of *Diamat* and at the same time tended to incorporate the most important achievements in post-Marxian philosophy and culture.

A thorough study of the classical works of Marxism, especially of Marx's early manuscripts, in a new perspective, led to the rediscovery of a profound and sophisticated humanist philosophy which, for a long time, has been either ignored or dismissed by a great many Marxist philosophers as being Hegelian. It became clear that the problems which the young Marx was grappling with – praxis, the conflict of human existence and essence, the question of what constitute true needs and basic human capacities, alienation, emancipation, labour and production, and other concerns expressed at that time – far from being sins of youth underlay all his mature work and, furthermore, remain even now the living, crucial issues of our time and indeed of the whole epoch of transition.

It did not take much time to realize that in the

writings of the classics of Marxism there were no answers to many problems of our time. How explain the fact that socialist revolutions did not occur in developed industrial countries of the West but in backward rural societies of the East? What really is a revolution if after its apparent victory a bureaucratic society can emerge? How to build up socialism in a relatively underdeveloped country? What does it mean for the state to wither away? How is a non-market modern economy possible? What is *Marxist* logic, ethics, aesthetics? Is there a Marxist anthropology? What is the essence of man with respect to which one speaks about alienation? If that essence is universal – how is history possible? If it is particular, how may we overcome relativism? If man is a being of praxis, and praxis is (among other things) labour and production, how can the standpoint of praxis be a standard of critical evaluation? How are we to reconcile the principle of determinism, according to which historical processes are governed by laws independent of human consciousness and will, with the principle of freedom according to which it is men who make their own history? What is the axiological ground for such normative dialectical concepts as *totality development, self-actualization, negation, transcendence*? How is it possible to conceive of the category of *matter* without either renouncing materialism or falling back upon absolute pre-Kantian dualism?

These and many other questions had to be thoroughly studied and discussed. Asking good questions resulted, on the one hand, in an opening out towards the whole of existing culture and on the other hand, in creating a proper intellectual community capable of a creative collective effort.

While, in the years of orthodoxy, immediately following the war and political revolution, Western culture was considered decadent and declining in almost all aspects (with the exception of ideologically neutral fields such as the exact sciences and technology) the picture became much more diversified and pluralistic in the early 1950s. Curiously enough that happened in the worst days of the Cold War, when intolerance and ideological prejudice reached the level of sheer madness in

McCarthyism and in Stalin's campaign against cosmopolitanism – indeed against any appreciation of foreign science and culture. On the contrary, in Yugoslav cultural life at that time ideological criteria tended to be replaced by aesthetic and scholarly ones. Socialist realism was generally abandoned as a caricature of a Marxist approach to the arts. A thoroughgoing process of emancipation from ideological censorship took place: at first in music, painting, sculpture and architecture, then in literature and eventually in all other fields. In the social sciences, especially in disciplines which at that time were suspected of being 'bourgeois sciences' (!) such as sociology and psycology, the pendulum even went to the other extreme when in reaction to 'historical materialism' certain primitive forms of empiricism were revived which at that time were considered *passé* in the West.

In philosophy a measure of general criticism of the basic assumptions of various existing trends of Western philosophy was always present but did not exclude a genuine interest in the concrete contributions of analytical philosophy, phenomenology, existentialism, and other schools. Under these influences much serious work was undertaken in the philosophy of language, the methodology of science, axiology, philosophical anthropology and meta-ethics – disciplines and problems which were completely outside the framework of orthodox Marxist philosophy.

A fortunate circumstance in those formative years after 1948 was the fact that the new, postwar generation quickly found suitable forms for a collective intellectual life. In 1950 the Serbian Philosophical Society was created. Later similar philosophical societies emerged in all the other republics. Since 1958 there has also been a Yugoslav Philosophical Association. During the decade of the 1950s dozens of philosophical conferences were held on problems which were considered essential at that time: the nature of philosophy, the relationship between philosophy and science, ideology, truth, alienation, the young and old Marx, Marxist humanism. These discussions were led in complete freedom and sincerity, in an atmosphere of genuine dialogue among spokesmen of several different Marxist orientations. A basic polarization occurred between those who continued the line of orthodox Marxism, which is to say, a mere defence and justification of the classical writings of Marx, Engels and Lenin; and those who radically opposed any orthodoxy, insisting on the further development of what is, in our time, still living and revolutionary in the classical sources.

The former orientation laid emphasis on the philosophy of the natural sciences, trying to employ recent achievements in that field to confirm an Engelsian conception of *Naturphilosophie*. Outside the domain of their interest remained Marx's critique of the political economy and especially the early humanistic writings of Marx. Therefore the basic philosophical problem remained for them the relation of matter and mind. The main objective of their research programme was the establishment of the most general laws in nature, society and human thought. This in fact was the programme of the whole orientation of dialectical materialism.

The latter orientation rejected 'dialectical materialism' as a dogmatic and essentially conservative orientation which at best leads to a generalization and systematization of existing scientific knowledge, but does not contribute to the creation of a critical epochal consciousness capable of directing practical social energy towards the liberation and humanization of the world. From this point of view the basic philosophical problem is the historical human condition and the possibilities for radical universal emancipation.

Within this humanist orientation there was from the beginning a clear distinction between those who tended to develop *Marxism* as a *critical science* and those who construed it as essentially a revolutionary *utopia*. From the former standpoint the essential limitation of dogmatism was the ideologization of Marx's doctrine. In order for this to be demystified it was necessary not only to return to classical sources and to reinterpret them, but also to develop a high degree of objectivity and criticism in dealing with contemporary problems; to re-establish the unity of theory and practice and to mediate the *a priori* philosophical vision of man as a 'being of praxis' and

communism as a de-alienated human community – with concrete knowledge about existing historical conditions and tendencies. According to this view Marx had transcended pure philosophy and created an all-embracing critical social theory. Such an approach required the development of a general method of critical inquiry: dialectic.

From the latter standpoint it was believed that the essential philosophical limitation of dogmatism was a positivist reduction of philosophy to a *quasi*-objective science. It is the nature of science to divide, fragment, quantify, reduce man to an object, study equilibrium rather than change, see changes only as variations of a fixed pattern. It was considered desirable, therefore, to separate sharply philosophy from science, to put philosophy into brackets as insufficiently relevant for the study of human alienation and emancipation. According to this view the philosophical thought of Marx expressed in his early writings was in fact utopian thought about the future, about what *could be*. Such an utopian thought is radical due to its implicit invitation to abolish existing reality. Scientific knowledge, on the other hand, remains within the boundaries of actually existing objects – that is the source of its conformism.

Although the representatives of these two tendencies used to clash whenever they met (and they have continued to disagree on some points up to the present) they also considerably influenced one another and began to fuse. What united them and at the same time opposed orthodox Marxists was their resolute criticism of dogmatism, resistance to Engelsian *Naturphilosophie*, a high appreciation for the humanism underlying all Marx's work, a self-critical attitude with respect to both Marxist heritage and the reality in which Marxist ideas were being implemented.

A decisive debate between humanists and orthodox Marxists took place at the symposium 'Problems of Object and Subject, Practice and the Theory of Reflection', organized by the Yugoslav Philosophical Association at Bled in August 1960.

During this lively, and at moments dramatic debate, orthodox Marxists tried to save the theory of reflection, the cornerstone of the epistemology developed by Soviet dialectical materialists and the Bulgarian philosopher Todor Pavlov. The main objections addressed to this theory were: first, it ignores the whole experience of German classical philosophy and goes back to eighteenth-century dualism of a material object *in itself* and a spiritual subject; secondly, there is an implicit dogmatism in the view that reflection is the essential property of all consciousness – how challenge products of mind which by definition are reflections of reality, i.e. true? Thirdly, the theory is false because, as a matter of fact, consciousness, far from passively accompanying and copying material processes, very often anticipates and projects not-yet-existent material objects. The attempt to define the theory of reflection by saying that in such cases we deal with 'creative reflections' made the impression of an *ad hoc* convention by which the concept of reflection was expanded in such a way as to become totally uninformative.

During this debate the view prevailed that the central category of Marx's philosophy was free, human, creative activity – practice. Dualism of matter and mind, object and subject was superseded by showing how these categories can be derived from the notion of *practice*. Objects we speak meaningfully about are not just given in themselves, they are objects of a historic human world, transformed by our practical activity, mediated by our previous knowledge, language, needs and indeed the whole of human culture at a given historical moment. The subject is not just a locus of reflection of external reality but a complex historical being, who not only observes and infers but also projects what is not yet there, yet might develop. Only within this context does the category of reflection become meaningful, only when it has been practically established that certain products of mind have their antecedent correlates in physical reality may they be considered reflections.

The Bled debate marks the end of a period of formation of the theoretical grounds for a new activist interpretation of Marxism. Orthodox Marxists subsequently completely withdrew from the philosophical societies and journals, and they played quite an insignificant role in philosophical life during the 1960s. On the other hand, humanists felt that after settling fundamental theoretical issues, a step towards more concrete activism had become urgent. Once it became clear that the role of a revolutionary philosophy cannot be reduced simply to a rational explanation of the existing reality, socialist as well as capitalist, that its essential task is the discovery of the essential limitations of the existing world and of the historical possibilities abolishing these limitations – it became necessary to transcend the initial, abstract, critical theory by a concrete, practically oriented, social criticism. Criticism reduced to a most general analysis of alienation of the contemporary would have the character of an alienated criticism because it would abolish alienation only in thought, not in reality. Concrete criticism, on the other hand, could not have been reduced to capitalist society only, because many forms of alienation characteristic of capitalism were still present in post-revolutionary society: the fetishism of commodities, the appropriation of surplus value by the ruling elites, political alienation and state power, nationalism, and above all, a professional division of labour and an enormous gap between the creative activity of the minority and the mechanical, degrading labour of the vast majority. To project alienation only into the external bourgeois world would amount to speaking about one's own problems in an ideological mystified way which would block further revolutionary activity. An authentic philosophical criticism had to be concrete in the sense of dealing with its own immediate historical grounds.

This new orientation was clearly formulated at the annual meeting of the Yugoslav Philosophical Association in Skopje in 1962, and in the collective work *Humanism and Socialism* produced by the Zagreb and Belgrade philosophers Supek, Petrović, Vranicki, Kangrga, Marković, Korać, Kršić and others.

Between 1963 and 1968 a series of extremely lively and fruitful philosophical meetings took place. The central themes discussed were: the meaning and historical novelty of socialism, criteria of historical progress, concepts of freedom and democracy, a critique of professional politics and bureaucracy, analysis of the limitations of the existing forms of self-management, a critique of the market economy, personal integrity in a society dominated by politics, the character of a new socialist culture.

An especially great role in the development of a philosophical social criticism was played by the Korcula Summer School, an informal summer meeting-place of Zagreb and Belgrade philosophers and sociologists with the participation of internationally known Marxists and Marxologists such as Fromm, Marcuse, Bloch, Habermas, the late Goldmann, Mandel, Bottomore, Ruel, Axelos, the late Mallet, Marek, Kolakovsky, Kosik, Cerrone, Lombardo-Radice, Heller, Fleischer, Wartoffsky, Tucker, Birnbaum and others. The same group of philosophers and sociologists who estalished the Korcula Summer School (Supek, Petrović, Vranicki, Kangrga, Grlić, Bošnjak, Kovacić – from Zagreb; Marković, Tadić, Korać, Krešić, Milić, Stojanović, Golubović, Zivotić – from Belgrade) founded the journal *Praxis*, the first issue of which appeared in 1964, edited by Petrović and Supek. At that time the journal of the Yugoslav Philosophical Association, *Filosofija*, edited in Belgrade, had a rather academic character, being open to all philosophical problems and all existing orientations. A new editorial board in 1967 gave it an equally and critical character. Selected articles from *Filosofija* and domestic editorials from *Praxis* are now being published in the international edition of *Praxis*.

III Development of the Praxis Group, 1964–74, under Increasing Pressure from the Establishment

Since most members of the Praxis Group actively participated in the revolution and because the critique of Stalinist dogmatism coincided with the general policy of the country in the 1950s, the official reaction was more or less favourable. It is true that Big Brother's eye kept watch closely and each philosophical meeting was attended by a few informers who would afterwards prepare detailed reports about what was spoken within the conference halls (and outside them). In 1957 a short period of improvement in Yugoslav–Soviet relations was used by an old dogmatist, Boris Ziherl, to attack 'revisionists' in a long article published in the party newspaper *Komunist*. His main point was that a group of younger Marxist philosophers read Western philosophers uncritically and were creating confusion by attempting to incorporate some of their ideas into Marxism. However, at that time it was possible to publish an extensive reply in the same newspaper and many of those who disliked Ziherl took this opportunity for rebuttal as an indication that the party no longer supported him.

Several top leaders listened with mixed feelings to tapes from the Bled debate. They did not have any illusions about the mediocrity and sterility of orthodox Marxists – the losers; but there was something on the winning side which they held suspect – an apparent touch of 'idealism', a complete sense of autonomy and self-reliance, an unusual boldness in taking up ideologically relevant positions without even consulting authorities, an exaggerated activism which seemed to neglect real conditions, a humanism that for some reason sounded 'elitist'. It was already customary in those years around 1960 to qualify this dominant philosophical trend as an *abstract* humanism. The true meaning of this derogatory term was: instead of practically supporting and affirming the efforts of the party to build up a new society here and now, philosophers discuss such abstract problems as alienation, human nature, praxis, emancipation, self-realization, true human community and similar themes that Marx dealt with only while he was young and immature. At that time politicians were not yet able to see how relatively harmless this *abstract* humanism was and how much more trouble with humanism they would have when it became *concrete*.

Since 1963 Praxis philosophers established that both forms of economic and political alienation still existed in Yugoslav society, that the working class was still exploited – this time by the new elites: bureaucracy and technocracy; that the market economy will inevitably reproduce capital–labour relations; that self-management exists only at the micro level in enterprises and local communities and organizations, and that consequently its further development requires a gradual withering away of professional politics and the formation of workers' councils at the regional, republican and federal levels; that the basic precondition for a really participatory democracy was at first a radical democratisation, and, later, the withering away, of the party.

In the period 1963–8 an attempt was made to mobilize loyal party theoreticians to oppose these critical views with ideological counter-criticism. But few able scholars were available and the counter-arguments were weak. 'How can the working class', asked these official spokesmen, 'being the ruling class in socialism, exploit itself?' Marx's critique of the market economy, they alleged, did not hold valid for a socialist market economy. 'The attack on bureaucracy', they held, 'is an anarchistic assault on organized society.' Any critique of the existing form of self-management they saw as a critique of self-management in principle. Integrated self-management at the republican and federal level was held to be a form of statism. Democratization of the party, in the sense of allowing minorities to continue to express and justify their ideas, amounted in their view to a demand that factions be allowed within the party, and so on.

The year 1968 was a turning point. Students' mass demonstrations in Belgrade on 2 and 3 June, and the occupation of all buildings of the universities in Belgrade 3–10 June, followed by similar events in Zagreb and Sarajevo, opened up the greatest political crisis in Yugoslav postwar society and produced a permanent fear that philosophical critical theory under certain conditions might inspire a mass practical movement.

A series of measures were undertaken in order thoroughly to reduce the field of activity of Praxis philosophers. Most of those who were members of the party were expelled, or their organizations were dissolved. They were eliminated from important social functions. Funds for philosophical activities, journals and other publications were cut off or became extremely scarce. Demands were expressed by top leaders that those philosophers who had exerted a 'corrupting', 'ideologically alien' influence on students, more specifically those from the University of Belgrade, had to be ousted from the university.

That in spite of all this the Praxis Group was able to continue to work, to publish, and in a sense still to dominate the Yugoslav philosophical scene can be explained by a fortunate combination of several factors.

First, and most important, after 1948 Yugoslavia had gone rather far in the process of democratization and the rejection of the theoretical and practical forms of Stalinism. The achievements of this process can no longer be fully undone since the mentality and life-style of millions of people has changed irreversibly. A whole new generation has grown up in the meantime, as well as a new generation of liberal and pragmatic functionaries who are lacking the earlier fanaticism and ideological militancy and who would hate to be indentified with Stalinists. There is a lot of foot-dragging when things reminiscent of old 'administrative' practices have to be done. No matter how little the principles of self-management are present in the higher political regions it is a reality in the micro-cells of the society, that is, in enterprises and also in the university faculties. One would have to violate the constitution and the laws in order to usurp the rights of workers' councils to decide about matters of internal organization and of personnel policy.

Secondly, the Praxis Group has had enough time between 1948 and 1968 to establish its scholarly and political reputation. In Yugoslavia, as in any other socialist country, ordinary people are ready to believe that there are all kinds of internal and external enemies. But unlike people in some other socialist countries they are no longer ready to believe that socialists turn overnight into enemies or that in reality they have always been anti-socialist, or that good comrades have to confess whatever has been demanded of them in some strange unconceivable interest of the party. Therefore all those abusive libels that were stamped on philosophers over the years: 'anarcho-liberals', 'opposition to the party', 'extremists', 'enemies of self-management' (!), and so on, have come to sound much more like expressions of someone's anger than real descriptions. Another relevant circumstance is that the Praxis Group plays an important role in keeping a complex ideological balance in Yugoslavia. Its disappearance would inevitably strengthen right-wing nationalists (especially in Croatia) and pro-Stalinist hard-liners (especially in Serbia). The Praxis Group played an important role in the struggle against those two dangerous conservative forces. In revenge both would gladly settle accounts with Praxis, and they keep on offering their services to the party, but the latter has to beware of such allies. Because the ideological situation is different in different republics and Yugoslavia continues to emphasize its federal structure, it is very difficult to synchronize pressure against Praxis in Serbia and in Croatia. The Croat leadership cannot possibly expel Praxis professors from the university yet at the same time tolerate dozens of those who in various ways were involved in the nationalist movement of 1971. The Serbian leadership, on the other hand, finds itself in an awkward position when it has to drive out of the Belgrade University the same kind of people who keep important functions at the University of Zagreb.

Thirdly, the international status and reputation that the country used to enjoy in the world is also a serious limiting factor. It is absolutely essential for Yugoslavia to preserve its present political and economic relations with non-socialist countries. Those relations have been somewhat strained since the party's 1972 crackdown on liberalism. Any further erosion of civil liberties and any harsh repressive measures against intellectuals would be interpreted as clear symptoms of a retrogressive trend and of a return towards Stalinism. This would eventually jeopardize all the achievements of a long, consistent policy of non-alignment and opening out towards the world.

Fourthly, and not the least significant, is the amazing solidarity not only within the group but also in the broader university community to which it belongs. There are well-known devices used a hundred times over by which the establishment reaches its objectives without actually using force. The essence of the technique is to disintegrate the

victim morally and then to bring him to the point where he strangles himself with its own hands. This is usually achieved by combining strong pressures, intended to scare possible supporters and to break the will of the victim (in this case: sharp, abusive attacks at meetings and via the mass media; banning issues of the journal: threats that the philosophy faculty will be dissolved and that its supporters as well as the main victims will lose their jobs; rumours that the people in question are foreign spies, therefore soon to be arrested; and so on) with opening up the prospect of a 'compromise', that is to say, splitting the issue into two parts, one which would have to be sacrificed for the other to be saved (in this case: *Praxis* could continue but must change its editorial policies, or it must apply self-criticism to past errors; the Belgrade professors will be given scholarly jobs but they must resign from their teaching position; or even that two of the eight have to go, so that the six may remain). After a sufficiently long and well-dosed pressure the victim usually feels isolated, becomes unnerved, and makes himself believe that by sacrificing something and by partial surrender he will be left in peace. But what he sacrifices is usually moral strength – the only weapon he has. And a surrender is never partial: bureaucracy takes its time and the principle of its absolute authority requires a corresponding principle of absolute surrender (which might technically be divided into several episodes).

None of those devices worked this this time. The scenario was well known in advance, the usual errors were not made, human relationships within the group, between the group and other intellectuals, between professors and students – all withstood the test. After six years of hard pressure they were even solidified. Student support from all three of the most important Yugoslav universities, Belgrade, Zagreb and Ljubljana, played a very important role. Students threatened to strike if anything happened to their professors and it was indeed difficult to forsee what kind of processes, in the given economic conditions, might have been triggered by such a strike.

For all those reasons the activity of the Praxis Group after 1968 was only reduced; it never stopped. A number of books were published in that period.

The journals *Filosofija* and *Praxis* survived. The sessions of the Korcula Summer School continue to take place each August. The Philosophical Institute in the University of Belgrade has engaged a number of co-researchers on several research programmes.

Since 1971 this institute together with the journal *Filosofija* and the Serbian Philosophical Society has organized winter meetings which concentrate on most current theoretical issues. These meetings take place in an atmosphere of considerable tension. The last one in February 1974 ended with security agents searching the rooms of several participants, interviewing some and confiscating the tapes intended for the publication of the *Proceedings* of the meeting. Eventually a participant, the poet Milan Ignjatović, was arrested and sentenced to three-and-a-half years in jail for the speech that he delivered at the meeting.

IV   Basic Philosophical Views of the Praxis Group

(1)   The Conception of Philosophy

The Praxis Group is composed of individual philosophers who not only specialize in different fields but also differ in certain basic conceptions. They must not be treated therefore as a homogeneous philosophical school. What unites them is much more a practical attitude than a theoretical doctrine, which does not exclude the possibility of formulating certain basic views which could be endorsed by all.

Concerning the nature of philosophy, for example, it is not controversial that the essential function of philosophy is to form a total critical consciousness able to enlighten and direct all human activity in a given historical epoch. Being *total* it differs from the fragmented knowledge of various scientific disciplines; being *critical consciousness* it is much more than a totality of positive scientific knowledge.

The main disagreement begins, however, when one embarks upon a more specific determination of the relation between science and philosophy. According

to Petrović, Kangrga, and Zivotić it makes sense to speak of a 'pure' philosophy, that is *a priori* with respect to science fully independent from it. According to Marković, Supek and Vranicki, philosophy in the tradition of Marx cannot be 'pure'; it develops from an initial abstract *a priori* vision towards an increasingly concrete and rich theory that tends to incorporate all relevant scientific knowledge.

(2)   The Philosophical Starting Point

The orthodox, *Diamat*, view that the central philosophical problem is the relation of matter and mind has been generally rejected as abstract, ahistorical, dualistic. The central problem for Marx was – how to realize human nature by producing a more humane world. The fundamental philosophical assumption implicit in this problem is that man is essentially a being of *praxis*, i.e. a being capable of free creative activity by which he transforms the world, realizes his specific potential faculties and satisfies the needs of other human individuals. Praxis is an essential possibility for man but under certain unfavourable historical conditions its realization may be blocked. This discrepancy between the individual's actual existence and potential essence, i.e. between what he is and what he might be, is *alienation*. The basic task of philosophy is to analyse critically the phenomenon of alienation and to indicate practical steps leading to human *self-realization*, to *praxis*.

This is believed to be the common ground of Marxist humanism. Undoubtedly it opens up a number of problems which are dealt with in various individual writings. Within the scope of this essay I shall mention only briefly a few distinctions which I have had to make in some of my works.

Praxis has to be distinguished from the purely epistemological category of *practice*. The latter refers simply to any subject's activity of changing an object and this activity can be alienated. The former is a normative concept and refers to an ideal, specifically human activity which is an end in itself, a statement of basic values and at the same time a standard of criticism of all other forms of activity.

Praxis must also not be identified with *labour* and *material production.* The latter belong to the sphere of necessity, they are necessary conditions for human survival, and must involve division of roles, routine operations, subordination, hierarchy. Work becomes *praxis* only when it is freely chosen and provides an opportunity for individual self-expression and self-fulfilment.

How may we conceive of potential human faculties? They must be universal, otherwise a general standard of criticism would be lacking and philosophy would have to be relativized – which is absurd. On the other hand, if they are unchangeable, history would lose all meaning and would be reduced to a series of changes in the realm of mere phenomena. The only solution is to conceive of universal faculties as latent dispositions which are the product of the whole previous history and which can be slowly modified or even replaced by some new future ones – depending on actual life-conditions over a long period of time.

But is human nature constituted only by 'positive' faculties such as: creativity, capacity for reasoning, for communication, sociability, and so on? How may we justify such an optimistic view? And how may we account for the tremendous amount of evil in human history? Again, the only solution is to modify somewhat Marx's optimism and to introduce an idea of polarity of human nature. As a result of millennia of life in class society man has also acquired some 'negative' latent dispositions such as: aggressiveness, egoistic acquisitiveness, will to power, destructive drives. All these enter into a *descriptive* concept of human nature which can be tested by historical evidence. Which of the conflicting latent dispositions will prevail and what sort of character will be formed in each individual case depends upon the social surroundings, upon the actual historical conditions. Thus when a philosopher builds up a selective, *normative,* concept of human nature he implicitly commits himself to a way of life, to the creation of such life-conditions under which certain desirable (positive) latent dispositions entering his normative concept, may prevail, while certain undesirable

(negative) dispositions would be blocked or slowly modified assuming socially acceptable forms.

On these grounds it becomes possible to distinguish between *true genuine needs* and *false, artificial* ones, or between a true and an illusory *self-realization.* The concept of truth in this context is much more general than the customary epistemological concept. One of its dimensions is adequacy to actual reality (the descriptive concept of truth). Another dimension is adequacy to an ideal standard, to an essential possibility (the normative concept of truth).

(3) Philosophical Method

Philosophers who agree on so many issues and have collaborated fraternally over such a long period of time, as is the case with the Praxis Group, must presumably have some common general methodological assumptions. But it is not easy to establish what they are. One of the things that unites all Yugoslav Marxist humanists is their rejection of the orthodox conception of dialectic.

Orthodox Marxists (*Diamatchiks*) believed that they should continue Engels's work and try to find new scientific confirmation for 'the laws of dialectic' discovered by Hegel and 'interpreted materialistically' by the classics of Marxism (these three laws were: the unity of opposites, the transition of quantity into quality and the negation of negation).

Dialectic, thus conceived, became a static and formal method – a set of ready-made, fixed, *a priori* rules that could be applied to any given content, celestial mechanics as well as the history of a revolution. While rejecting this interpretation of dialectic, some Praxis philosophers list all interest in the problems of philosophical method in general and dialectic in particular. As a consequence, one finds in their works quite sharp distinctions, an absence of mediation between opposites, a tendency to construe some key concepts such as human essence, alienation, revolution, human community, and so on, as transcendental rather than historical categories.

Other Praxis philosophers consider the question of method decisive for a theoretical orientation. They are convinced that the dialectic is the proper method for a critical philosophy and try to develop it, on the one hand by a deeper study of Hegel's *Phenomenology of Mind* and *Logic* together with the implicit dialectic of Marx's writings; on the other hand by critical examination of other contemporary methods (analytic, phenomenological, structuralist). The defining characteristics of dialectic, in contrast to those other methods, are the following regulative principles.

(a) Reality should be approached as a concrete totality rather than as an association of parts to be analysed in isolation from each other; such an approach reveals possibilities of radical change of the given system, not only of its modification.

(b) Making sharp dichotomic distinctions is only a first approximation in the process of conceptual inquiry; deeper analysis reveals mediating instances among opposites.

(c) A study of synchronic, structural relations must be supplemented by the study of dischronic, historic relationships. Each apparently stable object is only a phase of its history; it can be fully understood only in the light of its origin and its future possibilities.

(d) What moves all objects is the conflict of inner opposite forces and tendencies; what moves thought is the discovery of contradictions; all problems are contradictions of some sort; to solve the problem means to disentangle the contradictions.

(e) As distinguished from an external, rigid determination in the world of objects (and reified human beings) *praxis*, a specifically human activity, is characterized by self-determination, i.e. by a conscious purposeful commitment to realize practically one specific, freely chosen possibility among a set of alternatives.

(f) What constitutes a radical qualitative change of an object is the abolition of its essential inner limitation ('negation of its negation').

Dialectic according to this conception is neither a structure of an absolute, abstract spirit (as in Hegel) nor a general structure of nature (as in Engels) but a general structure of human historical praxis and its essential aspect – critical thinking. This conception, in contrast to the orthodox one, allows room for its further self-development, for the conceiving of or the creating of an object by this method means at the same time to enrich and make more concrete the method itself.

(4) Ontological, Epistemological and Axiological Implications

From the standpoint of a dialectic of praxis it does not make sense to speak about reality 'in itself', truth 'in itself', or values 'in themselves'. There certainly is an antecedent structured reality; without assuming its existence it would be impossible to understand how organized, coordinated activity is at all possible. But whatever we come to know and say meaningfully and concretely about material or cultural reality has been mediated by the specific, historically determined features of our practical activity.

For the same reason to speak about truth 'in itself' is either to confuse an epistemological category (truth) with an ontological category (fact) or to assume the existence of some mystical extra-human consciousness. As a measure of adequacy truth is a human, historical category.

The same holds for 'values in themselves'. There is not an ideal, a historical sphere to which they apply. There is not a Lotzean, Husserlian and, more recently, Popperian 'third world'. The world into which man has not practically penetrated is blind, meaningless, truthless, valueless. Objects and processes become values only when they are relative to human needs, which again in their turn are a product of the whole of preceding history.

An opposite procedure from this projection of especially human products into transcendental, extra-human realms is their reduction to mere things, i.e. their reification. In ontology, reification shows as a tendency to regard conscious human activity as merely an epiphenomenon of some primary objective structure: Being, Matter, Nature, inexorable Laws – independent of human consciousness and will. However, in the human word (with which philosophy deals) all objective structures are, in one way or another, mediated by human activity and relative to it. For example, laws that govern historic processes are nothing but relatively permanent patterns of human behaviour, repeated time and again while certain conditions are present. But conscious subjects can modify those conditions and change the patterns of their behaviour. In *epistemology* reification appears as a tendency to regard the model of natural sciences as the paradigm of knowledge in general. The transfer of concepts and methods of the natural sciences into the social sciences and the humanities does not only result in gross simplifications but also in a specific sort of conformism whereby mechanical, unimaginative, uncreative, reified forms of human behaviour (which are the result of extraordinarily dehumanizing conditions) are explained easily as the *natural* way of being. Analogously in *axiology* reification takes the form of a behaviourist reduction of all purposive, goal-directed activity to a stimulus/response scheme relegating thus all discussion of values to an archaic, pre-scientific era of theoretical development. This approach is capable of yielding interesting results only with rats and pigeons. It fails miserably in dealing with specifically human, that is spontaneous, free creative, imaginative, self-improving action. For example, no revolution could be accounted for in terms of mechanistic or behaviourist assumptions.

(5) Practical Social Implications

A philosophy based on the notion of *praxis* will naturally pay special attention to deriving practical consequences from its principles; furthermore, these consequences essentially will be steps that have to be undertaken in order to make true the idea of man as essentially a *being of praxis.*

Under what social conditions, in what kind of social organization can human activity become the objectification of the individual's most creative capacities and a means of satisfying genuine individual and common needs?

This question is much more general than the one usually asked by Marxists who ignore the philosophical roots of Marx's economic and political criticism. All questions about specific social institutions, such as private property, capital, the bourgeois state, and so on, boil down to the fundamental issue: what happens to man, what are his relationships to other human beings, does he actualize or waste all the wealth of his potential powers?

In this radical perspective (*radical* because the root, *radix*, of all issues is man) the basic purpose of critical inquiry is the discovery of those specific social institutions and structures which cripple human beings, arrest their development and impose on them patterns of simple, easily predictable, dull, stereotyped behaviour. Thus critique of various institutions of bourgeois society is a superficial sectarian critique if it remains an abstract negation of one particular form of social organization (capitalism) from the point of view of another particular form (socialism). The essential point of a radical, universally human critique is that these institutions inevitably bring about various forms of economic and political alienation. Thus: *provate property* produces a privatized, egoistic, acquisitive type of man; *professional division of labour* pins down complex human individuals to fixed simple roles which employ only a small fraction of their potential abilities; the regulation of production by the market reduces both the producer and the product to mere commodities, substitites the profit motive of production for the needs-satisfaction motive, turns production into an uncontrollable competitive process governed by blind economic forces; the *state* divides citizens into ruling subjects and ruled objects, turns decision-making on issues of general social interest into a specialized, professional activity in the hands of an alienated elite; the *party* is a hierarchical political organization with very little equality and genuine participation – it tends to create and preserve an artificial unity of will and of faith in an apparently just sense by ideological manipulation and compulsory discipline.

An important practical implication of the dialectical method is the important distinction between criticism as an 'abstract negation', aiming at total destruction of the criticized object, and criticism as a 'concrete negation', *Aufhebung*, aiming at the abolition of only those features of the criticized object which constitute its essential inner limitation, while preserving all those other features (properties, elements, structures) which constitute a necessary condition for further development.

Thus while it is in the nature of Marxist theory to offer 'a relentless criticism of all existing reality' – a characterization of the Praxis Group approach which infuriates bureaucracy – this criticism does not invite destruction but the *transcendence* of its object.

The practical form of transcendence in history is *revolution*. The defining characteristics of a social revolution are neither use of violence, nor overthrow of a government and seizure of political power, nor economic collapse of the system. Already Marx spoke of a possible peaceful social revolution in England, Holland and America. He also made very clear, explicit statements about seizure of power being only the first episode of a long process of social revolution, about political revolution (as distinguished from social revolution) having a 'narrow spirit' and leading necessarily to the rule of an elite. That economic collapse is also not a necessary condition of revolution follows from Marx's description of economic transition measures which a new proletarian government has to undertake after successful seizure of power. These measures are cautious and gradual, intended to preserve the continuity of economic functioning.

The Marxian concept of revolution is constituted by the following three basic elements: the first is the idea of a *socioeconomic formation*. Each concrete society belongs to a certain type, to a socioeconomic formation (feudalism, capitalism, etc.) which has definite structual characteristics; second is the idea of an *essential inner limitation* – some structural characteristics block any further development and prevent the realization of already existing historical possibilities of given society. (For example, private property prevents the socialization of production and its rational coordination as a whole.)

Third is the idea of *transcendence*, and it is irrelevant whether physical force is used, or whether change takes place in one discontinuous cataclysmic act or by a series of gradual transformations. The only relevant condition is the *abolition of the essential inner limitation of the given socioeconomic formation*.

From this point of view none of the twentieth-century socialist revolutions has so far been completed; what has taken place so far in Russia, China, Cuba, Yugoslavia and elsewhere were only initial phases or abortive attempts. Private ownership of the means of production was not transcended by really social ownership but modified into state and group property. Professional division of labour still largely exists, and work is equally long, monotonous, stultifying and wasteful as in capitalism. The market is no longer the exclusive regulator of production; it has been supplemented by state planning but this latter way of regulating production is still far from being very rational and democratic, and it still preserves a good deal of profit motivation. The bourgeois state was not transcended by a network of self-management organs but was only modified into a bureaucratic state which allows a greater (in Yugoslavia) or a lesser (in Russia) degree of participatory democracy in atomic units of social organization. The party as a typically bourgeois type of political organization tends to be perpetuated. It is true, the social composition of the rank and file membership of the 'communist' party shows a shift towards the working class but the organization is even more authoritarian and ideological indoctrination even more drastic. The fact that there is only one such organization which monopolizes all political power is hardly an advantage over bourgeois pluralism. Real supersession of political alienation will materialize only when all monopolies of power are dismantled, when authoritarian and hierarchical organizations such as the state and party gradually wither away and are replaced by self-governing associations of producers and citizens at all social levels.

This whole conception is labelled 'anarcho-liberal' by some politicians who speak in the name of Marx and of the Yugoslav League of Communists. The irony of the situation is that these are the ideas of Marx, ideas with which the Yugoslav League of Communists attracted the best minds of a generation of partisans and rebels against Stalin's domination.

These are the ideas explicitly formulated in the 1958 Programme of that same League of Communists.

The mortal sin of the Praxis Group seems to lie in taking these ideas seriously.

Summer 1974

14

Poetry as Political Criticism: The Case of Wolf Biermann

I

MICHAEL MORLEY

On the Songs and Poems of Wolf Biermann

In 1965 the East German regime imposed a ban on Wolf Biermann which has since prevented him from publishing or performing his works in the GDR. The ban was pronounced to the accompaniment of hymns of hate from the official press and a chorus of malicious and unprincipled criticism from coat-tail clingers masquerading as the authoritative interpreters of so-called socialist art. Since then, the vehemence of these attacks has abated somewhat, but the basic position is unchanged. Biermann, the most gifted writer of political and cabaret songs in either part of Germany, is still deprived of a public platform in the GDR. The official line has it that he does not exist as a writer to be taken seriously. However, when it is found that his presence and works do have some effect on circles in the GDR, he is subjected to 'inconveniences' which range from the bugging of his apartment in Berlin to the cancellation at the last minute of his visa for a trip to Russia as an ordinary member of a travel group.

Some poets thrive on isolation and choose life in a cocoon in preference to contact with society; Biermann, as a convinced Marxist, is not of this type. His cabaret songs and political *chansons* need the stimulus of an audience and derive much of their inspiration from the give and take between performer and listener. It is not being melodramatic to see in Biermann's isolation one of the tragedies of the contemporary German literary scene, though he himself would shy away from such high-flown pronouncements. Yet, for all his diffidence, it is clear from his conversation that he feels acutely the loss and continuing absence of an audience. He may – and indeed does – say that he is not as badly off as others; but without a platform, a singer may just as well retire to a tunnel, catching in the blackness only the hollow echo of his own voice.

Biermann has summed up his attitude to his present position in a lengthy interview published at the end of last year in the *Frankfurter Rundschau*. At the outset he acknowledged the fact of his isolation:

Yes, I am isolated, like everyone in this country; and it's not only here that people vegetate, wrapped up in handy family-size packets, cooped up in apartment-size rabbit hutches. But set against the norm, I'm probably one of the least isolated individuals in the GDR. That's not just a defiant turn of phrase which I use as some kind of pretence so as to cope better with my real sense of isolation. My live contact with many people in the GDR is the logical – if paradoxical – result of precisely that official policy of isolation that has been pronounced over me: the gag that the State has stuffed in the mouth of the song-writer acts like a microphone, the officious campaign of defamation acts like an enormous amplifier. The political singer is already at an advantage because of the popular form of the song itself: any ban can only serve to make him more popular.

One might object that such an argument is rather like an exercise in dialectical reasoning; and indeed, Biermann is inclined to use the rationale of Marxist dialectics to come to terms both with his own predicament and with that of the society in which he lives. Nevertheless, his knowledge of Marxism, and his fondness for its principles of argumentation, are not the result of a quick reading of the *Communist Manifesto* and the occasional dip into *Das Kapital*. His familiarity with the works of Marx, his heavily annotated copy of Hegel's selected writings on philosophy and art, and the way he uses their attitudes (fruitfully) in his own work and in discussion – all these are evidence enough that his attitudes to the important question of art and society are anything but easily acquired catch-phrases.

And yet for all that, the listener senses an uneasy fervour behind the explanations Biermann offers for his readiness to come to terms with his unenviable position. He concedes that the ban hits him hard and deforms him. But in the same interview he then qualified this by saying: 'It *forms* me too, for if one doesn't go completely to pieces, then the oppressive circumstances don't *only* have destructive consequences, but the artist's productivity' (it is revealing that he does not use the term 'creativity' – which he would classify as somewhat 'bourgeois') 'seeks out other paths.'

Biermann's latest poems give some indication of the direction of these other paths, but it is as yet too soon to say for certain whether his work will follow this direction in future, and if it will prove as rewarding as his earlier style. There is, however, little doubt that such recent poems as 'Brecht, your future generations' and 'On anxious friends' lose nothing in comparison with the best of his early verse. They

display the same skilful combination of irony and vigorous language, the same sense of a sharply individual voice speaking with urgent yet reasoned conviction, that is the hall-mark of the best of his poetry. At the same time, his musical settings for the songs and ballads from his latest collection 'For my comrades' – some of which I heard recently in Berlin, and which will, if all goes well, be released on record later this year – show that he has lost none of his remarkable skill as a song-writer.

One difficulty about describing the volume and range of Biermann's work is that it is at present impossible to give any accurate account of his achievement as a song-writer. Those songs of his which have already appeared in print are but the tip of the iceberg. According to his own vague calculations there are something like three or four hundred others as yet unpublished and unperformed – among these, adaptations of folksongs from several countries. As to assessing his achievements as a *poet*, there the situation is rather easier. It may seem as if I have erected a false division between the two aspects of Biermann's work. But he himself recognizes that there are two poets within him; or rather, there is the 'poet' and the writer of songs intended to be performed. To some extent, this is obviously a false division, inasmuch as his work in the latter genre inevitably colours and affects the style of the former. Yet he is uneasy at the course his poetry has taken over the last few years: because of the performing ban, he has become increasingly dependent on the book as the vehicle for his work. And it is not a development with which he is particularly happy – especially since there are only three records of Biermann's songs currently available. (Three records may seem a reasonable number, but only one of these is full-length Biermann – *Chausseestrasse 131*. Of the other two, one is a 45 EP, and on the other, recorded in 1965, he shares the recording with the cabarettist and conferencier Wolfgang Neuss.)

It is not as if there were no demand for his records in Germany – quite the contrary. But there are obvious difficulties in recording the songs in Berlin, and then transferring the tapes both from there and on to disc. These problems have, however, been overcome in the past. An enterprising British company might well consider the possibility of a record in English: Biermann knows English and is naturally interested in the possibility of his work becoming more widely known in the English-speaking world. It is a sad comment on the English publishing scene that, to date, no collection of his poetry is available – a situation that looks even more bizarre when one considers that in countries like Denmark, Sweden, France, Italy and even Spain (!) his work appears in translation almost as soon as it appears in Germany.

As a singer and performer, Biermann has few equals: he is a virtuoso guitarist, one minute scattering semiquavers like tracer, the next drumming out chords and an insistent, pulsing rhythm, the next coaxing forth, with ironic delicacy, the type of sentimental refrain so popular in German beer-halls, sung through smoke and a haze of *Gemütlichkeit*. For all his links with English and American folk-music, which are very real, he belongs to a definite German tradition, which began with Frank Wedekind (died 1918) and was carried on by a whole series of composers and poets in the 1920s – notably Kurt Weill and Brecht, and subsequently Hanns Eisler and Brecht. For Biermann, the supreme master of the political song was Eisler – even now, a composer sadly neglected in the West – and it is clear that he owes much to Eisler's encouragement and tuition. If his poetic style and fondness for popular forms derive ultimately from Heine and Brecht, then his musical idiom and approach to the relationship between text and music are conditioned by his work with Eisler and his extensive study of the latter's songs.

Biermann's position in the GDR as a committed Marxist who, because of his convictions and belief in principles he feels have been betrayed, sees it as his duty and right to criticize those aspects of the society he considers to be wrong, is not something that can be discussed in ready-made phrases like 'artistic independence' and 'political commitment'. Nor indeed is the role of his poetry and songs any easier to elucidate in a few words: from the selection included here, at least some of his themes and attitudes will be readily apparent. There are, to be sure, contradictions in some of his views, but at the same time, he is prepared to concede the possibility of error – on some points. On three of the most vital questions – the aim of his works, the Berlin Wall and political poetry – it is as well to return to his own words. First, on his work:

My entire work has the purpose of advancing the development of a socialist workers' democracy in those countries that call themselves socialist. I voice criticism of the monopolistic-bureaucratic system, and I voice those forces which, rather than accepting a petit-bourgeois liberalization being forced on them by the bankrupt old and neo-Stalinistic reactionaries – to shut them up – insist on the continuation of the socialist revolution.

On the wall:

I don't want the GDR to just disappear, and I certainly don't want those people who are discontented to clear out, for they are valuable for every society. We shan't pull down the wall just as soon as there are as many cheap cars in the GDR as in the West, but when there's someting here in which people can drive a whole lot better: socialist democracy.

Finally, his comments on the nature of political poetry are typically acute and witty and sum up his approach to literature with an image that is typically acerbic and satirical.

A song about apple-blossom in the middle of a war is something very political: something reactionary and a crime, as Brecht might perhaps say. But a song about apple-blossom sung by an armed peasant in a Vietnam pounded by bombs is also political in another way: it shows that the people survive hails of bombs and go on working at the task of peace – in the midst of war. But there are also songs that are peppered with political phrases and yet are ideological idylls. If a few song-writers pull the fishing-rod of easy living from the hands of the bourgeois garden dwarf, and shove back in its place a flag-pole, we're still stuck with a garden dwarf and not, by a long shot, with a political song.

II

WOLF BIERMANN

Poems

From the collection 'For my comrades'

On anxious friends

1

There are these anxious friends, anxiously, constantly urging me
To flee this country: You've *got* to escape
To the outside world! A singer must sing! Even the West
Is becoming Easternized. Communists are in short supply, and
Where now is there such a thing as communism?
Put by your daily art for those who come after us
Make safe your bundles of paper and
Protect your 140 pounds from the clutches of those
Who see the people as their property. Look:
They've not put you behind bars before now
Only because it would have cost them too much! But what
If it costs them too much *not* to put you behind bars?

2

Ah, people who talk like that
Don't need me

They can perfectly well go on living
Just as badly as before
And without me

They treat me worse
Than they treat a lump of dry bread

What sort of talent would that be, my friend
Which so urgently needs to be saved for the world
And yet you can do without? Comrade
What works of art are they meant to be that can be
Let loose on mankind
And yet you don't need them as much as you need bread?

I'll give it to you in writing: If you don't
Need me here, what
Is the world supposed to do
With me?
But if you needed me, what
Would I need the world for?

No! The world needs me
    here
And posterity needs me
    now!

3

Fine, say the anxious friends with relief:
Give it to us in writing
    – three copies
    – of the poem
    – about anxious friends
for distribution!

Little song of lasting values (to music)

1

And the great liars, just what – yes, what
Of theirs will ever endure?
Of theirs will ever endure:
    that we have believed them
And the great hypocrites, just what – yes what
Of theirs will ever endure?
Of theirs will ever endure:
    that we have finally seen through them

2

And the great despots, just what – yes, what
Of theirs will ever endure?
Of theirs will ever endure:
    that they were simply overthrown

And their Eternal Momentous Eras – yes, what
Of them will ever endure?
Of them will ever endure:
    that they were considerably shortened

3
They stuff the mouth of Truth with bread
And what will remain of the bread?
There will remain – yes, what? –
    that it was eaten up

And this shop-worn song – yes, what
Will remain of the song?
For all eternity will remain the fact
    that it was forgotten

State-saving confession of an enemy of the state

O high and mighty court, you see before you the
    incited inciter: yes
I am by far the most infamous of all perfidious fault-
    finders
I was a muck-raker of old dirt, I even dirtied it further
And various dead individuals, yes, I just would not let
    them rest in peace
Ah, I always saw only the worst side of everything
All I can do is destroy, as everyone knows, but
I can't be constructive, ah, I positively revel
In the exaggerated tales of horrors from the past
Over long-since forgotten miseries I snivelled in a
    manner calculated to provoke, but
I abused as party bosses those who work their fingers
    to the bone for the people
And whenever I happened upon 'them', our all too
    visible
Fighters on an invisible front: 'informers' was the
Name I gave those silent heroes, nothing but doubt
Dripped from my jaws into the well-scrubbed ears
Especially of the young. Even over this trial
The enemy without is gleefully rubbing his myriad
    hands
For thirty pieces of silver I have seriously damaged
    the state's good property!
Ah, in the name of our Great and Good Cause – pass
    sentence on me!

For those such as I must
    be eradicated!
        (by the rats)
And those such as I must
    be led to the slaughter!
        (by the swine)
In short: those such as I must
    be killed off
        by the state

For any man who does what I did, will never change
And even if he does change, then that changes
    nothing!
Even my repentance still reeks of incitement, no,
All conceivable confessions cannot stop up this
    bragging mouth
Therefore, have no pity on my pitiful self!
Down with my baseness! O, let this vermin be of
    some use:
This abject object lesson an instructive deterrent!

Pride cometh before a fall
In late summer this is the sermon
the maggots preach
to their early-ripened apples

When the children gather up the fallen fruit
    when the flies fly up our noses
        when the buxom women boil up the apple puree
            we shall calmly and in each case with all humility
                show a bold front to
                    all those who humiliate us

And from among the attitudes of our friends we
    prefer
    intelligence to understanding
        interest to curiosity
            and need love instead of charity
                and need anger and not rage

But in our own case we prefer
    passion to zeal
        and sadness to deep emotion
            and value knowledge higher than knowledgeable
                disclosures
                and praise pride in the face of the arrogant

And want to be
  tireless, instead of diligent
    quick, instead of hasty
      sharp and keen? OK!
        but not sharp-edged, nor cutting
          funny rather than funereal
            and to like witty people
              but not the witless

So, to the sound of unruly laughter, we discover
  lurking behind the dignity of the subtle distinction
    the brutal contradiction among men
      and thus know exactly where we are

O misprized fruit of the Tree of Wisdom!
How time and again with patient forbearance they
  betray Gravity's Law:
'Tis the sweeter apples that fall to the worm!

Brecht, your 'future generations'

'You who will surface from
the waves
Beneath which we sank . . .'

Those on whom your hopes rested
Are perishing along with your hopes
Those who were once to do it all better
Are getting better and better at following others'
  causes
And in these dark times they have
Made themselves comfortable with your poem
Those with the lines between their eyes
Those with their blocked ears
Those with their nailed-down tongues

  Brecht, your 'future generations'
  From time to time they close
        in
          on
            me

Fragments, dreams spread out before my eyes
Rubble, expectations raised aloft before me
They serve me up the scraps of early passions

They pour me out the flat dregs of former anger
On my head they scatter the ashes of former fires
A meagre legacy hangs there opposite me in the
  armchair
Burnt with the brands of bureaucracy
Fixed to the thumbscrews of privileges
Chewed to pieces and spat out by the political police

  Brecht, your 'future generations'
  From time to time they close
        in
          on
            me

And they are as if blinded by the darkness around
  them
And are as if deafened by the silence around them
And are as if struck dumb by the daily shriek of
  victory
They have learnt how to inflict
Ever more exquisite pain and
How to endure it and
Have not even begun to get to the
Bottom of the vast pot, not even begun to enjoy
The taste of the bottomless supply of
Bitterness and greasy poverty

  Brecht, your 'future generations'
  From time to time they close
        in
          on
            me

Romantic flotsam lies washed up within me
Metaphor-dripping driftwood of the Revolution
On brass plates can still be seen the great names
Of the 19th century. The sight of the wreck still calls
  to mind
The once proud ship. The sunken planks tell of
The drowned crew. The rotting hemp
Still drivels on about the ropes that tamed the ships
Yes, they have surfaced from the waves beneath
  which you
Sank and see now before them no sight of land

Brecht, your 'future generations'
From time to time they close

in

on

me

Even they, Master, are – and in prose – your
Future generations: the post-deceased pre-deceased
Full of forbearance with themselves alone
Changing their attitudes more often than their shoes
It's true their voice is no longer hoarse
– after all, they've nothing more to say –
Their features no longer a grimace, it's true:
For they have become faceless. Man has
Finally become a wolf towards his fellow man

Brecht, your 'future generations'
From time to time they close

in

on

me

When the guests finally depart, drunk on the
misleading
Truth of my ballads, inflamed by the false logic
Of my poems, when they depart, armed with confidence –

I remain behind: the ash of my own fires.
I stand there: a looted arsenal. And
I hang knocked out in the strings of my guitar

And have no longer a voice or a face
And am as if deaf from speaking and blind from
looking
And am afraid of my own fear and am

Brecht, your 'future generation'
From time to time I close

in

on

myself

Five finger exercises on Florian Havemann's flight

1

yet another daring attempt yet another successful
    attempt yet
another risks his life yet another of us has
left yet another has gone over the
wall yet another has found a
hole yet another turns his
back of the East yet an-
other escape to free-
dom yet another has
suddenly dropped
everything yet an-
other has burnt
his bridges
behind him
yet another
is over
there

2

he's gone he's cleared out he's run away he's
broken out he's hopped across he's
broken through he's taken republican leave he's
vanished he's done a
bunk he's
scrammed he's
flipped out
he's
over there

3

in the West he will make: money discoveries his
fortune babies contracts he will go:
into business on journeys off the rails
out on demonstrations will make:
plans for the future good marriages do: this and not the other go:
to parties nowhere to the
top bankrupt
think of coming
back

4

in the East he has left behind: Wolf Biermann Walter
   Ul-
bricht Robert Havemann Erich Honecker Anastas
boatman Karl Eduart von Schni grave-digger
Manni Strehlau Erich Mielke Franzi Popow
Thomas Brasch Klaus Gysi Sanda Weigl
Stangel Willi Stoph Bylle Havemann
Jürgen Tscheib Kohlen-Otto The
Fat Girl Dietrich Pantsch Flo-
rian Havemann

5

to a sickly-sweet waltz he danced
rock hard rock
oh yeah, the earth goes round, oh yeah
but not the flat spot you're standing on!

From the collection 'With tongues of Marx and Engels'

Portrait of an old man
Behold, Comrades, this man who changed the world:
   The world −
That he changed, but not himself
His works − *they* have reached their goal, but he is
   finished

Is he not like the ox yoked
to the Chinese wheel? He has drawn up
the water. He has quenched
the fields' thirst. The rice
shoots up green. And so he trudges
forward in a circle
and sees nothing before him but
for the umpteenth time the imprint of his own tracks
   in the mud
and so, year after year, in his splendid isolation he
   fancies
he is treading in the footsteps of the multitude. And
   all he does is
follow his own tail. He only catches up with
himself never finds himself
and remains furthest away from himself

Behold, Comrades, this man who changed the world:
   The world −
That he changed, but not himself
His works − *they* have reached their goal, but he is
   finished

Look upon that, Comrades. And tremble!

From the collection 'The wire harp'

Suburban Sunday (to music)
Shall we move on?
Yeah, may as well move on.
Nothing on here?
No, nothing on here.
Waiter, a beer!
Not many here.
Summer's been cold.
We're all getting old.
The Smiths had nice veal.
Quite enough for a meal.
Well, better move on.
Yeah, may as well move on.
He's already there?
He's already there.
Shall we pop in?
Well, may as well pop in.
You watching TV?
Yeah, I'll be watching TV.
They're playing a game?
Yeah, some sort of game.
Got any cash?
Yeah, still got some cash.
One for the road?
Yeah, one for the road.
Shall we move on?
Yeah, may as well move on.
You watching TV?
   Yeah I'll be watching TV.

Early morning

This morning, as I was lying snug in bed
a rude ring on the doorbell wrenched me from my
 sleep.
Furious and barefoot I hurried to the door and
 opened it
to find my son who
as it was Sunday
had gone out very early for the milk.

Those who come too early are not very popular.
But one drinks their milk afterwards.

The minstrel's maiden speech

Those who once stood before machine-guns with
 steadfast courage
now fear my guitar. Panic
spreads whenever I open my mouth and
the office-elephants' trunks run with the sweat of fear
when I hound the halls with my songs. Indeed
a monster, a pestilence, that I must be, indeed
a dinosaur dances in Marx-Engels-Square,
a booby-trap, a solid lump in the fat throat
of the 'responsible' members of society, who fear
 nothing so much as
responsibility.
    I see:
        you'd rather chop off your own foot

than wash it?! You'd rather die of thirst
than drink the bitter juice of my truth?!
For God's sake!
        let the shackles of fear fall from your breast!
Even if you are afraid that your heart might fall out
For God's sake!
        slacken the straps of fear off two or three holes
Let your lungs grow accustomed to breathing freely,
 shouting freely!
See, you are checked only by pressure from within,
 not from without!
Let us with clear resolution steal a march on the day!
Idiot! We were not born to turn our lofty dreams into
clandestine sneezes and blow them out into the world
 through a handkerchief!
The children of rebellion and freedom are our own
 fathers.
And so let us be true sons of our fathers: with
 irreverent insolence
let us tuck up our flapping shirt tails and sing!
                    shout!
                        laugh loud
                            with jaunty
                                impudence!

Translations by Michael Morley

15

The Hopes of Embattled Protest: Czechoslovakia, 1969–77

I

A Ten-Point Declaration on the First Anniversary of the Occupation

Addressed to the Federal Parliament, the Czech National Council, the Czechoslovak Federal Government, the Czech Socialist Republic, and the Central Committee of the Communist Party

One year has passed since representatives of the government and party were taken to Moscow and the so-called Moscow Protocol was formulated. This Protocol belittles a mature people, who have been unfortunate enough to become the pawn of two superpowers. The one that sent us its armies claimed that socialism was endangered in our country. It was not. What was at stake was the reputation of people who had preached socialism for twenty years.

The democratization of the country in 1968 convinced the people that mistakes can be corrected, that injustice can be undone, and that people can enjoy their work. At that time the government and the new Communist Party were on the way to proving that socialism is not necessarily connected with repression and economic scarcity. On the contrary, it can offer all the traditional freedoms that were fought for in previous revolutions and a blueprint for a society both economically and morally superior to any other. Our attempts were in harmony with the old ideals of the socialist movement, which since its beginnings has stood for national sovereignty and individual self-determination, and has condemned imperialism, shady diplomacy, and partisanship. It is the duty of everybody in the international socialist community not to interfere in our affairs, to treat us honorably, and to leave it to the Czechoslovak people to avoid restoring an outdated, reactionary social order.

For a whole year we have been living under conditions imposed on us. During this time our lives have become more difficult. The economy is faltering, prices are climbing, production goes unplanned, and the causes of these crises have not been discovered. Many able and gifted elected officials have had to leave their jobs. The Action Program of the Communist Party of Czechoslovakia has been revoked in its entirety, civic organizations have been paralyzed by the government's interference, the public has been excluded from the decision-making process, and not a single organ of political power is based on the will of the people. The mandate of the federal parliament has expired. And censorship makes it impossible to speak openly about these matters.

This state of affairs suits old opportunists and new careerists who say whatever they like, twist facts, slander other people, organize propaganda campaigns, and who are shameless enough to tell the people that it is now possible to speak and write the truth. The fact is that one has to look for truth sideways; nobody can guarantee that information is reliable. Many have been victimized – some even imprisoned – because they tried to fulfill the functions of a free press.

We are not satisfied with these conditions and will not remain silent. We have chosen to address the legislative bodies of the republic – the federal government, the state government, and the central committee of the Czechoslovak Communist Party – and have decided to make our case known, even if we risk the well-known reprisals.

(1) We condemn what happened a year ago because it violates our national sovereignty and discredits socialism. We stand for the fulfillment of all international agreements. Socialist governments should show the world how misunderstandings and conflicts between them are resolved by civilized means. We regard the occupation of our country by the Soviet Army as a cause of unrest and an obstacle to the restoration of friendly relations with the Soviet Union. We demand that the highest offices of our country begin negotiations for the withdrawal of the Soviet Army.

(2) We do not agree with the policy of retreat in the face of threats, which has led to the further entrenchment of the government bureaucracy and to purges in the state, party, and fiscal apparatus. We protest the repression of organizations whose activities do not violate any law. We condemn the prohibition against the coordinating committee of the union of artists, and government interference in the affairs of university students.

(3) We condemn censorship. It makes impossible the free exchange of thoughts and information, and the emergence of a well-informed public. It generates trashy literature, makes it difficult to check power, and encourages political immorality. It leads to a state where the arts and sciences are mere servants of the powerful.

(4) We do not believe that in the future the government will respect the laws of the land and that the institutionalized crimes of the 1950s will not be repeated. For those who have violated the law are not being prosecuted; they remain in key positions and are shielded from all criticism. The banning of the Society for Human Rights seems to us an evil omen.

(5) We do not accept the Communist Party as a power that stands above other organizations, which are responsible to the whole nation. It is reprehensible to make party membership a prerequisite for citizenship. We insist that the Communist Party must earn its leading role by serving the people better than any other organization. The relationship between the parties of the National Front should be balanced. Non-communists who represent a majority should not be forced to live in conditions they have no way of influencing. We applaud those communists who attempt to rid the party of its aberrations and who see it as their duty to realize 'socialism with a human face'. We support all those who insist that the legality of the Fourteenth Party Congress held in 1968 be fully respected.

(6) The occupation of our country by foreign troops has proved particularly harmful to our economy. The enactment of the law legalizing workers' councils is being postponed – and where they do exist, they are being phased out. Economic benefits are again being withheld and worker–management relations are arbitrarily established. This crisis is blamed on those who tried to put into practice economic reforms. The workers themselves are also blamed for their poor morale and low productivity. Yet, should they work for people who should have been removed from office a year ago? Should they work harder when a higher income cannot buy them what they want? We understand their mood.

(7) Everyone needs to know that his work has meaning and must be persuaded from day to day by his own experience that the leadership is acting in his own interest. Everyone should have the right to express his views regarding the economy. We believe that employees should have superiors whom they trust and respect, for it is unbearable to work for someone who is forced on you. Many of our problems

can be solved by replacing incompetent bosses. Trade unions should be allowed to do so. We demand, therefore, that a law on socialist management be enacted as soon as possible. This law should guarantee that experts – while taking into consideration the state plan – will make decisions about production and that workers will have the right to participate in decisions about investments and the distribution of profit. We demand that the rights of the trade unions be fully respected according to the Charter of the Association of Trade Unions. If we speak about the class interests of the workers, we recognize that these are the interests of everyone.

(8) We are glad that among the many reforms proposed by the Action Program of the CPC in 1968, at least one has been realized: the federalization of the state. We will oppose any attempt to create mistrust and conflicts between the Czech and Slovak nations.

(9) Censorship makes all criticism of the government impossible. Citizens are intimidated by the state's ruthless interference in their affairs, and state organizations and dishonest newspaper editors are creating an even more frightening mood. In the face of all this we declare unequivocally that to hold a different view from that of one's government is an age-old human right. As citizens who are striving for socialist democracy and humanism, and working against everything that offends our national traditions, we exercise our right to oppose, by all legal means, all that is unreasonable. We do not intend to act outside of the law, yet we will appeal to all state organs to defend our rights. We will try to create working relationships between national organizations. And in the same way that we deplore violence in international relations, we deplore violence as a means of solving national political problems. We will therefore demonstrate our hostility to functionaries who, under normal conditions, would have been fired a long time ago. We will do this by not seeing or listening to them, by not communicating with them in any way, and by not making use of their services. We declare our solidarity with all those who are persecuted for their political convictions.

(10) We believe that even the most intense repression is powerless to murder thought and subvert work. Every citizen should do his work well where possible, especially if it benefits his fellow man. Scientists, intellectuals, and artists should persist in their endeavors. Young people should continue to study and learn not only what they must but also what they choose. Even in political bondage a mature nation can still successfully define its own life-style and principles. Thus we may, though with some difficulty, improve housing conditions, create healthier working conditions, and fight against waste by economizing. We should cater to entertainment that is to our own taste and not accept entertainment we do not like. We should practice our hobbies. We know that the solution of our problems does not depend on us alone. We are not the center of the world and the driving force of the universe. There are times when we must simply persevere and appreciate our achievements. We are firmly convinced that progress cannot be stopped for ever.

(11) We conclude by refuting in advance all the accusations and insults we expect. We are not opportunists. We are not being hostile to the state; those who feel hurt have no right to identify themselves with the state. We only ask that the government function according to the constitution. We are not enemies of the party. Free discussions within the party would prove this. Nor are we against socialism; but we are for a socialism that is proper to a highly developed country and is devoid of those repulsive features imposed upon our country by a handful of narrow-minded, dogmatic, power-hungry careerists and unscrupulous despots. We have no reason to assume an anti-Soviet attitude insofar as the Soviet Union's internal policy is concerned. We object only to brutal interference in the affairs of other nations. We wish the best of success to the Soviet people. We support the democratic forces of the whole world in their fight for international demilitarization and the peaceful solution to all conflicts.

VÁCLAV HAVEL, writer
DR LUBOŠ KOHOUT, political scientist, university professor
VLADIMÍR NEPRAŠ, editor of the newspaper *Reporter*
LUDĚK PACHMANN, journalist

JAN TESAŘ, historian
LUDVÍK VACULÍK, writer
JAN WAGNER, deputy chairman of the Youth Council

II

Charter '77

Law No. 120, which was passed on 13 October 1976, incorporates the International Agreement on Civil and Political Rights and the International Agreement on Economic, Social and Cultural Rights, both of which were signed on behalf of our republic in 1968 and confirmed at the 1975 Helsinki Conference. These pacts took effect in our country on 23 March 1976. The freedoms and rights they guarantee have been the goals of progressive movements in the past, and their enaction can significantly contribute to the development of a humane society.

We welcome the fact that the Czechoslovak Socialist Republic has agreed to the Helsinki Agreements. However, their enactment is at the same time an urgent reminder that many fundamental human rights are violated in our country. For example, the right to freedom of expression guaranteed by Article 19 of the first pact is frequently infringed upon. Tens of thousands of citizens have been prevented from working in their chosen profession solely because their views deviate from the official line. They have suffered various forms of discrimination at the hands of authorities or social organizations, and have been deprived of the means to defend themselves. They are the victims of a new apartheid.

Others, numbering hundreds of thousands, have been deprived of the 'freedom from intimidation', which the preamble of the first pact guarantees, and

they live in constant fear of losing their jobs or other benefits if they express their views.

In violation of Article 13 of the second pact, which guarantees the right to education, many young people are prevented from pursuing higher studies because of their political or religious views or those of their parents. Countless others fear that if they openly state their convictions, they or their children will be deprived of an education.

The right to 'seek, receive and impart information freely, regardless of whether it is oral or printed' or 'conveyed through art, or any other means' – Point 2, Article 13 of the first pact – is denied not only outside but also inside the courts, as was evidenced by the recent trial of the Plastic People of the Universe, the rock band.

Freedom of speech is suppressed by the censorship of all mass media. No political, philosophical, scientific, or artistic view deviating even slightly from the official ideology is allowed in print; public criticism of the nation's crisis is prohibited; the possibility of defending one's self against false and offensive charges made by the official propaganda machine is foreclosed, although legal protection against libel is expressly guaranteed by Article 17 of the first pact; and open discussions of intellectual and cultural matters are out of the question. Many scientists and artists as well as other citizens have been discriminated against because years ago they published or openly stated views that are now condemned by the present regime.

Religious freedom, emphatically guaranteed by Article 18 of the first pact, is systematically curbed by the limits imposed on the activities of priests, who are constantly threatened with the revocation of their licenses, and by the suppression of religious instruction in schools.

Repression in Czechoslovakia results from the subordination of all institutions and organizations of the state to the ruling party and a few highly influential individuals. Neither the constitution of the CSSR nor the laws of the republic regulate the making of government policy. Policy-makers, therefore, are responsible only to themselves; yet they exercise a decisive influence on the legislative and executive branches of the government, the judiciary, trade unions, social organizations, other political parties, businesses, institutions, and schools.

The right of assembly and the right to participate in public affairs are both denied. Workers cannot freely establish organizations to protect their economic and social interests and right to strike, as Point 1 of Article 8 of the second part provides.

Other civil rights, stemming from the prohibition against 'government interference in private life, the family, home, and correspondence', are gravely violated by the Ministry of the Interior, which controls the life of the people by tapping telephones, searching private homes, censoring the mail, hounding individuals, and relying on a network of informers. The ministry has often interfered in the decisions of employers, encouraged discrimination, influenced the organs of justice, and supervised propaganda campaigns in the mass media. Its activities are not regulated by laws, and are so covert that the ordinary citizen is rendered helpless.

By engaging in political persecution, the organs of interrogation and justice violate the rights of defendants guaranteed by Article 14 of the first agreement as well as by Czechoslovak law. Prisoners are treated in ways that demean their human dignity and are hurt both physically and morally.

Point 2 of Article 12 of the first pact, which guarantees the right to travel abroad freely is generally violated, the pretext being to 'protect national security'. Foreigners are often denied entry visas because they have been in contact with persons who have been discriminated against in our country.

Some citizens have privately and publicly drawn attention to these systematic violations of human rights and freedoms, and they have demanded redress in specific cases. However, either their voices have not been echoed or they themselves have been silenced by government investigations.

The resposibility for preserving civil rights naturally rests not only with the government but with each and every individual. Our belief in the sharing of responsibility, in the value of civic involvement, and

in the need to find new and more effective forms of expression has prompted us to create Charter '77.

Charter '77 is a free, informal, and open community in which various convictions, religions, and professions coexist. Its members are linked by the desire to work individually and collectively for human and civil rights in Czechoslovakia and the world. These rights are guaranteed by the final agreements of the 1975 Helsinki Conference and other international treaties against war, violence, and repression. Thus Charter '77 is based on the solidarity and friendship of all people who share a concern for certain ideals.

Yet Charter '77 is not an organization. It has no statutes, permanent organs, or registered membership. Everyone who agrees with its ideas and works to realize them belongs to it.

Charter '77 does not constitute an organized political opposition. It only supports the common good, as do many similar organizations that promote civic initiative in both the East and West. It has no intention of outlining specific and radical programs for political and social reform but tries instead to initiate a constructive dialogue with political and state authorities, particularly by drawing attention to specific violations of civil and human rights – by documenting them, suggesting solutions, submitting general proposals to ensure that these rights are respected in the future, and acting as a mediator in disputes between citizens and the state.

As signatories of this declaration, we entrust Dr Jan Patočka, Dr Václav Havel, and Professor Jiří Hájek to act as spokesmen for Charter '77. They are authorized to represent it before the state and other organizations, as well as before the public at home and abroad. Their signatures guarantee the authenticity of all Charter '77 documents.

We hope that Charter '77 will help to insure that all citizens of Czechoslovakia will someday live and work as a free people.

Prague
1 January 1977

16

MARIA MÁRKUS AND ANDRÁS HEGEDÜS

Community and Individuality

One of the current basic problems of social progress is whether the undoubtedly fast development of the productive forces will permit a new way of life to take shape. There are two essential preconditions for this: social conditions which further the growth of personality, and aspirations which will act as an incentive to individuals to make use of the available opportunities and extend their framework. The question is thus whether it is possible to go beyond the objectified individualization of the consumer society that largely finds its expression in 'things', and if so in what way, and whether communal structures oriented toward human values and the development of the individual can take shape.

For Marx the end of private property was not simply the liberation of productive forces and the end of exploitation but precisely the emancipation of the individual from the rule of things, an emancipation which would ensure the growth and development of an authentic human personality.

This way of thinking inevitably links such usually separated notions as community and the individual, and collectivity and individuality. The growth of the personality in Marx's sense cannot be divided from that of social groups which function as communities, which are able to link everyday activities of individuals and larger social units, thus serving to overcome particularity, at least to some extent.[1]

Community links are not a value in themselves but are the necessary field for the development of a harmonious, many-sided and authentic personality. Conditions under which individual lives cannot be arranged without regard for those of others or stand in opposition to them can only exist within social groups functioning as communities.

Community functions can of course be carried out not only by institutions, organizations, and small groups but also by macrostructural units such as nations, social classes, and so on, together with their interests, ideologies, and value-systems. These, however, will not be discussed here, first of all because they would extend the scope of this essay too much, and secondly because in our view that sort of community experience is, as a rule, also transmitted by smaller groups, in which direct personal contact plays a larger role.

Not every such small group truly fulfills community functions, since they are often accidental (i.e. they are not based on a conscious choice of the participants), and what is more they often, by their own nature, strengthen particularity.

From the point of view of community function, the following types of social group can be discerned:

(a) Humanizing communities which further the growth of the personality of their members in the sense outlined above, realizing the sort of progress beyond particularity which leads toward realization of man's species-being.

(b) Collectivizing communities which serve progressive aims, but which cannot further the growth of personality since they completely subject the individual to the community.

(c) Dehumanizing communities which lock and

integrate their members into communities whose aim runs counter to the progress of man's species-being, thus producing distorted individuals.

(d) Quasi-communities which appear to be collective but really serve the particularity of their members.

(e) Compensatory communities which provide communal experience in some fringe area, often linked with a hobby.

All these are analytical categories, and in reality never appear in a pure state. Individual social groups need not perform the same function for all their members, and they can change their character in the course of time.

This essay deals with the community functions of various groups in the world of work. This essentially narrows down the subject and concentrates attention on a most important field in the life of modern man. If we bear in mind the fact that traditional community structures based on the family and neighborhood have lost much of their importance and are largely limited to private life, organizations at the place of work provide the principal framework for the growth of communities. This in no way implies a wish to limit the importance of those theoretical and practical experiments which endeavor to create new communities and ways of life in the private sphere, for example, by producing new types of family and neighborhood relations.

Largely because of the atomization of life, ways in which man can express and develop his personality must generally be looked for in the world of work, not only directly as part of his working activity, but also in the field of self-management and social control that is connected with it. Besides, man spends most of his time at work, which is a fact that cannot be neglected. A number of sociological investigations have shown that the nature of work and the position in the division of labor largely determine ways of life and aspirations.

The present problems of community life in the workplace are closely linked with the collectives that took shape amongst wage-laborers in the first stage of the industrial revolution, of which one of the most significant features is the absorption of the individual in collective communal norms. It differed essentially from the traditionalism of the 'naturally given' communities, and was an important step forward, particularly since it was not confined to the same extent to particularities derived from a social 'estate' or location. Nevertheless, this still gave little opportunity for the development of individuality.

Modern developments – in industrial societies – pushed this kind of collectivism into the background. The increasingly hierarchical structure at the workplace not only stratified the labor force, but at the same time extended the opportunities for individual advance. As a result, individual objectives relating to social mobility were given a greater importance.

All this has taken place within a framework where the growth of consumer goods and leisure have extended the scope for free choice of a way of life. This is true even where the choice is not between real needs but brands of consumer goods. As Kolakowski has argued: 'Petty bourgeois individualism is not the affirmation of personality but its degradation, by producing the sort of apparent personalities whose existence is not linked to activity and production, but to choice amongst finished goods.'

This refers primarily to the consumer society, which presumes a relatively high standard of living and a plentiful supply of consumer goods. In societies that have put an end to private ownership of the means of production, once the standard of living begins to rise this appears as one of the most attractive models of development. Its effect is increased by the absence, in theory and practice, of new ways of life that embody socialist values. This does not mean, of course, that these societies have not accumulated the kind of experience whose sociological analysis may help to work out alternatives for the future.

We must begin with a survey of the state of affairs *in statu nascendi*. A peculiar myth of collectivity took shape in the first years of socialism, particularly at the ideological level, which mainly concerned the structure of the workplace. According to this, individual interests and the growth of individual personality must be subordinated to 'higher', social, class, enterprise, and so on, interests, that were often presented as abstractions. Thus what we have termed the 'collectivizing' community function came to predominate. Two historical circumstances contributed to this. One was the difficulty of the conditions under which socialism came to power. This naturally concentrated attention on the defense of the new system against internal and external opposition, on the struggle against food shortages, and last but not least on the primitive accumulation of capital. This necessarily pushed individualization into the background and made it just about impossible on a larger scale. The second circumstance was that socialism won its first victory in a country where individualization, which as a mass phenomenon is the product of bourgeois development, was unable to develop because of the underdeveloped social conditions which prevailed in pre-revolutionary Russia, where primitive collectivism still survived in many aspects of life. The model which took shape there was taken over with only slight modifications by European countries, including countries where individualization had already reached a relatively high level.

Thus the principle of collectivization became dominant in a form that not only failed to further the development of the individual personality but also described it as being opposed to the common interest. A monolithically interpreted type of socialist man has turned into a principle.

These were all incentives for the growth of collectivizing communities of type (b), and not only at places of employment. The housing communes which developed in the Soviet Union straight after the revolution, and were based on the principle of the 'equality of poverty', are interesting in this respect. This was repeated in other countries, early on during the transformation period. Such communities generally played a positive role at first. They corresponded to concrete social relations in which homogenizing tendencies were the rule. Society had not become hierarchically structured as yet, and many factors counteracted this possible tendency.

The situation changed once a certain degree of stability was achieved. A structurized society took

shape in the socialist countries, in which individualization and individual interests were given an increasingly large role in economics and practical life, though their importance was denied by ideology for some time. Thus 'collectivizing' communities were not only unable to develop further, they actually regressed, and hierarchical and bureaucratic organizations took their place which generally functioned as 'quasi-communities'. A typical development in Hungary was the process which transformed the college movement, which was decidedly left wing and committed to socialism, into student hostels. Similar 'progress' took place in many other areas, and thus the contradiction between everyday facts and the proclamation of collective attitudes grew all the time.

A peculiar kind of illusion arose at the same time which presumed that the end of private ownership of the means of production by itself created a satisfactory basis for social integration and for the growth of a communal man, and that this would, so to speak, 'automatically' transform organizations at places of work into true communities. Those who support this view consider that communites which further the growth of personality already exist. Anything lacking in this respect, inasmuch as they take notice of it at all, is put down to subjective faults. However, the facts of everyday life do not bear this out but, on the contrary, indicate that there are objective reasons why the problem of community development by organizations at places of work remains unsolved.

The end of private ownership of the means of production has not given the workers' collectives any power of control over the productive process. This has remained the function of various administrative apparatuses of the economic organizations. Under such circumstances work remains wage-labor, in practice the worker sells his labor-power to an administrative institution. This is of course the reason for the quasi-community nature of the enterprise collective, since its basis is a matter of chance for the individual, that is, of the buying and selling of labor-power, not of free association. The interest of an individual worker is thus expressed by the advantageous selling of his labor-power and not the effective functioning of the institution. The high rate of labor turnover demonstrates this in a telling way.

The new system of management in Hungary promises a change in two directions. On the one hand, collectivist illusions are demolished by making the impossibility of production for direct social needs quite clear, thus offering a practical criticism of the proposition which declares that our society has already overcome wage-labor. At the same time, it affords the possibility that a conscious shaping of productive relations will allow the sort of social structures to take shape which will further the growth of real collectivities, at least in certain important fields.

This reform at the same time mobilizes certain individualizing tendencies which have a positive role in the dynamics of economic development and also in the extension of real opportunities for individual growth. The sort of attitude which completely renounces the principle of collectivism, considering it antiquated, and which wishes to replace it with an individualist system of values and ways of life oriented toward each person's own individual happiness, is a one-sided reflection of this. This is often linked with the nascent managerial-technocratic ideology in socialist countries, which considers collectivism to be an obstacle in the way of economic dynamism and optimization (and this in spite of the fact that recent research suggests that worker participation increases performance).

It is, of course, possible that collectivist attitudes will find themselves in opposition to the task of optimization at certain periods and for a limited time, and that, on the basis of concrete analysis, the latter must be given priority. In the long run, though, commitment to socialism demands the development of the sort of communities which stick to collectivist principles, ensure the growth of individual personality, and serve the purposes of economic dynamism.

The sort of totality and monopoly which was characteristic of traditional pre-capitalist and early working-class communities no longer occurs in these communities, nor are the limits of individual development strictly delimited, without the individual having a chance to change them. An active participation in the shaping of community relations and norms replaces the one-sided subjection of man to communal norms which is the rule in primitive communities. At the same time, the humanizing communal functions mentioned in our introduction cannot be limited to the activity of production, but transfuse all aspects of life in some form or other.

The question is whether movements that will result in such humanizing communities are likely to appear in the realm of work. This naturally gives rise not only to microstructural (e.g. work organization) problems, but also to macrostructural ones, since it is in this field that the question of to what extent communities at the workplace will be able to transcend the old forms and framework will be decided.

In order to strengthen such tendencies and allow them to become something that is qualitatively new, the organization of socialist enterprises must be re-examined, particularly the nature of the wage-labor system. At present, state and even cooperative enterprises and institutions simply buy the worker's labor-power and put it at the disposal of the administrative apparatus. As against this, and to the extent that technical conditions permit, one could build on the basis of workers associated in groups, provide them with the means of production, and determine their income on the basis of the labor supplied. The administrative apparatus would exist primarily to serve the interests of such associations.

Modern business management, going right back to Taylor, idealizes the break-up of the work process into units which are then reassembled by management experts, without the participation of those doing the work. Changes have lately been carried out on the original Taylor principles, but they do not affect the essence, and are merely devices to lessen the monopoly. Whatever their practical use, they do not change the principle that workers are given partial tasks by others; not only do the teleological functions of determining the objective belong to someone else, but even the way in which the partial process is carried out is not determined by those who actually carry it out. Elton Mayo subjected Taylorism to sharp and justified criticism, but even he does not imply essential changes; what he tries to do is to produce community experience at the microstructural level, changing not the conditions but the methods of management. Taylorism has had an influence on socialist society too. In the 1920s it seemed the only scientific system of management which appeared rational in the context of the technological level. These methods were further developed in the interests of an increase in productivity, but no one criticized them from the point of view of Marxist humanism.

The practical consequence of such Marxist criticism would not be a return to the primitive collective spirit which preceded 'scientific' labor management, but the growth of communal forms of the sort which were outlined above. One must bear in mind, though, that traditional communities still survive in certain fields of production, and that these are in many cases linked with illusions about their being the embryos of a new collectivism. Organizational forms preserving such primitive collectivism were fairly general in work such as navvying in Hungary, where the worker-collective provided just about the only form of socializing for workers living away from their families. These frequently showed the same norms as their home communities, which only increased their closed nature. This type of community survives to this day without profound changes, in types of work which take people away from their homes such as work in oilfields, seasonal work on state farms and forests, and also of course navvying.

We had the opportunity to investigate a group of over twenty navvies working in a Transdanubian state farm who all came from the same Trans-Tisza village. Its internal structure was relatively homogeneous and strongly patriarchal. The charge-hand, who had organized the group himself, had considerable power, without in any way making use of administrative means. The basis of his power was a set of strong collectivist norms which were inhuman and strict in many respects, excluding just about every manifestation of individuality. Sticking to them in closed circumstances nevertheless provided the members of the group with security, and defended them against various influences of the outside world which they did not consider desirable. Group norms determined all their activities, including eating and entertainment. Their wages were saved for their families, they cooked together, their food was poor and traditional, they also entertained each other. Neither party nor trade union organizations had any influence on them.

The new principles of organization which have replaced such traditional ones in most places not only provide no substitute for the communal experience but, polarizing the workers, they put them at the mercy of the administration to an even greater extent: 'I should like to work in the way', one of the labourers said, 'in which we used to work, at least eight or ten of us together. Not in a large group like this year.' Or another: 'What upsets me is that a man can't choose those he works with, they send someone along and you've got to work with him, that's not right, that has an effect on the shaping of a good collective.' The question is whether this dream can be fulfilled by creating the sort of new forms which can transcend primitive communities, new humanizing communities which do not conserve the old way of life and which do not hinder the individual in his quest to develop. The other problem is whether such a type of organization fits into a modern enterprise, and if so then in what form.

Let us look at certain attempts to include this type of organization (which we shall henceforth call enterprise associations) in more or less modern labor management.

One such attempt was made by brigades of telephone line fitters. This permitted a clash of views concerning these organizational forms to be observed. The type of work demands communal life. The eight to ten members of the brigade spend the whole of the week away from their families in temporary quarters. The time for starting and finishing work is determined, and transport to and from the location is provided by the enterprise. There are work-norms, pay is according to individual performance but cannot exceed average wages. The alternative that the group should undertake the work as an association, see to its food and shelter itself, and work in its own rhythm, without fixed working hours, seemed obvious. Thus continuous supervision and direction would be replaced by acceptance of the completed work.

This alternative looked advantageous from the enterprise's point of view too, since it would have made direction simpler, besides alleviating the shortage of labor. But the trade union made serious objections. One was that the workers, bearing in mind that their pay was low, would exploit their labor-power at the expense of their health, that they would lengthen their working hours and work with greater intensity. Others said that by employing this alternative one could do a week's work in two or three days. At the same time they opposed the idea that the brigade should get money in lieu of food and shelter since they presumed that this would involve a significant drop in standards.

Some of these objections are justified in themselves, but they do not touch the essence of the transformation, which would still hold good even if the negative aspects of it were reduced. One might say, to start with, that labor-power is exploited to the detriment of health by other types of organization of labor too, perhaps not in basic official working hours but outside of them. A true notion of leisure has not yet taken shape amongst the first generation of workers, and not only for material reasons. Time outside of work can only be employed doing nothing, satisfying purely physiological demands; that is why they wish to extend their working hours, especially where poor financial circumstances and special needs are involved, bearing in mind that the demand for differentiated consumption has increased considerably in Hungary in recent years.

In cases like this, workers often try to expend as little energy as possible at their place of work, and employ their strength (often at the expense of their health) in increasing their income outside their proper working hours. The fact that the unofficial price of labor-power is double the official one is also a contributing factor. A builder, for example, is paid 12 to 13 forints an hour by state enterprises, and 25 to 30

by small private tradesmen. Discrepancies thus arise between the consumer goods that can be obtained and state and cooperative incomes which give rise not only to the phenomena we have mentioned but also to many kinds of corruption. The association model would encourage processes in which an increase in the intensity of work would permit needs to be largely covered within normal working hours. Though this would not be a barrier in itself to self-exploitation, it is likely to show better results in this respect than the control regulations suggested by the trade unions. A real solution, however, demands the sort of general change which provides other objectives for people than the mere acquisition of worldly goods.

Studying the Szekszard State Farm, we were able to observe the results of many years' experience, and also had the benefit of research conducted on the spot by Ferenc Funszabo. The first such groups were organized for work on ploughed land, and that is where they are still operating most successfully: 1,700 to 2,400 yokes of arable land are entrusted to eleven to fourteen men. Not only the land but the necessary machines and chemicals are also at their disposal. The management only controls the execution of previously determined operations. On principle, and lately in practice also, the brigade itself decides what work is done where and by whom, and who is on leave or absent and when. No work-process is measured or standardized by the management: the single standard is the amount produced. They are paid according to the value produced at predetermined rates, a minimum income being guaranteed. The members themselves decide how the income is to be allocated amongst the members of the brigade. The principle is one of equal distribution in proportion to the number of days worked by each. Neither expertise, not strength, not seniority is taken into account. This does not give rise to any special problems, since the groups are relatively homogeneous. Draft contracts are renegotiated yearly.

The first complex planting brigade was established in 1964; the following year saw another two. By 1967 these three brigades worked three-quarters of the planted area. This form of labor organization is also employed in the vineyards and in animal husbandry, and is beginning to spread to other state farms in the area, which are benefiting from this experience in this type of labor organization.

There are greater difficulties in industry, where the division of labor is greater and processes are broken down into their parts. As a result, such associations are developing more slowly. The greater individualization of city life, with the choices it offers, and the internal structure of industry itself, are the two chief sources of the difficulties. The most characteristic feature, besides the division of labor, is a strong hierarchization. Nevertheless there are endeavors to establish communal forms, though they do not reach the degree discussed above. The most elementary form is the replacement of payment for individual performance by payment for group performance. This creates a group interest and facilitates the development of communities at the place of work.

Conditions are better in industrial development research, where the nature of the work demands that people with a variety of skills cooperate. The teams which are formed there in many ways resemble what we have called enterprise associations. Every research project carried out in this area shows increasing attempts to form teams freely in laboratories and similar places to replace the ones which were previously established in a bureaucratic manner, and attempts too to emancipate them from bureaucratic direction by the enterprises. The strengthening of this tendency is one of the most important contributing factors to the increased efficiency of research and development work. This is borne out both by the surveys conducted and by practical experience. All this allows one to conclude that enterprise associations may well fit in with more advanced types of labor organization. It is true, though, that these experiments were not prompted by any sort of commitment to collectivist attitudes but by a variety of entrepreneurial interests, such as labor shortages and lack of interest (and therefore lack of efficiency). This is in fact a proof that the time is ripening for a practical point of view too, where the classical type of work and labor organization will be gradually replaced by a growing number of various types of association amongst workers.

When the socialist brigades were formed the problem was formulated in a more extended way. There was the recognition, to start with, that our society has not given rise to any new way of life. As against previous individual competition, the emphasis was not put on the collective, an emphasis which was interpreted as covering life outside work, too. A number of sociological surveys and a study of brigade logbooks, however, showed that these attempts had largely formal results, that they did not succeed in producing a genuine movement, and that even the brigades which were considered the best often concealed a quasi-community.

In fact the primary objective of the attempts was not to create opportunities for the kind of collectivist association of workers which had a real content, and which workers could freely choose or accept, but to include as large as possible a percentage of workers, even if purely formally, in socialist brigades, or in such as were competing for this title. This was often linked with direct financial incentives: this is particularly demoralizing when it is considered that the original idea was that socialist brigades in themselves, without any kind of material incentives, would create more advantageous conditions and a more pleasant way of life.

What also helped to make socialist brigades purely formal was the fact that they were clearly integrated into the hierarchy of the enterprises. The instructions laid down by the Presidium of the Trade Union Council clearly stated that 'the leader of brigades competing for the title of socialist brigade will be chosen by the members', but surveys showed that as a rule they are chargehands chosen at a higher level, who as such already have a place in the administrative hierarchy, and who receive a fee for this activity, even though they are not completely relieved of all manual labor.

The fact of inclusion in the official structure is a sufficient obstacle in itself to hinder the enhancement of the associative and communal character of the brigades. What we called humanizing communities presuppose a certain kind of spontaneity: without it, the movement's character cannot be preserved, and it is necessarily formalized and turned into an organization.

A movement, in our interpretation, is a continuous struggle for progress beyond the present state of affairs, and for renewal in such a way that the degree of responsibility undertaken by the participants is not determined by their particular interests but by their budding collectivity. Thus their area of movement must be determined by themselves and not from outside.

This kind of humanizing community is necessarily linked with the movement for real social control, one of whose main characteristics is that it cannot be and must not become an organization, since its purpose is not to take over the administration but to place it under the control of the masses. The aim is therefore not some new state of affairs, but the growth of social control as a dynamic process, the production of conditions where men continuously, and not only in the course of a revolutionary situation every now and then, take part in what happens in society and in the determination of their own fate.

Although we have looked primarily at work, we are well aware that all these processes making for collectivization cannot be divided from society as such, and cannot be realized in one isolated enterprise, or even in one section of the economy. They are an integral part of the reforms which affect society as such, and it is only thus that they can be put into effect in a systematic way.

Note: Chapter 16

1 For the use of the terms 'particularity' and 'individuality', see Georg Lukács, *Ästhetik*, 4 vols (Neuwied: Luchterhand, 1972–6), and Agnes Heller, 'Marx's theory of revolution and the revolution in everday life', in Andras Hegedüs, Agnes Heller, Maria Márkus, and Milhály Vajda, *The Humanization of Socialism. Writings of the Budapest School* (New York: St Martin's Press, 1976).

PART FIVE

European Culture: Memory and Vision

17

STANLEY HOFFMANN

Fragments Floating in the Here and Now

Is There a Europe, Was There a Past, and Will There Be a Future?
or
The Lament of a Transplanted European

I

Let us take any Western European nation in the nineteenth century – say, France, the one I know best. At any given moment, a visitor could have heard vigorous discussions of its past: the nature, flaws, and benefits of the old regime, the causes of its fall, the respective virtues and crimes of the different phases of the revolution, the reasons for the restless and unsuccessful quest for political stability that followed it, the effect on the nation of the dramatic fracture in its history brought about by the revolution, the lasting impact of Bonapartism. All of these questions were constantly examined along clear-cut ideological lines and were reassessed by each generation of historians. History played a large part in the school curriculum, and the nation's past was imprinted thereby on the minds of its future citizens. 'At age thirteen', says Jean-Marie Domenach – now in his mid-fifties – 'my image of France was solidly formed. It linked the recent glory of the fatherland to Greek and Roman antiquity, with the help of classical humanities, which consisted in . . . an aesthetic and moral impregnation.'[1] At the same time, intellectuals and politicians were offering various models of the future. Even a society as keen on tight self-protection

against economic and social upheavals as that of nineteenth-century France never stopped arguing about what the future might bring and, above all, never stopped believing that it was ultimately up to its citizens to shape that future – whether by the restoration of a beneficial past or by the realization of one or another vision of progress. What struck observers most was the depth and multiplicity of disagreements. But the concern with the past and the future – the conviction that the latter would emerge from acts inspired by a proper reconsideration of the past; the belief that past and future were inextricably linked, less by historical determinism than through one's own consciousness of them; the idea that one was seeking one's future in one's stand toward the past; and that the future ought to be the enactment of the lessons learned from the past – all this seemed perfectly obvious and appropriate.

It may, therefore, appear obvious and equally appropriate to ask whether the same questions are raised in Western Europe today. But when its citizens consult the mirror on the wall to find reflections from the past or intimations of the future, they find a broken mirror and a blurred image. For Europe remains a virtuality, the past is mere spectacle, and the future is a riddle. Why this is so takes us into the story of postwar Europe's political, social, and cultural transformation, as well as of Europe's role in the world.

II

A superficial observer might marvel at the way in which the Europeans seem to have left behind the feuds and alienations of their past. Whatever happened to hereditary enmities? Spain, so marginal to European history for so long, except in the tragedy of its civil war, hurries to restore the old connection. If Northern Ireland fascinates, it is not only because of the Irish, it is also because there is something anachronistic about such hatreds and passions in Western Europe. And yet, if the hostilities entailed by separate pasts appear to have evaporated, the separate pasts have not; each European country is still concerned only with its own history, insofar as its people look back at all. Attempts at producing common history textbooks have succeeded only in smoothing the edges. To be sure, scientific history often deals with someone else's past – the best history of modern France in a long time is that of Theodore Zeldin – but in only a few countries is there a tradition of transnational investigation. The French have thrown little light on Germany's past, and Elie Halévy has had no successor. Popular history and the mass media deal almost exclusively. with the national past. The media, of course, sometimes report on a neighbor's present – communism in Italy, for instance, is of concern to the French. But generally, television delves into a neighbor's past only when it is connected with its own national experience: German television showed *The Sorrow and the Pity* and a recent film on Pierre Laval because of Germany's involvement in wartime France.

The fundamental questions therefore are: how is the national past being examined? and what parts of it are considered important? The two queries are linked, for what is striking is a concentration on the recent past and a way of looking at it that I would call escapist. Here again, the media are informative. Television, the movies, and popular history have

mass-produced stories about the troubled past of the 1930s and 1940s. What could be more normal, given its traumatic nature? The parades of the 1930s and the shadows of the war years fill French screens; Mussolini and Hitler obsess the Italians and the Germans; the British endlessly contemplate their finest hours; and Spanish novels and films, before Franco's death, posed poetic or picaresque riddles about and around the civil war. Does this preoccupation demonstrate a willingness to come to terms with a harrowing experience and to derive once again, for present and future behavior, painful lessons from it? I wish I could be sure. Instead I find in it something far softer and more superficial, perhaps because much of this quest is driven by little more than curiosity about the behavior of people who are still alive and present, or nostalgia about one's own earlier years. (Thus what seems like a turning to the past is really little more than an attempt to catch the beginnings of the present before they fade away.) Perhaps a deeper look, a confrontation with the tough moral questions raised by these grim years, is still too painful or (as the Occupation is for France) too divisive; nations, like individuals, repress the humiliating and the harrowing and would rather look at the picturesque than ponder shame or guilt. And so, what we get – in the case of Spain, for example – is a longing for humane normalcy, rather than a search for the reasons behind past inhumanity. Sometimes, as in Germany, there is a fascination with now-incomprehensible phenomena of mass hysteria and evil that has very little to do with soul-searching. One looks at the spectacle as if what happened had been either a collective hypnosis perpetrated by one extraordinary man or a march behind the pied piper undertaken by only a part of the people, most of whom followed him into the abyss. Sometimes, as in France, we encounter an intellectual appetite for exercises in ambiguity; it is another way of putting distance between oneself and one's past. The German way tells us that what happened was exceptional, and from the exceptional there is little to learn. The French way tells us that each of us, like Lacombe Lucien, could have been a resister or a collaborationist or, like some of the characters in *The Sorrow and the Pity*, a hero, a criminal, or a coward; this is a subtle way of debunking the past, or reducing it to a moral shrug. Sometimes, as in England and in Italy, one re-enacts the heroic hours – the Battle of Britain or the Italian resistance – a melancholy yet exalting way of escaping from the sadness of the present and of reassuring ourselves about our highest potential. Thus one tries to bolster one's self-esteem: it has not been all bad, indeed some of it has been glorious. But when one finally realizes that one has been drugging oneself, what a sense of fall – witness *We All Loved Each Other So Much* or *The Glittering Prizes*.

For such concern with the recent past to transcend curiosity and spectacle, one needs elites – governments, intellectuals, educators – determined to connect the present and the whole of that recent past, not just its heroic or inspiring features, but also the ugly ones, in order that they may never be reproduced or that they may be finally erased. This is not what we find. Governments, politicians, those who are loosely called opinion leaders, have been willfully selective or evasive. They have either (like the British) diverted their people from looking at their present or (like Adenauer) protected them from their past by plunging them into the imperatives of the present. (Even scholars have occasionally behaved like hurt citizens when a foreigner has revealed an unwelcome truth: Robert Paxton's fine book on Vichy France[2] was not well received by an establishment that prefers to see in Vichy a set of grievous, often well-meaning blunders rather than a deeply rooted logic of reactionary defeatism.) It is easier to tell oneself that moral choice is a matter of temper and circumstance, that one has been heroic, or that what made one evil is gone, than to tell people that their recent performance has often been shameful or that their recent valor has not prepared them at all for the very different challenges of the present (and indeed may have bled them white). To proclaim the former is easily dismissed as masochism or as an obstacle to getting people to improve their current lot, for one does not inspire others by rubbing their noses into past dirt. To proclaim the latter is equally discouraging – it rubs their noses into present dirt.

Lacombe Lucien, with its romantic yet degrading love affair between the Jewish girl and the young collaborationist, was far more popular than the stark and unsparing *Black Thursday*, which showed the French police rounding up Jews for the Germans. As for the intellectuals, while some – a Böll, a Grass – have done what they could, many others, like Sartre, have used the terrible experiences of the recent past only as demonstrations of universal timeless paroxysmic dilemmas. Such a paradoxical, and in the end narcissistic, contemplation of one's finest or most villainous hours, such a variety of escapes, however useful in the present, have not only amounted to a refusal to draw any valid lessons; they have also often incited the next generation to rebel against their too easily satisfied parents, whether the rebellion takes the form of mere cynicism or of actual terrorism – the gentler or the stronger form of nihilism. But this connection has not been and still is not widely recognized.

At least the recent past is alive , if only as a horror show, a pageant, or a pep pill. What is striking is the growing disconnection from the more distant past. Of course, scholars continue to study it, often with great verve, new methods, and original interpretations. But their works rarely reach the general public, except when the authors have, thanks to television, become fashionable or objects of a cult (in which case their books are bought because of the author's fame rather than read because of their substance). One can sometimes hear learned writers arguing fiercely on the radio or the television about bygone events or personalities (one of the most heated debates I ever heard on France's famed *Dossiers de l'écran* concerned the fate of poor little Louis XVII). But these programs deal with the froth or the scum, not with the waves and their movements. The past is becoming an object of erudition or diversion, rather than a part of one's own being, through family or school transmission. What the French called *le passé vécu*, the experienced past, is displaced by the past as a product of specialists, a consumer product, a subject matter for scholars, or a spectacle.

One might be tempted to look for the explanation in the process of democratization. In traditional societies the elites derive their authority from the past and preserve it through the maintenance of customs and values (such as deference) whose very purpose is to delay change and to safeguard hierarchies. In democratic societies, preservation of the rites and habits of the past needs justification; the individual defines himself through his achievements and demands that authority be grounded either on his consent or on its own accomplishments; no democratic generation believes it has either much of a debt to its predecessors or much of a duty to do as they have done. If, as Tocqueville argued, the drive toward equality is the motor of modern society, the matrix of modern history, then the past always risks being rejected, both because it is a prehistory of inequality and because, if it were allowed to become a straitjacket slipped by each generation on to its successor, it would cripple that dogma of perfectibility, that belief in progress, which Tocqueville described as one of the biggest differences between democratic and aristocratic peoples.

But we must beware of such sweeping generalizations. For if we look around us, we find democratic societies in which *le passé vécu* has not receded. It may well be that the ideal type of democratization (the one Tocqueville tried to erect in the second volume of his great work) entails a destruction of ties, both to the past and between the members of that vast crowd of similar and equal men and women, restlessly left to their egoistic pursuits and panting to give themselves small, vulgar pleasures amidst the collapse of old beliefs and barriers.[3] But in order for this severing of ties to happen, democratization must be accompanied by a number of other quite separate and distinct destructions. This is precisely the situation we find in postwar Europe – but not everywhere. Let us admit that democratization may push away the past; still, we find by looking at some countries (say, Switzerland) that the distance between past and present can be either quite small or, when countervailing forces temper the innate 'present-orientation' of democracy without preventing democratization itself, can even be non-existent. In most of Western Europe, however, we find not counterweights, but reinforcements.

The most obvious of these is the speed of social change, the sweeping away of old customs and rites, the disappearance or transformation of old occupations, the reshaping of class distinctions, the revolutions in mores and morals, and the collapse of traditional modes of social control, all of which have been catalogued by sociologists (serious and pop). Yesterday the past was all around us, and the relative stability of the social order preserved the relevance and meaning of old and durable controversies about the past. As long as traditional institutions, practices of social ascent, economic structures, religious dogmas, and personal values persisted, there were people who wanted to preserve them and others who argued for change; both groups had to evaluate the past for their enterprise. Today so much of the past is dead that there is little left of it to preserve. The old solidarities and communities are gone; often even the old landscapes, along with the rituals, customs, and costumes, have disappeared. The advocates of change argue from the inequalities and perils of the present. Yesterday there were conservatives and reactionaries; the former were rooted in the past (and tried to prevent rapid change, political or economic); the latter thought there was enough still left of the blessed past to make it possible to bring back what had, unfortunately, been toppled. Today a conservative is someone who merely wants to slow down the pace of change or (like Pompidou) to make inevitable changes smooth for the individual. The reactionary is the real radical: he argues – as a particular New Right does in France – not for a return to the past, but on behalf of abstract principles – inequality between races and sexes, hierarchy and authority – which he is wise enough not to connect with any particular time or place.

The speed of change is one of the reasons the past seems so little relevant, but there is another related, but slightly different reason: a gradually growing sense of radical discontinuity. After the ordeals of the 1930s and the war years, the loss of the colonies, the seizure of political predominance by the superpowers, Western Europeans feel, more or less confusedly, that their normal historical development has been interrupted, that their past has been devalued, that their highest achievement – nationality – has plunged them into disaster followed by impotence, that they have moved from the age of self-determination to that in which the outside world determines their fate. The more distant past thus seems alien – not a prelude to the present; it is perhaps even a reproach.

This discontinuity is both expressed in and magnified by modern European historiography. Romantic history is gone, replaced by scientific history. Of course, romantic history was symbolic with the nation-state; it was indeed a form and an agent of nationalism. It showed how the modern nation emerged from the tribes and the tribulations of the Dark Ages or triumphed over the machinations and oppression of foreigners. Present-day historians still operate, with a few grand exceptions like Braudel, within the limits of a nation; but the nation is no longer their object. The focus is often on culture and *mentalités*, but the approach is ethnographic, not political; it is the investigation of worlds we have lost, a sampling of vanished riches, not a celebration of how every stone fits into the national monument and every jewel into the nation's crown. Indeed, it often becomes an indictment of the nation, a kind of digging up of the bones of all those local cultures, cults, or customs that were killed by the national Molochs. It allows one to contrast the beautiful diversity of the past and the frantic ugliness of the present; but, unlike romantic history, it stresses both the discontinuity between past and present and the impossibility of reviving the dead. If, as one Frenchman put it, culture is what is left when everything else has been forgotten, the quest for bygone folkways is what is left when one wishes to forget everything else. Often, biography fills most of the gap opened by the demise of traditional history; it at least attracts many readers. But biography too is a kind of denationalization: in romantic history, the hero was the people, suitably idealized or idolized; today we indulge either in the nostalgia of past peoples or in curiosity about individuals.

A third accompaniment of democratization has contributed to the demise of the past: ideological disillusionment. We never used to see the past 'objectively'. We looked at it through the lenses of ideologies – liberalism, socialism, varieties of conservatism, Christian democracy. (I shall come back to this point in my discussion of the future.) None of these old prisms seems sufficiently helpful for examining the present stage, whether it is the social scene – with its (often immigrated) *Lumpenproletariat*, its stratified and not-at-all pauperized working class, and its proliferating and largely salaried middle classes, or the political scene – with its welfare states in precarious coexistence with a free, but by no means competitive market, and its formidably organized and encrusted interest groups. The situation of the individual – part-time member or free rider of one of these groups, part-time rebel against state and groups, integrated yet overadministered citizen, or 'marginalized' and helpless victim – is unlike any that these earlier visions of the meaning and movement of history predicted. Thus, through speed and the savagery of history, we have not simply lost touch with the world that is behind us; it also appears that this world said many things that turned out to be false and thus has nothing more to say to the average European. There are three ingredients in this disaffection. First, the predictions turned out to be incorrect, and the past as the matrix of all good things to come stands discredited. Secondly, there were too many predictions: it is as if they had cancelled each other out or annihilated one another, as religious dogmas do when too many sects argue about their meaning. There never was a single common faith in Western Europe. The closer a country comes to having one – for instance, in England – the less disconnected it is from the past (although there is some disconnection precisely because past creeds and present realities seem unrelated). The differing views of the past that, only yesterday, made history seem present to the French or the Italians, have, by losing much of their meaning in the present, devalued the past for them. Finally, some of the predictions were not merely wrong, they were murderous; they turned Europe into a field of ruins: 'the ideologies of nation, race, and class have fed the fire. Everything, or almost, is burnt out now.'[4] The fading away of the past is part of a general repudiation of totalitarian ideologies and of the totalitarian implications of ideologies.

Why does the same disconnection not exist to any comparable degree in the United States? Because, I believe, the three destructive forces I have listed have not operated here. In the first place, social changes have been vast and often disruptive, but they have come as organic changes within an established democratic society rather than as the searing agents of democratization – that is, as the gravediggers of values, hierarchies, social patterns, and constellations that were still predemocratic, a mixture of fading aristocratic and narrowly bourgeois societies. Paradoxically, because there has been, ever since the nation's birth, an expectation of quick mutations – the shedding of old skins and the growing of shinier ones that will, in their turn, be discarded when progress next requires it – change looks not like instability but almost like the condition of stability. The past can still be seen as the incubator of the present. This implies, of course, that such change must not be catastrophic. And indeed, in the second place, America has had no reason to experience radical discontinuity: this is the century of its emergence as the most powerful nation on the world stage, a rise for which its whole history has prepared it. In America we are still in the age of romantic history, in the midst of a love affair with the nation. Finally, and most important, we must go back to Tocqueville, or Louis Hartz, and the liberal consensus or common faith. The speed of social change may well be the same as it is in Europe (although one could argue that postwar Europe has been hastily catching up with America's brand of industrial society); but the irrelevance of past beliefs does not appear at all obvious to Americans. Whatever its transformations, their policy still seems in harmony with an unfolding of the 'Lockean faith'. Tocqueville would probably have some trouble recognizing his pre-industrial small-town America; but the basic principles are still there, and the new institutions that have developed since his day are based on them.

The American creed has survived because the United States has been (or appears to the world and to its own people to be) a success story. Both this creed and other powerful bonds – ethnic loyalties, religious communities, class solidarities, or neighborhood associations – have mitigated the effects of social change and crises. In Europe such ties have, on the contrary, been weakened or destroyed by a combination of factors: the speed and magnitude of change, a disastrous history, the corrosion of religion (and of such a quasi-religious force as the early working-class movement) by secular ideological involvements and struggles, and the poverty of associational life in centralized nations. Therefore, contrary to what might have been expected, the democratic society *par excellence*, the United States, is closer to its past than the historical societies of Europe – a fact that confirms the impossibility of deriving any firm conclusion about politics or culture from a social ideal type such as democracy. The bones tell us nothing about the flesh or about the spirit.

A collective image of the past and the possibility of being inspired by this image thus depend on the preservation of collective ties, in the form of institutions or common values, among the citizens. Religion, the nation, and ideologies (which played so large an integrating role) partook of both forms. In Western Europe there used to be one group that defined its mission either as the defense of established institutions and values or as the mobilization of the people to create new ones: it was the intelligentsia, a kind of secular priesthood that owed its audience to the decline of organized religion and old regimes and to its frequent association with liberalism and nationalism (even though its prestige and authority were firmly rooted in persistent aristocratic values – which may help explain why it never played a comparable role in this country). Today, however, its attitude contributes to the erosion or erasure of the past. The relation of the intelligentsia to the past is, needless to say, far from simple. Let me take only the case of France. There we find every possible attitude, on the part of the intelligentsia, and yet somehow every one of these contributes to the break with the past. Malraux, in his quest for death-defying acts, became a celebrator of mankind's past artistic achievements and of France's national record. But his very style – his dazzling ellipses and his instinct for the difficult or the inaccessible, his heroic yet impractical hope of bringing the highest to the common man, his sumptuous threnodies, his fascination with exceptional men, and his part-whimsical, part-desperate doubts about humanity's future – somehow widened the distance between the past and us. Sartre, with his frenzied view of consciousness defining itself (and all of us) by throwing itself into and acting toward the future and his somewhat Manichaean view of the historical process as a discontinuous series of surges of spontaneity that fall back into the *pratico-inerte* as soon as organization and institutions take over, looks at the past both as a struggle of alienated beings driven by scarcity and as a record of failure. By contrast with Malraux, he was never concerned with its meaning for us (since we shall find meaning only through what we do next). Yet in his long confrontation with Marxism, he at least proclaimed that whatever meaning history has lies in the acting out of human consciousness. Other intellectuals have rejected history altogether, or tried – to use the jargon of the time – to 'evacuate the conscious subject': Lévi-Strauss asserts the importance of structures that owe nothing to man-made history and expresses his nostalgia for those societies that live outside history, 'surrounded by [its] substance and . . . impervious to it';[5] Althusser reduces Marxism to a set of structural laws; Foucault discovers hidden structures of knowledge that dictate their rules to men; Deleuze and Guattari see man as a mere collection – not of feelings, desires, or ideas that can properly be called his own but of *machines désirantes* that drive, or rather push and pull him. It is not surprising that the confrontation with events has made it difficult for several of these writers to be consistent: events are clearly man-made, not just structural outputs; and in such confrontations, when writers had to decide – concretely – who was at fault, who caused the harm they deplored (and not simply what structure or what clash of machines resulted in what action, institution, or *discours*), they fell back not on history but on ideology. Foucault has shifted from the archaeology of knowledge to capitalist alienation, and the authors of *L'Anti-Oedipe*

have denounced captialism (and indeed, the whole modern system of production) as the root of poor Oedipus's schizophrenia.

Is there, then, nobody who wants to preserve the connection to the past? Surely many do, but for reasons that turn out to have rather little in common with the desire to nurture a sense of historical continuity or to use this sense as an enrichment of the present or an inspiration for the future. (De Gaulle was the last postwar statesman, along with the aging Churchill, to look at history in this way; and it is not merely a matter of age, since Adenauer, for many reasons, did not do so.) Ancient monuments are, of course, being piously restored: but is it because of what they mean today or because they are part of the 'aristic patrimony' of the nation and, therefore, of its overall resources? Old buildings are being renovated and visited by eager groups, but is it a way of keeping the past in one's midst, or is it an alternative to a relief from the unmistakable horrors of much of modern European architecuture? Old regional feasts and fairs are turned into festivals, but is this a means for reaching into the past or into the pocketbooks of tourists? National holidays are being celebrated, but is this done for the reasons a Robespierre once gave when he advocated such ceremonies or in order to provide governments with a moment of contrived harmony, and citizens with a day off?

The real reachers for the past fall into two groups. Paradoxically, the Marxist left and its intellectuals – the heralds of change – have become the curators of the revolutionary museum. Radicalism has become a tradition. Since the present has a mixed record, the past can be used to show the depth – in time and scope – of the present evils. (For example, *Que la fête commence*, a quite wonderful film, uses the regency of 1715 as a way of denouncing the social and political ills of today.) The past can also be used to assure the faithful that the day of reckoning will come, as well as to put them on guard against repeating the errors that have doomed revolutions in the past. But when turning to the past as a way of lecturing us about the present and expressing hope in the future becomes the last resort of revolutionaries, what appears at first as reconnection turns out to be one more escape. (I am thinking of the abundance of French literature about the commune and of recent plays about the revolution.) For such a turn is no longer a search and a scrutiny of the past. It is a consolation for the present – a series of parables that keeps us warm for a while in the middle of a very cold here-and-now. One leaves such books, plays, or movies feeling, contrary to the authors' wishes, that insofar as things were always so bad, there is little hope indeed; the past mainly serves as an explanation of and a diversion from present failure. Often today the best historians are either Marxists who are, personally, sufficiently unrevolutionary – that is, conservative – to use Marxist insights as a tool of historical research rather than using historical examples as an ersatz goad to Marxist revolution; or else they are ex-communists who have given up the promised land of utopia for the historian's territory. So we again find scientific history as a repudiation, overt or covert, of ideology, and as a way of looking at the past that disconnects it from the present.

The other group that goes after the past is made up of ethnic and regional minorities: as the majority grows distant from its past, these groups rediscover (or invent) theirs. The present is the age of *their* romantic history. This, too, is an old story – that of nationalism among peoples long deprived of sovereignty, for whom a digging-up of alleged or real antiquity is a rebellion against the oppression of the recent past and the present. But just as there is something pathetic about the *passéisme* of Marxist revolutionaries, there is something ungainly about that of Corsican, Occitan, or even Scottish rebels. For here, the past is used not, as it was among the Germans, Italians, or Slavs of the last century, as a cultural basis for a modern creation – a nation – but as a protest against (largely) economic inequalities. Usually there is insufficient popular support (or often even desire) for establishing a separate nation in a Europe where the present nation-states suffer from multiple impotence (which new ones would only reproduce) and yet still have the capacity to defend themselves against secession.

In the educational system the teaching of history regresses. It used to be a major component of mass primary education and of the secondary education that a minority of privileged *and* gifted not-so-privileged youngsters received. Today, this pre-eminence is challenged by more practical or by more scientific disciplines. In a democracy, the authority of the teacher *qua* teacher is rather low. It rests on his expertise, not on his calling; and the prestige of his expertise depends on the usefulness of the knowledge he imparts. In France, the traditional supremacy of letters and history has ended: glamour glistens on mathematics. High school history is being diluted into social studies – the study of the contemporary. The hold of history in the school thus depends, above all, on the importance of the school as a seminary for teaching a civic faith that is rooted in history. In the United States, schools are often still such seminaries; on the other side of the Atlantic, they no longer are.

Those who find silver linings in every cloud might want to stress one advantage of this demise: will not young Europeans stop learning, internalizing, and reliving the ideological and national quarrels of the past? Maybe; and yet, such potential gains in tolerance and détente (the French word for which has become *décrispation*) are more than offset by important drawbacks; for the unexamined past lives on, and disconnection from it merely makes it more difficult to understand and cope with its formidable resudues. It lives on, first of all, in the form of would-be but unfit masterkeys. Since the human mind craves comprehensive explanations for complex events and general causes for disparate effects – especially in countries such as those of Western Europe, where education used to be a missionary branch of the Enlightenment rather than a service for practical adaptation – what is more natural than trying to account for the bewildering array of contemporary changes in the sweeping terms of a seemingly 'scientific' philosophy of history? Hence the persistence of Marxism, despite repeated, careful demonstrations of its inadequacy (à la Raymond Aron)[6] or periodic denunciations of its temporal incarnations (à la *nouveaux philosophes*, twenty-five years after Camus). A system of thought rooted in history has become an obstacle to understanding much of the present precisely because the growing evidence of its divorce from historical evolution is obscured by the decline of historical consciousness.

The past lives on, also, as a series of problems, tensions, atavisms – old institutions, modes of authority, or, to quote Michel Crozier,[7] models of rationality that no longer fit the advanced industrial societies of Western Europe, and constitute so many obstacles to individual desires, group aspirations, or collective efficiency. If the problems of class conflict are muddled rather than clarified by a clinging to old dogmatic formulas, the problems of persistent but counter-productive authoritarianism are made worse by the frequent failure to examine its historical roots, to understand why it has proven so resilient despite vast changes in social organization and in values, and despite the transformation or the weakening of many institutions (such as the family, the church, and the school system) that used to be its props. The lack of historical reflection thus breeds the illusion of quick remedies or encourages the growth of anti-authoritarian utopias (like *autogestion*) that are too impractical, too naive in their hope of doing away with power altogether, to do much harm to their foe; or, on the contrary, they foster the belief that new challenges to social order can best be met by 're-enforcing authority' (as in West Germany's reaction against terrorism). What a writer recently called postwar West Germany's confusion of democracy with anti-communism,[8] like Italy's confusion of democracy with bureaucracy legitimized by universal suffrage, is the joint result of an inadequate confrontation with the recent past and a growing estrangement from the more distant one.

It has been said that bad conscience – fed by the failures or crimes of the past – may at least have the virtue of instigating commitment. But when it is pure of historical understanding, it leads to blind nihilism. And when that same purity is not accompanied by any bad conscience, the failure of memory through disconnectioin from the past leads to a failure of imagination and will in connection with the future: the destruction – partly willed, but largely unwitting – of the past has not been the prelude to the construction of a new destiny.

III

The future too, of course, is viewed in national terms because of the same idiosyncrasies that have kept the Western European nations from building a common state; they are partly deep residues of the past, partly distinctive features of their present political and social systems. Old blinders or worries, present crises and opportunities loom large in such visions. The British, after years of vivisecting their malaise (the 'British disease'), see a brighter future thanks to the combination of luck – the North Sea oil, and traditional virtues – rediscovered self-restraint and incomes discipline. The Germans, despite a party system that strikes foreign observers as more consensual than any outside the United States, worry about law and order and argue about the best way to protect a democratic system whose fresh roots are growing in a society where liberalism remains conditional – dependent on efficiency. Italians are entirely absorbed by the drama of the permanent crisis, and see as the only alternatives either a total breakdown – followed by some still unpredictable rule of violence and terror – or a coalition of the two huge secular churches – the Christian Democrats and the Communists. This coalition would feed the skepticism or anxieties of those who belong to neither party, those who trust one but not the other, and those who fear that the union of the two mastodons would give a colossal, final proof of impotence. The French oscillate between a new pragmatism that may turn out to be another word for complacency and immobility and an addition to political divisions whose only merit is to keep alive the illusion of real choice. What is remarkable is how little each national vision is affected by the others. It is even more remarkable that none of them amounts to a national design.

They have one thing in common: a combination of two sets of experiences and expectations, which does not beget a vision of the future. For many years, Western Europeans have lived on the moving escalator of economic growth. The social dislocations and political changes it has brought about have, as I have already stated, riveted their minds on the present. At the same time, especially as governments for so long have suggested that (or acted as if) the solution to all tensions would be provided by further growth, the citizens were led to believe that the future could be summed up as a continuing and growing manna – the condition of the fulfillment of individual ambitions and desires, the prerequisite of greater social justice, and the way to equality of opportunity and results. In this sense, the imagined future was no more than a projection of what was most welcome in the present and the hope that what was currently unwelcome would be eliminated or tamed. The British, whose growth was smaller, told pollsters that they felt happy, happier than the continentals. But their own leaders worried about the effects of the lower rate, and the continentals showed a remarkable consensus in rejecting any thought that their tensions and frustrations might be relieved by a slowdown. If we mean by the word *political* a consideration of one's relation to others, to groups, to the community, and to the state in terms of values, beliefs, and power, the prevailing vision was singularly apolitical: its blandishments were bland, its appeal lay in its being so easy.

It was precisely because this vision of quantitative happiness, this somewhat mindless faith in a self-propelled expansion that apparently required no more from each citizen than his labor and a minimum of social integration, this failure to imagine another model of society, another kind of individual fate, another destiny for the nation seemed so tepid or boring to many of the young, that the 'events' of May 1968 occurred. But a rebellion is not a construction: no alternative vision came out of it. May 1968 showed how the death of *le passé vécu* and the failure to bring a new design to life are linked. The young rebels may have thought they were reliving a revolutionary past, but they were only going through the motions: they acted, they did not re-enact. A liquidation of what had become second-hand or bookish memories led nowhere – except to a deluge of books. Most of the young, whether they took part in this 'happening' or not, seemed, in fact, to accept the common vision and to think of their own future in terms of individual security amidst general prosperity.[9] There seemed to be nothing between unlimited alienation and limited horizons, a rejection *in toto* of the prevailing values or a somewhat passive acceptance of them.

Then came the experience of the recession. It shattered the expectations of an ever-rising escalator. It revived old critiques of capitalism, old discussions about its final crisis. But no new alternative vision has emerged; it is as if people remained glued to the motionless escalator and waited for it to get well. The Europeans' own 'revolution of rising expectations' made its sudden stop that much more jarring. But despite some talk about new models of growth or qualitative rather than quantitative growth, governments and citizens were joined in a desire to put the escalator back in motion; the only disagreements between or within nations have been over rates of recovery, fears of inflation and unemployment, and obligations of mutual solidarity. In other words, little has been learned from the troubles that have blurred the easy vision. No more-political action or proposal has appeared. This older and somewhat uninspiring vision – what French rebels had called *métro, boulot, dodo* – has simply been proven unreliable. The recession and its inequities confirmed the rebels in their rejection of the model (and probably helped turn some of them from spontaneous psychodrama to organized terror), while the passive acceptance of this model by the others lost some of its former complacency. And the millions, neither rebels nor conformists, who subscribe to the critique of capitalism offered by the Marxist left, nevertheless live a double life or practice double-entry bookkeeping. They have seen their reasons for distrusting the model vindicated, yet they see no future other than one of economic growth. (They only wish the authorities in charge to be less distant, unreliable, greedy, or unfair than the profit-makers who have managed it so far.)

This brings us to a query about the institutions and forces that used to be, so to speak, the incubators of designs, the shapers of the collective will, or the sources of collective utopias. Among the most potent of these were the ideologies political forces offered to the citizens. What visions of the future do they now propose? Nothing much, really. One can divide these forces into several categories, which do not always correspond to distinctions between parties. First, there are the managers: the French *majorité*, the Italian Christian Democrats, the bulk of the three West German and the British parties, and the Spanish establishment that developed under Franco's shadow. They are the high priests of the prevailing model of growth, and all subscribe, with national or party nuances, both to Pompidou's conviction that the state's role is to straighten or smooth out (nothing more) the natural effects of continuing industrialization, and to Giscard's dictum that governing is just the art of *gérer l'imprévisible*. There may be a vision here, but the least one can say is that it lacks inspiration. To quote the earlier French president – de Gaulle – 'marrying one's century' may well be necessary, but does it prepare one for the next? De Gaulle, it is true, was not simply a manager; he had a vision, both of the past and of the future, and he still believed in national history and national will in the grand double drama of internal togetherness and external struggle. But his was, above all, a vision of rallying for and acting on the world stage. He talked of French and European might, not of French or European social and political organization (beyond the need for a strong state). When, at the end, he realized that this was the area in which a vision was most needed (given France's and Europe's limited range on the world scene) and when he came to see that without such a vision no dream of the world stage, however modest, could ever be realized, he fell – both because many of his own supporters showed no desire for imagination and because his own was ill at ease in this realm.

Next to the managers, there are the challengers: the communists, the Labor and SPD left, and the French socialists. They too have had trouble with the future. Sometimes, as in England, their vision is so insular and goes so much against the common scriptures of growth as to appear almost perverse – thoroughly unappealing to the unconverted and singularly austere even to the faithful. Sometimes, their programs are not prophecies or calls to arms but mere critiques of present injustices and acute expressions of present discontents. Sometimes, as in the case of the French socialists, they seem caught between residual

(or is it revived?) utopianism – as in the drive for *autogestion* – against 'professional politics' and against the centralized state that pretends to express the general will. The drive comes, if not like de Gaulle's view of France, *du fond des âges*, at least from the oldest socialist and syndicalist fund[10] – as well as from rather routine sources of social democracy. Sometimes, as in the case of the communists, the challengers are split between those who seek, at least temporarily, to collude diffidently with the managers – because of the scars left by past fascist experiences and, therefore, the need to give priority to the establishment or survival of democracy (however 'formal') – and those who, like the French, cling to a Leninist model of revolutionary break with the established order while trying to de-Leninize the model just enough to capture voters whose ideal for the future is definitely not Leninist. In other words, they behave like a church that is afraid both of losing its distinctiveness by throwing out too much of a now-unappealing dogma and of losing its appeal by not throwing out enough (not an inaccurate description of the present Roman Catholic Church). The compromise is neither stable or popular within, nor convincing outside.

Thus, the great ideological 'spiritual families' of the past have either disappeared or propose no relevant future. What do Christian democrats offer, except a plea for law and order, a spectacle of decay, or a touching faith in European integration as the *deus ex machina*? Has socialism succeeded in preserving its identity? Or has it not rather been endlessly torn between the managerial temptation, a stern egalitarianism, and a welfarism that accepts, in order to reform it, capitalist society; and when the costs of welfarism become unbearable as growth slows down (and welfarism tends indeed to slow growth by drying out investment), what more does socialism offer than a nostalgia for a new *projet de société* it cannot quite define? Has liberalism succeeded in moving beyond the reconciliation of political liberty with democracy, or the compromise between the market and some government control, which date from much earlier times? What can old conservatism offer when whatever is wanted to conserve is gone? What is the communist ideal, once you erase the Soviet Union from it – and even if you leave it in? The notion of the death of ideology has been accepted too easily and buried too soon. Its celebrators grandly overrated, in their Saint-Simonian faith in science and production, the degree to which the advent of post-industrial society would inject pragmatism, erase class differences, tame class conflicts, modernize party systems, and eliminate Luddite extremists. Ideologies are still there, though, especially on the left – as is normal since the left is the refuge and hope of those who dislike the established order. Traces of ideological thinking can be found all over the picture; but insofar as ideologies offered plausible visions of the future, the much-rejected notion was not so wrong. Either there are no such visions or else they are not plausible, like those spun out by hundreds of *groupuscules*. They describe the ideal future as what will miraculously arise when the present society has been entirely destroyed – a grand release of spontaneity, a fusion in fraternity, but no discernible social order. And the visions are based less on faith than on hate, as in the beautiful scene of destruction at the end of Antonioni's *Zabriskie Point*. Marxism is still present – often omnipresent – and diffuse. But it serves as a tool for analyzing the flaws of the status quo and as a goad for proposing the demise of the present – not as a blueprint for the future. Societies that depend on growth, and whose citizens expect it even when they criticize its present motors; societies, moreover, that have been bitten, or have barely escaped being bitten, by the 'carnivorous idols' Bernanos talked about in the 1930s, ask formidable questions of each ideological vision of the future. The questions were often either not raised before or were deemed secondary. Will it work? At what costs? Societies that have suffered from the disease of unrestrained ideologies on a rampage, and have put their hopes in the benefits of economic growth, now impose a reality test on political visions, even if their own vision of the future is singularly unpolitical and unreal.

Those who announced the end of ideology believed that the advent of a pragmatic age would propel Western Europe toward a plannable future – post-industrial society. But such pragmatism presupposes either that political problems have been reduced to technical ones (to be solved by experts) or that the old ideologies are to be replaced by a new one – the ideology of advanced liberal capitalism – which would dampen and thus help resolve disputes. If both postulates are wrong and the old ideologies are dead or dying, one is left immersed in a dreary present, a jungle of group conflicts, with no standard for their solution. And the very intensity of the struggle for power and product, the very absence of any grand cause, the very myopia of each class, profession, and association concentrating on its claims makes it almost impossible for any vision of the future to emerge.

The other forces from which such visions used to emanate are in no better shape. I have already mentioned the Catholic Church. Its image of the future used to be shaped by its conception of the past, by the accretion of values and dogmas transmitted from generation to generation. Inevitably, now that this heritage is being liquidated – partly because it is incompatible with the dynamics and mores of the modern world and partly because it has been compromised by past collusions between the church and anti-democratic political ideologies and elites; the church is left without a vision of the future and exposed to another kind of collusion – with the political and social activists of reform or even revolution. Yesterday's involvement with secularism condemned the church to unpopularity; but the secularists on whom it used to lean had borrowed their own design and dogmas from the church. Today, it is the church that does the borrowing – from people caught in or drifting amidst the troubles of the present.

The army also used to offer a vision of the future. But it was one of a struggle against other European nations for revenge or supremacy, or against the barbarians for law and order and civilization. Of course, the willingness to resort to force, the usefulness of force, indeed the greatness of force, were essential to this vision: as de Gaulle wrote, 'the sword is the axis of the world, and greatness cannot be divided'.[11] Force today is doubly devalued:

pragmatically because the risks are too great and the rewards too slim, and intellectually because its prestige in Europe has not survived the orgies of violence of two world wars. Armies reduced to deterrent and latent or oblique functions or to 'punctual' rescue operations have trouble finding volunteers or keeping draftees from displaying their boredom. At any rate, they too are in a limbo, between a past they can only celebrate with ambivalence and a future they cannot like.

Again, the intelligentsia offers no more vision of the future than of the past. It may once have played a role as the purveyor of utopias, but there are not many utopias to be found today. Marxists abound – as critics of the present. But they are now bereft of a future. It was relatively easy to propose one – as there was no socialist society anywhere – before 1914. Now there are too many, and the most orthodox is the biggest disappointment of all. When reality begins to shackle the imagination and to betray hope, resentment alone remains – and sometimes indeed, as in France in the past months, the resentment turns away from the present toward a wholesale repudiation of Marxism altogether. To be sure, Italian and French syndicalists and their sympathizers have, as I said before, articulated the utopia of *autogestion*; but in their drive to appear responsible – that is, not utopian – the revolutionary force of the idea, which was still considerable after May 1968 and the 'hot Fall' of Italy, has been eroded. Pragmatic proposals have replaced the Sorelian myth. Intellectuals are still the experimenters, but their experiments have been, so to speak, privatized: they deal with the realms of aesthetics, linguistics, theater, and the movies, with psychoanalysis, and with poetry. Sometimes their experiments carry them into local social-welfare operations, like the French *Lacaniens* and anti-psychiatrists after 1968; but this occurred precisely because the wider political scene had proven so disappointing.[12] As Crozier points out, the traditional role of the intellectual – to serve as a self-appointed conscience and guide of the nation, and thus to propose ideals and to speak out about its present and its future – has to a considerable extent disappeared.

Sartre's last active years as a writer have been spent on his negative identity, called Flaubert.

For a while, in the 1960s, it seemed that the old intellectual would be replaced by the new problem-solving social scientist, who would lend his expertise to the managers and lead them to careful reforms. But on the one hand, the multiplication of 'perverse' (or counter-intuitive) effects, the latent dissatisfaction of many of the experts with a role that seemed to them like a fall from the pedestal of the past and like mere service of the prince, the impatience of the managers with experts more concerned with their own research priorities than with those of the state – all doomed or at least dwarfed that experiment. On the other hand, social science, especially when it divorces itself from public philosophy, rarely goes beyond what Max Weber called the disenchantment of reality – revealing, unveiling, and debunking. Now, any vision of the future must go beyond this point or, rather, stay on this side of total lucidity, if it is to be a call or guide to action. For one cannot act without somehow underestimating difficulties or overestimating those whom one wants to rally. Intellectuals *qua* prophets had idealized the People; the social scientists' job is to describe the real, not the imaginary people. Action simplifies, social science complicates.

Insofar as social engineering continues, with carefully reduced expectations, it reflects what I said about the citizenry as a whole: its practitioners have demonstrated little imagination about the future and have proven that even its limited promises may not be kept after all. Members of the intelligentsia who have turned away from that troubled partnership in social engineering have gone in one of two directions, and sometimes in both. One is specialized, scientific research or arcane experimentation. This choice preserves that distance between the intellectual and the average man, that equation between intellectual work and prowess that is a legacy from the aristocratic age – although it is now divorced from the nineteenth-century artist's desire to lead the masses into a promised land. Of course, among those who choose this direction, very little is being said about the problems of everyday life, ethics, institutions, work, and leisure. The second direction is a residue of this grand claim — a kind of debased nostalgia for it: it is the desire to be 'popular', fashionable, a media *habitué* or a media event, a troubadour of spontaneity or a mod synthesizer of concepts that are in or on the air. (Witness the sudden discovery in France, in 1977, that power is everywhere. What would Molière have done with that?) But in this case, the once-prophet becomes a mere critic, who peremptorily denounces what the powermongers have done, but who refuses to say what they should have done, since all politics is contemptible. A narcissistic, self-appointed spokesman for the victims of the universal Gulag, he abdicates all responsibility for imagining a better world, merely calls for resistance whenever the powers-that-be step on the little man's toes, or sympathizes with the longings of adolescence. This has happened to the *nouveaux philosophes* (they were not reluctant), and it also characterizes much of the writing of Alain Touraine. Even a work as careful in its attempt to avoid both esotericism and grand rhetoric as the Crozier–Friedberg call for a new kind of social theory strikes one as singularly ahistorical and modest about the future:[13] change must come through experimentation *à la base*, through the gradual learning of new collective capabilities; there is no way to describe it in advance, nor should too much of it be attempted at any given moment, since people cannot stand a heavy dose of upheaval. It is as if much of the European intelligentsia, after witnessing the shambles and crimes perpetrated by the 'isms' it used to embrace, had turned away in horror, not merely from such 'isms' but also from the kind of *prospective* they provided and perverted. The welcome rediscovery of those virtues dear to Camus — modesty and limits — has led to a retreat from political thought altogether. Since the air was foul, those who helped make it so have decided to stop breathing.

The intellectuals, through their writings and through the role they played in and around political parties, used to peddle visions of the future. While their wares may have reached only a small portion of the public, their influence was much broader; their ideas became known not only through the parties, but also because of another transmission belt — the system of education. Nowhere was schooling merely a

set of training techniques, a transmission of accumulated usable knowledge, or a machine for 'social reproduction'. Not only in the *Gymnasium, lycée*, or public school attended by the few, but in primary education for the many, the school system transmitted values, formed citizens (some as responsible participants, some as obedient subjects), and provided them, more or less overtly, with images of the future. The educational system of the Third Republic, whose textbooks were written by distinguished scholars and intellectual administrators, propagated a vision of the future that combined the preservation of traditional French bourgeois values and the progressive unfolding of the Enlightenment — science, rationality, material gains, and increasing possibilities of self-determination for individuals long oppressed by routines or dogmas, as well as for nations. It was a remarkable blend of the traditional and the revolutionary, well fitted to a society that resisted rapid changes in behavior and habits yet was permanently in love with the idea of change, the ideal of emancipation, and a self-image as a beacon of light. It is not a coincidence that the most influential intellectual godfather of schoolteachers before the First World War was Jaurès, a visionary who was also the finest product of his nation's culture and the very symbol of nineteenth-century optimism.

As in the intellectual world, we are now witnessing an eclipse of the future in the school system. It has been replaced with 'present shock': a proliferation of options and subjects, an often frantic or overstuffed attempt at putting into the hands of the young as many tools as possible to help them understand and navigate in the present (hence a high rate of obsolescence and a breathless, permanent revision of curricula). To be sure, there is much of this kind of scurrying in America as well; but there the beliefs of the *angewandte Aufklärung*[14] surround and give meaning to the disconnected bits and pieces. This is not the case in Western Europe. The public cult of growth is not a substitute, for it is a cult of means, not ends; and if there is one group that is often sullen, bitter, and hostile toward the cult, it is the teachers. Not only is their prestige falling, as I have pointed out before. But, trained to transmit established knowledge to pupils whose function it is to receive it, they are confronted instead with the need for their own permanent re-education, with the duty to transmit methods and data that in a short time may prove to be wrong and with young men and women who are increasingly impatient with the old-style pedagogy. Both in reference to what is to be taught and how best to teach it, the very speed of change, already found partly responsible for the receding of the past, also contributes to the blackout of the future. The school is caught between students concerned above all with their own opportunities in nations marked by disruptive changes – as well as by vast surges for collective social ascent – and teachers who do not always comprehend the changes, and who often feel that in growth-obsessed societies they have lost much of the high ground they held in the days when efficiency, consumption, and the production of goods were not the highest values. The only function of the school seems to be running after (or behind) adjustment: its fate parallels that of European societies, which used to see themselves on top of their own fate in a world shaped by them. Yesterday the school was a force for social integration that taught values drawn from the past and expectations about the future. Today, if it is such a force at all, it is as a purely functional agent of preparation for the present.

If 'no model of civilization emerges from the present-day drifting culture, no call for reform and pioneering',[15] if radical criticism so often turns out to be no more than criticism without a vision for replacement of what is to be destroyed, there is still another reason: the displacement of the intelligentsia by the media, or perhaps the rush of the intellectuals themselves to become (pardon the expression) 'communicators' rather than creators. This is often seen as a means of remaining 'relevant' in nations where the public no longer turns to its great writers for guidance – unless they write for mass consumption or appear on the screen. Indeed, the media have become a screen between the intellectuals and the public. The former feel that their only alternatives are isolation (which they fear) and capitulation (which they often seem to crave). I call it capitulation – not merely joining what one cannot fight – because the media impose their own constraints. Whether – depending on the country and the medium – they revel in muckraking or in celebration, they too tend to emphasize the present, either to condone or to condemn it. The past is a source of entertainment, the future a dangerous bone of contention. A few movie-makers may invent futures, but it is rare, and usually only to warn us about present trends (for example, Truffaut's *Fahrenheit 451*, which is based on a story by American Ray Bradbury). Television, in Europe, shuns the controversial for political reasons (as in France), scrutinizes the present to heighten citizen awareness (as in England and West Germany), or endlessly serves up old movies and adaptations of novels. The press, with few exceptions, sees its role as purveyor of information and analyses of the present; the recently created 'ideas' page of *Le Monde* almost seems designed to highlight the plight of the modern intellectual – he sounds esoteric when he talks of his own research, and puerile when he tries to walk in the steps of the older thinkers and muse about anything outside his own field.

If the media are the daily opium, the provider of food in the citizen's daily life is the bureaucracy. Just as the media have pushed aside or domesticated the intellectuals, who used to invent futures, the bureaucrats have taken over the state, which used to choose one and build it. Ruling has become managing, and the bureaucracy manages us all, or almost all of us. 'Marginalized' people – immigrant workers, or workers and employees who live in the shadow economy on which the visible one often relies for survival (as Suzanne Berger has shown),[16] shop-keepers, artisans, and peasants on their way out, or students parked in university ghettos with no job possibilities when they come out – may fall outside the bureaucracy's net. They are either living in a hopeless present or 'recuperated' by nihilists. The citizens who perform in the carnival of growth, those who are under the net – with their bargaining power, institutions, and associations that are the essence of modern corporatism – are, for all the weapons at their disposal, *administrés*. Pressuring the bureaucracy on whose benefits, directives, incentives, and guidelines they depend is their constant concern as producers or consumers. (This is one reason why the use of the word *corporatism* is misleading: in orthodox corporatist theory, the groups are autonomous and have taken power away from the state; today, they are tied to it in symbiotic alliance or contest.) The bureaucracy also contributes to the general immersion in the present. True, there is some official concern with planning the future, but it is less a matter of vision than a question of deterrence; without foresight, without an evaluation of trends, an extrapolation of curves, there will be disasters, and the bureaucracy's role is to ensure smoothness. But, almost by definition, it cannot begin with a utopia and provide the means to bring it about. It must start with the present, with today's notions of what is desirable (full employment, no inflation, better housing, the stability of families, adequate health care and schooling, growing productivity, sufficient supplies of energy, better working conditions); it then tries to ensure that tomorrow will meet the standards and demands of today. I do not mean to suggest, as Henry Kissinger did, that bureaucracy is the born enemy of creativity and imagination; I would only point out that this is not its domain or its duty. The vision must come from somewhere else; when there is none, when no people or leader give them directives about the kind of future that ought to be created, then the bureaucracy's essence – the middle range, coping with what exists, trouble-avoidance, and predictability – occupies the whole scene. Its own weight, its importance in the daily affairs of Western European societies, tends to be rather overwhelming anyhow (much more so than in the United States, even in a country such as Italy, where the state is weak and the bureaucracy is far from efficient). The reasons are many: parliaments cannot cope, or else they try to do little more than protect special interests; so many ministers are managerial types or are easily tamed by the bureaucrats; the margins of choice are so small; and, above all, the economic and social functions of the state are so large. This situation not only seriously limits the leaders' capacity to realize whatever vision they may have; it also inhibits their ability to shape any vision at all. Everywhere in the capitalist world, the state that wants to avoid recession and inflation finds that its margin of maneuver is severely constrained by the dynamics, domestic and international, of the capitalist economy; the more extensive the functions and bureaucracy of the state, the more visible these constraints and the more inhibited the state's capacity to imagine and prepare a different future. It was fascinating to watch, in the French Socialist Party, the struggle between the utopians and 'realists' (and, sometimes, between utopian and 'responsible' fragments of a same personality, such as Michel Rocard). Societies doomed to constant efficiency and success are deadly not only for ideologies but for all far-reaching visions of the future.

Thus, none of the forces or institutions that used to breed visions of the future, and that also served as instruments of social integration and control, perform as innovators anymore. Another factor obliterates visions of the future. There are no outside models to inspire one and to allow one to say: see, my future is no utopia, since it already works somewhere else. Neither superpower is an inspiration. There are many reasons why America is not – even though Europe's model of growth and the techniques for promoting growth are borrowed from the United States. To Europeans, America is a supermarket, not a religion; one turns to it for recipes and goods, not for its spirit or for its value as a model of society. There is also the simple fact of America's power and presence; can the heir to a long and glorious past, the dreamer of a united Europe (whatever the failure of will and the blurred image of the past) legitimately accept the master's way of life as an ideal? Indeed, the more they lift or imitate, the more Western Europe's societies begin resembling America, at least superficially, and the more they are bound to proclaim that the borrowing is a means to something original. The difference in world power strengthens and inflames an old European tendency to cultural snobbery – how can one take as an ideal a nation whose cultural achievements do not measure up to one's own? This pose remains important, even in places such as England and Germany, where the next reason is not so strong. Europe's traditional ideologies, however irrelevant or faded in their power to describe a future, remain, with the single exception of liberalism, distant enough from American experience to serve as screens between it and the Europeans. It is not surprising to find in France, side by side, a Marxist critique of American capitalism and imperialism and a right-wing onslaught on American egalitarianism, commercialism, homogenization of cultures, pernicious universalism, and lack of aesthetic sense. 'A corpse in good health', a source of perversion, degradation, and infection, a country which 'drops everywhere the eggs of its ugliness' – these themes are spun by some Gaullists and also some neo-fascists.[17] (However, the critique of capitalism and imperialism sometimes comes from the right, the aesthetic critique from the left, as in Werner Herzog's unforgettable movie *Stroszek*, whose anti-hero finally kills himself in the wasteland of America, the country of the cold and of artificial hens gone mad in an amusement gallery.) Moreover, as Aron has pointed out, America is a country whose idea of the future is nothing but the fulfillment of its ideals at birth:[18] it is not a prophecy, but a vindication (so that any crisis of values or institutions breeds a kind of fundamentalist revival). The Western Europeans find no such decalogue at their origins: their revolutions are either unfinished or have failed. For all these reasons, there have been more piecemeal imitations than overall celebrations of the American model. Finally, America's own ideal (but do Americans understand it?) is highly nationalistic: it is the realization of America's mission, it is the triumph at home and abroad of a certain conception of man's relation to God and to government, which was born in rebellion against and developed in separation from Europe. And so we have come full circle.

If America never became the ideal even when it was the example, the Soviet Union has ceased being either. 'Eurocommunism' is not a very helpful concept. But what the three communist parties of France, Italy, and Spain have in common is a deliberate distance from the Soviet Union – whether in the form of an open attack on the essence of the Soviet system, as in Carrillo's case; as jerky repudiations of key elements of the Soviet state and ideology, as in Marchais's; or in polite and friendly estrangement, as in Berlinguer's. The French example shows that it is more difficult to jettison the Nessus's tunic of a Leninist organization and frame of mind than to get rid of the concept of proletarian dictatorship and the single-party state. Yet the lesson is clear: no significant Western European communist party, except Portugal's, proposes the Soviet Union as a model of socialism; each one explains that Western European circumstances make it irrelevant. Moreover, the new generation of communist voters knows more about the crimes of Stalin, thanks to the media, than older party members were ever allowed to guess. As for the savage kinds of communism or extremist Marxism, they are orphans. Whether they were of Trotskyite origin or not, they had always looked askance at the Soviet Moloch. They used to believe that the sun would rise in the Far East, in Mao's China; but the end of the Cultural Revolution and the fall of the Gang of Four have made them aware of a bitter fact: the Chinese model may not be so different from the Soviet one after all, whatever the national enmities and differences in levels of development and policies between the two. (One such orphan, the *Tel Quel* group of French intellectuals, having moved beyond Red China, has now discovered the United States as a country where, given capitalism's constraints, little may be accomplished but a lot is permitted: artistic experiments, group rebellions, experimentations – who would have thought that the search for spontaneity would cross the Atlantic, or rather the Pacific?)[19] Yugoslav workers' control is a dubious case; Guevara is dead; Castro is a Soviet client; and Régis Debray is a prize-winning novelist.

V

We have once again come full circle. The fading of the national past could have meant the giving-up of a narrow identity in preparation for and in favor of the adoption of a new broader European one. But this would have required an image of, a will for, a common future. *Tout se tient*: with no clear visions of the future, how can Frenchmen, Englishmen, and so on, desire a *projet* for Europe? And if they are encased in their national present, how can they do anything but lose contact with a past that is both increasingly less vivid, less present, less relevant, and something of a reproach? How can they be more than conformists complying with a perplexing present, half-citizens half-protestors, or pure rebels whose revolt, when it does not merely express itself in terror, takes, as in May 1968, the form of a half-finished blend of disparate, uprooted old ideas thrown into a Cuisinart for quick concoction? For a vision of the future as pure release, à la *Zéro de Conduite*, what slogan is more telling than 'under the pavement, the beach'?

The disappearance of the past is partly a disappointment with that past – with what history and human action have wrought; thus it is very different from that deliberate historical break that revolutionaries intent on building a new order and creating a new man provoked in 1792, or in 1917, or in 1949 in China. It means exhaustion, not energy; drainage, not arson. In turn, the lack of a sense of the future has further depressed, devalued, and discolored the past; when one does not know where one is going, when there seems to be nowhere to go and nothing new and better to accomplish, what is the point of retracing one's steps? It takes a combination of faith in, ideas about, and will to build one's future to keep an interest in the past from becoming mere scholarship or leisure. There has been enough democratization, in the sense of a liquidation of the residues from the non-democratic past, enough demationalization – even in France – enough 'dis-ideologization' (pardon the word) to disenchant the past. But the result is a vacuum, not a will to build either a common European future, or a new national one. As we have seen, this is a story in which cultural, political, economic, and social factors all mix.

In the nineteenth century the nations of Western Europe were marked by an original combination of lively, even heated ideological quarrels about different visions of the future, especially the political future; there was broad public consensus about the social order, the general direction, and the nation's role in the world. Those who felt left out had their own vision. Today the quarrels are more about the present, and the public consensus, almost everywhere, is what I once called, for France, a consensus by default – the present is embraced less for its virtues than for its benefits (when they flow), less for its values than because any alternative is seen as either worse (whether it is the return of a frightening past experience or the imposition of the Soviet model) or more divisive. As a result, the continent that has always prided itself on its sense of roots and innovation appears more uprooted and less creative than the other model that makes Europeans so uncomfortable – the United States. Tocqueville's nightmare of disconnected individuals under a tutelary state is more present in Europe than in America. What he did not foresee was that individuals would also be disconnected from the past and the future, that voluntary associations (in which he saw a corrective to disconnection) would often only add group egoism to individual acquisitiveness, and that the state would be both bloated and trapped.

We are left then with two questions for morose or worried speculation. First, can one live for ever in the economic present, comforting oneself with comparative statistics and a half-cozy, half-worried enjoyment of goods, freedom, and rights? Secondly, to what extent are the poverty of inspiration and imagination, the concentration on the here and now, related to the European nations' fall from international eminence? Are images of the past and visions of the future tied either to struggles for national identity or to the possibility of strutting on the world's stage, to fighting or speaking out for a great cause, national or not? France's intellectuals lost their voice at the moment when France ceased to be a pacesetter for other nations and a leader in world affairs. Britain's inability to have a clearer vision of its future than its partners cannot easily be explained as a result of the cult of growth (although it results in part from the penalties that must be paid for forgetting the criterion of efficiency). It can be explained in part by the 'end of ideology'; for even though the scope of ideological battles was not as wide there as on the continent, Britain was once inspired by deep political and religious creeds. Still, this explanation does not go far enough. Was not Britain's image of its future always associated with a vision of a great role in the world – and was not de Gaulle's intuition about the necessity of such a role as a goad to internal creativity correct after all? If there is such a connection, the plight of Western Europe is not likely to end. For if the fall from the heights has broken that part of the *élan vital* that expresses itself, not in daily work and often-successful responses to the challenges of growth, but in the ability to find stimulation in the past and to will a future, then the very imprisonment in the present, the vital impulse's engulfment in the daily adjustments and crises, make the recovery of a sense of time (backward and forward) and the discovery of a common will unlikely. And so, each nation remains encased in its present self, giving an occasional backward glance at the recent past for remorse or consolation and a worried glance at the near future. Only a uniting Europe that could look at the whole of its fragmented past would be able to will a future. But how can it emerge, if its members have neither the drive nor the necessary incentives to transcend themselves into Europe?

References: Chapter 17

I want to express my gratitude to my friend and colleague Judith Shklar, whose comments and suggestions have been invaluable – as usual.

1 Jean-Marie Domenach, *Ce que je crois* (Paris, 1978), p. 82.
2 Robert Paxton, *Vichy France* (New York: Knopf, 1972).
3 See *Democracy in America*, Vol. 2, chs 5 and 6 or Part Four.
4 Domenach, op. cit., p. 201.
5 Quoted in Mark Poster, *Existential Marxism in Postwar France* (Princeton, NJ: Princeton University Press 1975), p. 327.
6 See Raymond Aron, *L'opium des intellectuels* (Paris: Calmann-Lévy, 1955), and *Plaidoyer pour l'Europe décadente* (Paris: Lafont, 1977).
7 In Michel Crozier, *The Crisis of Democracy* (New York: New York University Press, 1975), pp. 39 ff.
8 Jane Kramer, 'Hamburg', in *The New Yorker*, 20 March 1978).
9 See Gérard Vincent, *Les Lycéens* (Paris: Colin, 1971).
10 See Jacques Julliard, *Contre la politique professionnelle* (Paris: Editions du Seuil, 1978).
11 Last sentence of C. de Gaulle, *Vers l'armée de métier* (Paris: Editions Berger-Leurault, 1934).
12 See Sherry Turkle, *Psychoanalytic Politics* (New York: Basic Books, 1978).
13 *L'acteur et le système* (Paris: Editions du Seuil, 1977).
14 See Ralf Dahrendorf's book by that name (Munich: Piper, 1963).
15 Crozier, op. cit., p. 33.
16 See Suzanne Berger's 'Reflections on industrial society: the survival of the traditional sectors in France and Italy', forthcoming.
17 See *Nouvelle Ecole*, 'L'Amérique', no. 27–8 (1975), esp. pp. 64, 93 ff.
18 Aron, *Plaidoyer pour l'Europe décadente*, p. 136.
19 See *Tel Quel*, 'Etats-Unis', no. 71–3 (Fall 1977).

Bibliographical Essay

As the purpose of this anthology has been primarily to be a teaching aid, the selections presented here were designed to be indicative rather than exhaustive of the range of cultural thought in contemporary Europe. The introductory essay attempted to suggest how developments in European culture could be understood in the context of twentieth-century social and political history. The selections were meant to be points of departure for further explorations in the varieties of cultural criticism they represent. This closing bibliographical note in turn makes an effort to offer some suggestions for further reading on the general problem of the relation of culture and society as well as some hints concerning sources that we consider useful extensions of the themes emerging from our selections.

Besides the works included in the references to the introductory essay, all of which bear on the general theme of the relation of culture and society, other important theoretical contributions to the subject include Karl Mannheim, *Essays on the Sociology of Culture* (London: Routledge & Kegan Paul, 1971) and Leo Löwenthal, *Literature, Popular Culture and Society* (Englewood Cliffs, NJ: Prentice-Hall, 1961). Raymond Williams, *Keywords. A Vocabulary of Culture and Society* (New York: Oxford University Press, 1976), is a companion volume discussing the meaning of the central terms of his earlier classic. The same author's *The Long Revolution* (Westport, Conn.: Greenwood Press, 1961) and *The Country and the City* (London: Chatto & Windus, 1973) continue and supplement the explorations of *Culture and Society*, while his latest work, *Marxism and Literature* (Oxford: Oxford University Press, 1977), offers a lucid discussion of his theoretical principles. The older works by Ernst Cassirer, *The Logic of the Humanities* (New Haven, Conn., and London: Yale University Press, 1960), which discusses the problem of a humanistic culture, and Herbert Read, *Art and Society* (New York: Schocken Books, 1966), retain always their relevance for a broad understanding of cultural phenomena. The problem of culture in 'post-industrial' society is discussed in Daniel Bell, *The Cultural Contradictions of Capitalism* (New York: Basic Books, 1976), and Herbert J. Gans, *Popular Culture and High Culture* (New York: Basic Books, 1974), while Eugene Goodheart, *Culture and the Radical Conscience* (Cambridge, Mass.: Harvard University Press, 1973), discusses some of the political dimensions of cultural criticism in contemporary society. For representative current European views of the problem of the content of cultural expression, one may consult the works by Robert Escarpit, *Le littéraire et le social* (Paris: Flammarion, 1970) and *Sociologie de la littérature* (Paris: Presses Universitaires de France, 1958), as well as Jacques Leenhardt, *Lecture politique du roman* (Paris: Editions de Minuit, 1973).

A major example of in-depth literary interpretation in contemporary European cultural criticism is the voluminous biography of Gustave Flaubert by Jean-Paul Sartre, of which three volumes have been published. It would be interesting to attempt to determine to what extent this biography constitutes an application of, or a departure from, the analysis of the social situation of the authors presented in *What Is Literature?*. Both Lukács and Brecht offered applications of their theoretical views in their respective interpretive and literary works. Commentaries and continuing interpretive controversies on the views of these foremost framers of contemporary European cultural thought, as well as on the contribution of Benjamin, are too numerous to mention here but the debate between them recently collected in the volume *Aesthetics and Politics*, with an afterword by Frederic Jameson (London: New Left Books, 1977), should not escape the attention of the concerned student. On the cultural thought of Lucien Goldmann a very good and comprehensive survey in English is Robert Sayre, 'Goldmann and modern realism', *Praxis*, vol. 1, no. 2 (Winter 1976), pp. 129–49.

A number of useful collections of pertinent texts supplement and broaden the themes represented in this volume. Among them the interested reader might consult with profit James B. Hall and Barry Ulanov (eds), *Modern Culture and the Arts*, 2nd edn (New York: McGraw-Hill, 1972), and Irving Howe (ed.), *The Idea of the Modern in Literature and the Arts* (New York: Horizon Press, 1979). Along similar lines, the series Literary Taste, Culture and Mass Communication, edited by Peter Davison, Rolf Meyersohn, and Edward Shils (Cambridge: Chadwyck-Healey, 1978) reproduces in its fourteen valuable volumes many important essays, including several classics of cultural criticism, supplemented by suggestions for further reading.

W. Eugene Kleinbauer (ed.), *Modern Perspectives in Western Art History* (New York: Holt, Rinehart & Winston, 1971), offers a substantial introduction to contemporary modes of art appreciation, which place particular weight on the psychological, sociological, and historical dimensions of artistic creation. On the articulation of specifically political concerns through literature the sensitively selected and commented-upon texts in Philip Green and Michael Walzer (eds), *The Political Imagination in Literature* (New York: The Free Press, 1969), constitute a valuable source, while Walter Laqueur and George L. Mosse (eds), *Literature and Politics in the Twentieth Century* (New York: Harper & Row, 1967, originally published as *Journal of Contemporary History*, vol. II, no. 2, 1967), and George Panichas (ed.), *The Politics of Twentieth Century Novelists* (New York: Crowell, 1974), contain interesting essays on several twentieth-century European authors. Roy Pierce, *Contemporary French Political Thought* (London: Oxford University Press, 1966), includes perceptive essays on the political philosophy of, among others, Simone Weil, Albert Camus, and Jean-Paul Sartre.

When we turn to a concrete consideration of the problem of culture and society in the European context, a necessary point of departure is a good acquaintance with the historical background and the range of political and social problems that form the parameters of cultural life. Good surveys of twentieth-century European history with adequate attention to cultural phenomena are offered by H. Stuart Hughes, *Contemporaty Europe: A History* (Englewood Cliffs, NJ: Prentice-Hall, 1966), George Lichtheim, *Europe in the Twentieth Century* (New York: Praeger, 1972), and Robert O. Paxton, *Europe in the Twentieth Century* (New York: Harcourt Brace Jovanovich, 1975). Two volumes in the series The Rise of Modern Europe directed by William Langer are particularly useful for their well-written chapters on cultural life and rich bibliographical suggestions: Oron Hale, *The Great Illusion 1900–1914* (New York: Harper & Row, 1971), and Raymond J. Sontag, *A Broken World 1919–1939* (New

York: Harper & Row, 1971). More specifically on different aspects of European intellectual history the following works by H. Stuart Hughes are essential: *Consciousness and Society: The Reorientation of European Social Thought 1890–1930* (New York: Knopf, 1958) and *The Obstructed Path. French Social Thought in the Years of Desperation* (New York: Harper & Row, 1966). The most recent general cultural history of twentieth-century Europe, Michael D. Biddiss, *The Age of the Masses. Ideas and Society in Europe since 1870* (New York: Harper & Row, 1978), is comprehensive and very well written and has an excellent bibliographical survey.

On the cultural climate of contemporary Europe, two recent special issues of the journal of the American Academy of Arts and Sciences, *Daedalus*, Winter and Spring 1979, surveying the European scene, are particularly informative and up to date. These two *Daedalus* issues on Europe are designed to update an earlier issue on Europe that appeared also as Stephen R. Graubard (ed.), *A New Europe?* (Boston, Mass.: Beacon Press, 1964), and included many important essays on cultural life. On the issue of the 'Americanization' of European culture, see C. W. E. Bigsby (ed.), *Superculture. American Popular Culture and Europe* (London: Paul Elek, 1975), and Daniel Snownan, *Britain and America. An Interpretation of their Culture 1945–1975* (New York: Harper & Row, 1977), both of which, though oriented more toward sociological phenomena, are suggestive. Along similar lines, the collection *Arts in Society*, edited by Paul Barker (London: Fontana/Collins, 1977), surveys the character of cultural phenomena in the Anglo-Saxon world in an age of mass communications. Perry Anderson, 'Components of the national culture', *New Left Review*, no. 50 (July–August 1968), pp. 4–56, is a remarkable survey of the failure of academic British culture which he relates systematically to the character of British society.

Regarding the cultural outlook of the different continental societies, the following works are helpful. On France, see Jacques Charpentreau, *Le Livre et la lecture en France* (Paris: Editions Ouvrières, 1968) and Jean-Paul Aron, *Qu' est-ce que la culture française?* (Paris: Editions Denöel, 1975). Stanley Hoffmann, *Decline or Renewal? France since the 1930s* (New York: Viking, 1977), relates cultural phenomena to contemporary political history and social change. On Germany, Walter Kaufmann, 'German thought after World War II', in *From Shakespeare to Existentialism* (Freeport, NY: Books for Libraries Press, 1960), offers a sobering diagnosis on the earlier part of the postwar era, but a more comprehensive and hopeful picture is presented in the pages of *Postwar German Culture: An Anthology*, edited by Charles E. McClelland and Steven P. Scher (New York: Dutton, 1974). On Italy, the relevant chapters in H. Stuart Hughes, *The United States and Italy*, rev. edn (Cambridge, Mass.: Harvard University Press, 1965) are lucid and informative, while the collection *Il caso italiano*, edited by Fabio Luca Cavazza and Stephen R. Graubard (Milano: Garzanti, 1974), includes some interesting essays illuminating different aspects of Italian cultural thought. For some representative sources one may consult Norberto Bobbio, *Politica e cultura* (Torino: Einaudi, 1955, repr. 1974), and Palmiro Togliatti, *La politica culturale*, edited by Luciano Greppi (Rome: Editori Riuniti, 1974), which argue from opposite ideological viewpoints, as well as Eugenio Montale, *La poesia non esiste* (Milan: 1971), which offers a critical commentary on the place of representatives of culture in society. On the political context of cultural life in Spain under the dictatorship, José Maravall, *Dictatorship and Political Dissent. Workers and Students in Franco's Spain* (London: Tavistock, 1978), is a relevant source, while Raymond Carr and Juan Pablo Fusi Aizpurua, *Spain: Dictatorship to Democracy* (London: Allen & Unwin, 1979), is an outstanding survey of the transition and contains an excellent chapter on culture. The collection *Eighteen Texts*, edited by Willis Barnstone (Cambridge, Mass.: Harvard University Press, 1972), offers a sample of dissident literature against the Greek dictatorship. On the political and cultural climate of post-junta Greece, one might refer to Paschalis M. Kitromilides, 'Democratic Greece – stumbling towards modernity', *Dissent*, Winter 1978.

Among the proliferating writing appearing in England on and from Eastern Europe, the following sources are especially relevant for the purposes of this volume: George Gömöri and Charles Newman (eds), *New Writing of East Europe* (Chicago, Ill.: Quadrangle Books, 1968); Abraham Brumberg (ed.), *In Quest of Justice. Protest and Dissent in the Soviet Union Today* (New York: Praeger, 1970); George Saunders (ed.), *Samizdat. Voices of the Soviet Opposition* (New York: Monad Press, 1974). The facts of dissidence and protest are surveyed and discussed in V. Mastny (ed.), *East European Dissent, Vol. I: 1953–64, Vol. II: 1965–70* (New York: Facts on File, 1972), and R. Tökes (ed.), *Dissent in the USSR* (Baltimore, Md: Johns Hopkins University Press, 1975). Gerson S. Sher, *Praxis: Marxist Criticism and Dissent in Socialist Yugoslavia* (Bloomington, Ill., and London: Indiana University Press, 1977), is a history of the Praxis Group. The best way to gain a complete sense of the issues and aspirations involved in the pursuit of a 'Marxist humanism' in East European thought is through the texts of the dissidents themselves. Gajo Petrovic, *Marx in the Mid-Twentieth Century* (Garden City, NY: Doubleday, 1967), and Leszek Kolakowski, *Toward a Marxist Humanism* (New York: Grove Press, 1968), provide a Yugoslav and a Polish perspective respectively on the earlier phase of philosophical protest, while more recently Jiri Pelikan, *Socialist Opposition in Eastern Europe* (London: Allison & Busby, 1976), adds a Czech angle on the meaning of socialist humanism. Finally Rudolf Bahro, *The Alternative in Eastern Europe* (London: New Left Books, 1978), still insists that by means of a 'cultural revolution' that would break the fetters of bureaucratic ossification, true human liberation through socialism can be achieved in Eastern Europe.

Editorial Note

The essay by Georg Lukács, 'The ideology of modernism', is reprinted in its entirety from *The Meaning of Contemporary Realism* (London: Merlin Press, 1962), pp. 17–46. The selection by Jean-Paul Sartre is reprinted from *What Is Literature?* (Magnolia, Mass.: Peter Smith, 1978), pp. 144–54. The title has been supplied by the editors. Bertolt Brecht, 'A short organum for the theatre', is reprinted from John Willett (ed.), *Brecht on Theatre* (New York: Hill & Wang, 1964), pp. 179–83, 204–5. Paragraphs 47–73, which deal with principles of acting and directing, have been omitted. Walter Benjamin, 'The work of art in the age of mechanical reproduction', is reprinted from *Illuminations* (New York: Harcourt Brace Jovanovich, 1968), pp. 220–43. The author's preface and epilogue and his notes have been omitted.

Lucien Goldmann, 'The revolt of arts and letters in advanced civilizations', is reprinted in its entirety from *Cultural Creation in Modern Society* (St Louis, Mo.: Telos Press, 1976), pp. 51–75. Hans Magnus Enzensberger, 'The industrialization of the mind', is reprinted from *The Consciousness Industry* (New York: Seabury Press, 1974), pp. 3–15. The author's notes have been omitted. Michel Crozier, 'France's cultural anxieties under Gaullism', is reprinted from William Andrews and Stanley Hoffmann (eds), *The Fifth Republic at Twenty* (Albany, NY: SUNY Press, 1980). Krishan Kumar's essay has been written especially for this volume. Heinz Ludwig Arnold, 'From moral affirmation to subjective pragmatism: the transformation of German literature since 1947', is published here for the first time.

Antonio Bar's essay has been especially prepared for this volume. Umberto Eco, 'The modes of cultural fashion in Italy', originally appeared in his book *Il costume di casa* (Milan: Valentino Bompiani, 1973), pp. 33–9, and is here translated into English for the first time. D. N. Maronites, 'The poetic and political ethic of postwar Greek poetry', has been especially translated from the author's book *Poietike kai Politike Ethike* (Athens: Kedros, 1976), pp. 11–23, 73–80.

Mihailo Marković, 'Marxist philosophy in Yugoslavia: the Praxis Group', is reprinted from M. Marković and Robert S. Cohen, *Yugoslavia: The Rise and Fall of Socialist Humanism* (Nottingham: Spokesman, 1975), pp. 11–40. The author's notes have been omitted. The selection entitled 'Poetry as political criticism: the case of Wolf Biermann' (editors' title) is made up of Michael Morley's note 'On the songs and poems of Wolf Biermann' followed by Wolf Biermann, 'Poems', both reprinted from *Index on Censorship*, vol. II, no. 2 (Spring 1973), pp. 23–6. The texts 'A Ten-Point Declaration on the First Anniversary of the Occupation' and 'Charter '77' are reprinted from Hans-Peter Riese (ed.), *Since the Prague Spring* (New York: Random House, 1979), pp. 3–8, 11–14. Maria Márkus and András Hegedüs, 'Community and individuality', is reprinted from András Hegedüs, Agnes Heller, Maria Márkus, and Mihály Vajda, *The Humanization of Socialism. Writings of the Budapest School* (New York: St Martin's Press, 1976), pp. 91–105.

Stanley Hoffmann's 'Fragments floating in the here and now: is there a Europe, was there a past, and will there be a future? or the lament of a transplanted European' first appeared in the Winter 1979 issue of *Daedalus*: *Looking for Europe*, vol. 108, no. 1, pp. 1–26.

Grateful acknowledgement is made to all copyright-owners who have granted their permission to reprint the texts in this collection.

Notes on Contributors

The following authors prepared new material for this casebook:

HEINZ LUDWIG ARNOLD is an Editor of *Text und Kritik* in Göttingen, West Germany.

ANTONIO BAR is Professor of Political Science and Constitutional Law at the University of Zaragosa, Spain. He was a Research Associate of the Harvard University Center for European Studies in 1979–80.

KRISHAN KUMAR is Reader in Sociology at the University of Kent at Canterbury, England. He was a Visiting Fellow in the Harvard University Department of Sociology in 1979–80.